Scotland in Revolution, 1685–1690

In Memory of David Raffe, 1951–2015

Scotland in Revolution, 1685–1690

Alasdair Raffe

EDINBURGH
University Press

Edinburgh University Press is one of the leading university presses in the UK. We publish academic books and journals in our selected subject areas across the humanities and social sciences, combining cutting-edge scholarship with high editorial and production values to produce academic works of lasting importance. For more information visit our website: edinburghuniversitypress.com

© Alasdair Raffe, 2018

Edinburgh University Press Ltd
The Tun – Holyrood Road
12 (2f) Jackson's Entry
Edinburgh EH8 8PJ

Typeset in 10.5/13pt Sabon by
Siliconchips Services Ltd, UK

A CIP record for this book is available from the British Library

ISBN 978 1 4744 2757 9 (hardback)
ISBN 978 1 4744 2758 6 (webready PDF)
ISBN 978 1 4744 2759 3 (epub)
ISBN 978 1 4744 5221 2 (paperback)

The right of Alasdair Raffe to be identified as author of this work has been asserted in accordance with the Copyright, Designs and Patents Act 1988 and the Copyright and Related Rights Regulations 2003 (SI No. 2498).

Contents

List of Figures	vi
Acknowledgements	vii
Abbreviations and Conventions	ix
Map: The Royal Burghs of Scotland in 1685	xii
Introduction: Scotland in Revolution, 1685–1690	1
1 King James's Scotland	9
2 James's Religious Experiment	31
3 Multiconfessional Scotland	56
4 James and the Royal Burghs	80
5 The Revolution in the Localities	106
6 The Revolution Settlement of 1689–1690	131
Conclusion: Revolutions, Settlements and Scotland's Political Development	157
Notes on the Sources	164
Notes	166
Bibliography	216
Index	248

Figures

1.1 *By the King. A Proclamation* (Edinburgh, 1687) 21
4.1 Earl of Perth to the magistrates and council of Kirkwall, 16 Sep. 1686 88
6.1 'The humble adres of the Nobelmen, Gentilmen and Royal Borows, within the Shyre of east Lowthian' 139

Acknowledgements

Though I have been reading and thinking about the revolution of 1688–90 for over fifteen years, I began the main research for this book in the summer of 2013. My first archival trips were funded by Northumbria University; I later received support from the University of Edinburgh and a small grant from the Royal Society of Edinburgh. I am grateful to these funders for allowing me to visit so many interesting parts of Scotland.

In conducting my research, I depended on the assistance of many librarians and archivists. Some made special arrangements for me to read items in their care. I particularly appreciated the help of Anna Louise Mason at Blair Castle, who photographed manuscripts for me at very short notice. For permission to quote from privately owned manuscripts, I am grateful to the earl of Moray and to Mr D. Maxwell Macdonald.

Numerous colleagues offered suggestions, references and encouragement. Especially helpful were Aaron Allen, Karin Bowie, Thomas Brochard, Gordon DesBrisay, Lionel Glassey, Julian Goodare, Mary Hardy, Tim Harris, Alan MacDonald, David Onnekink, Ben Rogers, Leona Skelton and Laura Stewart. Audiences at seminars and conferences in Oxford, London and Edinburgh helped me to develop my interpretations. Parts of Chapters 2 and 3 previously appeared in my article 'James VII's multiconfessional experiment and the Scottish revolution of 1688–1690', *History*, 100 (2015), pp. 354–73. I am grateful to the editor for permission to reproduce material here. For commenting on draft chapters, I am indebted to Julian Goodare and Laura Stewart.

As the book took shape, I was often in the mountains, finishing off the Munros. The friends who accompanied me bore patiently my impromptu lectures on King James – before tactfully changing the subject!

One of the satisfactions of publishing my first book, *The Culture of Controversy*, was that my father read and appreciated it. Regretting that he won't read *Scotland in Revolution*, I dedicate it to his memory.

Abbreviations and Conventions

AA	Angus Archives, by Forfar
ACAA	Aberdeen City and Aberdeenshire Archives
AM	Annan Museum
APES	E. W. M. Balfour-Melville (ed.), *An Account of the Proceedings of the Estates in Scotland, 1689–1690*, 2 vols (SHS, 1954–5)
APS	Thomas Thomson and Cosmo Innes (eds), *Acts of the Parliament of Scotland*, 12 vols (Edinburgh, 1814–75)
AyA	Ayrshire Archives, Ayr
Balcarres, *Memoirs*	Colin Lindsay, earl of Balcarres, *Memoirs touching the Revolution in Scotland, MDCLXXXVIII–MDCXC*, ed. A. W. C. Lindsay (Bannatyne Club, 1841)
BC	Blair Castle, Blair Atholl
BL	British Library, London
CAC	Caithness Archive Centre, Wick
DCA	Dundee City Archives
DGA	Dumfries and Galloway Archives, Dumfries
DL	Dumbarton Library
ECA	Edinburgh City Archives
ELA	East Lothian Archives, Haddington
ESTC	English Short Title Catalogue
EUL	Edinburgh University Library
Fasti	Hew Scott, *Fasti Ecclesiae Scoticanae: The Succession of Ministers in the Church of Scotland from the Reformation*, rev. edn, 8 vols (Edinburgh: Oliver and Boyd, 1915–50)

FCAC	Fife Council Archive Centre, Kirkcaldy
GCA	Glasgow City Archives
GUL	Glasgow University Library
HAC	Highland Archive Centre, Inverness
HMC	Historical Manuscripts Commission
Leven and Melville Papers	[William Leslie Melville (ed.),] *Leven and Melville Papers: Letters and State Papers chiefly addressed to George Earl of Melville, Secretary of State for Scotland, 1689–1691* (Bannatyne Club, 1843)
LL	Lanark Library
MHC	Moray Heritage Centre, Elgin
NLS	National Library of Scotland
NRAS	National Register of Archives for Scotland
NRS	National Records of Scotland
NRS, Secretary's warrant books	NRS, Warrant books of the secretary for Scotland, 5 April 1683–15 December 1691, SP4/8–15
NUL	Nottingham University Library
ODNB	H. C. G. Matthew and Brian Harrison (eds), *Oxford Dictionary of National Biography*, 61 vols (Oxford: Oxford University Press, 2004)
OLA	Orkney Library and Archive, Kirkwall
PCL	Paisley Central Library
PKCA	Perth and Kinross Council Archives, Perth
RPC, 3rd ser.	P. Hume Brown, Henry Paton and E. Balfour-Melville (eds), *The Register of the Privy Council of Scotland*, 3rd series, 16 vols (Edinburgh, 1908–70)
RPS	Keith M. Brown et al. (eds), *Records of the Parliaments of Scotland to 1707*, <http://www.rps.ac.uk/> (last accessed 6 July 2017)
RSCHS	*Records of the Scottish Church History Society*
SAUL	St Andrews University Library
SBA	Scottish Borders Archives, Hawick
SBRS	Scottish Burgh Records Society
SCA	Scottish Catholic Archives, Aberdeen University Library
SCAS	Stirling Council Archives Service, Stirling
SHR	*Scottish Historical Review*
SHS	Scottish History Society

SM	Stewartry Museum, Kirkcudbright
SP	ScotlandsPeople Centre, Edinburgh
StrM	Stranraer Museum

All quotations retain the original spelling and punctuation. Biblical quotations are from the King James Version. Sums of money are in £ Scots unless otherwise indicated. £1 sterling was equal to £12 Scots. One merk was worth 13s.4d. Scots. Unless otherwise stated, dates are in old style. The year began on 1 January.

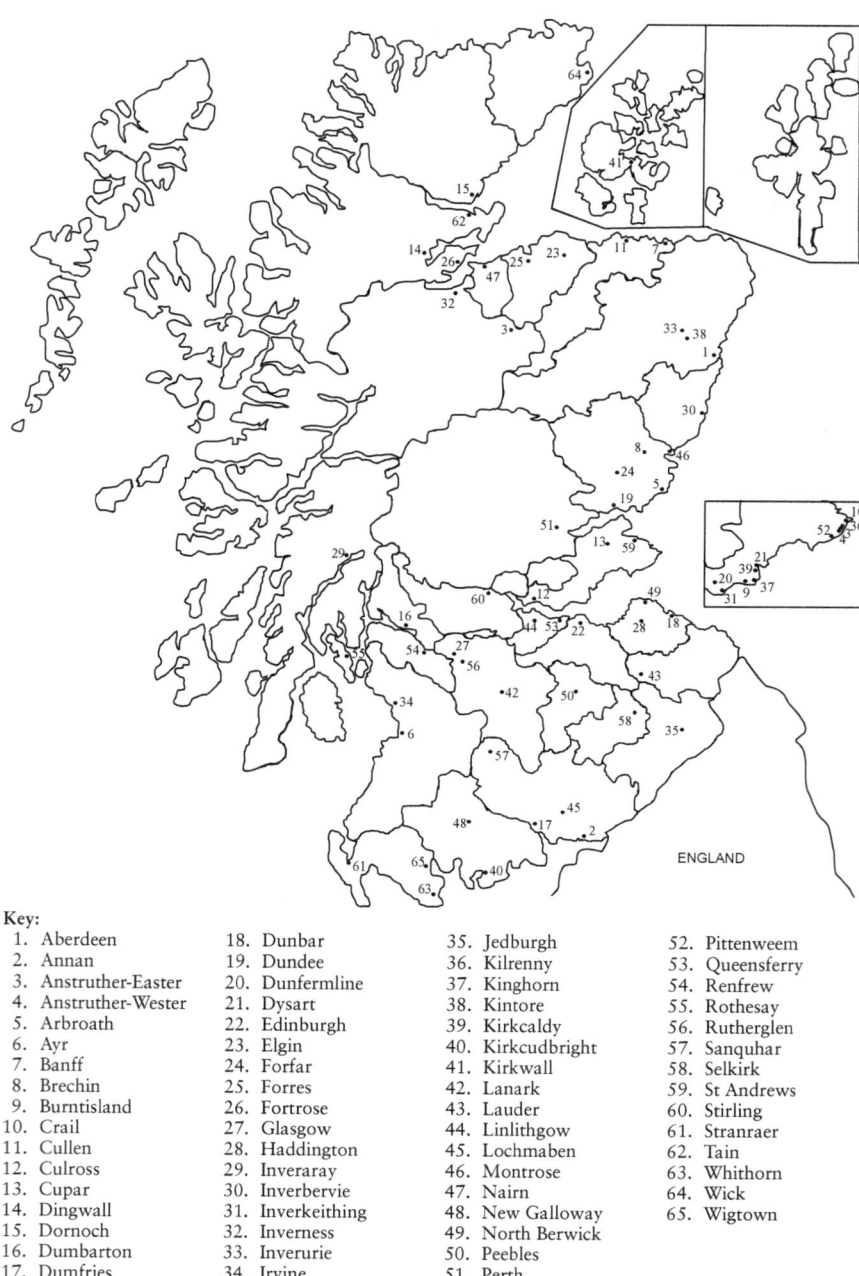

Key:
1. Aberdeen
2. Annan
3. Anstruther-Easter
4. Anstruther-Wester
5. Arbroath
6. Ayr
7. Banff
8. Brechin
9. Burntisland
10. Crail
11. Cullen
12. Culross
13. Cupar
14. Dingwall
15. Dornoch
16. Dumbarton
17. Dumfries
18. Dunbar
19. Dundee
20. Dunfermline
21. Dysart
22. Edinburgh
23. Elgin
24. Forfar
25. Forres
26. Fortrose
27. Glasgow
28. Haddington
29. Inveraray
30. Inverbervie
31. Inverkeithing
32. Inverness
33. Inverurie
34. Irvine
35. Jedburgh
36. Kilrenny
37. Kinghorn
38. Kintore
39. Kirkcaldy
40. Kirkcudbright
41. Kirkwall
42. Lanark
43. Lauder
44. Linlithgow
45. Lochmaben
46. Montrose
47. Nairn
48. New Galloway
49. North Berwick
50. Peebles
51. Perth
52. Pittenweem
53. Queensferry
54. Renfrew
55. Rothesay
56. Rutherglen
57. Sanquhar
58. Selkirk
59. St Andrews
60. Stirling
61. Stranraer
62. Tain
63. Whithorn
64. Wick
65. Wigtown

The Royal Burghs of Scotland in 1685.

Introduction: Scotland in Revolution, 1685–1690

IN DECEMBER 1688, THE authority of King James VII, Scotland's last Catholic ruler and most self-consciously 'absolute' monarch, collapsed. As recently as the summer, James's government had seemed strong. The political instability convulsing his southern kingdom of England, where James had prosecuted seven bishops for refusing his commands, had no visible parallel in Scotland. North of the Tweed, the king's highly innovative policies – religious toleration, the promotion of Catholicism and systematic intervention in local government – were unchallenged. But in November, the invasion of southern England by William of Orange, James's Dutch nephew and son-in-law, quickly undermined the government in Scotland. Despite gathering his army to confront William's forces on Salisbury Plain, James failed to resist the invaders, withdrawing to London on 23 November.[1] News of the king's retreat accelerated the unravelling of his authority in Scotland. On 10 December, the departure from Edinburgh of James Drummond, fourth earl of Perth, James's chancellor and the leading noble convert to Catholicism, triggered an anti-Catholic riot, destroying the chapel royal at Holyroodhouse. This signalled the beginning of the end of the royal policy of religious toleration, and shattered the credibility of the king's Catholic ministers of state.

As December advanced, further bad news came from the south. With little hope of defeating William, James fled for France, leaving London on 11 December. Though James was intercepted and briefly brought back to the capital, William was in control of London by the 18th. James made his second, successful, departure for France on the 23rd. Observing these developments, many of Scotland's political leaders hastened to London, to make terms with the conquering William. Attendance at the privy council, the body responsible for governing Scotland, dwindled.[2] James's

Scottish army had been transferred to England before the invasion, and the relatively dysfunctional militia was stood down in early December.[3] By the end of the year, violent crowds were attacking the houses of Catholics and evicting the ministers of the protestant established Church from parishes across southern Scotland. Neither the central government nor local magistrates had the strength to preserve order.

James's regime had collapsed, but there was no obvious revolutionary party waiting to assume power. Indeed, the king's fall was followed by a period of political uncertainty and administrative breakdown. The commissioners running the Scottish treasury ceased to sit in early January 1689, and it appears that privy council meetings stopped at the end of the month. Though in December the treasury had made new arrangements to fund military and cavalry divisions, by late January it was proving difficult to pay the troops. The refusal of taxation, a problem as early as November, became more widespread.[4] Scots assumed that the resolution of the crisis, like the evaporation of James's authority, would be driven by events in England. On 25 and 26 December, William of Orange was invited to assume executive control of England by assemblies of the English peerage and former MPs.[5] On 5 January 1689, the prince requested a similar gathering of the Scottish peers and gentlemen present in London. The Scots met on 7 January and sat for four days. James Hamilton, earl of Arran called for the king's return, but the rest of the meeting concurred in asking William to take responsibility for Scotland's government, and to summon a convention of estates that would agree a political and religious settlement.[6]

In the short term, however, little was done to end the chaos in Scotland. According to one well-placed observer, the country was 'abandon'd to the aduenture of all the disorders its capable of'.[7] Only with the meeting of the convention in Edinburgh on 14 March did order begin to return. The estates quickly resolved that James had forfeited his right to the throne. Before offering the crown to William and his consort Mary, who had become king and queen of England on 13 February, the convention approved the Claim of Right and Articles of Grievances, documents expressing the faults of James's government and requesting specific reforms. Over the following months, as the convention – now declared to be a meeting of parliament – started to enact a settlement, William began the demanding job of governing Scotland.

Contemporaries were quick to call the events of 1688–9 a 'revolution'. In January 1689, the soldier Lord David Hay wrote to his father John Hay, second earl of Tweeddale, confessing his uncertainty about how to act after 'all the passage's of this revolution & of the Kings second goeing away'.⁸ In the same month, Placid Fleming, abbot of the Scottish Benedictine monastery in Regensburg (Ratisbon), Germany, expressed his 'sorrow and grief ... for these unhappie revolutions'. '[T]his sudden revolution cannot but be most sad and lamentable to all the kings faithfull subjects', he wrote.⁹ Colin Lindsay, third earl of Balcarres, in the account of events he addressed to the exiled King James in 1690, also lamented 'these unhappy revolutions'.¹⁰ By contrast, the government official Sir Patrick Murray described James's overthrow and the settlement of the crown on William and Mary as 'so hapie and great a revolution'.¹¹ In 1690, James Fall, recently removed from office as principal of Glasgow University, referred to 'the great Revolution which followed upon' William's invasion.¹² In some of these statements, the word 'revolution' clearly signified the transition of power from James to William and Mary. In others, revolution apparently referred to a more general political upheaval. But if some seventeenth-century writers thought of revolution as a cyclical revival of former political conditions, akin to an astronomical rotation, there is little indication that Scots understood recent events in these terms.¹³ Contemporaries did not, it seems, find the idea of revolution as restoration adequate to describe the developments of 1688–9, and nor is such a characterisation of much use to historians.

In the centuries since 1688, of course, 'revolution' has become a still more ambiguous and contested concept.¹⁴ The French Revolution of 1789 and the Russian Revolution of October 1917 established 'scripts': patterns serving as an inspiration for later attempts to topple governing regimes, and sets of ingredients that scholars have found in other great revolutions.¹⁵ Thus the historical sociologist Jack Goldstone argues that revolutions have occurred in states experiencing fiscal crisis and serious divisions among the elites, and in which there was a potential for popular mobilisation.¹⁶ Like the French Revolution, Samuel Huntington suggested, the outbreak of most western revolutions can be precisely dated and attributed to episodes taking place in the state's capital city, before being replicated elsewhere.¹⁷ Scholars who associate revolutionary change with the modernisation of society have also looked for evidence that revolutions transform social structures.¹⁸ The 'English Revolution' of the 1640s and 1650s is sometimes said to have effected permanent social change, and recently Steve Pincus has linked the events of 1688–9 to the long-term re-ordering of society in England.¹⁹ But most early modernists are unconvinced that upheavals in political and religious institutions had a causal impact on the very gradual evolution of hierarchies and patterns of organisation in pre-industrial societies.

Because of this, Charles Tilly's definition of revolution in essentially political terms is better suited to early modern cases. For Tilly, the transfer of political power – a 'revolutionary outcome' – was a possible (but not inevitable) result of a 'revolutionary situation', in which sections of a divided political elite competed to control the state.[20] This model fits a large number of early modern revolutions; as we shall see, it helps to expose the peculiarities of the Scottish revolution.

The complexity of defining and analysing revolutions has given rise to wildly differing interpretations of the Scottish events of 1688–9. Ian Cowan, by stressing the vacillations of the leading politicians in Edinburgh, and the lack of an alternative government in waiting, suggested that there were few serious divisions among the Scottish elites after William's invasion.[21] This was scarcely a revolutionary situation, and the Scots were reluctant revolutionaries at best. With his focus also on the nobility, Bruce Lenman produced a complementary reading: few landed Scots were strongly committed to either side.[22] More recently, Tim Harris has uncovered the scale of popular mobilisation in 1688–9, and emphasised the radicalism of the convention of estates' demands. Energised by the enthusiasm of the crowd, he argues, the Scottish revolution quickly jettisoned James and erected a scaffolding for major political reform.[23] Perhaps this was to be expected: as Ginny Gardner and Clare Jackson have taught us, Scots figured prominently among the organisers and ideologues of James's overthrow.[24] In 1688–9, the current scholarship suggests, there was a genuine struggle for control of the political agenda, resulting in far-reaching changes to Scottish politics and religious life. A revolution resembling many others in the early modern world took place.

But this interpretation risks overlooking one fundamental point about the Scottish revolution. Its primary cause was not division among the country's elites, far less fiscal crisis, but rather William's successful invasion of England. Scotland and England had shared their kings since 1603, and the fall of the monarch in one kingdom could easily bring a collapse of royal authority in the other. Under Charles I, the revolt of the Covenanters in Scotland helped to trigger civil war in England.[25] Now the shock of invasion brought down James's regime in both countries. Once the king had fled to France and William was in control of London, it was unlikely that James would recover his northern kingdom. In these circumstances, William succeeded in Scotland in large part because he had already triumphed in England. This is not to say that developments in Scotland followed a path laid out in England.[26] Of course, there were similarities between the revolutions in the two kingdoms, but these arose because revolutionaries in both reacted against the policies of the same king. It is also misleading to call William's Scottish partisans reluctant. We can identify a number of politicians who consistently supported William. They took part in some subversive activity, notably intercepting posts between London and Edinburgh in November 1688.[27] Other Scots armed themselves and stood ready to assist the prince of Orange.[28] But they did little – they needed to do little – to seize control of the government. Debates about who should occupy the throne had less impact on the elections to the convention of estates than has sometimes been thought, and it was not until March, with the opening of the convention, that a coherent Williamite response to the crisis emerged.

Between the fall of James and the construction of a new regime, then, there was a period of at least three months. This interval cannot easily be characterised in terms of competition between political leaders for national power, as in Tilly's revolutionary situation. There was no attempt by James's supporters to defeat their rivals, and William's partisans made little effort, apart from paying court to the prince in London, to prepare for government.[29] Instead, early 1689 saw a patchwork of local upheavals: struggles for office, protests against Catholic worship and competitions for control over parish churches. These events involved some overt expressions of support for William, and in general helped his cause, but they were primarily a reaction against James, stimulated by his downfall. More than in England in 1688–9, and more than in most other revolutions, there was a sharp disjunction in Scotland between the collapse of one government and the appearance of its successor. The most obvious struggles over the future of Scotland occurred in the months after William had claimed the throne almost by default. Much more than before the prince of Orange became king, there was now a real debate about how the country's religion and politics should be reconstituted. There was also a brief civil war, in which Jacobite forces under John Graham, viscount of Dundee confronted a Williamite army. The absence of a typical revolutionary situation in the winter of 1688–9 should not make us conclude that there was no revolution. Like contemporaries, we can use the word to refer to the transfer of power between James and William and Mary. But we should recognise that in early 1689, Scotland departed from familiar revolutionary scripts. Scotland was part of a multiple monarchy, and the breakdown of its government and the construction of a successor regime were enabled by the invasion of, and successful seizure of power in, England.

This analysis, which is justified at length in Chapters 5 and 6 below, is the result of a new approach to the reign of James VII and the revolution.

Most histories of the period focus primarily on the noblemen who governed Scotland, the plotters who promoted revolution, and the intellectuals who justified it. The resulting interpretation is dominated by the national capital. Even Tim Harris's work, with its attention to crowd violence across Scotland, draws largely on sources describing events in Edinburgh, or reflecting the experiences and opinions of people living there. In this book, I use a wide range of local archival sources to understand the diverse experiences of Scots across the country. In doing so, I seek to correct the metropolitan bias of previous histories, which has resulted from their reliance on printed sources and the records of central government. A case is sometimes made that events in provincial England strongly influenced the outcome of William's invasion. Revolts and the defection of noblemen in the north and west, the unreliability of county militia forces, and William's stage-managed entries into the towns on his route to London weakened James's resolve to fight.[30] Nevertheless, London was pivotal to the outcome of the revolution in England.[31] Though Edinburgh saw some of the first disturbances of the Scottish revolution, in keeping with Huntington's model, the capital played a surprisingly small role before March 1689. The evaporation of central authority made way for turmoil in towns and parishes across Scotland, and revolutionaries in these communities did not necessarily look to Edinburgh for inspiration.

But there is a further, more important reason for studying Scotland in this period through its local records. More than is sometimes recognised, the convention of estates' Claim of Right justified the overthrow of James VII by denouncing those of his policies that destabilised, or increased royal interference in, local communities. In 1685, he continued the approach of his brother Charles II by commissioning military officers to enforce justice against religious dissenters, bypassing the jurisdiction of local magistrates. In the following year, he began to intervene in the royal burghs, suspending their council elections and nominating magistrates and councillors. In his most radical policy, James granted toleration to the great majority of Christians, allowing them a choice about how to worship. To adopt the more general sense of 'revolution' known to contemporaries, Scotland witnessed continuous upheaval and was thus 'in revolution' throughout the reign of this energetic, assertive and experimental ruler. Before charting the reaction to his rule in 1688–9, therefore, we must analyse the impact of James's government in the Scottish localities.[32]

The first four chapters of this book explore James's attempts to solve the problems of governing his poor, geographically diverse and religiously divided northern kingdom. In Chapter 1, after a narrative of the main events of the reign, we assess how the king and his advisers emphasised the 'absolute' character of royal power. James, it was claimed, had the authority to suspend laws and to appoint local magistrates. Royal orders were to be obeyed 'without reserve'. This understanding of monarchical authority drew on statutes passed under Charles II and the royalist discourse of the period, which James pushed to new extremes. But James could do more to ramp up his rhetoric than to amplify his power in terms of military might and administrative capacity. Compared with his government in England, and especially when measured against the would-be absolute monarchs of continental Europe, the authority of James's Scottish regime was constrained. Despite his theoretical absolutism, the king's power was limited and fragile.

Nevertheless, James built innovative policies on the foundation of his absolute authority. Most strikingly, he attempted a radical solution to the problems of religious dissent that had bedevilled Scottish politics since the Restoration. In his declarations of indulgence of 1687, and in his declaration for England of the same year, James allowed freedom of worship for almost all Christians. In Chapters 2 and 3, I argue that we should think of the king's Scottish policy as a 'multiconfessional experiment'. Multiconfessionalism, a recent historical coinage, refers to 'the legally recognized and politically supported coexistence of two or more confessions in a single polity'.[33] Multiconfessional policies were a challenge to the ideal of religious uniformity, promulgated by the peace treaties of Augsburg (1555) and Westphalia (1648), and pursued by the monarchs of Scotland and England for much of the early modern period. Scholars have traditionally argued that early modern rulers used religious uniformity to enhance their control over their territories, a set of processes often labelled 'confessionalisation'.[34] In support of this agenda, protestants and Catholics defended the repression of religious dissent, making use of reasoning inherited from the middle ages. Generations of intellectual historians have traced the emergence, especially in the seventeenth century, of principled arguments in favour of toleration.[35] Increasingly, however, scholars emphasise that, before tolerationist ideas gained a foothold, practical arrangements were made to allow people of different religious persuasions to live side by side in relative peace. Sometimes multiconfessionalism resulted from informal habits of coexistence in divided communities; in other cases, it was enacted by governments.[36] James imposed multiconfessionalism from above, and though it permitted the sudden appearance of religious pluralism, there was less popular enthusiasm for the principle of toleration in Scotland than in England.[37] In his religious policy, moreover, James was experimenting with Scottish society. He created a freer market in religious services than had previously existed, fuelling significant competition between religious groups. By fragmenting parish communities, however, James's experiment undermined the registration of births and marriages and compromised Scotland's systems of poor relief and ecclesiastical discipline.

Chapter 4 turns to the king's policy in the royal burghs. James had less scope in Scotland than in England to remodel the government of counties and districts by appointing loyal men to local offices. Thus James's interference in the elections of the royal burghs constituted his main attempt to influence local communities, and ultimately to gain the support of the burghs' representatives for his agenda in parliament. Whether his policy in the burghs would have had this effect is unclear: he summoned no new parliament after 1685. But while the king's orders were generally obeyed in the towns, his intervention stirred up considerable discontent, as became clear in the upheavals of 1688–9. Chapter 5 reconstructs the events of this interval – from the collapse of James's regime to the meeting of the convention of estates – in detail.

Finally, in Chapter 6 we analyse the outcomes of the revolution. As we shall see, debates and divisions delayed the conclusion of a settlement until the summer of 1690. It is for this reason that I use the phrase 'revolution of 1688–90' to encompass the various developments following from William's expedition and culminating in the legislation re-establishing presbyterianism in June and July 1690. If James proposed radical solutions to religious diversity and local autonomy, the 'revolution settlement' of 1689–90 was an alternative attempt to resolve these problems. The revolution settlement restored religious uniformity and the independence of the royal burghs. But religious dissent did not disappear, and the increasingly assertive Scottish parliament was a new source of instability. The book's Conclusion argues that it took a second settlement, implemented from 1707 to 1712, to lay out a lasting framework for Scottish government. The 'union settlement' of 1707–12 gave formal recognition to religious pluralism for the first time since the multiconfessional experiment. While the autonomy of the burghs, and of other local magistrates, was confirmed in 1707, many functions of central government were transferred to London. The union settlement was a further response to the problems of government with which James grappled. More than the settlement of 1689–90, it was to decide the country's future.

1

King James's Scotland

THIS CHAPTER INTRODUCES THE political culture and summarises the main events of James VII's Scottish reign. After the Restoration of the monarchy in 1660, it argues, the most important aspects of political life were, first, the challenges of religious diversity and, second, the evolution of an absolutist understanding of royal authority. These themes were to shape events through to James's accession. In fact, James had a significant influence over his own political inheritance. As duke of Albany and York, he was resident in Scotland in the years 1679–82. He presided over the Scottish parliament of 1681, which continued a process of magnifying royal authority that had begun at the Restoration and accelerated once he came to the throne. After sketching the Restoration background, the chapter provides a narrative of political developments from 1685 to 1688. Unlike in the following chapters, the focus is largely on high politics – the development of the king's policies and the reactions of the political elites to them – rather than on the impact of royal initiatives in Scottish communities. The purpose of the narrative is to establish a context for the analysis in Chapters 2, 3 and 4, which draw largely on local sources. In the final part of this chapter, we assess James's claims to absolute authority in more detail. How did contemporaries think about the royal prerogative, and what were the limits to James's power?

* * *

In order to understand the politics of King James's Scotland, we should trace two important themes from the start of the reign of Charles II into that of his brother. The first concerns the nature of the Church of Scotland and the government's policies towards religious dissenters.

By re-establishing bishops and excluding ministers who remained committed to the presbyterian system that had been in place since the Covenanting revolution of 1638–41, the Restoration Church settlement created a serious problem of nonconformity. Especially in southern Scotland, the presbyterian ministers who refused to accept the settlement retained the loyalty of a significant proportion of the population. Some presbyterians began to preach at irregular services not condoned by the established Church. As a result, many episcopalian clergy – both former presbyterians who conformed and new men – struggled to win and preserve the respect of their parishioners. The Church was especially weak in the south-west, where large numbers of experienced presbyterian ministers had been replaced by younger, less respected episcopalian conformists, and where numerous parishes remained vacant for years after the return of bishops.[1]

Importantly, the Church settlement overturned the religious toleration introduced under Oliver Cromwell, restoring an older assumption that the civil magistrate was obliged to enforce uniformity.[2] Using a mixture of threatening laws and military force, the government in the Restoration period attempted to compel all Scots to attend services in the established Church. Various statutes of the 1660s and 1670s defined the penalties for withdrawing from church, attending nonconformist services (often called 'conventicles') and employing unlicensed ministers to conduct weddings and baptisms.[3] As presbyterian dissent became widespread, the government resorted to increasingly coercive measures against those participating in illegal worship, helping to provoke armed presbyterian risings in 1666 and 1679. Yet the laws were not consistently enforced, and nonconformity flourished, especially in the 1670s. In the indulgences of 1669 and 1672, moreover, the crown licensed selected presbyterian clergy to exercise their ministry in specified parishes, mostly in the south-west.[4] This policy acknowledged that it was proving difficult to suppress dissent and include all Scots in the established Church. But by introducing the indulgences, as we shall see in Chapter 2, the crown neither abandoned the basic goal of religious uniformity, nor allowed more than a restricted toleration to a specified group of presbyterian ministers. And by the mid-1680s the policy had been dropped in favour of a more systematic enforcement of the laws against dissent. It was the pursuit of religious uniformity, a consistent objective of the crown's policy since 1661–2, that was to be repudiated by James in his multiconfessional experiment.

Our second theme in Restoration politics is the period's absolutist understanding of royal authority. After the return of Charles II, a wide range of Scots, including parliamentarians, episcopalian clergy and legal and political theorists, expressed their loyalty by affirming the king's powers. There was an 'obligation lying upon' the first parliament after the Restoration, its members claimed, 'to oune and assert the royall prerogatives of the imperiall croun of this kingdome, which the king's majestie holds from God Almightie alone'.[5] In a series of acts in January 1661, therefore, parliament specified the king's roles in civil, military and ecclesiastical affairs, the areas in which it was perceived that the Covenanters had invaded royal authority. It was 'an inherent priveledge' of the crown of Scotland, parliament declared, to have the 'sole choise and appointment' of officers of state, privy councillors and judges in the court of session. The monarch also had exclusive control over the holding of parliaments and conventions, and of the waging of war.[6] Restoring bishops in 1662, parliament stated that 'the ordering and disposall of the externall government and policie of the church' was an 'inherent right' of the crown. In 1669, a further statute – passed to give retrospective legal backing to the policy of indulgence – confirmed that the king had 'supream authority and supremacie over all persons and in all causes ecclesiasticall' within Scotland.[7] The political elite coalesced around these royalist principles, and were rewarded with offices and influence in Charles's government. Meanwhile, preachers and lawyers published theories of the divine right of kings and non-resistance to monarchical commands, while historians recounted the antiquity of the Scottish royal line and the traditional loyalty of its subjects.[8]

These twin themes – the pursuit of religious uniformity and the assertion of royal authority – continued to dominate politics during James's visits to Scotland in 1679–82. Though the government introduced a more liberal policy of indulgence after the defeat of the presbyterian rising of 1679, Charles II changed tack in 1680 and increasingly limited the opportunities for presbyterians to preach outwith the Church.[9] The Scottish bishops called for more to be done against nonconformity; they received a sympathetic hearing from the duke of Albany and York. In March 1682, Bishop John Paterson of Edinburgh praised James, among other things noting his 'particular care that all our conventicles may be suppresst by a moderat but steddie execution of the laws'.[10] Meanwhile, the parliament of 1681 upheld the principle of religious uniformity by ratifying laws in favour of the established Kirk and against Catholicism. Of more practical significance was the new oath – the Test – that parliament imposed on holders of public office. By requiring its swearers to disown all 'popish or phanaticall' principles, the oath intended to exclude from political life those who failed to conform to the established

Church.[11] Parliament restated its commitment to religious uniformity, and by the end of 1682, it seemed to the archbishop of St Andrews that presbyterian dissent was everywhere in decline.[12]

At the same time as Scottish politicians renewed their insistence on uniformity, they loudly declared their enthusiasm for royal power. In November 1680, at the start of James's second stay in Edinburgh, the privy council wrote to Charles, explicitly rejecting the arguments of the English whigs who sought to exclude the duke from the succession to the throne. Echoing two decades of royalist rhetoric, the councillors thanked Charles for giving them a 'renued occasion of letting the world see that no humours or jealousies shall for the future divert that dutifullness in the royall line which our predicessours have mantained for so many ages'.[13] In the following August, parliament passed a law asserting that kings derived their power from God alone, that the succession to the throne was hereditary and unalterable, and that the next monarch, regardless of his religion, would assume royal authority 'immediatlie' after Charles's death. The implication was that it was not necessary for kings to swear the coronation oath.[14] No doubt this was deliberate: James would have refused to take the oath, which obliged kings to suppress Catholicism. In a separate act, parliament declared that, because 'all government and jurisdiction ... does originally reside' in the king, Charles, his successors and those commissioned by them were entitled to judge in any cases before any of the subordinate magistrates of Scotland.[15] This measure recognised that the king could bypass local courts, and send men of his own choice to enforce the laws. As we shall see shortly, this presaged some of the most violent measures employed against religious dissent in the mid-1680s.

James's Scottish visit also saw the government give sustained attention to a subject of increasing importance in Scottish politics: the country's economic position and prospects. In January 1681, drawing on the model of earlier parliamentary commissions, the privy council established a committee for trade, empowering it to interview merchants and make proposals for economic development. The committee heard detailed evidence of the unfavourable balances of trade between Scotland and its main commercial partners, the Netherlands, France and England. As well as prompting royal proclamations to forbid imports of foreign commodities, the committee suggested the two approaches to economic amelioration that would be tried several times over the following two and half decades.[16] The first was an independent Scottish imperial strategy. The settling of an American colony was canvassed in the committee, and in 1682 Charles gave his approval to Scottish participation in the settlement of South Carolina. As king, James offered further encouragement to Scottish colonists in East New Jersey.[17] The second proposal for economic growth was to change the Anglo-Scottish relationship. If this could not be done through 'ane union betwixt the kingdoms', which seemed impossible, or with 'ane union of traid', then it might be hoped that English 'impositions and prohibitions ... so grievous to our traid' – a reference not only to tariffs but also to the restrictions on shipping in the navigation acts of the 1660s – would be repealed or modified.[18] As we shall see, the considerable appeal of closer union between Scotland and England meant that it was proposed at two crucial moments before the end of the decade: in the parliament of 1686 and the convention of estates in 1689. Representatives of the royal burghs, furthermore, repeatedly urged parliament to restore their exclusive rights in foreign trade, which had been removed in 1672 in an attempt to encourage more widespread economic development.[19]

While resident in Scotland, James took the opportunity to cultivate support from the country's landed and professional elites. In Edinburgh, he patronised several cultural projects, notably the founding of the Advocates Library in 1680 and the Royal College of Physicians in 1681. He also visited Linlithgow, Stirling, Glasgow and Dumbarton, making valuable contact with the burgh notables.[20] As we shall see in Chapter 4, however, it is questionable how much knowledge James ever acquired of the leading men in Scotland's smaller towns. Among aristocratic politicians, James built good working relationships with many of the privy councillors who would serve him as king. More generally, he attempted to restore harmony among the nobility and gentry after the rivalries engendered by the political career of John Maitland, duke of Lauderdale.[21] On the other hand, James's role in the trial and forfeiture of Archibald Campbell, ninth earl of Argyll, who refused to swear the Test oath without qualification, alienated some Scots, while Argyll's escape from Scotland in December 1681 made him a focal point for future opposition to James.[22]

* * *

Charles II died on 6 February 1685, after a short illness. In the early hours of 10 February, the Scottish privy council met to receive the news. Later, between nine and ten o'clock, the councillors reassembled, swore the oaths of allegiance and the Test, and ordered the proclamation of James as 'King of Scotland, England, France and Ireland, defender of the faith, etc.'.[23] In accordance with the statute of 1681 asserting the succession, therefore, James succeeded seamlessly, and he was not asked to swear the coronation oath. He soon indicated that there would be no obvious break between the last days of his brother's reign and the opening of his. In narrating the main political developments of James's rule, then, we begin by stressing the continuities across the years 1684–5. In his approach to religious matters and his relations with the Scottish elites, James pursued the programmes laid out under Charles. It was only in 1686 that he adopted a significantly different religious policy, coupled with a more aggressive assertion of his royal prerogative.

James came to the throne during the most violent phase of the Restoration state's campaign against presbyterian nonconformity. In general, dissenting worship was less common after 1680. Its character shifted, as more of the services that took place were large, outdoor meetings, attended by armed men who were prepared to fight the government troops sent to investigate. These were the field conventicles of the United Societies, or Cameronians, a radical group that had crystallised in 1679 under leaders who repudiated their allegiance to Charles II and declared war on the government.[24] Though the group's activities were curtailed by the deaths of its first ministers by the summer of 1681, the emergence in late 1683 of James Renwick as the Societies' preacher allowed for a new wave of field conventicles. The government responded with vigour. In January 1684, it named commissioners for the shires of Lanark, Dumbarton, Dumfries, Wigtown and the stewartries of Kirkcudbright and Annandale, charging them to prosecute participants in the rising of 1679 and those who disowned royal authority.[25] Meanwhile, the central courts brought a growing number of prisoners to trial and execution.[26] The crown then appointed more local justiciary commissioners, in September 1684 for the southern and western shires, and in December 1684 for the Lothians, Fife, Kinross and the Inverness area, giving them a wide remit to enforce the laws against dissenters from the established Church. As well as taking the problem of dissent out of the hands of potentially negligent local magistrates, these commissioners were instructed to use militarised force and lethal violence against the recalcitrant.[27] On 20 September, moreover, Renwick, who had refused to appear before the commissioners, was declared a fugitive from the law, and assisting him was forbidden.[28]

The Societies' response, in November 1684, was the 'Apologetical Declaration', a statement reiterating the group's previous threats to attack public officials and episcopalian clergy.[29] The government countered by imposing the death penalty on lay people who refused an oath abjuring the Declaration.[30] This order made way for many of the summary executions that led contemporaries and presbyterian historians to call the years 1684–5 the 'killing times'.[31] Two famous episodes illustrate the pressure now experienced by followers of the Societies. On 1 May 1685, soldiers under John Graham of Claverhouse shot dead John Brown, of Priesthill in Muirkirk, Ayrshire, who was an active member of the Societies, had accommodated the field preacher Alexander Peden and declined the oath of abjuration. Also refusing to swear, Margaret Wilson and Margaret Maclauchlan were sentenced to be drowned in the Solway Firth at Wigtown in May.[32] The crown's policy, therefore, was to deploy the judicial and military resources of the central government in dramatic interventions in the localities. As the dates of the executions show, this approach continued after James's accession. In March and April 1685, new commissions were issued, first to Colonel James Douglas and then to Lieutenant-General William Drummond, for the apprehension of 'desperate rebells sculking up and down in some southern and western shires'.[33]

In the last months of Charles's reign, the crown sought to reconvene the Scottish parliament. On 8 November 1684, the king informed his privy council that the parliament elected in 1681 would assemble in March, again with James as commissioner.[34] But before parliament could meet, Charles died and his commissioner inherited the throne. One of James's first actions as king was to summon a new parliament for April, in which, he said, he was 'graciously resolved to prosecute the same good designes' intended by the late king.[35] Opening on 23 April, the parliament once again provided a stage for the loyal gestures and royalist rhetoric that had characterised political life since 1660. Parliament's letter to the king assured James that his Scottish subjects aspired 'to exceed all their predicessors in extraordinary marks of affection, and obedience to your majesty'. Then, in an act of fiscal generosity exceeding even the court's expectations, parliament gave the crown the permanent right to collect the excise on domestic and foreign commodities. James also benefited from an act increasing the rate at which the cess, the tax on income from rents, was paid.[36] And parliament gave its support to the severe measures against dissenters, passing an act imposing the death penalty on all preachers at nonconformist services held inside and outdoors, and on lay people caught at field conventicles.[37]

As parliament was sitting, the earl of Argyll launched a rebellion in the west of Scotland against the king's authority. Since fleeing execution, Argyll had spent much of his time in the Netherlands, where he had agreed to coordinate his rising with that planned for southwestern England by Charles II's illegitimate son James Scott, duke of

Monmouth. Argyll's rising, of which the government had warning by 28 April and which got under way in Kintyre in mid-May, was diminutive and short-lived. After raising men and pursuing confused objectives in Argyll itself, the earl attempted to reach Glasgow. During the march, much of his army disintegrated; Argyll slipped away in disguise but was captured near Inchinnan, Renfrewshire, on 18 June.[38] Not only had the earl's campaign been badly organised, but he gained too little support to pose a serious threat to the regime. He struggled to raise his Campbell kinsmen, and the Cameronians – his other potential followers – were divided over whether to participate. Rallying to the government's side, on the other hand, were large irregular military forces recruited by John Murray, marquis of Atholl from highlanders hostile to Argyll.[39] Parliament responded with predictable loyalty, agreeing an address to the king that denounced the rising. Parliament also ratified the forfeiture of Argyll in 1681, put the former earl's offices and jurisdictions at the king's disposal, and annexed to the crown the estates of various other rebels and participants in the rising.[40] The emergency created by Argyll's rising had subsided by the end of June. The highland troops were stood down on 23rd, and Argyll was executed on 30th.[41] The episode suggested that the great majority of Scots were reluctant to rebel against James's rule. As well as continuing the eclipse of the Campbells in the highlands, bolstering Atholl's position in the region and in national politics, the failure of Argyll confirmed the king's authority in Scotland.

In the second half of 1685, James began to formulate his policy in favour of Roman Catholics. The chief obstacle he faced in giving employment to his co-religionists was the requirement that officials swear the Test oath. Prior to the meeting of parliament in 1685, James instructed his commissioner, William Douglas, duke of Queensberry, to secure an act obliging all protestant landowners to swear the Test. Parliament duly complied.[42] But despite giving the oath his backing, at least as a measure to deny presbyterians access to public life, James sought to prevent Catholics from being troubled by the Test. Already in May 1685, the king asked the privy council's secret committee whether to seek parliamentary approval of a new oath of allegiance, instead of the Test, which would abjure the Covenants and resistance, but would 'exclude no loyall Subject from taking thereof'.[43] George Douglas, earl of Dumbarton was that month made commander in chief of the forces, and was added to the secret committee, the inner circle of James's Scottish executive, in spite of his Catholicism.[44] In November, James instructed the privy council that, while he expected that most of the commissioners of supply named by parliament to collect the cess would take the Test in accordance with the law, he was exempting a list of Catholic commissioners from swearing.[45] In December, James explicitly dispensed his chancellor, the earl of Perth, a recent convert to Catholicism, from the Test.[46] He followed this by instructing the privy council that not even protestants should be pressed to swear the oath.[47]

In the spring of 1686, James and his ministers prepared for a new session of parliament, which the king hoped would repeal the laws against Catholicism. Prior to the session, James attempted to win advocates for his policy. Archbishop Arthur Ross of St Andrews and Bishop John Paterson of Edinburgh were at court in March, where they agreed to support James's agenda.[48] In Edinburgh, however, the privy council's secret committee was unenthusiastic. In response, James summoned William Hamilton, third duke of Hamilton, Lieutenant-General Drummond and Sir George Lockhart, president of the court of session, to court in an attempt to convince them.[49] They persuaded the king to consider introducing a measure of toleration in favour of moderate presbyterians. James referred this option to the secret committee for its deliberation, and the idea was not among the inducements to support the king offered in parliament. The secretary of state, John Drummond, viscount of Melfort, and his brother Perth insisted that any such toleration of presbyterians, if granted, would be by the royal prerogative, rather than by statute. This would make it easier to suspend the toleration, if James were to 'find it inconvenient'. Meanwhile, the business of parliament was to relieve Catholics from the penal laws and preferably also to abolish the Test and the oath of allegiance.[50]

When parliament sat down on 29 April, then, James's letter to the assembled commissioners made no promises in favour of protestantism, but instead attempted to win support by offering economic reforms. In line with the recommendation of the committee for trade in 1681, James promised to make 'the opening of a free trade with England our particular care'. He let it be known that his envoy at the French court was lobbying for the removal of a tariff on Scottish imports. And the commissioner, Alexander Stewart, fifth earl of Moray, proposed restoring the royal burghs' exclusive trading privileges, while stressing that the crown would not seek a further grant of taxation.[51] Despite these blandishments, the reluctance of members to act in favour of Catholics became clear when there was a lengthy debate over parliament's response to the king's letter, particularly about whether the use of the term 'Roman Catholics' gave the king's religion too much legitimacy.[52] A small majority of the Articles, the committee that prepared legislation, was willing to accept a draft act that would have protected Catholic worship in private houses, while leaving the penal laws on the statute book.[53] After debates in the full parliament, the draft went back to the Articles, whose members added a clause explicitly leaving in force the Test and the oath of allegiance.[54] Though this version fell far short of his initial hopes, James was willing for it to be put to a vote in parliament, if Moray was certain that there would be a majority in its favour.[55] Either way, the king was convinced that 'he Can doe mor' for Scottish Catholics than the act granted by means of his assumed power to suspend laws.[56] Melfort pressed Moray to ensure that there was a respectful discussion of the suspending power in parliament, presumably to provide a prospective vindication of the king's next steps.[57] Recognising the scale of opposition to toleration, Moray opted not to introduce the act in full parliament. The session was adjourned on 15 June and parliament did not meet again in James's reign.[58]

By the summer of 1686, the government was aware of widespread hostility to the toleration of Catholic worship, both among parliamentarians and in the country more generally. The most spectacular evidence had come in January and February 1686, when Edinburgh witnessed significant rioting against Catholics. The first protest, on 24 January, targeted a service taking place in the house of Peter Bruce (or Breusch), the German engineer who would subsequently become James's Catholic printer. Larger riots followed on 31 January and 1 February, affronting many of the elite Catholics resident in Edinburgh, including Perth himself.[59] The government also worried that ministers of the established Church, if their sermons reflected on popery, would stir up popular opposition to James's religious policy. James Canaries, minister of Selkirk, preached a forceful anti-Catholic sermon in Edinburgh in February, leading to his suspension from office by Archbishop Alexander Cairncross of Glasgow. But Cairncross secretly supported Canaries, encouraged him to print the sermon and ultimately lost his own job in part because of the episode.[60] In March 1686 and again in July 1687, James instructed the bishops to identify and censure any clergy who 'suggest unto, or amuse our Subjects with fears & Jealousies as if the established Religion was in hazard or danger'.[61] On 17 June 1686, a royal proclamation complained that 'divers Ministers, and others ... Do take upon them in Sermons, and other Discourses, To Allarm the People, and to raise dislike of Our Person and Government in their Hearts, Defaming and Slandering Our Designs'. Anyone found guilty was to be punished as a slanderer of the king under the terms of a statute of 1584. The pulpit was seen not only as the source of the disease, however, but also its cure: the proclamation was reissued in September, with instructions that ministers read it out in churches quarterly after their sermons.[62]

Meanwhile, James had reconfigured the upper echelons of his Scottish government. As the parliamentary session of 1686 was meeting, he removed from office several ministers and councillors who were reluctant to support toleration. Especially significant were Sir George Mackenzie of Rosehaugh, who lost his position as lord advocate in May, and Robert Bruce, removed from the bishopric of Dunkeld on 3 June. The judge Sir Alexander Seton, Lord Pitmedden was ejected from the court of session.[63] But the most important change in 1686 was the fall of Queensberry, whose position as treasurer ended with the introduction of a treasury commission in February 1686, and who lost his other offices in June.[64] These developments tended to confirm the power of the three leading converts to Catholicism: Perth, Melfort and Moray. Because Queensberry had been a firm defender of the established Church, historians writing from a British perspective often describe his fall as equivalent to that of the staunchly Anglican earls of Clarendon and Rochester in England. Likewise, the rise of the Drummonds is seen as akin to the consolidation of an English Catholic party around the earl of Sunderland.[65] But between Queensberry and the Drummonds there was as much a personal antagonism as a difference over religious policy. Moreover, Queensberry saw the protestant Hamilton as among his chief enemies.[66]

Perth, as chancellor, and Melfort and Moray, as the two secretaries of state, held the most influential offices after the treasury was put in commission. In 1686, James advanced further Catholics including George Gordon, duke of Gordon, Kenneth Mackenzie, earl of Seaforth and Charles Stewart, earl of Traquair to the privy council and other offices.[67] As we have seen, when James sought the advice of his Scottish councillors, he tended to work through the secret committee of the council, a body first appointed in 1683, perhaps at James's suggestion, when it numbered eight.[68] But despite these trends, and the execution of Argyll and the removal of Queensberry, James's regime did not become as unrepresentative of the Scottish elite as is sometimes alleged.[69] Among the country's magnates, Atholl held a central place in the government, while Hamilton was not alienated until after the collapse of James's authority. Unlike in England, after the fall of Cairncross James retained the support of the Scottish episcopate. Depending largely on the crown for their own survival, the bishops were committed to the last to the doctrines of divine-right monarchy.[70]

Having failed to secure the toleration of Catholics in parliament, James took his subsequent steps in religious affairs by means of the royal prerogative. More than was the case in early 1686, policy was devised at court and there was little room for discussion among councillors in Scotland. Writing in December 1688, the well-informed English dissenter Roger Morrice described Melfort as 'a principall man in laying down and promoting the late Methods both in Scotland and England, for the setting up of the Dispensing Power and all things depending thereupon'.[71] Whether Melfort was as important as this suggests, the king's failure to consult his councillors in Scotland makes it hard to assess what James thought he was doing, and what he expected the effects of his orders to be. Writing to the privy council on 21 August 1686, the king alleged that 'It was not any doubt Wee had of our Power' to safeguard Catholics in their worship that 'made Us bring in our Designes into our Parliam[en]t ... but to give our loyall Subjects a new opportunity of showing their Duty to Us, their Justice towards the Innocent, and their Charity towards their Neighbours'. Finding that he needed to instruct his subjects in the ways of justice and charity, James ordered that Catholic worship in private homes be protected, and that a Catholic chapel royal be established in Holyroodhouse.[72] For the time being, the beneficiaries of James's policy were Catholics, and his promises in favour of presbyterians remained unfulfilled.

In the following February, James's first indulgence suspended the penal laws against Catholics, allowing them to worship in houses and chapels, but not to hold public processions in royal burghs.[73] Quakers were granted full freedom to worship. The proclamation introduced a new oath of allegiance, replacing the various declarations and assertory oaths adopted under Charles II, including the Test. Eschewing religious details, the new oath focused solely on the king's 'Absolute Power' and asserted the doctrine of non-resistance to royal authority. 'Moderat Presbyterians ... willing to accept of Our Indulgence' were to be allowed to conduct services in private houses (see Figure 1.1).[74] But on 1 March, James instructed the privy council that no 'Presbiterians be allowed to Preach, but such only as have your Allowance for the same, and that they at receiving the said Indulgence take the Oath' specified in the declaration of indulgence.[75] Presbyterian ministers objected to the absolutist tenor of the oath, and probably none was prepared to swear it. Thus the king sent a further letter to the council, dated 31 March, allowing it to tolerate the worship of presbyterians who refused to swear any oath.[76] Perhaps because ministers were reluctant to apply for the council's permission to preach, or because toleration remained limited

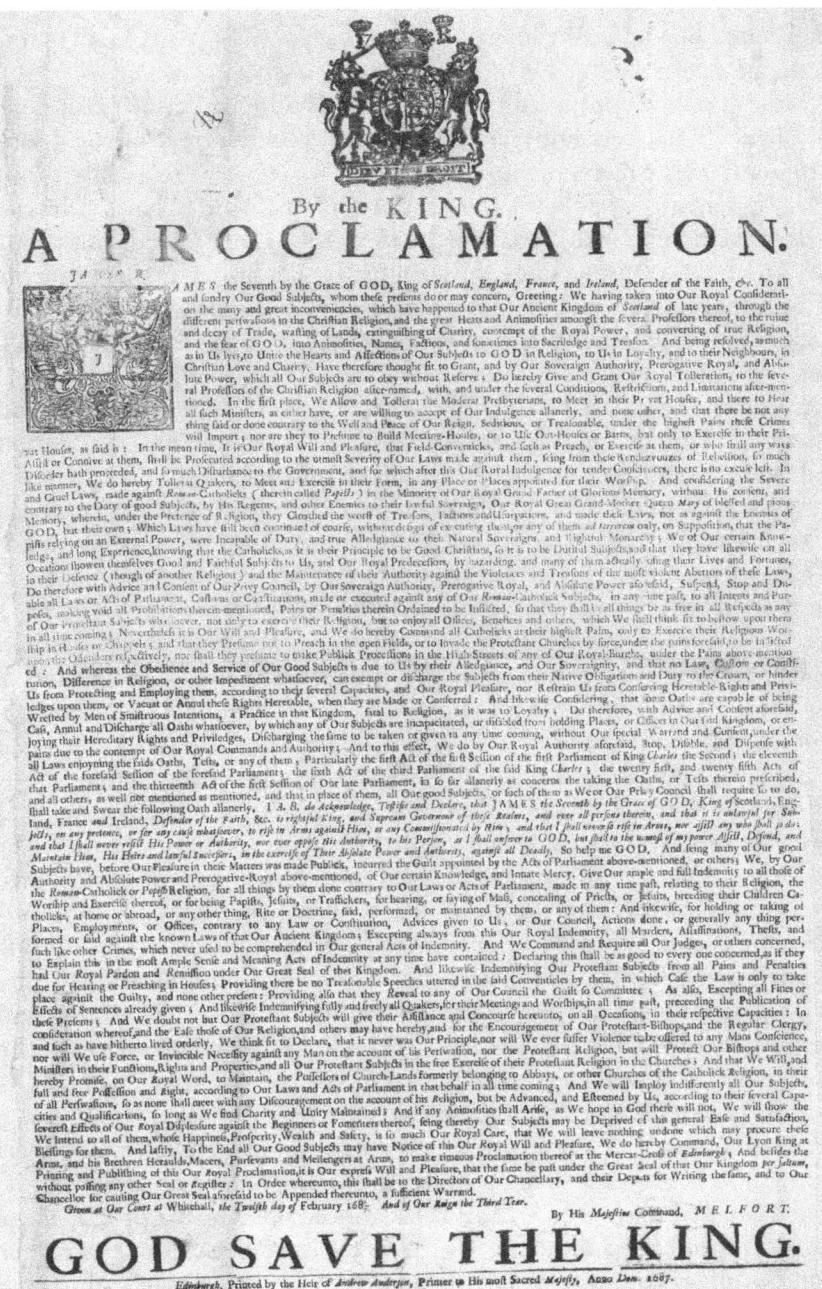

Figure 1.1 *By the King. A Proclamation* (Edinburgh, 1687), Wing J249, NLS, J.133.c.4(61). Reproduced by permission of the National Library of Scotland.

to private houses, few or no presbyterians seem to have taken advantage of the new terms.

James's policy continued to divide opinion among the Scottish political elite. On 16 September 1686, the privy council read a royal letter purging from its membership five noblemen. These were mostly prominent opponents of the royal agenda, and included Charles Erskine, earl of Mar, who had voted in the Articles against the act in favour of Catholics.[77] On the same day, councillors considered the letter they had drafted in response to James's order of 21 August, and there was a dispute about whether the king's actions could be described as 'legal'.[78] This argument reflected the court's insistence that all councillors should sign important letters to the king, thus sharing responsibility for their contents. Hamilton and his sons-in-law James Maule, earl of Panmure and John Cochrane, earl of Dundonald refused to sign the council's letter acknowledging the first indulgence. Hamilton suffered an official rebuke; Panmure and Dundonald were removed from the council.[79]

The order that did most to initiate a multiconfessional experiment in Scotland was the king's second declaration of indulgence. In this document, dated 28 June 1687, James admitted that 'sinistruous Interpretations ... either have, or may be made of some Restrictions' in the February indulgence. In response, he reaffirmed his commitment to protect the established Church, while suspending all laws against dissenting worship, except those prohibiting services held outdoors, now the special practice of the United Societies. When the new indulgence was printed, the broadside included the minute of the council, listing those present on 5 July when the text was ordered to be proclaimed, again to reflect the councillors' approval of the policy.[80]

The response of presbyterians to the second indulgence was generally enthusiastic. We shall see in Chapter 2 that while ministers and their congregations were not entirely free from restrictions, they were able to organise parallel Church structures in a way that repudiated Restoration uniformity. Further developments of James's religious policy, including his efforts to promote Catholicism, are discussed in Chapters 2 and 3. Here we should note that the king did not attempt to reverse his experiment, though some of his Catholic and episcopalian councillors may have wished him to.[81] On 7 May 1688, indeed, he issued a proclamation restating the second indulgence. This may have been done, as Robert Wodrow suggested, to coordinate Scottish policy with that in England, where James had taken the fateful decision to require Anglican clergy to read the declaration of indulgence in their churches. The same was not demanded of Scottish episcopalian ministers, but James took the opportunity of the proclamation to contradict unspecified critics, probably including presbyterian ministers, who said that the toleration 'will not be lasting'.[82] In fact, the multiconfessional experiment was to continue until the fall of the king.

* * *

It is now time to evaluate James's assertions of 'absolute' power. As we have seen, these claims were fundamental to his religious policy, which depended on the rights he exercised to dispense individuals from the Test oath and suspend the laws against Catholicism and protestant dissent. James's interpretation of the royal prerogative can be seen as an evolution from earlier seventeenth-century understandings. In religious affairs, Charles I's imposition by means of the prerogative of canons and a Prayer Book served as precedents for what a monarch might pretend to do. With respect to the royal burghs, we shall see in Chapter 4 that James VI and Charles I used the powers of nomination assumed by James. More particularly, James's view of his prerogative built on the statutes passed in the 1660s, which gave more specific definition to, and recognition of, monarchical powers than had previously existed. But James's desire to employ Catholics and impose multiconfessionalism led him urgently to emphasise his authority, in a series of official statements more aggressive than those made under Charles II. Indeed, James became more assertive of his power as his reign advanced. In March 1685, he instructed Queensberry, the commissioner in that year's session of parliament, to propose an act abolishing the periodic rendezvous of the militia required by a law of 1669, substituting instead more infrequent musters at royal command. While parliament was sitting, however, James sent another instruction cancelling the first, because it was his intention 'to have nothing brought into Parliament w[hi]ch wee may doe by our Prerogative alone'. Unfortunately, this attempt to preserve the royal prerogative over the militia failed. Before receiving the king's second instruction, Queensberry promised parliament that it would legislate on the matter, and it was thought fit to allow the intended act to pass.[83]

In March 1686, in advance of the second session of parliament, the privy council's secret committee sought the advice of the bishops about the king's plans for Catholic relief. Responding angrily, James defended his right to dispense individuals from the laws and to suspend statutes entirely. As well as asserting his prerogative to employ any of his subjects, regardless of their religion, James claimed that:

> it is inherent in Us, and an undoubted Prerogative of our Crown, to dispense with, and to suspend all Sanguinary & Penall Laws for any Crime or Delinquency whatsoever, and in like manner to suspend all Oathes relating to the Goverment [sic] or obedience to Us, as the Test, Supremacy, Allegiance &c.[84]

Though James wished that parliament would repeal the penal laws affecting Catholics, he was already convinced that he could suspend the legislation. But unlike in England, where the court case *Godden* v. *Hales* vindicated James's dispensing power, there was no explicit judicial ruling on the king's claim to free individual office-holders from the Test.[85]

In his first declaration of indulgence, James made an uncompromising public statement about his power to suspend standing laws. The toleration of Catholic worship was to take effect by the king's 'Sovereign Authority, Prerogative Royal, and Absolute Power, which all Our Subjects are to obey without Reserve'.[86] In a hostile commentary on the declaration, the Scottish clergyman Gilbert Burnet, in exile in the Netherlands, claimed to find these phrases new and alarming. He acknowledged that the concept of absolute power might be traced to the Roman law formulation, *princeps legibus solutus* ('the prince is unconstrained by the laws'). But requiring Scots to obey 'without reserve' was 'carrying Obedience many sizes beyond what the *Grand Seigneur* [Louis XIV of France] has ever yet claimed'. Not only did the declaration exaggerate the Scottish king's power, Burnet suggested, but James's despotic presumption exceeded that of Louis, generally seen in Britain as the quintessential arbitrary tyrant.[87] But while the king's language was provocative, it was not new. The 1685 act of parliament granting the inland excise to the crown in perpetuity referred to the 'king's sacred, supream, absolute power and authority', and to members' resolution 'to give their entire obedience to his majesty without reserve'. The phrase 'without reserve' had been used in a similar context by Perth in his speech at the opening of the parliamentary session. If the language of absolute power and obedience without reserve was first propagated by a member of the government, it had nevertheless been approved by parliament two years before the first indulgence.[88]

The fact that Scottish subjects had themselves called the king 'absolute' seemed, to James's supporters, to justify the subsequent steps of his policy. During the 1686 meeting of parliament, Melfort argued that Scots had already 'given too much to stop nou', and refuse to accept

Catholic relief, 'as is most evident by the act of Excise in the last sessione'. But Melfort also wondered whether the statute of 1685 might in fact free the king from seeking parliament's consent to suspend the penal laws.[89] When James reiterated his indulgences, in his proclamation of 7 May 1688, he referred to parliament's recognition of his authority in 1685.[90] And while there was no real challenge to the king's suspending power, Scots who were sceptical that he had absolute power were given assurances that James planned to seek parliamentary approval for his religious policy. To the general meeting of presbyterian ministers, which had addressed the king in gratitude for the second indulgence, Melfort wrote that as James had 'begun to disable' the penal 'Laws by his Soveraigne & Absolute Power so he will ratify what he has done, in his next Parliament, for his People's ease & Security in all time coming'.[91] Though there was no sign at the end of the reign that a new parliament was imminent, the crown recognised that a significant number of Scots would like to see the actions of absolute power reviewed by the representatives of the nation.

James, then, had absolute power in a theoretical sense. As the possessor of undivided sovereignty, the staff of St Andrews University declared, he was the true author and fountain of law and justice.[92] He could thus claim the right to suspend penal laws restricting worship outwith the established Church. We shall see in Chapters 2 and 3 that the result was a transformation of religious life, lasting from the summer of 1687 to the end of James's reign. But his religious policy was a deregulation, or a giving up of power. It was a negative exercise of royal authority: James forbade inferior magistrates from enforcing particular laws, thus giving protection to those who wanted to break those laws. But how freely could James rule in a positive fashion, by giving commands and having them obeyed? In practical terms, how much power did he have in Scotland?

In recent years, we have learned much about the power of the government in seventeenth-century Scotland. Beginning in the fifteenth century, Julian Goodare argues, Scottish monarchs asserted their authority in new ways, creating an 'absolutist state' capable of serving the interests of the crown and landed subjects alike. Under James VI, there was a 'Stewart revolution in government' increasing the centralisation and capacity of the Scottish state.[93] Then in the 1640s, the Covenanting regime expanded public revenues with new taxes and borrowing, while improving the state's military effectiveness and its ability to intervene in the localities.[94] Though they repudiated the political reforms of the Covenanters, Charles II and James VII accepted several of their fiscal innovations, notably the inland excise and the cess. The result was that, by the 1680s, Charles II's income was perhaps three times that of his father.[95] And if this was the long-term trajectory of the crown's position in Scotland, it seems that in the 1680s the English state experienced still more rapid development. In that decade, J. R. Western established, the English state became more efficient, better funded and militarily stronger.[96] More recently, Steve Pincus has described James II as a modernising king of England, who was determined to reform his armed forces, increase his control over the press and public discourse and achieve greater influence in the localities.[97] While Pincus exaggerates the coherence of the royal agenda in England, he identifies the impatience with which the king often proceeded. In Scotland, James's approach resembled not so much a programme of modernisation as a series of experiments. We shall see that he had high hopes for his religious and administrative policies, but no way to envisage many of their consequences. Nevertheless, James certainly sought to increase the power of the central government in Scotland. The following paragraphs offer a brief assessment of his endeavours, though there remains much scope for further research.

We will consider three aspects of the king's fiscal-military capacity and executive authority. First, how large was the crown's income, and was it growing in the period? Using the audited accounts of the treasury, we can calculate that the king's average daily revenue from March 1686 to August 1688 was £4,490.15s.3d.[98] His annual income in this interval was thus on average £1,639,128.6s.3d. Scots, or about £136,594 sterling. This means that James's Scottish revenue was about one fifteenth of what he derived from England, with its population of perhaps five times that of Scotland.[99] Scotland was poorer and less heavily taxed than its southern neighbour, and we might note that in the long term, Scotland's revenues shrank relative to those of England. In 1659, Scottish taxes raised a sum equal to 9.5 per cent of the amount collected in England; in 1707, article eight of the union specified that Scotland would in future pay land tax at 2.4 per cent of the rate levied in England.[100]

But in Scotland as in England, James was a significantly more prosperous monarch than Charles II had been. Charles's average daily Scottish income from February 1676 to March 1679 was £2,864.11s.1d.[101] The mid-1680s saw a large rise in royal revenues, which can be attributed partly to growing receipts from the customs and foreign excise, but especially to regular payments of the cess imposed by the convention of estates in 1678, continued by parliament in 1681 and increased in 1685.[102] Thus James benefited from rising royal revenue during his brother's final years, which his central role in the administration helped to secure. He was also a prudent spender. Though the treasurer's accounts show that spending exceeded income in the two years ending in March 1686, the Scottish state was in surplus by May 1688.[103] Moreover, James tried to promote more efficient means of tax collection. In February 1686, he insisted that the inland excise should be collected directly – by crown employees – and not farmed to private collectors. Direct collection had worked in England, and James was prepared to ignore the advice of his Scottish treasury commissioners that the system would raise less than the previous farm. It soon appeared that the commissioners were right: the king's preferred method of collection led to plummeting yields, though there were some gains in heavily populated areas such as Edinburgh, Glasgow and Haddingtonshire. The commissioners claimed that brewers, who paid the majority of the excise, had ceased operation, but the falling income may have been partly the fault of dishonest collectors.[104] With the king's permission, new farms of the excise were agreed in November and December 1686.[105] Though his reform of the excise backfired, James enjoyed a 6.9 per cent rise in revenue between the periods April 1685 to March 1686 and March 1686 to August 1688.[106]

Military force was a second dimension of James's power.[107] The king spent greater sums on his army than on anything else. Again he was in a stronger position than Charles had been, and was the beneficiary of growing investment in the army since the 1670s. Military expenditure was particularly high in the mid-1680s.[108] Partly this was due to the costs of mobilising against Argyll's rising, but the spending also allowed for an increase in the size of the Scottish standing army between June 1684, when the crown budgeted for 2,564 officers and men (excluding the artillery and garrisons), and November 1685, when the army was to number 3,252.[109] As well as responding to the emergency of Argyll's invasion, this growth reflected James's preference for standing forces over the militia, which led to the end of annual militia musters.[110] But after 1685, the king tended to retrench, reducing his forces by 120 men in March 1686, and by a further fifty-four in June 1687.[111] Only in March 1688 was there renewed growth, when James recalled those of his subjects who served as soldiers and seamen in the Dutch republic. There was incomplete obedience to the king's order, especially among the rank and file, but the return of John Wauchope and others from the Scoto-Dutch regiments allowed a new Scottish regiment to be levied.[112]

In general, however, we can conclude that James did not sustain the high levels of military spending of the start of his reign, and the expansion of the army ceased to be his objective until 1688.[113] By contrast, the king invested consistently and heavily in his English army, which grew by over 200 per cent between his accession and William of Orange's invasion. At the start of the reign, the king's Scottish army was, relative to the kingdom's population, perhaps 40 per cent larger than his English forces. But by late 1688, when James drew together his English, Irish and Scottish soldiers to resist William, his English troops were, proportionately, at least 60 per cent more numerous than the Scottish army.[114] James had larger standing forces than Charles II, but he had much greater capacity to fund a big army in England than in Scotland, and made more of a priority of military expansion in the southern kingdom. If his English army was increasingly comparable with those of continental princes – probably in 1688 it was a little larger as a proportion of the population than the Habsburg army, though it was surpassed by the forces of Louis XIV – James's Scottish army was left behind.[115] There were strict limits both to the country's military potential and to the king's ambitions for his Scottish armed forces.

A third facet of the king's power was the administrative capacity of his government. Despite rising royal revenues, the central government remained small in Restoration Scotland. The number of officers of state and administrators receiving royal salaries changed little under Charles II and James VII. It is impossible to derive precise totals from the lists of fees approved by each king, but across the period to 1688, there were probably around seventy or eighty paid officials of the central government.[116] Relative to national population, the Scottish administration was a little smaller than its counterpart in England, where Gerald Aylmer was able to count 517 servants of the crown in June 1673, and 470 a decade later.[117] But both bureaucracies were dwarfed by the civil service of Louis XIV's France.

An important contrast between Scotland and England lay in the ability of the king to intervene in the localities and influence the conduct of local government. We have seen that Charles and James sometimes exercised their power in Scottish communities by bypassing the established authorities. This reflected their concern that local magistrates failed to enforce the laws against religious dissent with sufficient vigour. More generally, James faced a problem familiar to his royal predecessors in Scotland: most of the courts responsible for justice and administration in the counties and districts were in private hands, and were passed on heritably within families. Thus the majority of the thirty-three sheriffs (who held the king's courts in the shires) and the more numerous lords possessing regalities (who exercised most of the king's powers of justice over about half of Scotland) could be neither removed nor appointed by the king.[118] In 1682, the refusal of sixteen possessors of heritable jurisdictions to swear the Test gave the crown the opportunity to nominate the holders of twenty-two regalities and sheriffdoms.[119] But during his reign, James named men to only nine sheriffdoms that were in his gift (two of which were vacated in 1682), revoking one of his commissions in the interest of a hereditary holder.[120] Under James, the other crown presentations to local offices in rural Scotland were five bailies of regalities and other estates (three of which offices had changed hands in 1682), and temporary lieutenancies and justiceships of seven regions, mostly in response to Argyll's invasion in 1685.[121] James also renewed the commission with judicial oversight of the highland counties first established by his brother in 1682.[122] Some of these appointments helped to change the balance of power in particular regions; especially significant was the displacement of Argyll's authority in the western highlands, a process that began with his forfeiture in 1681. But otherwise James's impact on the personnel in charge of Scotland's rural communities was small. In Scotland, he could not undertake the sort of remodelling of local magistracy he implemented in England, where lords lieutenant and justices of the peace (JPs) unsympathetic to the king's religious policy were removed to make way for apparently more supportive men.[123] And he lacked local officers comparable to the intendants of France, royal appointees, who were usually independent of local interest groups, with the authority to impose the king's will in the regions.[124]

The most substantial difference that James could make was by nominating the magistrates and councillors of the royal burghs. Though there were precedents for this policy in earlier periods, no previous Scottish monarch had intervened in the towns' government to the same extent. By suspending council elections and naming provosts and bailies, James hoped to ensure that the burghs' representatives in a future parliament would support his policies. If his interventions created tensions in some towns, there was no significant obstruction to his commands. But we shall see that there were limits to the efficiency with which the policy was implemented. Moreover, close inspection of the local records reveals that James made less difference to the composition of burgh councils than has sometimes been imagined.

James made more deliberate strides towards absolutism – in theory and practice – than his brother had done.[125] Though the steep rise in Scottish revenues and the crown's military capacity dated from the late 1670s, James increased both his income and the size of his army in 1685. Thereafter, however, he enjoyed only a modest growth in revenue and did not significantly expand his armed forces. He took charge of the personnel of urban government, and used temporary commissions to exercise justice in place of sitting local magistrates. But he did not wrest control of the majority of Scotland from the jurisdiction of courts held by private landowners. In Scotland, we might suggest, he was an equivocal moderniser, whose programme lacked the obsessive enthusiasm to increase central power evident in his English government. Nevertheless, as we shall see in the following chapters, James was an innovative, experimental, risk-taking king of Scotland. He brought about a series of upheavals in the country's politics and society. And when he was toppled in the revolution, there was a violent reaction to his rule.

2

James's Religious Experiment

THIS CHAPTER ANALYSES THE impact of James's indulgences of 1687, which granted freedom of worship to the great majority of Scots. The king's policy was a radical experiment: no previous Scottish ruler had allowed such wide-ranging religious toleration, with such unpredictable results. Indeed, the indulgences constituted a clean break from the crown's previous approach – pursued with vigour until the mid-1680s – which used penal laws to enforce religious uniformity. Though there had been a series of indulgences in favour of presbyterian ministers in 1669, 1672 and 1679, none of these had resulted in the unrestricted religious pluralism that developed in the years 1687–9. Whereas Charles II sought to mitigate the problem of presbyterian dissent while maintaining a uniform national Church, James repudiated the assumptions on which religious uniformity rested. Not only did he stimulate a revival of Catholicism, by allowing the public celebration of the mass, funding Catholic institutions and promoting Catholics to political office: he also turned his back on the traditional view that it was the duty of magistrates to suppress schism and preserve common standards of religious belief, practice and organisation. He hoped to maintain order in Scotland, in spite of religious diversity, and insisted that the field conventicles of the Cameronians would not be tolerated. Yet it is unclear whether James anticipated the principal effects of his indulgences: a massive resurgence of organised presbyterianism in southern Scotland, and a corresponding decline in support for the established Church.

It is difficult to interpret the thinking behind James's policy, and probably impossible to decide whether he sincerely favoured toleration for protestant dissenters. From Robert Wodrow to Peter Hume Brown, most historians of Scotland assumed that James wanted to impose Catholicism on the country.[1] In this reading, the liberty for presbyterians was at best a diversion, at worst a sham. More recently, scholars including Maurice Ashley and W. A. Speck have seen James as essentially tolerant.[2] And yet other historians stress that, because he tended to view protestant dissenters as rebels, his commitment to freedom of conscience is questionable. The Scottish government's suppression of presbyterian dissent, during James's visits to Edinburgh as duke of Albany and York and after his accession to the throne, suggests that he was not consistently opposed to persecution.[3] As we saw in Chapter 1, in the spring of 1686 some of the king's protestant councillors called for toleration to be extended to presbyterians as well as Catholics. James was in no hurry to accede, and it was only after the second indulgence, issued on 28 June 1687, that a revival of presbyterianism could take place.

Aside from the rhetoric of the successive letters and declarations, however, there is little evidence of the king's motives in launching a multiconfessional experiment. His letter to the privy council of 21 August 1686, ordering the protection of private Catholic worship, called for the government to prosecute Scots who said that the king 'intended to make any violent alterations'. '[I]t is far from our thoughts to use any violence in matters of Conscience', James continued.[4] The first declaration of indulgence, of 12 February 1687, lamented that religious divisions created 'Heats and Animosities', undermining trade and breeding contempt for royal authority.[5] We do not know if James really believed that the indulgences would solve these problems. Undoubtedly the king hoped to stimulate a flood of conversions to Catholicism. But the emphasis of the first indulgence, which primarily benefited Catholics and Quakers, allowing only a restricted toleration of presbyterians, might make us think that James was reluctant to allow widespread competition among protestants. And yet perhaps the changes made by his declaration of June 1687 indicate that he had not been well advised about the likely response of presbyterians to the first indulgence, and that he had sought to liberate them all along. We shall see that presbyterians, though they gained from the king's policy, generally distrusted his motives. Rather than speculate further about James's intentions, however, this chapter concentrates on the effects of his religious experiment.

The main consequences of the indulgences are well known, and were first summarised by Robert Wodrow, whose *History of the Sufferings of the Church of Scotland* (1721-2) has been the basis of most subsequent accounts. Wodrow printed the main documents illustrating the king's evolving policy, together with some important information about the response of the leading presbyterians. But his discussion is otherwise anecdotal, and gives little detail about the effects of the indulgences beyond Edinburgh and Glasgow.[6] Other scholars have depended on Wodrow, and more generally on impressionistic sources written from the perspective of Edinburgh. So as to give a more substantial account of the impact of James's toleration, this chapter is based on a much wider body of source material. As well as sources illustrating the central government's policy, it draws on a full survey of the records of the established Church's synods and presbyteries, as well as those of the synods and presbyteries set up by presbyterians from 1687. To these regional and district-level sources are added a large sample of parochial kirk session registers, the surviving Quaker records and correspondence from the Scottish Catholic Archives.[7]

The chapter begins by charting the evolution of James's religious experiment, and assessing the ways in which the indulgences departed from the crown's previous policies. We then examine the responses to toleration of the dissenting religious groups. A small but growing Catholic mission provided priests for existing Catholic communities, and achieved a high profile at Holyrood, thanks to the crown's investment in the chapel royal and a Jesuit college. The Quakers expressed gratitude for the king's favour, but do not seem to have attracted many new members. Excluded from protection under the indulgences, the Cameronians continued to preach outdoors in protest against the king's rule. But by far the most significant response to the indulgences was that of the mainstream presbyterians. They quickly organised themselves in the south of Scotland, and in a few places further north, setting up church courts, renting meeting houses and collecting funds. Many presbyterian ministers came out of retirement, returned from exile, or were newly ordained. Together they attempted to meet the demand for preaching. After the overthrow of James, they were assisted by presbyterian ministers fleeing the war in Ireland. If the scale of presbyterian resurgence was more limited than some previous scholars have recognised, presbyterians entirely eclipsed their episcopalian rivals in some places, and offered vigorous competition to the established Church elsewhere. By the end of the discussion, then, the scene will have been set for Chapter 3, in which we examine the multiconfessional competition between Scotland's religious groups.

* * *

Together, the king's declarations and indulgences were a dramatic reversal of earlier royal policies concerning religious dissent. The change can be understood in three main ways. First, James explicitly suspended the catalogue of penal statutes passed against Catholicism since 1560. These laws sought to forbid or restrict Catholic worship and education. Their starting point had been an act of the Reformation parliament of 1560 prohibiting the mass. This statute, ratified in 1567, threatened confiscation of goods for both celebrants and worshippers, and banishment and death for repeat offenders. An act of 1594 specified the death penalty for all found guilty of hearing mass.[8] A string of laws targeted priests and their protectors; from 1592, the clergy and their harbourers were considered guilty of treason.[9] Another category of legislation aimed to restrict the education of children in schools on the continent and of Catholic children at home.[10] The package of penal laws was ratified after the Restoration of the monarchy, in an act that envisaged banishment as the standard punishment for priests. Parliament also called for lists of suspected lay papists to be compiled, and for the children of Catholics to be educated under protestant supervision.[11] Subsequently, there were periodic orders for the enforcement of the penal laws, including by the parliament of 1681.[12] In James's first parliamentary session as king, a short act was passed to ratify all laws in defence of protestantism, without specific reference to the penal laws.[13]

James's experiment had less effect on the lives of Catholics than might first appear, because the laws against Catholicism were rarely enforced after 1660.[14] Indeed, the successive measures against Catholic recusancy in the Restoration period were essentially hollow gestures, designed to compensate for the unpopular re-establishment of episcopacy in the Kirk. According to Sir George Mackenzie of Rosehaugh, 'whenever any thing was done in favours of Episcopacy, there was at the same time also somewhat done against popery, for allaying the humour of the people'.[15] But if Catholics who worshipped discreetly could live without much interference after the Restoration, under James they gained new confidence to celebrate mass in public. Catholic worship was becoming visible, in Edinburgh at least, by late 1685 and early 1686, prompting the riots discussed in Chapter 1. The indulgence of February 1687 confirmed that Catholic priests would be able to conduct worship openly, and to seek new converts.

A second way in which James rejected earlier assumptions was by abandoning all state oaths that contained a religious test. In particular, the first indulgence suspended the oath of allegiance of 1661, which denied the pope's ecclesiastical authority, and was formerly taken by all officers of state, session and exchequer, by sheriffs, commissaries, magistrates and councillors of royal burghs.[16] The indulgence also discharged the Test oath of 1681, with its requirement that swearers profess their adherence to protestantism.[17] By superseding these engagements, James opened public offices to all those prepared to swear the new oath specified in the first indulgence, removing the need for a specific dispensation when a Catholic or presbyterian was nominated to office. As we noted in Chapter 1, many presbyterians objected to the absolutist terms of the new oath, but it was designed to be acceptable to loyal Catholics. Whereas parliament had tried to prevent Charles II from giving offices to dissenters from the established Church, James asserted his right to employ whichever of his subjects he chose, regardless of their religious principles.

James reversed previous policies in a third way: by rejecting the ideal of uniformity among protestants. Here there was a precedent in the religious toleration allowed in Scotland under Cromwellian rule in the 1650s. Yet the earlier toleration had less practical effect than James's experiment, not only because it excluded Catholics, but also because the large majority of Scottish protestants were then presbyterians. Nevertheless, the Cromwellian toleration permitted considerable public discussion of religious doctrines, leading a small number of Scots to become Quakers, Independents and Baptists, protestant dissenting groups of English origin or inspiration.[18] At the start of the 1650s, furthermore, a fault-line opened within presbyterianism, dividing Protesters from Resolutioners over how to respond to the failed Scottish intervention in England of 1648, the accession of Charles II and the Cromwellian invasion of Scotland. In a few localities, rival preachers competed for hearers.[19] Meanwhile, various deposed and excommunicated presbyterian ministers conducted irregular marriages and baptisms with impunity.[20] But while there was a degree of fragmentation in the 1650s, few Scots had a choice about where to worship and most continued to attend their parish churches. Compared with the situation in 1687–9, there was little multiconfessional competition.

James's experiment was foreshadowed by the Cromwellian toleration, but it rejected the policies pursued since the emergence of widespread religious dissent in the early 1660s, which were based on the enforcement of uniformity. To understand this point, it is important to recognise the differences between James's indulgences and those issued under his brother Charles in 1669 and 1672. The earlier indulgences nominated presbyterian ministers to preach in particular vacant parishes, located in areas where there was strong hostility to the episcopalian settlement. These ministers were allowed to preach within their parishes only, and restrictions were imposed to prevent them from attracting worshippers resident in parishes where episcopalian ministers had been settled. And the presbyterian clergy were not permitted to organise presbyteries and synods of their own. The presbyterians were not fully accommodated into the established Church, as they would have been under the scheme proposed by Bishop Robert Leighton in 1670, but the Kirk's uniform structures were preserved. Unlike in 1687–9, there was to be no competition between episcopalian and presbyterian clergy for followers, and as little movement across parish boundaries as possible.[21] In 1679, a further indulgence, part of the peace settlement after the defeat of the presbyterians at the battle of Bothwell Bridge, allowed presbyterian ministers to hold house conventicles across most of southern Scotland under council licence.[22] This might have allowed a situation closer to the multiconfessional competition of 1687–9. But in May 1680, pressure from the bishops led the crown to place new restrictions on the 1679 indulgence. Almost all the ministers who had benefited from the measure were again prevented from preaching by the end of 1680.[23]

As we saw in Chapter 1, the early and mid-1680s saw the government adopt new and more vigorous measures against presbyterian dissent. Meanwhile, the privy council gradually moved against presbyterian ministers indulged under the arrangements of 1669 and 1672, cancelling their licences for various infractions of the indulgences' conditions. In January 1684, for example, the council silenced four indulged ministers who had failed to limit their ministry to one parish. They had refused to observe the national thanksgiving day for the discovery of the Rye House Plot in September 1683, and some had failed to keep the annual thanksgiving day for the Restoration on 29 May.[24] Then in December 1684, the council's justiciary commissioners in south-west Scotland were instructed to require indulged ministers to find caution to cease preaching or to leave the country.[25] This order signalled the end of the Restoration model of indulged presbyterian preaching, obliging moderate dissenters to attend episcopalian services. Prior to the indulgences of 1687, the government's actions against dissent increasingly focused on the Cameronian militants, and the disappearance of moderate presbyterian nonconformity seemed a real possibility. James's policy in 1687 suddenly abandoned the expectation that moderate presbyterians should conform, though Cameronians remained subject to a coercive campaign.

James's experiment initiated an ultimately uncontrollable presbyterian resurgence. But the king continued to hope that, like Charles II's privy council, his government could regulate presbyterian nonconformity. Thus the second indulgence required presbyterians to notify the privy council or local magistrates of their places of worship and preachers.[26] At least one of the new presbyterian congregations followed this instruction straight away.[27] But in August, the duke of Hamilton wrote that 'ministers observe no methods in their preaching or in fixing them selves to places & giveing notice to the magistrat where they are to preach'.[28] This sort of complaint resulted on 5 October 1687 in an act of the privy council, which threatened to prosecute ministers who preached without informing magistrates.[29] The council's records include eighteen reports, received from October 1687 to July 1688, listing the activities of forty-four ministers, who preached in places across Fife and Kinross-shire, in Edinburgh, Glasgow and the surrounding areas, as well as in Kincardineshire and Dundee.[30] There were presumably also lost notices, and others were made to local officials.[31] But already in November 1687, one magistrate described weekday services that had taken place without prior warning, and wrote that 'our indulged cleargiemen and their church officers are wearie off this formalitie' of reporting their meetings in advance.[32] It is possible that the practice entirely ceased several months before the revolution.

In 1688, the appointment of national thanksgiving days for the pregnancy and successful childbirth of James's consort, Mary of Modena, further highlighted the presbyterian congregations' freedom from government oversight. Following the example of the authorities in England, the Scottish privy council ordered thanksgivings in January and June. In both cases, the council's orders related only to parish churches – then possessed solely by the episcopalian clergy – and did not require presbyterian meeting houses to observe the thanksgivings.[33] Possibly this was a precaution taken to avoid provoking opposition to the thanksgiving days: presbyterian ministers, as we noted above, were reluctant to observe special worship appointed by civil authority alone.[34] On the other hand, many of the celebrations of the queen's fecundity were organised by royal burghs, and would have involved residents of different religious persuasions.[35] But the privy council's failure explicitly to demand presbyterian support for the royal succession is noteworthy. In rural areas of the south and west, where presbyterian ministers had gained many followers since the second indulgence, the thanksgivings for James's great triumph must have been widely disregarded. By the summer of 1688, presbyterians, who at first received little encouragement from James's religious experiment, had almost complete control over the times and locations of their worship.

* * *

By suspending the penal laws, the first indulgence allowed Catholic priests to operate freely. But the Catholic mission remained a small affair. In 1687 and early 1688, there were six or seven clergy settled in parts of the highlands where Catholicism was traditionally strong, with an additional twelve active in the north-east lowlands and other highland and Hebridean areas.[36] By the end of August 1688, there were over forty priests in Scotland; in addition to the northern heartlands, missionaries were now based around Edinburgh, Glasgow and the southwest. This enlarged total included six Jesuits resident in the college at Holyroodhouse, and at least four who were ill or dying.[37] Though some priests reported growing numbers of communicants, they thought that the mission would 'thyue much better if God's Goodnesse uold Giue us a bishop'.[38] It is probably correct to say that the mission was hampered by its lack of leadership, and by the rivalries among the priests. The proposed appointment of Scotland's first Catholic bishop since the Reformation stimulated much gossip and clerical jostling for position. In February 1687, the secular priest David Burnet blamed the Jesuits for obstructing the nomination of any of his brethren.[39] A year later, Lewis Innes, principal of the Scots College, Paris, complained that the delay in choosing a bishop was 'openly scandalous', divisive and made Scotland an 'object of dounright laughter and mockery to our neighbours'.[40] It was rumoured in September 1687 that James saw no reason for haste; yet in the following summer, he sent to Rome a shortlist of two candidates: Innes and Thomas Nicolson, a priest working in Scotland. The project was aborted by the revolution, though Nicolson was made bishop and vicar apostolic in 1694.[41] In parallel to the discussions about a bishopric, the government aimed to recreate the monastic foundation at Holyrood Abbey. Again there was little unity of purpose among the clergy, as Augustinians and Benedictines competed for the prize.[42]

The proclamations of indulgence denied Catholics the use of protestant church buildings, and there was little new construction to accommodate Catholic congregations. An exception was at Enzie, Banffshire, where a chapel dedicated to St Ninian was built, opening in 1688 with room for 1,000 worshippers.[43] And in May 1688, after lobbying from the local priest Robert Strachan, the king ordered that Trinity Church in Aberdeen, a former protestant property, should be used for Catholic services. Sermons were preached there from late June.[44] But significantly more governmental and clerical attention focused on the Catholic chapel royal at Holyrood. Initiated after the king's letter to the privy council of 21 August 1686, the chapel was at first located in the former council chamber in Holyroodhouse. In September, the king instructed the treasury commissioners to pay for fittings in the room, at the direction of the earl of Perth.[45] An altar, images and vestments were brought from London, and the chapel was consecrated on St Andrew's Day 1686.[46] By February 1687, the chapel was deemed too small, and building works were ordered for its enlargement.[47] Then on 28 June, the king decided to move the chapel royal from Holyroodhouse itself to the nave of the adjacent abbey church, the surviving remains of the former Holyrood Abbey. This required the ejection of the Canongate parish congregation of the established Kirk, which had worshipped in the nave and was now relocated to Lady Yester's Church, pending the construction of a new church in the Canongate. Lady Yester's, a building otherwise surplus to Edinburgh's requirements, was then accommodating a French protestant congregation, which in turn moved to the town college's common hall.[48] The new, larger royal chapel was to be the focal point of the recently revived Order of the Thistle, of which the Drummond brothers and other Catholic noblemen were the first members.[49] It was thus an elite project, which raised the profile of Catholicism in the capital, but could not provide services to the large majority of Scottish Catholics.

Another important Catholic response to toleration, which also tended to concentrate resources at Holyrood, was the establishment by the Jesuits of a school in the royal palace. As with the chapel royal, James gave considerable financial backing to the Jesuits' efforts. Beginning in August 1687, rooms in the palace were allocated for their use; that December, the king promised £500 sterling to the project.[50] Conveniently, the chapel royal that had been refurbished inside the palace, but had been superseded by the chapel in the abbey, was available for the school.[51] The school opened to pupils in February or March 1688. In March, the diarist Lauder of Fountainhall noted the appearance of *The Rules of the Schools*, a broadsheet setting out the new institution's regulations.[52] This publication announced that children would be taught for free, without regard to religious background, and that 'every one shall be promoted according to his Deserts'. 'There shall not be, either by Masters or Scholars, any tampering or medling to perswade any one from the Profession of his own Religion'. Protestants were entitled to excuse themselves from attending mass. Whether these tolerant principles were observed in reality is questionable, because *The Rules of the Schools* probably gives little indication of the local characteristics of the Holyroodhouse school. The broadsheet was almost identical to two sets of rules issued by Jesuit schools in London, at least one of which was published before the Holyrood text. The one significant change made to the London broadsheets was to add philosophy to the Latin, Greek, poetry and rhetoric that the schools promised to teach.[53] This suggests that the Jesuits at Holyrood were seeking to compete not only with local grammar schools, but also with the protestant town college.

Though the Catholic population was much larger in the north, Holyrood became the main focus of the Catholic revival in Scotland. Resources were concentrated in and around Holyroodhouse, at royal direction and because of the presence of elite Catholics in Edinburgh and the Canongate. As we shall see in Chapter 3, the residence of numerous priests, the worship of the chapel royal and the operation of a prolific Catholic printing press in Holyroodhouse helped to make the royal palace and its vicinity a centre of multiconfessional interaction and confrontation.

* * *

As far as Scotland's small Quaker population was concerned, the indulgences probably made little difference. Quakers had been fined and incarcerated in the 1660s and 1670s, especially in their stronghold of Aberdeen. In 1679, their position improved when, apparently as a result of James's influence, the imprisoned Aberdonian Quakers were released. Thereafter, James protected the Friends from further prosecution.[54] After the first declaration of indulgence, the Aberdeen Quakers' monthly meeting received a letter from its prominent member Robert Barclay, then in London, urging it to follow the example of English Quakers in addressing the king in gratitude. Approving the suggestion, around sixty Friends in Aberdeen and Montrose commissioned Barclay to act on their behalf. The resulting address thanked James for clemency towards Scottish Quakers since 1679.[55] A second address, referring more specifically to the recent indulgence, was sent from the Quaker meeting at Heads, in Glassford, Lanarkshire.[56] It is difficult to detect any change in the Quakers' practices as a result of the toleration, partly because of gaps in their records.[57] It is clear, however, that in 1688–9, Quakers in Lanarkshire shared the fate of local episcopalian ministers, and of Catholics in various parts of Scotland, in being subjected to crowd violence and intimidation. This was probably the work of Cameronians, and may not have been condoned by the Quakers' more moderate presbyterian neighbours.[58]

The crown's attitude towards the United Societies changed little across the reign. As we have noted, the Cameronians were excluded from the indulgences of February and June 1687, which called for the continued enforcement of laws against field conventicles. Though the vigour of the government's action against the Societies had tended to decline after 1685, periodically the report of a field conventicle triggered an investigation.[59] Efforts were made to apprehend the Societies' preachers. On 9 December 1686, a reward of £100 sterling was offered for the capture of the minister James Renwick, dead or alive. In the following October, the same reward was promised for the arrest of Renwick and his fellow preachers Alexander Shields and David Houston. Houston was subsequently taken in Ireland, but was rescued in Ayrshire in June 1688. Renwick was captured and executed in February 1688.[60] Though weakened by this blow, the Societies continued to operate as a small group based chiefly in the south.

Claiming to represent presbyterian orthodoxy, the Cameronian ministers denounced the indulgences and the moderate ministers who benefited from multiconfessionalism. In common with most Scottish protestants, the Cameronians upheld a traditional hostility towards toleration. Though the conscience should not be forced, they reasoned, it was the magistrate's duty to prohibit idolatrous worship and restrain false teachers.[61] While full liberty to presbyterianism would have been welcome, the Cameronians found James's indulgences unacceptable for two principal reasons. First, the Societies condemned what they saw as the sinful objective of the toleration, which was to advance popery. James had 'presumed by absolute power to suspend all Laws, made for the protection of our Religion', the Cameronians argued, and 'when he will, he may repeal all Laws for its establishment'.[62] To seek the overthrow of protestantism was characteristic of such a zealous Catholic, James Renwick asserted in one of his final sermons, since 'it is his Principle to be treacherous, and to keep no Faith to Hereticks'.[63] In the meantime, moreover, the toleration sought to promote harmony between protestants and Catholics, 'with whom we should have an Irreconcilable War'.[64] It was the duty of presbyterians to protest against the Catholicising tendency of James's policy, the Cameronians asserted. Despite this, the so-called moderate ministers were not only silent about the threat, but (as we shall see shortly) addressed the king giving thanks for the toleration.[65]

The Cameronians also argued that the toleration placed illegitimate restrictions on the work of ministers. Because the second indulgence ordered that 'nothing be Preached or Taught ... which may any ways tend to Alienat the Hearts' of the people from their king, ministers would be unable to warn of the dangers of multiconfessionalism.[66] The requirement that presbyterians report the time and place of their services made the ministry depend 'upon the Courts of Men'.[67] For the Societies, this latter encroachment on clerical freedom recalled the government's policy in 1669 and 1672 of indulging presbyterian ministers to preach in specified parish churches. The earlier indulgences were divisive; some presbyterians had argued that those ministers who complied with the initiative recognised the crown's supremacy over the Church and thus compromised presbyterian principles.[68] According to Renwick and Alexander Shields, the granting of yet another restricted indulgence renewed the obligation on faithful ministers such as themselves to preach with full freedom in the fields. They argued that outdoor worship was convenient, offering security and secrecy to the crowds who flocked to hear the small contingent of itinerant Cameronian ministers. And because James's indulgences explicitly excluded field meetings from protection, worshipping outside constituted a 'very significant Testimony in itself, against this *Popish Toleration*'.[69] Moreover, Renwick's final statement before his execution – part of the genre of scaffold speeches perfected by Restoration presbyterians – portrayed his death as a further protest against James's toleration.[70]

* * *

The response of mainstream presbyterians to the second indulgence was fundamental to the emergence of tolerated religious pluralism in Scotland. The presbyterians decided to embrace the indulgence within weeks of its proclamation on 5 July. Presbyterian clergy from across Scotland met in Edinburgh, probably on 20 July, and began to organise the provision of worship.[71] On 21 July, the meeting drew up an address 'to offer our most humble and hearty Thanks' to James for the indulgence. Many presbyterians accepted at least some of the Cameronians' concerns about the king's motives; as a result, some mainstream ministers seem to have opposed the adoption of an address. But while the document professed unshakeable allegiance to James, its authors subtly qualified their loyalty by referring to the Westminster confession of faith:

> [A]s we have amidst all former Temptations endeavoured, so are firmly resolved still to preserve an entire Loyalty in our Doctrine and Practice, (consonant to our known Principles, which according to the Holy Scriptures, are contained in the Confession of Faith generally owned by *Presbyterians* in all Your Majesties Dominions:)[72]

A subsequent address of the 'Citizens and Inhabitants ... of the Presbyterian Persuasion in the City of Edinburgh and Canongate', though more fulsome in its thanks to the king, likewise alluded to the Westminster confession.

The lay presbyterians hoped that their behaviour would 'make it appear that there is no Inconsistency between True Loyalty and Presbyterian Principles'.[73] The addresses' definition of loyalty should be understood in the context of the controversy over the indulgences of 1669 and 1672. By explaining their acceptance of the June 1687 indulgence in terms of the Westminster confession, the addressers hinted that they did not recognise the royal supremacy, since the confession asserted Christ's headship of the Church, set limits to the magistrate's ecclesiastical authority, and was thought to entail divine-right presbyterianism.[74] At least implicitly, moderate presbyterians repudiated the Restoration concept of ecclesiastical supremacy.

Essential to the resurgence of presbyterianism was the reconstitution of a hierarchy of church courts, which oversaw local organisation and managed the recruitment and ordination of ministers. The presbyterians' gathering in Edinburgh in July 1687 began a series of 'general meetings', which provided national coordination until the first general assembly of the re-established presbyterian Church in October 1690.[75] The meeting of July 1687 adopted twenty-four 'overtures for making the liberty practicable', a blueprint for the reorganisation of presbyterianism. The overtures called for the creation of local courts: where there were enough ministers, presbyteries were to be settled in their traditional bounds; where there were fewer clergy, they were to unite across larger areas. The presbytery meetings were to be held monthly, and all presbyterian ministers were expected to attend.[76] Three was considered the minimum number of ministers for a viable court.[77] Not all the registers of the reconstituted presbyteries survive, but we know that by the end of August 1687, meetings had been held in Irvine, Ayr and Glasgow (which was united with Paisley and Dumbarton presbyteries).[78] Hamilton presbytery (joined with Lanark) met in September; Kintyre, Dumfries and Linlithgow in November.[79] Twenty-six ministers of the synod of Glasgow and Ayr met in August, and six sat as the synod of Argyll in September.[80] Twenty-four ministers attended a meeting of the synod of Lothian and Tweeddale in July 1687; this court supervised the settling of ministers across a large region centred on Edinburgh.[81] As the presbyterians did not have access to the buildings of the established Kirk, most meetings took place at ministers' residences or meeting houses.[82]

The local courts set about listing all surviving presbyterian ministers and probationers, with the aim of placing them in parishes as soon as possible.[83] It was widely assumed that the older presbyterian ministers who had been deprived of churches after the Restoration retained a pastoral connection with their former congregations. Thus the general meeting encouraged congregations to call their erstwhile ministers home.[84] Some ministers did preach in their old parishes. David Williamson, previously of the West Kirk, Edinburgh, was provided with a meeting house in the parish, then on the city's outskirts.[85] Patrick Simson resumed preaching in Renfrew, remaining its minister until his death in 1715.[86] But some clergy who were settled in parishes before 1661 had since moved to more important stations. John Gray, formerly minister of Orwell, Kinross-shire, may have returned briefly to the parish, but transferred to Dunfermline, and was replaced at Orwell.[87] Having been called to a meeting house in Edinburgh, James Kirkton did not settle in his former charge at Mertoun, Berwickshire.[88] Duncan Campbell spurned repeated requests to go back to Dunoon, his former parish, though he was reportedly in nearby Paisley presbytery.[89] Anne Hamilton, duchess of Hamilton was among the local presbyterians entreating John Inglis to return to Hamilton, though he demurred on grounds of ill health.[90]

Some of the presbyterian ministers active after the second indulgence had recently been in exile. Among the places of refuge at greatest distance from Scotland, the return from which was correspondingly difficult, were the American colonies. One minister to come back from north America was William Trail, who returned from Maryland to settle at Borthwick (Dalkeith presbytery) where his brother-in-law had been the minister.[91] In 1685, Archibald Riddell had joined George Scot of Pitlochie's colonial venture in East New Jersey, settling at Woodbridge. After the revolution, Riddell attempted to return to Scotland. He was captured by a French man-of-war, and imprisoned in France until his release was negotiated by the Scottish secretary of state in autumn 1689.[92] Complicated for different reasons was the return of William Dunlop, the post-revolutionary principal of Glasgow University. In 1687, he was in Carolina, separated from his wife Sarah Carstares, who remained in Scotland. In letters of 1686 and early 1687, she repeatedly promised to cross the Atlantic with their children to join Dunlop in the colony. But on 29 June 1687, hearing of the second indulgence, the ministers William Moncrieff, Ralph Rogers and William Crichton wrote to Dunlop, asking him to return to his ministry in Scotland.[93] Thereafter Sarah began to hope that the family could be reunited in her home country; she and other friends and relatives pleaded with Dunlop to return.[94] Business commitments delayed his departure, and it was only in May 1688 that he announced his decision to leave Carolina. He did not reach British territory until September 1689.[95]

Other ministers had sought refuge much closer to Scotland. Gabriel Semple, formerly minister of Kirkpatrick-Durham in the presbytery of Dumfries, had spent some of the 1680s preaching at Ford and Etal in Northumberland. In February 1688, his Scottish parish invited him to return. Though he paid short visits to Dumfriesshire in 1688 and 1689, he was reluctant to stay there, and ultimately settled in Jedburgh.[96] More straightforward was the homecoming of Gilbert Rule, who had served as a minister in Dublin before being called to Edinburgh in December 1688. In 1690, he became principal of Edinburgh's town college.[97] As we shall see below, Rule was joined in Scotland by a majority of the presbyterian ministers active in Ireland, who fled the conflict there in 1689.

But the most numerous Scottish exile community was in the Netherlands. Ministers who returned from the United Provinces included the aforementioned James Kirkton, Patrick Warner (or Verner), who had an interview with William of Orange before departing for Scotland to become minister of Irvine, and William Spence, who had been secretary to the earl of Argyll during his rising in 1685, and later preached at Kinross and nearby Fossoway.[98] By contrast, William Carstares, the prince of Orange's chaplain, whom the Scottish authorities had tortured on suspicion of his involvement in the Rye House Plot, was unwilling to preach under the indulgence. Though in August 1687 he received a call to go to Glasgow as a minister, he declined the request, lamenting the continued involvement in the government of 'men from whom I have suffered so much'.[99] Carstares waited in the Netherlands, accepting a call to the British Church in Leiden, before participating in William's invasion of England and becoming an adviser at court.[100] Yet another reaction to James's policies and the revolution can be seen in the career of Robert Fleming, a minister at the Scots Kirk, Rotterdam, who remained in the Netherlands until his death. The presbytery of Hamilton wrote urging him to return to his former parish of Cambuslang, but he sent a formal demission of his charge there.[101]

Some parishes waited for the local presbytery or synod to provide them with ministers, but many communities acted on their own initiative. On 7 July 1687, two days after the second indulgence was published, presbyterians in South Leith took out a lease on a building suitable for use as a meeting house. They invited the minister William Wishart senior to preach the next Sunday, informing a local magistrate that the service would take place.[102] At Queensferry, a group of locals – mostly laymen, but including at least two ministers – began to run a meeting house in October 1687. They resolved to ask preachers to conduct services weekly until a fixed minister could be settled.[103] If at first these congregations operated autonomously, both sought the assistance of the local presbytery or synod when they called a permanent minister.[104] In doing so, they acted in accordance with presbyterian norms, which dictated that presbyteries should oversee calls, and that a minister should be present when a call was signed.[105] Indeed, the election of ministers often followed the procedures laid down by the general assembly in 1649. When a congregation had identified a suitable candidate, its elders were supposed to liaise with the presbytery to draw up a formal call.[106] In many parishes, as we shall see below, there was no recognised presbyterian eldership in 1687–8, and it was impracticable for new elders to be created before a minister was settled. In these cases, congregational leaders without the status of eldership dealt with the presbytery to make a call.[107]

Ideally, a call to a minister was unanimous, with agreement from across the social spectrum.[108] Unanimity was sometimes difficult to achieve. In January 1689, the presbytery of Hamilton received two rival calls from presbyterians at Avondale, where the episcopalian minister had been violently evicted in late December. One call favoured Robert Young, who had been an indulged minister in the parish in the 1670s. The other call was to Robert Langlands, formerly an associate of the United Societies; it is possible that Langlands' supporters objected to Young for his complicity with Charles II's indulgences. The calls were followed in June by what the presbytery called 'a protestation against the settling of avendale or any other parish within the kingdome with a gospell ministrie'. This was perhaps a Cameronian address objecting to all mainstream presbyterians. Counselling the parish's residents to practise forbearance, the presbytery warned that divisions would serve the cause of presbyterianism's enemies.[109]

Presbyteries were responsible for the formal trials of candidates for the ministry, and for their ordination. Traditionally, ordination among Scottish presbyterians was carried out by the ministers of the presbytery in the presence of the congregation the new minister was to serve. It therefore differed from the practice in the Restoration Church, whose clergy received their orders from a bishop, usually in a church close to his residence, and were instituted to parish livings by a separate, more public process.[110] At first it was unclear whether presbyterians would revive their customary pattern of ordination. In March 1688, the presbytery of Hamilton recorded that 'for what is known to the presbytrie publick ordination of ministers hath not been in use' since the second declaration of indulgence. Thus the brethren decided that Robert Muir should not be ordained in Kilbride, where he was to be the minister, but rather at the presbytery's scheduled place of meeting, with representatives of Kilbride in attendance.[111] A similar practice had been followed by the presbytery of Dumfries in December.[112] These ordinations suggest that presbyterians were cautious about how visible their activities should be. On the other hand, public ordinations before the congregation took place at Bo'ness in Linlithgow presbytery in December 1687, and near Peebles in March 1688.[113] By February, Irvine and Ayr presbyteries had agreed that ordination 'ought to be publick att the meeting house of the parish whereto the person was to be ordained'.[114] In April, the synod of Glasgow and Ayr recommended this form of ordination to all its members.[115]

These attempts to impose uniform practice in ordination were influenced by concerns about the behaviour of itinerant preachers, especially those catering to the Cameronians. During the Restoration period, many presbyterians had necessarily conducted a mobile ministry. In the 1680s, the United Societies had their field-preaching ministers ordained 'indefinitely', that is without being dedicated to a specific congregation. The presbyterians' meeting of July 1687 resolved that 'all who have not been ordained to particular flocks' should give information of the circumstances of their ordination to their nearest presbytery, and that in future, none was to 'be ordained indefinitely'.[116] Of course, the Cameronians disregarded this instruction. In the summer of 1688, presbyterians in western Scotland were worried by reports that the United Societies sought the ordination of two of their members in the Netherlands.[117] In fact, the only Cameronian ordained at this time, Thomas Linning, was subsequently among the three Societies' preachers who submitted to the general assembly after the re-establishment of presbyterianism in 1690.[118] Nevertheless, in 1688, indefinite ordination looked likely to perpetuate the problem of ministers who preached itinerantly without informing the restored presbyterian courts.[119] Presbyterian ideas of order, and a pragmatic concern for harmony in an unstable political environment, required that ordination should be carefully regulated.

The great number of parishes without settled presbyterian ministers were encouraged to petition the local courts for a temporary supply of preaching. At its early meetings from August to October 1687, the presbytery of Ayr arranged for six parishes to have a day's service each; in at least one case, the temporary preacher was subsequently ordained to the congregation he supplied.[120] But even as the number of presbyterian preachers increased, not all requests for supply could be granted. In June 1689, the presbytery of Peebles and Biggar denied a petition for supply from Lamington parish, 'the Number of Min[iste]rs being so few and their Charges so Great'. Moreover, residents of Lamington could attend services in Biggar, a few miles away. Later that month, the presbytery could satisfy only one of two requests for supply from other nearby Lanarkshire parishes.[121]

From 1689, presbyteries received assistance in their attempts to meet the popular demand for preaching from an influx of ministers fleeing the conflict in Ireland. Prudently, in light of the Cameronian preacher David Houston's Irish connections, the general meeting obtained a list of the Irish ministers 'who walked orderly in the presbyterian way'. The list, compiled by some of the Irish presbyterians in May 1689, revealed that of the seventy-nine ministers and eleven probationers known to be in Ireland earlier in the year, forty-six ministers and nine probationers were by then in Scotland.[122] Unsurprisingly, these men found themselves much in demand. In June, the presbytery of Dumbarton advised representatives of three parishes seeking supply to go to Glasgow, where

> a course is to be taken by the ministers there joyntly w[i]t[h] the ministers of Ireland who by providence are in this kingdom for the tyme [tha]t such parishes as desire any of [th]e s[ai]d Irland ministers may have their service in the work of [th]e ministrie for such a tyme as they can conveniently stay w[i]t[h] them.[123]

Later in the summer, the presbytery of Dumfries sent Gabriel Semple to a meeting at Ayr, where he was to negotiate for some Irish ministers to preach in the Dumfries area. Two Irishmen were duly supplied; within weeks, both had received calls to Dumfriesshire parishes.[124] Some Irish ministers settled in particular Scottish communities, usually reserving the right to return home when this became possible.[125] Two well-documented Irish ministers who preached in Glasgow during the Jacobite wars were Robert Craghead, formerly of Donaghmore, County Donegal, and Thomas Kennedy, of Donaghmore or Carlan, County Tyrone. Both returned to Ulster, Craghead to Derry in 1690, Kennedy to his former charge in 1693, though Craghead spent another short period in Glasgow at the end of the 1690s.[126]

As well as a settled pastor, the newly constituted presbyterian congregations were thought to require lay elders, to sit with the minister in the kirk session and exercise discipline in the parish. When Patrick Simson returned to Renfrew in 1687, he recorded, 'it was not thought fitt that wee should be without a Eldership and Church session'. As well as a deacon, there were only two surviving presbyterian elders, one of whom was, 'upon weighty accounts', thought unsuitable to serve.

Simson arranged a fresh nomination, and an enlarged eldership was in place by early 1688. But Simson had to confront possible objections to his nominees. Two of the proposed elders, as heritors, had entered 'into some degrees of Compliance to avoide that terrible persecution of the year 1684', perhaps by swearing the oath of abjuration or the Test, or participating in the prosecution of Cameronians. The men were willing to 'declare their hearty sorrow for it with a very apparent remorce', and were admitted as elders.[127]

In many parishes it was harder than at Renfrew to find suitable men, and no eldership could be settled for several years after 1687. In some places, the problem lay in local divisions, the small size of the presbyterian congregation or the new minister's unfamiliarity with his flock. At Cambuslang (Hamilton presbytery), Archibald Hamilton was ordained minister in June 1688. Because 'the tymes were then troublesome, and he unacquainted with the paroch; he could not get [an] eldershipe orderly setled for a considerable while thereafter', probably until 1690.[128] Elsewhere, however, the difficulty was that men of sufficient standing to become elders had often countenanced episcopacy before 1687, by swearing state oaths against presbyterianism, or serving in episcopalian kirk sessions. Like Simson, presbyterian ministers frequently demanded that such men apologise and show penitence for their conformity. Thus Irvine presbytery noted, in February 1688, that 'the offences given by some of the elders of Irwin by [thei]r fainting in the hour of temptation' had been satisfactorily 'removed'.[129] In Dumfries, where a presbyterian eldership was reconstituted in August 1689, it was found that several nominees 'had been in the tyme of the late violent Tryalls and troubles hurried into a sad complyance with some illicit ingadgements'. The men in question were required to express a sense of guilt for their offensive behaviour, which in most cases constituted swearing the Test.[130] In October 1689, the synod of Glasgow and Ayr recommended a standard solution to the problem: because 'several persons qualified for the office of elder, are guilty of such scandals as render them offensive to the people', local days of humiliation were to be held for the 'removeal' of this offence.[131] Nevertheless, whether because of the weakness of presbyterian organisation, or insuperable local obstacles, many southern parishes lacked an eldership as late as 1690.

Kirk sessions, or the groups of presbyterian volunteers that acted in place of sessions, performed two further roles, sometimes in consultation with presbyteries. First, as we have noted, they rented or built meeting houses for their worship. More new meeting houses seem to have been constructed under James's indulgences in Scotland than in

England, where most presbyterian congregations waited until toleration was enacted by parliament in 1689.[132] Nevertheless, there were relatively few meeting houses in the northern half of Scotland. Inverness's meeting house opened in December 1687.[133] Perth had one by August 1689, though episcopalians alleged that it was five times larger than was required for the diminutive congregation.[134] In September 1688, moreover, it was reported that the entire synod of Aberdeen, an episcopalian stronghold, had only one meeting house.[135]

In southern and central Scotland, on the other hand, presbyterian places of worship were plentiful. Glasgow had two meeting houses, and there was another in nearby Rutherglen.[136] Edinburgh's presbyterians received royal permission to hire the halls of the burgh's incorporated trades for services. But these premises were reportedly 'far short of containing the numbers that resort unto them'.[137] Thus presbyterians of the Old Kirk parish were 'at considerable Expences in repairing & furnishing' the Magdalen Chapel, the property of the hammermen, 'with Lofts & Seats'.[138] In July and August 1688, moreover, Edinburgh's dean of guild court approved the construction of two new presbyterian meeting houses, one of which was to occupy a plot of seventy by forty feet.[139] There were as many as nine places of presbyterian worship in Edinburgh, plus venues at Corstorphine and Cramond, and meeting houses in the West Kirk parish, the Canongate and Leith.[140] In some places elsewhere, newly constituted presbyterian congregations took over disused church properties. The presbyterians of Dreghorn, Ayrshire, successfully petitioned the king for the use of the church at Pierstoun, formerly a separate parish. The church was given to John Spalding, minister of Dreghorn at the Restoration and indulged preacher in the 1670s.[141] Ayr's presbyterians, including John Muir, a former provost who resumed that office in 1689, simply purchased the empty St John's Kirk. As well as holding services, it became the meeting place for the presbytery.[142]

Local presbyterian organisers also arranged the collection of funds to pay their ministers. The Edinburgh diarist Thomas Kincaid recorded going to the Magdalen Chapel on a Saturday in October 1687, and giving 'some money to the ministers'.[143] At its first meeting, the Queensferry presbyterians appointed six of their number 'to speake and com[m]une with the inhabitants to see what they will [con]descend yearly to give in order to [th]e settling of a Presbyterian Minister'. Two of them were later sent to the adjacent parish of Dalmeny, 'to deall with the substantiall persons ... in order to their joyning in procureing a maintenance to a Presbiteria[n] Min[iste]r'.[144] At Dumfries, a group of prominent local men, including several former magistrates, drew up a maintenance roll in support of the minister George Campbell. This document listed 304 people who agreed to contribute sums ranging from 5 merks (£3.6s.8d.) to 10s.[145]

Before settling a minister in a parish, presbyteries looked for evidence that an adequate income would be provided. Following a call from Tweedsmuir to James Thomson in the summer of 1688, the united presbyteries of Peebles and Biggar sent a member to enquire of the parishioners 'anent a Competencie for his maintenance and securitie'. The brethren postponed Thomson's ordination until a satisfactory report was received.[146] In August 1687, some parishioners of Craigie presented the presbytery of Ayr with 'a paper offering five hundred merks' for the support of John Campbell. The presbytery 'desired them to give security' for the sum.[147] The promised maintenance was below the Kirk's official minimum stipend of 800 merks (a little over £44 sterling), but was comparable with clerical incomes in some poorer parishes.[148] Clubbing together, the neighbouring Kirkcudbrightshire parishes of Terregles, Lochrutton and Troqueer offered £32 sterling (576 merks) to Robert Paton, 'and also to provide ane house wher he may conveniently live, together with peats for his fire and grasse for an horse and a Cow'. Unfortunately, the funds proved not to be forthcoming, and Dumfries presbytery allowed Paton to move elsewhere.[149]

Some parishes were too poor to provide a preacher's income. In October 1688, hearing that Irvine presbytery was contributing 100 merks to the maintenance of a minister on the island of Cumbrae, the synod of Glasgow and Ayr agreed to collect 100 merks from its other presbyteries, 'in regard of the inability and povertie' of the island's people.[150] A laird in the parish of Kilcalmonell and Kilberry told Kintyre presbytery that 'his tennents refused to call or encourage any minister at this time (in regard of there povertie) otherwayes then as they are served alreadie', by the episcopalian incumbent.[151] In some cases, the difficulty of raising voluntary contributions frustrated the return of a presbyterian minister to his pre-1662 parish. Encouraged by the presbytery of Dumfries, Kirkbride invited home its former incumbent Thomas Shiels. He was apparently willing to return, but by February 1690 it was clear that Kirkbride was 'not able to maintain or encourage' him.[152] Partly because of this and similar cases, an act of parliament of April 1690 granted the surviving pre-Restoration ministers a right to the stipends and access to the manses of their old parishes.[153] This legislation finally allowed Shiels to return to Kirkbride.[154]

* * *

How might we assess the scale and impact of the presbyterian resurgence? Previous historians have tended to rely on two categories of evidence. First, there are the rather generalised and tendentious accounts written by episcopalians after the revolution. In 1690, John Sage alleged that 'within a few Weeks' of the second indulgence, 'Meeting-houses were Erected in many places; especially in the Western Shires ... and the Churches were drain'd'.[155] Other episcopalians painted a similar picture.[156] The second type of evidence consists of colourful local examples, usually drawn from individual parishes. William Bullo, who had become minister of Stobo in Peebles presbytery by an alleged abuse of episcopal power, had 'non to hear him [preach] except his own familie and on[e] persone who is debitor to him in greater soumes then he is able to pay'.[157] In Carrington (Dalkeith presbytery), we are told, by November 1688, all but four or five of the residents had left the established Church for the newly settled presbyterian meeting house.[158] Unfortunately, the evidence we have of Stobo and Carrington comes from potentially unreliable sources: petitions against their episcopalian ministers submitted to the convention of estates and privy council after the overthrow of James. And we have no way of knowing how many other episcopalian churches were similarly deserted.

Whatever the shortcomings of the evidence, the broad regional patterns of protestant adherence after the second indulgence are clear. A majority of parishes north of the Tay experienced little or no presbyterian revival. Many communities south of Perth, and more particularly south of the Forth, saw considerable numbers leave the episcopalian Church for presbyterian meeting houses.[159] But an examination of detailed local evidence demonstrates that presbyterians were constrained in their capacity to meet the demand from worshippers in the south. Most obviously, the number of preachers was insufficient to cater to the 'vast majority of parishioners' who, according to Ian Cowan, abandoned the established Church in the counties of Ayr, Dumfries, Kirkcudbright, Lanark, Renfrew and Wigtown.[160] From 1687, there were small, but growing, numbers of hard-working presbyterian ministers in Ayrshire, Dumfriesshire, Lanarkshire and Renfrewshire. But Galloway was less well served. In May 1689, when its synod began to meet, there were fourteen ministers present, of whom at least seven were from Ireland.[161] Further east, a similar pattern prevailed. Presbyterian clergy were plentiful in Edinburgh, and they could meet some of the demand for their services in Linlithgowshire and Peeblesshire. But there seems to have been less capacity in the south-eastern counties of Berwickshire and Roxburghshire. Even where there were enough preachers, it could be difficult to settle them permanently in specific parishes. Some congregations took time to agree on a call to a minister, others struggled to raise the necessary funds. Though there was a palpable surge of support for presbyterianism in the south, there was a great deal of variety in the responses of local communities to James's religious experiment.

In a few parishes, the records can give us a fuller sense of the decline of an episcopalian congregation and the appearance of multiconfessionalism. At Lenzie Easter (Cumbernauld), presbytery of Glasgow, members of the episcopalian congregation, including most of the elders, started attending presbyterian services in July 1687. The minister tried threatening the many absentees from church, and excommunicated 360 heads of families who failed to appear for the thanksgiving sermon on 14 October, the king's birthday. From late October to August 1688, when the kirk session minutes cease, the clerk recorded the attendance at church. This fluctuated between thirteen and forty people, in a parish of over 1,000.[162] In this exceptionally well-documented community, which is almost as extreme an example as Carrington or Stobo, there were not many episcopalians left.

In some other places, however, episcopalian congregations were more resilient. Lenzie Easter apart, kirk session clerks did not regularly record the size of the parish congregation, or note the number of worshippers who left to join the presbyterians. Instead, evidence of Sunday churchdoor collections must serve as the best indicator of the size of the episcopalian congregations. This evidence is difficult to interpret, and because the sums raised fluctuated considerably from week to week, it has been necessary to calculate average collections across long periods. There is no indication that the scale of individuals' donations declined in the period, though it is conceivable that Scots who continued to attend their parish churches increased or decreased their donations in response to James's indulgences. Nevertheless, it is more likely that the average collection across a period was roughly in proportion to the size of the congregation.

Around Edinburgh, the parishes of the West Kirk and South Leith both had presbyterian meeting houses soon after James's second indulgence. The average weekly collection for the first six months of 1687 was £6.19s. in the West Kirk and £16.17s.1d. in South Leith. In the first half of 1688, the average collections were £4.11s. and £11.6s.6d. respectively. There was thus a fall of slightly over a third in the West Kirk and around a third in South Leith.[163] This might be compared with Trinity College parish in Edinburgh itself, where there was a fall of under 18 per cent between the same two periods.[164] Similar calculations for

Dysart, Fife, show a fall of a little over 37 per cent between the average collection for the first half of 1687 (£7.4s.9½d.) and that for the same months in 1688 (£5.5s.3d.). Dysart was in dire straits economically, but the fall might be explained in part by the presence of a presbyterian minister in the burgh.[165] Perhaps the most revealing figures can be calculated for Penicuik (Dalkeith presbytery) and Dumfries. We do not know if Penicuik had a resident presbyterian minister by early 1688, and whether, like nearby Carrington, the parish church was now empty. But it is surely significant that the average weekly collection fell by over two thirds from the first half of 1687 to the first half of 1688.[166] At Dumfries, where there was a presbyterian meeting house by December 1687, there was a fall in average collections of 44 per cent from the first half of 1687 to the same period in 1688.[167] Dumfries was a royal burgh, and we shall see in Chapter 4 that it had a nominated council at least some of whom were unsympathetic towards presbyterianism. These factors may have allowed the established Church to retain more support in Dumfries than in its rural hinterland. But if the episcopalian congregation of early 1688 remained at least half as large as the pre-indulgence congregation, we might also conclude that there was some popular commitment to the parish church in Dumfries. There was no uniform desertion of the Kirk, even in south-western Scotland, and the response of a community to James's religious experiment depended on many local dynamics.

Dumfries illustrates one final point about the reappearance of organised presbyterianism from the summer of 1687: the response of elite men and women had a considerable influence. The magistrates and councillors of royal burghs seem to have been reluctant to give corporate recognition to the meeting house congregations. This may have been because, as Chapter 4 explains, all councillors of royal burghs at this point held office by virtue of the king's orders. But there was probably a more general tendency for magistrates and councillors to attend the burgh church, of which they were formally patrons. Though in February 1688, the senior bailie of Queensferry, accompanied by the burgh treasurer, 'appeared publickly in the meeting hous' to welcome the newly ordained minister, in August, the magistrates refused to rent a pew there for the council's use, and were instead offered seating as private individuals.[168] The Ayrshire burgh of Irvine was thus unusual in the willingness of its leaders to commit themselves as a body to presbyterianism. The town gained its first settled episcopalian minister since the Restoration as late as 1687, and he quickly lost what support the magistrates had been willing to offer. In January 1688, the councillors declared that they would 'associate themselves into the societie of these of the [pres]byterian persuas[ion]', and install for their use 'four pewes or das[ks]' in the meeting house. The house seems to have been glazed at public expense, for in December 1689, when the re-establishment of presbyterianism seemed likely, the council voted to remove the glass to the parish church, promising nevertheless that 'If the parochiners s[ha]ll be constrained to leave the Church, And to returne to the s[ai]d meitting house', its glass would be refitted.[169]

In rural parishes, the attitudes of small landowners towards presbyterianism were presumably crucial. We do not have to accept the cynical claims of one episcopalian pamphleteer, who attributed the exodus of lay people from churches to the intimidation of zealous landlords, to recognise the influence of such men in their communities.[170] Men identified as lairds and knights signed calls, and some sat on kirk sessions and presbyteries.[171] But it is difficult to evaluate the role of these individuals. More visible were the nobles prepared to support presbyterianism. Wodrow highlighted the participation of such men and women in presbyterian worship 'in Paisley, Leslie, Weems [Wemyss], Ormiston, Struthers, and other places'.[172] Here he alluded to the presbyterianism of John Cochrane, second earl of Dundonald, Anne, countess of Rothes, Margaret, countess of Wemyss, Adam Cockburn of Ormiston and William Lindsay, eighteenth earl of Crawford. William, twelfth Lord Ross, the duchess of Hamilton, her daughter Katherine, and Katherine's husband, Lord John Murray, later the first duke of Atholl, were also among the nobles who countenanced presbyterianism.[173] A smaller proportion of the nobility joined with the presbyterians than had sided with the Covenant in 1638, but presbyterianism now enjoyed more elite favour than it had done since 1660.

These final conclusions help to explain the context in which presbyterianism was re-established in 1690. But the broader aim of this chapter has been to examine how Catholics, Quakers and especially moderate presbyterians emerged as rivals to, but not necessarily replacements for, the established Church in 1687–9. If in some parishes, presbyterians quickly gained the upper hand, elsewhere episcopalian congregations retained the support of large parts of the community. In much of southern Scotland, and in scattered areas further north, James's second indulgence created a multiconfessional situation, in which rival ecclesiastical groups competed for followers. It is to the character and implications of multiconfessionalism that the next chapter turns.

3

Multiconfessional Scotland

THIS CHAPTER EXAMINES THE nature of multiconfessionalism in King James's Scotland. As we saw in Chapter 2, James's second declaration of indulgence prompted a very rapid response from presbyterians. Knowing that presbyterianism would be re-established in 1690, and that episcopalian clergy would be removed from most southern parishes, historians have understandably emphasised the collapse in support for the established Church evident in some places. They have prioritised evidence of deserted parish churches, and paid too little attention to the competition between the main religious groups. By contrast, this chapter illustrates the groups' attempts to win worshippers in a multiconfessional marketplace. There is little evidence that the Quakers aimed to expand their membership, but presbyterians and Catholics sought to attract new followers, while episcopalian clergy hoped to hold on to their formerly dominant position. The competition was most vigorous in southern Scotland, but can also be observed in parts of the north. A multiconfessional situation persisted in this form for the eighteen months from July 1687 to December 1688. As we shall see in Chapters 5 and 6, the dynamics of confessional competition then changed with the collapse of James's government and the creation of the Williamite regime. In the winter of 1688–9, most Catholic priests fled and many episcopalian ministers were forcibly ejected from their churches or deserted. Though a large number of episcopalian ministers retained parishes after 1689, especially in the north, the presbyterians took time to organise themselves there, and did not at first offer as much competition to the episcopalians as they had in the south during James's reign.

Multiconfessional Scotland, this chapter argues, can be conceived as a religious marketplace. Learning from the sociologists who have brought economic principles to the study of religious pluralism, we can interpret the indulgences of 1687 as a 'supply side' reform. James's religious experiment constituted an almost complete deregulation of a formerly restricted market in religious services. The king granted Scotland's religious groups the freedom to compete for worshippers, giving them the potential to stimulate demand.[1] We shall discuss some of the motives that individuals had for switching from one group to another, though there is more evidence of the groups' efforts to gain worshippers. We know too little about the consumers in the religious marketplace, but we can recognise the ways in which the suppliers marketed their religious services by emphasising their distinctive qualities and talking down the competition.

Before returning to these theoretical points in its conclusion, the chapter discusses the efforts of Catholics, presbyterians and episcopalians to gain converts and retain existing adherents. Much of the evidence of conversion to Catholicism concerns members of the landed elite who decided, for spiritual or political reasons, to adopt the king's faith. As we saw in Chapter 2, there were not enough priests in Scotland to make conversion to Catholicism a realistic possibility in many parts of the country. Nevertheless, Catholics competed with protestants in some communities. More importantly, perhaps, the chapter shows how protestants responded to what they perceived as a threatening Catholic revival. Meanwhile, there was vigorous competition between the main protestant groups. While episcopalian ministers retained the majority of their followers in the north and some places in the south, it was the presbyterians who had most to gain from competing for worshippers in the newly liberalised religious marketplace. After discussing the presbyterians' efforts to distinguish themselves and attract recruits, the chapter examines some of the effects of multiconfessionalism. The registration of marriages and baptisms, one of the established Church's functions, was compromised as people abandoned their parish churches. Poor relief became more difficult to collect and distribute. And the competition between religious groups made it simpler than ever before for Scots to evade ecclesiastical discipline.

* * *

As well as easing the lives of existing recusants, a chief objective of James's religious experiment was to encourage new conversions to Catholicism. During the king's reign, a small but influential body of nobles and clan chiefs announced that they had adopted the Catholic faith. For some, especially members of traditionally Catholic families, whose erstwhile protestantism had been nominal or vague, the decision to convert must have been taken lightly. Examples include Alasdair MacDonald of Glengarry and Coll MacDonald of Keppoch. Neither man was especially committed to Catholicism; indeed, Keppoch claimed to be a protestant in 1692.[2] Other conversions were more surprising, or were brazenly opportunistic. One of the more cynical converts was Archibald Campbell, Lord Lorne and later tenth earl and first duke of Argyll, who temporarily renounced protestantism and attached himself to James, before joining William of Orange's invasion in 1688.[3] Less well known is the case of Sir Godfrey McCulloch of Myrton, Wigtownshire, who professed Catholicism and sent his son to the Jesuits' school at Holyroodhouse. It was alleged that the motive for his conversion was to ingratiate himself with the earl of Perth, who thereupon allowed McCulloch access to the rents and properties of his estate, control of which he had lost by escheat after failing to pay his debts.[4] Another convert who added little lustre to the Catholic cause was Philip Stanfield. He was convicted of involvement in his father's murder and was received into the Catholic Church after calling for a priest to attend him in his prison cell. Thomas Nicolson, the priest who visited Stanfield, regretted that the case allowed protestants to 'calumniat us saying none turne Papists but reprobat and wicked persons'. In fact, Stanfield regretted his brief dalliance with Catholicism and was accompanied to the scaffold by protestant ministers.[5]

But it is too easy – and misleadingly simplistic – to emphasise the worldly reasons for conversion among Scotland's elites. In fact, there were strong pressures discouraging the adoption of Catholicism. One Catholic, dedicating a book to Perth and the lords of session in 1686, recognised that most Scots were hostile towards opportunistic converts. '[I]f a Man find himself convinced to become a *Catholick* at this time', he wrote, 'the very fear of being thought to turn upon the account of Gaining or continuing in Favour, is no small Stumbling-Block to Persons of Honour'.[6] James Ogilvy, third earl of Findlater disinherited his son Lord Deskford after the latter converted to Catholicism.[7] Newly convinced Catholics were certainly taking a risk while it looked like the king's successor would be his protestant daughter Mary. For most of the leading converts, indeed, there would be no way back to protestant respectability in the anti-Catholic 1690s. Having adopted Catholicism by November 1685, the earl of Seaforth remained a Catholic and a Jacobite after the revolution, and he was repeatedly imprisoned.[8] The conversion of the earl of Moray, secretary of state and commissioner to the 1686 parliament, might be seen as a political act, though Moray was likewise sufficiently sincere not to seek rehabilitation after 1688.[9] The Drummond brothers, Perth and Melfort, were perhaps too close to King James to envisage reviving their careers under William and Mary. But whatever the reasons for Melfort's conversion, his elder brother certainly became a committed Catholic. No doubt Perth exaggerated when he claimed that no circumstance of his life deserved to be 'noticed except that of his Conversion from Heresie to Truth'. Yet we should recognise that in playing a pivotal role in the crown's efforts to promote Catholicism, and in 'leading the World by example', as a clerical supporter put it, Perth was gambling with his career and reputation.[10] His commitment to Catholicism secured his position in the years 1685–8, yet he had spiritual as well as political advancement on his mind.[11]

Perhaps the case that most vividly reveals the dilemmas posed by James's policy is that of Sir Robert Sibbald, one of Scotland's leading physicians and antiquarians. He briefly became a Catholic, before recanting and returning to the established Church. Writing after the event, Sibbald claimed that controversy among protestants had weakened 'the attachment I had for our owne Religion'. Yet the biggest influence on his conversion was Perth, at whose house Sibbald was persuaded of the truth of Catholicism in late 1685. Soon afterwards, Sibbald was a target of the anti-Catholic riot in Edinburgh on 1 February 1686. A crowd of 300 or 400 descended on his house, apparently in the belief that he was responsible for Perth's conversion. Sibbald fled for London, where he met the king. Nevertheless, after a short illness, Sibbald began to regret his conversion. He returned to Edinburgh and began to attend episcopalian services. His protestantism was formally acknowledged by the bishop of Edinburgh in September. As the attentions of the crowd attest, Sibbald's religious odyssey was widely discussed. His adoption of Catholicism was welcomed by courtiers, condemned in sermons in Edinburgh, and it was soon rumoured that he had received a pension from the king. His recantation was still more important; according to Sibbald, 'good men thought I by my returne had done' the Catholic interest 'more damage then my joining had profited [the]m'.[12] The famous intellectual's rejection of Catholicism, in spite of the personal advantages that his conversion might have brought, was a seminal event.

To the disappointment of the court and the Catholic mission, the number of converts remained small. Missionaries repeatedly observed that more new Catholics were received in the north than in the south, in the country than in the towns.[13] Responding to this situation, the priests resolved to baptise the illegitimate children of protestants, potentially increasing the number of families received into the Church.[14] But as we saw in Chapter 2, the supply and distribution of missionaries had a large influence on the fortunes of the Catholic revival. The deployment of priests in the north-east served the mission quite well, but the concentration of others in and around Edinburgh yielded more meagre results. And in parts of Scotland, Catholics were scarcely more visible than before James's accession. Yet arguably the significance of the Catholic revival lay not in the precise numbers attracted to the faith, but in the perception – held by Catholics and protestants alike – that the mission offered vigorous competition to the protestant groups. As we shall see, both episcopalian and presbyterian ministers felt impelled to attack popery more vociferously than the threat of re-Catholicisation would seem, in hindsight, to have warranted. From a few places, we have detailed evidence of the struggle between protestants and Catholics for supporters.

Aberdeen was one such hard-fought locality. As early as March 1686, the town council suspended the clause of the burgess oath designed to exclude Catholics and Quakers from civic privileges.[15] According to a Catholic witness, the episcopalian clergy preached loudly against popery, and made a show of their charity towards Huguenot exiles. George Garden, minister of the East parish, 'was so zealous as to go through the privat houses ... & quester pour une famille de la Religion unhappily come to Aberdene', who were 'now honored there as Confessors who have suffered under [thei]r Nero or Herod'.[16] This seems to have given rise to the special church collection, held throughout the dioceses of Aberdeen and Brechin, in favour of the Huguenot Andrew Bovier, then living in poverty with his family in Aberdeen.[17] On the other hand, the Catholic cause may have gained some advantage from a legal dispute that prevented the settlement of an episcopalian minister in one of the burgh's livings for several years after 1684.[18] The priest Robert Strachan resided in Aberdeen from the autumn of 1687, and other Catholic clergy were present intermittently. After securing the use of Trinity Church for Catholic worship in May 1688, Strachan hoped to see the foundation of a convent in the town.[19] Whether or not there was a genuine threat to protestant hegemony in Aberdeen, many breathed a sigh of relief when James's regime collapsed. In January 1689, Aberdeen was one of the Scottish towns to stage an elaborate anti-Catholic procession, after which the bells of Trinity Church were rung.[20]

The best evidence of the coexistence of protestants and Catholics comes from the Canongate, the district to the west of Holyroodhouse, then outside Edinburgh's walls but effectively a suburb dependent on the capital.[21] Between the riots of January and February 1686 and those signalling the collapse of the regime in December 1688, the revival of Catholic worship in the Canongate was peaceful. Of course, developments at Holyroodhouse alarmed many. John Brand, later a presbyterian minister, resided in the Canongate in 1688. He heard the Catholics there 'boast great things, & threaten all who would [n]o[t] turn' Catholic.[22] But some locals responded to the Catholic revival in less suspicious and fearful ways. The Edinburgh diarist Thomas Kincaid, who conformed to episcopacy until the second indulgence but thereafter attended presbyterian services, often visited the Abbey. He expressed conventionally anti-Catholic attitudes in December 1688, but did not record a negative judgement on the chapel itself.[23] Moreover, the Benedictine James Bruce reported that curiosity led many to go to mass at the chapel.[24] In April 1687, a tailor attending mass was 'so impertinent as to make urine upon' members of the congregation; apparently this was a result of incontinence, rather than malice.[25] Catholic priests gained influence among Edinburgh's students. Alexander Cunningham, one of the town college's regents, was said to worship at the Catholic chapel; his colleague Andrew Massie allegedly kept company with priests. Some students were more receptive to the Catholics' claims than was John Brand, and one departed for the college of Douai. Meanwhile, a missionary from Douai gained admittance to a class at Edinburgh's town college in the hope of winning further converts.[26]

Holyrood became a focal point for theological dispute. In November 1687, a protestant paper questioning Catholic attitudes towards worship was posted up at the Abbey. The priest on duty declined to answer in writing, but addressed the paper's queries in his sermon. The evidence we have of the queries suggests that they derived from *A Request to Roman Catholicks*, by James Gordon, episcopalian minister of Banchory-Devenick, near Aberdeen.[27] This pamphlet was published in London, perhaps indicating that the privy council's actions against anti-Catholic bookselling in Edinburgh had some success, and that local protestants had to rely on manuscript copies of works printed elsewhere.[28] Catholic literature, on the other hand, was in plentiful supply. Probably in 1686, King James appointed the Catholic James Watson as printer to his 'family and household'. Watson was provided with premises in Holyroodhouse; on his death in late 1687, the German Catholic Peter Bruce was named in his place.[29] Importantly, the king supplied financial assistance. In May 1687, the treasury commissioners were instructed to donate £100 sterling to 'particular Charities' and to spend another £100 on printing books; both sums were to be distributed by Perth.[30] The result of this investment was that Watson and

Bruce published at least forty-four books, pamphlets and broadsides, together with four issues of London newspapers, in the years 1686–8. This was in spite of a fire near to the printing house in February 1687, which consumed some of its productions.[31] Seventeen or eighteen of the publications were Catholic devotional or polemical books; these included works by Thomas à Kempis and more recent Scottish, English and French writers.[32] By the standards of the Scottish book trade, this output was considerable. In comparison, members of the established Church published around forty-one devotional and controversial works in Scotland in the entire period from 1662 to 1688.[33] We have little evidence about how widely the Catholic books circulated, though it seems that Kincaid, in Edinburgh, read some of the Holyroodhouse press's output.[34]

* * *

For as long as it appeared that Catholicism was gaining ground, it was necessary for Scotland's protestants to respond to the popish threat. Uncomfortably for the episcopalians, the established Church was compromised by the king's expectation that its clergy should help to advance his religious policies. The willingness in 1686 of Archbishop Ross of St Andrews and Bishop Paterson of Edinburgh to support the repeal of the penal laws became notorious.[35] John Strachan, professor of divinity at Edinburgh, preached in favour of Catholic toleration at the Edinburgh synod meeting held immediately before the 1686 parliamentary session. Unsurprisingly, he was considered 'very moderate tow[ards] Papists' in his divinity teaching.[36] Responding to reports of episcopalians' sermons, as we noted in Chapter 1, the crown on several occasions urged the bishops to prevent anti-Catholic preaching.[37] The king also interfered to stop Catholic converts from being excommunicated from the Church.[38] At least three episcopalian ministers themselves became Catholics, though none was an influential figure.[39] Thomas Burnet, a regent of Marischal College, Aberdeen, defended the king's absolute power in his graduation theses of 1686, which were dedicated to the Catholic duke of Gordon. Burnet was rewarded with a pension from the king and, thanks to Gordon's influence, was offered the next vacant position in Edinburgh's town college, against the will of the principal. It was falsely rumoured that Burnet was a Catholic; hearing these reports, the parents of students threatened to remove them from Burnet's class.[40] The complicity of this prominent lay episcopalian in James's policies caused churchmen considerable embarrassment.

In spite of the Church's treatment by the crown, and the equivocations of some of the bishops, most episcopalian clergy seem to have sustained, or perhaps elevated, their customary anti-popish rhetoric after 1685. This was notably the case in the north-east, where Catholic recusancy was a longstanding problem. After the first indulgence, but apparently not before, the moderator of Ellon presbytery regularly exhorted his clergy 'to prevent the apostacie of ther people to Poprie Quakerisme and the other dangerous errors of the tymes'.[41] While visiting parishes in its bounds, the Restoration presbytery of Fordyce habitually enquired about the clergy's efforts against Catholic and Quaker errors. This practice was maintained after the indulgences. During the visitation of Rathven in August 1688, the minister was praised for his diligence in 'preventing apostasie to poprie'.[42] Despite the king's wish to unite Scots in multiconfessional harmony, candidates undertaking ministerial trials by north-eastern presbyteries continued to be examined on anti-Catholic topics, such as the number of Christian sacraments, transubstantiation, auricular confession and the nature of Church government.[43] As we have noted, collections were made to support Huguenot refugees, heightening awareness of the threat of militant Catholicism. With such actions, episcopalians showed that they were not cowed by pressure from the court, they remained opposed to Catholicism and were reluctant participants in the multiconfessional experiment.

Presbyterian ministers likewise warned against popery. Of course, the second indulgence insisted that presbyterian sermons should not alienate Scots from the king or his government.[44] After the revolution, episcopalians alleged that presbyterian ministers had avoided preaching against popery under James.[45] But there was much in their sermons that was critical of James's religion. In December 1687, one observer reported that Scottish presbyterians 'preach constantly of the Antichrist, and of the Whore of Babilon'.[46] If this was an exaggeration, Gilbert Rule would nevertheless claim that the presbyterians did 'not neglect to instruct people in the controverted points of our Religion, nor to hold forth the evil and danger of Popery in particular'.[47] Indeed, the sermons surviving from this period show that, when explaining points of doctrine, presbyterian ministers periodically referred to the errors of Catholicism. Preaching in Burntisland in May 1688, William Tullideff challenged the Catholic attitude towards miracles: 'seing they maintain docktrain contrare to [th]e scripturs they ought to confirme [the]m by reall miracles'.[48] In a sermon given in the same year, William Erskine criticised those who trusted in works of supererogation. 'Lord pity such Ignorants, and send them the light of the knowledge of God'.[49] In Irvine, Patrick Warner condemned idolatry, arguing that 'if we consider the time when the Lord charges Israel with worshiping of devils ... Ye will not think it strange if we charge the Church of Rome with it'.[50] Lay presbyterians were not spared anti-Catholic polemic, in spite of the king's orders.

More significantly, presbyterians often expressed disquiet about the crown's policy, and about the wider threat of Catholics to the survival of protestantism. Mainstream ministers did not preach 'to the times' as routinely or aggressively as did the Cameronians, whose sermons we sampled briefly in Chapter 2. And unlike their radical rivals, moderate presbyterians seem not to have criticised the king directly. Nevertheless, some faltered on the fine line between condemning the sin and insulting the man. Alexander Orrock was accused of calling the king an idolater; according to Robert Wodrow, he had merely wished James free of 'heart idols'.[51] Moderate presbyterians could not ignore the domestic and international context in which Catholicism was suddenly enjoying a revival. John Hardy was prosecuted for seditious speech (and acquitted) after preaching of the hazards of allowing legal recognition for popery.[52] Preachers frequently drew attention to the suppression of protestantism on the continent. In July 1688, Matthew Crawford mentioned the 'havock' caused by Catholic oppression in France, the Savoy and Piedmont, and warned of 'the many designs of Antichrist and [th]e projects for ruine to the church at this day'.[53] Others invoked the history of Catholic violence against protestants, including in Britain and Ireland. Referring to the bonfires of Marian England and the Irish Catholic rising of 1641, a preacher in March 1689 asked: 'can we expect a milder potion from them if ever the like advantage should againe be given them[?]'[54] And while this minister was perhaps emboldened to cite British and Irish evidence at a time when the Catholic threat was passing, Warner had spoken out explicitly while the danger was at its height. In 1688, he suggested that:

> if ye see fears of Poperie, ye may from thence take occasion to speak to your nighbours, what need they have to be established in the true religion: what reason they have to bring up their children earlie in the knowledge of God & his truth, least Poperie come in as a deluge upon them & sweip them away before they be confirmed in the truth.[55]

In another sermon, Warner advised parents to train their offspring in the 'grounds of the true religion in these days wherein poor children may meit with God knows what temptations to imbrace Poperie & idolatrie'. The danger of widespread conversion seemed still more live when Warner cautioned that 'if the multitude of Scotland were once gone over to idolatrie & Poperie, I am affrayd there would be few to stand against the shock'.[56] His hearers could not have doubted that he feared the consequences of multiconfessionalism.

* * *

As well as facing up to the threat of popery, presbyterian ministers found themselves in competition with episcopalians and radical Cameronians. The aim of the moderate presbyterians was to unite local communities in reconstituted and newly formed congregations, and thus to draw worshippers away from the established Kirk and the field conventicles. Among the overtures approved by the general meeting in July 1687 was a proposal 'That care be taken, in meekness and love, to reclaim all persons, preachers, or others, who have stepped aside in the hour of temptation'. Presbyterians particularly hoped to accommodate 'those who are given to wild courses', the Cameronians.[57] In fact, it was only after the revolution that significant numbers of the United Societies became reconciled with their parish congregations.[58] In 1687 and 1688, ministers serving areas where the Cameronians were active could do little more than denounce their divisive and violent courses. Preaching at Pollok, near Glasgow, Matthew Crawford lamented 'the divisions & delusions that are amongst us', and that some had 'come to that hight that they cast at all the Ministers in Brittan & Ireland'.[59] In June 1688, there was an opportunity for more public condemnation of the Societies, after a party of Cameronians rescued their preacher David Houston as he was transported through Ayrshire in military custody, killing six soldiers. The privy council responded by calling meetings of enquiry in the south-western shires, to which the nobility, other landowners and tolerated presbyterian ministers were summoned. At the Dumfriesshire meeting, three ministers sought to be excused from participation, submitting a petition in which they disowned 'these murthering principells and practices quhich some to the great scandall of religion are guilty of'. Ministers made similar statements to the meetings in Ayrshire, Lanarkshire and Renfrewshire.[60] These and other declarations added to the pressure on the Societies. In August 1688, their general meeting complained that 'the tolerated Presbyterians are inveighing bitterly against us'.[61] It is unclear to what extent the mainstream presbyterians, by condemning their rivals, expanded their own congregations.

A more significant objective for the presbyterians was to win over erstwhile conformists to episcopacy. The logic of multiconfessional competition dictated that the presbyterians should distinguish themselves from their episcopalian rivals, emphasising the purity and spiritual power of their doctrine and worship. Presbyterian ministers sought to set themselves apart from the establishment in various ways. First, they asserted clearly that their theological beliefs were those stated in the Westminster confession of faith. As we saw in Chapter 2, the presbyterian addresses thanking the king for the second indulgence explicitly referred to the confession. By clarifying their doctrinal principles in the addresses, the presbyterians distanced themselves from the episcopalians, some of whose leading clergy had adopted broadly Arminian understandings of salvation.[62] In baptism, moreover, presbyterian ministers did not require the father to assent to the apostles' creed, which was perceived as an episcopalian practice. Some ministers instead asked for the parent's approval of the Westminster confession; more hardline presbyterians apparently demanded a commitment to the National Covenant and the Solemn League and Covenant as well.[63] Especially in their preaching, presbyterians upheld the tenets of orthodox Calvinist theology.[64] This helped to ensure that when presbyterianism was re-established in 1690, the Westminster confession was itself granted the statutory authority that it had received in 1649, but which was rescinded after the Restoration.[65]

Presbyterians also tried to assert the distinctiveness of their style of public worship. In terms of prayer, the most obvious difference between episcopalian and presbyterian worship was that presbyterian ministers did not say the doxology or the Lord's Prayer in their services.[66] But there was an arguably more significant contrast between the groups, which has been noticed less often. At their meeting in July 1687, the presbyterian clergy agreed not only to preach, if possible, 'twice every Lord's day, and week days', but also to 'lecture as formerly'.[67] The practice of lecturing had evolved in the 1640s and 1650s, decades in which presbyterian worship became increasingly informal and extemporary. Introduced in place of the reading of chapters from the Old and New Testaments before the sermon, lectures consisted of a short reading – often less than a full chapter – followed by a sermon-like analysis of the text. In the Restoration period, bishops criticised lecturing and their synods tried to suppress it, though some conforming ministers were reluctant to revert to unadorned reading.[68] The presbyterians indulged by the government in 1669 started lecturing, but the privy council prohibited the practice, arguing that it 'was never used in the Church before the late trowbles, and is not warranted by authority'.[69] Nevertheless, politicians who investigated the issue observed that the presbyterian laity were 'superstitiously fond of' lecturing, while their ministers feared that complying with the council's order would alienate their congregations.[70] As late as 1683, the episcopalian minister John Cockburn found that there was 'no Bible belonging to the Church' of Ormiston, the Haddingtonshire parish to which he had been presented, 'the people receiving great prejudice by the want of reading'. Cockburn's predecessor, the presbyterian John Sinclair, had presumably retained the practice of lecturing, before being removed from the parish for refusing to swear the Test oath in 1681.[71] In 1687, therefore, the presbyterians' deliberate decision to lecture revived a popular form of worship, which was of presbyterian origin and had been disowned by the episcopalian establishment.

A third strategy in the presbyterians' attempts to attract former episcopalians was to persuade potential worshippers that the imposition of episcopacy in Scotland had been illegitimate and regrettable. Warner's preaching in Irvine gives a flavour of the tactics used. After his arrival in the town in 1688, he gave a series of nine sermons on Jeremiah 3: 1 ('thou hast played the harlot with many lovers; yet return again to me, saith the Lord'). The contemporary resonance of Warner's text became explicit when he asked his congregation to 'Consider what a dreadfull & lamentable falling from our first love there hath been among us: that love to the cause of God, to the interest of Christ & to the pure religion that shyned in our forefathers, how far is it gone in our days?' Scotland was guilty of a 'dreadfull defection' from presbyterianism.[72] Mainstream ministers were cautious in their allusions to the National Covenant and the Solemn League and Covenant. As recently as 1685, parliament had declared it treason to defend the Covenants as lawful or binding engagements. And the Cameronians loudly argued that the continuing force of the Covenants justified their renunciation of James VII.[73] But moderate presbyterians were not silent about Scotland's breach of the Covenants since the Restoration.[74] In January 1689, Matthew Crawford warned his hearers to repent of their various sins, including the swearing of 'contradictorie oaths & in breaking our covenants with God by false suearing & perjurie'.[75] Around the same time, the synod of Glasgow and Ayr adopted a declaration for a day of fasting, which regretted Scotland's 'general apostasie & backslydeing from solemn engagements'.[76] The process of persuading people of the errors of the episcopalian past and the righteousness of presbyterianism continued through 1689 and beyond. Most controversially, the act of the 1690 general assembly appointing a national fast, which was observed in January 1691, repudiated multiple aspects of the Restoration Church, including episcopacy, the royal supremacy and the swearing of oaths contradicting the

Covenants.⁷⁷ Through preaching, prayer and fasting, ministers endeavoured to forge a presbyterian identity for their re-formed congregations.

As well as attracting lay followers, presbyterians took the opportunity to recruit a few ministers who had formerly served under episcopacy. Presbyterians were naturally suspicious of such men, and it was not until the 1690s that the presbyterian courts comprehended significant numbers of episcopalian clergy, partly under royal pressure. Nevertheless, a few erstwhile episcopalian minsters sought to join the presbyterians during the period of multiconfessionalism. In October 1687, John Dalgleish, who had been minister of Roxburgh in the 1670s, successfully applied to the general meeting to be accepted as a presbyterian. The meeting heard that 'he behaved himself soberly even during the time of his conformity', now expressed 'his sincere disatisfaction with the course of conformity', and was 'of presbiterian principles'. Dalgleish then preached to the presbyterian congregation at Queensferry, before returning to Roxburgh; in 1700, he became minister of Dundee.⁷⁸ Ministers who were perceived to have suffered for their opposition to the Test oath of 1681 were more likely than most episcopalians to be accepted by the presbyterians. David Thomson claimed to have been deprived of the church of Manor, near Peebles, for refusing the Test. In 1689, the presbyterian presbytery first appointed its ministers to give Thomson charity, and then recommended him as a suitable preacher to supply vacant parishes.⁷⁹ But the most famous one-time episcopalian to join the presbyterians was George Meldrum. Before refusing to swear the Test oath, Meldrum was one of the ministers of Aberdeen. He began preaching again soon after the second indulgence, without giving the expected notice to the authorities. He was settled as the minister of Kilwinning, in Irvine presbytery, in March 1688. In later life, he was professor of divinity at the University of Edinburgh and a moderator of the general assembly.⁸⁰

Probably the most controversial convert from episcopacy to presbyterianism was Angus McBean, minister of the first charge, Inverness, since 1683. He disowned episcopalian government after the second indulgence, and absented himself from presbytery meetings. McBean told Michael Fraser, the minister asked by the episcopalian presbytery to speak to him, that he had doubted episcopacy at the time of his ordination; his presbyterian sentiments 'now returning with greater force upon his Conscience, he could not overcome them'.⁸¹ In October 1687, the synod of Elgin appointed a committee to try to persuade McBean against separating from the Church. But before these ministers could meet, on Sunday 23 October McBean preached a sermon against episcopacy, publicly demitting his office as an episcopalian minister in Inverness.

The following Sunday, he conducted worship at a meeting house in Ross-shire. On 6 November, he was back in Inverness, preaching to a presbyterian congregation. '[S]o begann his schisme, in one of the most Loyall, orderly and regular Cities, in the Nation', the episcopalian presbytery recorded. Fraser was sent south, to ask for the archbishop of St Andrews' assistance in 'suppressing the Schisme begun at Inverness'.[82] McBean visited Edinburgh, perhaps to meet with presbyterian clergy. Presumably as a result of Fraser's lobbying, McBean was summoned by the privy council on 29 November. His enemies in Inverness had reported that his preaching was disloyal, and McBean was questioned about the lawfulness of resistance, the murder of Archbishop James Sharp and the Bothwell Bridge rising of 1679. His answers were evasive, and he was briefly imprisoned. Released under caution to appear again, McBean returned to Inverness and preached. On 3 February 1688, the privy council summoned him, warning him to cease his ministry; on 27 February, he appeared before the archbishop and other clergy at Edinburgh, and was formally deposed from the ministry and excommunicated.[83] He was imprisoned in Edinburgh, dying two months after his release in December.[84] McBean's actions brought the multiconfessional experiment to Inverness, as he and his episcopalian critics denounced each other's principles from the pulpit.[85]

For episcopalians, then, the king's multiconfessional policy was enormously frustrating. In parts of the north-east, there was a renewed risk that lay people would abandon the Kirk for Catholic worship. And in the south, the re-emergence of a strong presbyterian alternative to the establishment sapped the clergy's morale. In October 1687, the moderator of Dalkeith presbytery urged his brethren to remain 'couragious and resolute, stedfast & immoveable', notwithstanding 'all the discouragements and difficulties they encountred with through [th]e disorders of the times and giddines [tha]t possess foolish people puft up [wi]t[h] [th]e present liberty'.[86] But while some ministers stood firm, perhaps especially where they enjoyed the support of landowners or burgh councils, others witnessed significant declines in the size of their congregations. It is to the wider consequences of these changes that the next section turns.

* * *

As well as jeopardising the spiritual and pastoral effectiveness of the episcopalian clergy, multiconfessionalism disrupted the administrative functions of the established Church. One seemingly minor but revealing issue concerned the income of parish officers such as kirk session clerks, precentors and beadles (often a single person fulfilled two or all of these roles). The first indulgence promised to protect the 'Functions, Rights and Properties' of the Kirk's clergy, while the second indulgence guaranteed protestants the 'Quiet and Full Injoyment of all their Possessions'.[87] But it soon became clear that, when Scots left the established Church for meeting houses, episcopalian kirk session officers lost a significant proportion of the fees paid to them by people seeking marriage, baptism and burial. In January 1688, the clerk of the Barony parish, Glasgow, recorded in his register of marriages that, since the second indulgence, many locals had married in presbyterian meeting houses, without acquainting the episcopalian minister 'or paying the half croune of consigna[tio]ne' money.[88] This was evidently a widespread problem. In the previous month, the privy council felt it necessary to enact that session clerks and others 'should not be prejudged of their Rights and accustomed Fees and Casualties, arising to them by Baptisms, Marriages and Burials (the ordinar mean of their Subsistence;)'. Presbyterian dissenters (and indeed Catholics) who married, were baptised and buried outwith the Church were thus required to pay the episcopalian officers for the privilege.[89]

The council's act was to be read in churches, but it is unclear how well it was enforced. Soon after the act, Dalkeith kirk session noted that a couple intending marriage 'being proclaimed in the [presbyterian] meeting house of dalkeith payed the dues of the Church according to the act of Councell'.[90] But the session apparently made no more minutes to this effect, and we cannot assume that the council's act was generally observed. The kirk session of Bathgate (Linlithgow presbytery) recorded a collapse in income from 'mariage mo[ne]y since the Indulgenc[e]'.[91] In July 1688, the precentor of an Edinburgh meeting house gave his episcopalian opposite number a list of persons married and baptised in the meeting house, so that the episcopalian precentor might 'operat against the persons concerned for what is due to him'. The episcopalian refused to accept the list, perhaps considering the recovery of his lost fees too difficult.[92] Sometimes civil magistrates intervened to ensure that episcopalian officers received their dues. The kirk session of Spott, in Dunbar presbytery, resolved to ask the JPs to make presbyterians pay the fees to the kirk officer.[93] In October 1688, the schoolmaster of Stitchill, Roxburghshire, complained to the local baron court about four men who had not given him the accustomed dues for baptisms and marriages. The court ordered the men to pay and threatened a fine against any who refused to do so in future.[94]

As well as reducing the incomes of session officers, the presbyterians' reluctance to pay compromised the registration of births and marriages. In November 1687, the session of Kirkliston (Linlithgow presbytery) sent one of its number to visit parishioners who had had presbyterian ministers baptise their children, 'to get ther names & the names of thosse [tha]t baptizd them'. We do not know if successful enquiries were made, but the recording of baptisms and marriages seems to have ceased and there is nothing in the parish register from the end of 1687 to 1692.[95] The presbyterians' general meeting instructed the new congregations to keep their own registers. There is evidence that presbyterians did make records of baptisms and marriages, and some took over the existing parish registers. In communities where the meeting house attracted a large majority of the population, the presbyterians effectively superseded the established Church in this function.[96] But inevitably in divided parishes there was the potential for confusion. In September 1687, Glasgow burgh council ordered all residents, including presbyterians, 'to booke their mariages, and what children they shall baptize, in the publict and authentick register as formerlie', so that it would in future be possible to establish every child's age (and, presumably, legitimacy). The burgh's presbyterians and episcopalians kept separate registers, at least until January 1688, when the episcopalian record stops; it is unclear whether episcopalian marriages and baptisms were publicly recorded after this point.[97] In Edinburgh, the town council complained in May 1689 that, since the toleration, 'no accompt' of marriages and baptisms in presbyterian congregations had been given to the clerk of the episcopalian kirk sessions, who kept the burgh's 'publick registers'. In fact, a few baptisms by presbyterian ministers were recorded in the Edinburgh registers, but they are probably far from complete.[98] Not only did the competition between religious groups undermine the Kirk's capacity to vouch for baptisms and marriages, but the period's upheavals led to the loss of some records. The former episcopalian clerk of Renfrew claimed that the registers in his custody disappeared in late 1688 or early 1689, when 'his house was by the mob Rabled and any books or papers he had riffled and taken away'.[99]

More immediate problems arose with respect to poor relief. Though the poor law devised in 1574 allowed for compulsory local levies to fund relief, the majority of Scottish parishes in our period relied on voluntary church collections, which were distributed to the needy by the kirk session. Recent research, especially studies concentrating on towns, suggests that the frameworks of poor relief that evolved in the seventeenth century were not as inadequate as was once thought.[100]

Nevertheless, the system was fragile, and even in the relatively prosperous 1680s, some kirk sessions struggled to satisfy demand for their charity. In September 1687, the Midlothian parish of Ratho, finding that 'the Collections upon the Lords day were so inconsiderable [tha]t the [poor's] box was not able to maintaine' all the claimants, took the unusual step of agreeing that landowners would make a compulsory contribution of victual to support the local poor.[101] Moreover, when poor relief depended on the charity of the congregation, reliable elders were needed to oversee collections and keep accounts of the sums raised.[102] Unfortunately, elders sometimes failed in their duty. In Kelso, it was complained in January 1688 that some elders 'do not attend the collections when it is incumbent to them', and thus 'the poor of the parish sustain much prejudice'.[103]

It is unclear whether the Kelso elders' negligence or the insufficient collections in Ratho can be attributed to presbyterian dissent. Elsewhere, however, multiconfessional competition evidently made it more challenging for the established Church to raise adequate funds and administer poor relief. In Lenzie Easter (Cumbernauld), as we saw in Chapter 2, most elders started to attend presbyterian services after the second indulgence. It became difficult to collect for the poor's box, and the minister proposed that residents should pay a levy of 8s. per year to fund poor relief.[104] By November 1687, the boxmaster in charge of the poor's money of Dron, Perthshire, together with the other elders, had 'deserted the ordinances in the Church', presumably to worship with Alexander Pitcairn, the parish's former presbyterian incumbent. The episcopalian minister was necessitated 'to take the key of the box himself' and to become personally accountable for the receipts and gifts.[105]

Even in places where the administration of funds was not so obviously affected, multiconfessionalism had a significant impact on poor relief. Most obviously, shrinking episcopalian congregations received smaller collections. In Spott, the kirk session noted in January 1688 that the 'poor are daylie Incressing And the ordinar collections daylie declyning throw [th]e contempt & separa[tio]ne of dissenters'. This parish, which had previously experimented with a compulsory stent to support the needy, now sought to recover money from the fines levied by JPs for offences of profanity, a proportion of which were, by an act of parliament, intended for the poor.[106] The session repeatedly hoped to gain access to these funds, noting in March 1689 that there was now 'small or noe collectione for the poor through the peoples dishaunting the Church'.[107] As we saw in Chapter 2, where detailed accounts survive, we can be more precise about the effects of presbyterian dissent on the episcopalian churches' collections. In Bathgate, the accounts show that there was a fall from £61.3s.4d. collected in a period of nine and a half months in 1686 to £11.6s.8d. raised in the seven months beginning with October 1687. This constituted a drop of three quarters in average weekly income. The kirk session attributed the collapse in its collections to the indulgences.[108] In the Barony parish, Glasgow, to cite a more extreme case, the records tell us that, after August 1687, with the departure of all the elders and the great majority of the congregation, no accounts were made of collections at all, there being 'littill or nothing given but by the Mini[ste]r and his famelly'.[109]

As with the registration of baptisms and marriages, it is likely that problems with poor relief were mitigated by the efforts of presbyterians. The general meeting instructed the new congregations to collect for the poor.[110] In October 1687, David Williamson, the presbyterian minister active in the West Kirk parish, Edinburgh, offered 'to take off the burden of the poore of West Port, Bristo, Potterow & Pleasance', and the episcopalian session agreed to concentrate its payments in the parish's other districts.[111] It is possible that, in the excitement of committing themselves to presbyterianism, members of the new congregations became more charitable. In South Leith, where we have information about the collections of both the episcopalian and presbyterian congregations, the donations made in the meeting house were apparently greater than the decline in weekly collections in the church following the second indulgence. Considerable sums from the presbyterian collections were distributed to the poor, though perhaps the minister's stipend was funded from the same source.[112]

But even if presbyterian congregations ran their own poor relief, a heavy demand continued to fall on the increasingly straitened episcopalian kirk sessions. In July 1688, the episcopalian presbytery of Duns recorded that 'tho our poor be daily increasing', church collections grew 'every day le[ss] & le[ss], by reason of the wandring of our parishoners, to schismatical & fanaticall meetings'.[113] In April, the presbytery of Linlithgow complained to the local JPs about 'a great many who have deserted' the Church and declined to make contributions for the poor, as well as failing to pay dues for marriage and baptism. In July, the JPs ordered the goods of those who had not paid to be poinded (distrained).[114] Together with the case of Spott, this evidence highlights the role of JPs in poor relief, which had developed earlier in the century, especially in periods of crisis, and was particularly significant during the period of multiconfessional competition.[115] The justices do not seem to have appointed overseers of the poor, as they were instructed to do in

1661,[116] but they may have attempted to distribute funds to places of need. Thus in the spring of 1688, the archbishop of Glasgow instructed the episcopalian presbytery of Lanark not to comply with requests from the local JPs to pay over mortifications and money collected for the poor and the purchase of communion elements.[117] Conceivably, the JPs intended to use these sums to ameliorate poverty among the presbyterian laity. In parts of southern and central Scotland, this suggests, the civil magistrate intervened in response to problems created by the competition between episcopalians and presbyterians. Multiconfessionalism had undermined a model of poor relief that depended on religious uniformity.

The poor relief system was at its weakest in the period 1689–90, when the authority of episcopalian kirk sessions collapsed and there was a delay until June 1690 before presbyterianism was finally settled. In Cramond, near Edinburgh, 'The Ordinar poore wanted their monthly pensions for two moneths, viz March and Aprill [1689], by reason of the smallnes of Collections, few comeing to the Church'. The session also found it difficult to collect the income on the parts of the poor's money that had been invested.[118] In February 1689, 'many' of Edinburgh's deacons, whose job was to collect and distribute poor relief, refused to do so, 'upon pretence they goe to hear the word in the meeting house'.[119] It seems that several of the established Church's sessions in Edinburgh struggled to raise enough for the poor until the restoration of presbyterianism in 1690.[120] In parishes where the incumbent was forcibly evicted or deprived by the civil authorities, regular church services and collections ceased. At Spott, it was noted in August 1690, there were 'Noe Collections since Sept[embe]r 8 [1689] The Minister being deprived by the [privy] Consell [on] Sept[embe]r 10 1689'.[121] Multiconfessionalism had weakened the system of poor relief, but the effects of the revolution were still more disruptive. The large number of vacant parishes resulting from the revolution and the presbyterian settlement continued to disrupt the provision of support to the poor through the 1690s.[122]

Multiconfessionalism created fundamental problems for the established Church's discipline. In areas where Scots could choose to abandon the Kirk's services, they were soon able to escape the intrusion of its courts into their lives. The Church's intense scrutiny of moral conduct, one of the characteristics of Scotland under religious uniformity, was potentially under threat. Before 1687, of course, Quakers, Catholic recusants and the more consistent presbyterian nonconformists had evaded discipline.[123] In 1686, Dingwall presbytery heard that Ewen McHucheon vic Ewn, an adulterer in the parish of Kilmorack, had 'profest himself a

Papist to shun the censure of the Church'.[124] The problem became more visible and widespread after the indulgences. The episcopalian minister of Rutherglen, Lanarkshire, told his elders in November 1687 that he had spoken to a suspected fornicator, who denied the allegations against him, 'bot being ane Papist refused to compeare befor' the session.[125] In December 1687 and January 1688, the Trinity College parish in Edinburgh investigated two cases of fornication involving Catholics. One of the accused men appeared before the session, 'declared himself a Roman Catholick but confest his guilt'; the other couple was simply referred to the civil magistrate.[126] Where overlapping ecclesiastical and secular jurisdictions complemented each other, as in Edinburgh, the refusal of discipline by Catholics and other nonconformists did not necessarily allow them to escape justice. Nevertheless, multiconfessionalism weakened the operation of discipline by the church courts.

In some cases, opportunistic offenders attempted to avoid the consequences of their sinful behaviour. Identified as the father of an illegitimate child killed shortly after birth by its mother, George Ronaldson, of Temple, Midlothian, persisted in denial for over two years. After multiple enquiries, it was reported in April 1688 'that he [wi]t[h]drew from the Church and went constantly to [th]e [presbyterian] meetings'.[127] In fact, Ronaldson's parish minister soon brought him before the episcopalian congregation, and asked him to deny his paternity on oath. This caused many worshippers, who thought Ronaldson guilty, 'to tremble and raised a huge noise amongst [the]m many of [the]m weeping to hear it and see him so ready to suear it'. Hoping that this reaction would awaken Ronaldson to the dire consequences of perjury, the minister halted proceedings. But Ronaldson, who remained willing to swear, continued to outwit the church courts.[128] Meanwhile, John Wilson, a weaver in Dalkeith, aimed to take advantage of Midlothian's disciplinary confusion to marry his deceased wife's niece, an unlawful match. On pretence that his intended spouse was an unrelated woman in Edinburgh, Wilson sought a testimonial that he was a widower from Alexander Heriot, Dalkeith's episcopalian minister. Wilson then applied to the kirk sessions of Edinburgh, hoping that he could proceed to marry his niece undiscovered. Further investigations revealed that Wilson, who attended presbyterian services, had approached Heriot after the local presbyterian minister had refused to countenance the marriage.[129]

These examples suggest that the established Church's discipline, though compromised by confessional competition, had not quite ceased to be effective. But episodes involving more dedicated presbyterians show that they were increasingly able to escape the oversight of the episcopalian courts. In July 1686, the presbytery of Dingwall heard that John McCalich of Kiltearn parish allowed two of his children to die unbaptised. Though the presbytery pursued him for contempt of the sacrament, it was probably the episcopalian clergy he despised. He failed to respond to summons and was referred to the bishop. In August 1687, it was reported that he declared himself a presbyterian, and the episcopalian presbytery 'thought it not their concern to follow him further untill they adwise with the B[isho]p and Synod'.[130] Probably McCalich was never brought to account by the established Church.

If the multiconfessional experiment encouraged offenders to try to evade discipline, it also called into question the authority of the established Church's courts over recalcitrant parishioners. In May 1687, the presbytery of Paisley investigated the case of Simon Vadie, a resident of Paisley accused of fornication. Called before the presbytery, Vadie submitted a protestation, alleging among other things 'that the kings royall proclamatione for libertie of conscience, did free him from all obedience to the discipline of the Church'. Responding that 'ther is no such thing as is alleadged in the fors[ai]d proclamatione', the presbytery received the archbishop of Glasgow's permission to continue pursuing Vadie.[131] After the indulgence of June 1687, however, more Scots attempted to decline the jurisdiction of the church courts. Since the spring of 1686, David Risk, of the Stirlingshire parish of Strathblane, had consistently refused either to admit or formally to deny adultery, despite the confession of his alleged partner. In February 1687, the episcopalian presbytery of Dumbarton initiated a process of excommunication against him. Then in September it was reported of Risk and several other delinquents 'that they refuse to answer before ane Judicatorie and that they count themselves not obliged to purge themselves of these scandalls and crimes formerlie laid to their charge In respect of the libertie granted by his majestie of late'.[132] This prompted the presbytery to refer the case to the archbishop and synod of Glasgow. The synod resolved that episcopalian courts should pursue instances of alleged 'scandalous carriage antecedent to this late indulgence', and the presbytery continued its process against Risk.[133] Nevertheless, the implication of the synod's decision was that kirk sessions in the established Church should no longer exercise discipline in the parish community as a whole, but merely among those who chose to remain episcopalians.

In two other revealing cases, the episcopalian courts conceded that presbyterians would no longer be subject to their oversight. Shortly before the second indulgence, James Coliart of Hawick had been summoned by the kirk session there for sabbath breaking. He did not appear, and his minister referred the case to the presbytery of Jedburgh. He likewise failed to respond to the presbytery's summons. Then in August 1687, the presbytery recorded 'that he was gone to the meeting house and so deserted our dicipline'. Though he was again cited, Coliart told the presbytery's officer 'that he had joyned himselfe to the [presbyterian] meeting house and so was not oblidged to answer to our diciplen, neither would he'. The presbytery suggested that John Langlands, the minister of Hawick, represent the case to the sheriff. But in November, Langlands told the presbytery that, 'in respect ther wer so many separatists In the lyke transgressione who disowned all disciplen of the present Established Church', he thought 'it needlesse to give any addresse to the sherif for that effect or the presb[yte]r[y] any furder trouble'.[134] The court gave up on Coliart, leaving him to the supervision of the presbyterians.

It was probably true that some local magistrates were more willing to assist the established Church's courts than others. In September 1688, the episcopalian minister of Bathgate obtained an order from two local JPs to imprison a woman who had failed to satisfy the kirk session.[135] Nevertheless, in the case of John Johnston of Peebles, the civil magistrate's involvement helped to establish the principle that the Church could impose discipline on its own members only. Following an incident of drunkenness, Johnston confessed and performed repentance before the presbyterian congregation, which he had joined soon after the second indulgence. But he was pursued for the offence by the episcopalian kirk session, whose authority over him he declined to recognise. On the instruction of the archbishop of Glasgow and his synod, Johnston was summoned to appear before the episcopalian presbytery of Peebles. For at least five months, Johnston was repeatedly cited, and refused to appear.[136] In April 1688, the newly constituted presbyterian presbytery recorded that the 'prelatick pairtie Intendit a process of excommunica[tio]ne' against Johnston for his contumacy. The presbytery resolved to ask the sheriff depute to stop the episcopalians' pursuit, and by May the resulting intervention of the civil magistrate had brought a halt to the case.[137] This solution seems to have encouraged local presbyterians to take responsibility in other matters of discipline, as the general meeting envisaged that the new congregations would.[138] Thus the presbyterian presbytery instructed its minister in Stobo to process the repentant adulterer John Simpson, who declined to satisfy the episcopalian session, even though his partner in the offence, Jean Veitch, had done so.[139] The lack of presbyterian elders in some parishes, which we noted in Chapter 2, was an obstacle to the presbyterians' exercise of discipline. Indeed, the occurrence of moral scandal in a congregation could prompt the local presbytery to settle an eldership.[140]

From the episcopalian point of view, James VII's second indulgence soon disrupted the exercise of discipline in areas of multiconfessional competition. Risk, Coliart and Johnston vexed the episcopalian courts, but other newly presbyterian delinquents escaped episcopalian discipline with little comment. Summoned before Dalkeith kirk session in March 1688, John Little appeared and 'declined the session leaving a paper w[i]t[h] his defences'.[141] Thomas Watson, a fornicator in Newbattle, took the opportunity of his offence to become a full member of the local presbyterian congregation. Though his partner Bessie Jackson satisfied the episcopalian session, Watson failed to respond to citations from the session and presbytery. In March 1689, the session heard that he had been absolved in the presbyterian meeting house. The presbyterians' record noted that Watson, having 'joyned with' the meeting house congregation 'formerly, did now upon the acknowledgment of his Offence, desire to be received into their fellowship, which was granted'.[142] As this case suggests, then, presbyterian courts claimed to oversee the behaviour of men and women who joined presbyterian congregations only. Kintyre's presbyterian presbytery, indeed, suspended its meetings for much of 1689, in part because 'all the present delinquents in q[uho]m the presb. might be concerned' sought to satisfy for their offences before the episcopalian authorities.[143] In areas of Scotland where both presbyterians and episcopalians had a significant presence, therefore, each group imposed discipline on its members only. The multiconfessional experiment had fractured Scotland's uniform worship, discipline and ecclesiastical organisation, creating parallel Churches on the voluntary model envisaged by John Locke.

* * *

The multiconfessionalism initiated in Scotland under James VII saw the country's religious groups compete for followers. The years 1687–8 should be understood not in terms of the eclipse of the episcopalian Church, but as a period of unprecedentedly free religious pluralism. Of course, where there was competition in northern Scotland, it was more often between episcopalians and Catholics than among the major protestant groups. Nevertheless, the logic of the religious marketplace influenced the rhetoric and actions of churchmen and lay people across the country.

By conceiving of Scotland as a deregulated religious marketplace, we can focus with some precision on the most common change in religious affiliation in the period: the shift from worshipping in the episcopalian Church to attending presbyterian services. For the individual consumers of religion, this was a transition with relatively low costs.[144] There was no longer a threat of prosecution for dissenting from the established Kirk, though some feared that James's indulgence would be temporary. In many places, groups of like-minded men and women became presbyterians together, without risk to their social connections. Indeed, for those who believed that presbyterian worship offered more vivid religious experiences, or minimised the threat of exposure to corrupt doctrines or teachers, it made sense to hear presbyterian preachers rather than episcopalians. If some elite figures thought that presbyterian dissent was not socially respectable,[145] other Scots gained the esteem of their godly neighbours by worshipping at the meeting house.

Thinking in economic terms, it is more obvious that, for at least a significant minority of Scots, religion was a matter of choice after June 1687. Historians have tended to imply that the surge in support for presbyterianism enabled by James's indulgences was somehow inevitable, as if the majority of Scots were naturally presbyterians. Yet we should recall that the great body of the population conformed to episcopacy at the start of the king's reign, and recognise that some of those with the opportunity to become presbyterians in the interval 1687–9 did not do so. As we shall see in Chapters 5 and 6, the market in religious services was seriously constrained after the collapse of James's regime, and in most areas of the south there was then little option but to be a presbyterian. But this does not detract from the possibility that Scots who became life-long presbyterians in 1687–8 made a (comparatively free) choice.

4

James and the Royal Burghs

THIS CHAPTER ANALYSES JAMES VII's intervention in the government of Scotland's towns. By nominating the magistrates and councillors of the towns represented in parliament, the king expressed his displeasure at the refusal of the 1686 session to repeal the laws against Catholicism. Because the appointed councils would choose their burghs' commissioners to the next meeting of parliament, James hoped to engineer a more pliant membership and ultimately to secure statutory approval of his religious experiment. Indeed, the policy had the potential to neutralise opposition to the court among the burghs' representatives in parliament, who amounted to approximately a third of that unicameral institution. As we saw in Chapter 1, James's policy towards the royal burghs was his only systematic attempt to reshape the patterns of local office-holding in Scotland. He could do little to change the holders of judicial office in large parts of rural Scotland, where most sheriffdoms, regalities and other jurisdictions were possessed heritably. By contrast, the king manipulated the membership of the councils in forty-eight of the kingdom's sixty-five parliamentary burghs. It was his principal effort to alter political attitudes on a national level through local meddling.

James's policy offers plentiful evidence of the aspirations and limitations of his 'absolutist' government. Though the crown had been interfering in burgh elections for more than a century, and albeit Charles I's government proposed that councils should be named by the king, James was the first Scottish monarch to invade the privileges of all the royal burghs at a stroke. Suspending the routine elections in sixty-five burghs, and nominating men in forty-eight, depended on swift and diligent action by officials in the central administration and the localities. In the main, the policy was implemented efficiently, though there were some failings. More significantly, close study of the crown's choice of magistrates and councillors shows that James made less difference than has sometimes been assumed. Nevertheless, in some towns the royal nominations served to exacerbate the factionalism of local politics. The king's policy thus contributed to the sense of experimental and revolutionary upheaval characteristic of his reign.

The treatment of the royal burghs was also an important issue in the overthrow of James. His interventions in urban government featured prominently in the Scottish *Declaration of Reasons* issued in 1688 to justify William of Orange's expedition. James's policy was, the *Declaration* urged, a 'manifest violation' of the right of free elections guaranteed by burghs' charters, and was 'done by meer Arbitrary Power, without any Citation, Trial or Sentence'.[1] In April 1689, the convention of estates echoed these complaints. According to the Claim of Right, James's nomination of councils had been 'without the pretence either of sentence, surrender or consent'. Furthermore, the Claim asserted that 'many' of the magistrates nominated by James were 'avowed papists' and noted that burghs were required to pay for the delivery of royal letters naming their magistrates. The Claim also objected to the exacting of tax without parliamentary approval; we shall see that this complaint related to James's relations with the royal burghs.[2] By the time of the Claim of Right's adoption, the convention had begun to reverse the king's policy, ordering new council elections in which all ordinary burgesses (freemen) were entitled to vote.[3] And the revolution stimulated action to address some of the royal burghs' wider grievances, bringing about the restoration of their monopoly of overseas trade that had been lost in 1672.

The chapter begins by reviewing the formal status and economic circumstances of Scotland's royal burghs. Next it tracks earlier control of their elections by the crown, arguing that James's interventions, though of unprecedented scope, were in continuity with previous developments. We then examine the implementation of James's policy, showing the channels of communication between the king, his privy council and burghs across Scotland. There is some evidence, albeit fragmentary, that aspiring urban politicians cooperated with the crown, suggesting nominees or seeking promotion to office. The central part of the chapter then analyses the impact of the king's appointment of magistrates and councillors. Contrary to the Claim of Right's assertion, few Catholics were put in charge of towns. On the other hand, James nominated a significant number of landed gentlemen who might not normally have held office, together with a group of prominent functionaries of the central government. But a majority of nominees seem to have been members of the conventional urban elites, and only a minority of towns had obvious outsiders imposed on them. If this suggests that there was little reason to complain about the crown's policy, the final section of the chapter explores reasons for discontent, showing that some towns had to endure unpopular magistrates, and others faced new tax burdens.

* * *

The royal burghs were those towns that held their lands and privileges directly from the king. In feudal terms, they were tenants-in-chief. With this status came the right to self-government under the crown, in the form of councillors, bailies and often a provost selected by members of the urban community itself. One of the chief functions of the council was to manage the town's property – called the common good – on behalf of the inhabitants. The royal burghs were entitled to be represented in parliament, and collectively they were obliged to pay a sixth part of the grants of taxation agreed there.[4] In contrast, burghs of barony and regality – so-called 'unfree' towns – were subordinate to particular noblemen, and the residents of these settlements often had no say in the choice of their magistrates. The unfree burghs were taxed with the counties of which they were a part, and did not send commissioners to parliament. Strictly speaking, St Andrews, Glasgow and Brechin were ecclesiastical burghs subordinate to their respective bishops, rather than royal burghs. Nevertheless, they took seats in parliament and had the other privileges of royal burghs.[5] There were sixty-one towns represented in the parliament of 1686, sixty-four at the convention of estates in 1689 and sixty-five in parliament in 1690.[6] In addition to participating in parliaments, royal and ecclesiastical burghs sent commissioners to regular meetings of the convention of royal burghs, which decided on matters of shared economic and fiscal concern, and prepared the towns' collective response to parliamentary proposals.[7]

Traditionally, the most important of the royal burghs' privileges was their monopoly of overseas trade. By the Restoration period, however, the burghs of barony and regality increasingly evaded the restrictions on their participation in this activity. In 1672, parliament overturned the royal burghs' exclusive right to import and export most commodities, but did not require a bigger contribution to taxes from the other towns that would benefit from the reform.[8] The royal burghs' leaders thus considered the new statute an assault on their economic well-being, at a time when they found it difficult to meet their fiscal obligations.[9] The convention lobbied for the restoration of the burghs' lost privileges, and in 1681, parliament considered proposals to modify the act of 1672.[10] These came to nothing, and observers thought that other legislation in 1681 had further disadvantaged the royal burghs.[11] At the time of the 1686 parliament, the convention favoured a draft act to restore the burghs' monopoly, but this was again abortive, not least because of the failure of the king's religious proposals.[12]

Most of the royal burghs faced economic difficulties in the 1680s. This was partly due to growing competition from burghs of barony and regality, but also because the towns' traditional incomes from rents, customs and other duties were typically too small to meet their spending commitments. In 1692, a major survey of the royal burghs' finances reported that most bore a heavy burden of debt. Even if this enquiry exaggerated the poverty of the burghs, it identified the widespread need for new sources of local revenue.[13] We shall see below that the search for fiscal solutions was a controversial aspect of the crown's relationship with the royal burghs under James VII. For the time being, however, we should acknowledge the diversity of the royal burghs, in size, social complexity and economic viability. A few of the weaker towns could not afford to make even the smallest of contributions to the estate's tax dues. In 1672, Cromarty, Anstruther-Wester and Kilrenny began the process of resigning their status as royal burghs for this reason, though only the first town ultimately ceased to pay tax and send men to parliament.[14] Some other royal burghs scarcely functioned as such. Dysart lacked magistrates during James's reign, reportedly because a collapse in the town's trade had led to depopulation, discouraging potential bailies from serving.[15] A few other towns whose council minutes are missing for this period may have been in a similarly parlous state.[16] The king's decision to suspend council elections probably made little difference in some of the poorest burghs; most of the weaker towns did not receive nominations of councillors and magistrates. Though the larger and wealthier burghs were typically in debt, control of their shared resources could be lucrative, and partly for this reason there was often factional competition for local offices. As a result, James's nominations in several such towns caused considerable controversy.

* * *

How innovative was James's interference in urban government? Because the monarch was the feudal superior of the royal burghs, he had ultimate responsibility for resolving disagreements and abuses of power within them. In response to one such dispute, the sett or constitution of Edinburgh had been varied after a judgement (the decreet arbitral) made by James VI in 1583.[17] Across the sixteenth and seventeenth centuries, moreover, national political priorities had at times prompted the crown to remove and appoint burgh magistrates. As Michael Lynch argues, this was more common during royal minorities than when an adult monarch was on the throne. In 1583, as the government of James Stewart, earl of Arran reacted against its radical protestant predecessor, the crown secured the appointment of its chosen men as provosts in nine of Scotland's twelve largest burghs.[18] This was an unusually widespread manipulation, but the adult James VI again attempted to impose burgh magistrates in 1593. On this occasion, the council of Edinburgh unsuccessfully tried to resist. In fact, the capital had, since the 1550s, experienced frequent royal regulation of its elections.[19]

In the early seventeenth century, the crown's involvement was occasional if erratic, but the need to enforce its religious policies encouraged the central government to take more notice of local magistrates. In 1637, Charles I involved himself in the elections of six important towns, including Edinburgh; he also envisaged the creation of 'constant' councils with no annual elections. This reform – perhaps a blueprint for James VII's policy – remained unrealised before the 1680s.[20] The closest that earlier regimes came to implementing systematic oversight of burgh councils was in the purges of town councils following the defeat of the marquis of Montrose's royalist military campaigns in 1645 and the army of the Engagement in 1648.[21] On these occasions, however, the national authorities were attempting to remove men associated with failed counter-revolutions, not to promote a body of magistrates dependent on the central government, and willing to do its bidding.

The scale of James's interference in urban government was unprecedented, then. But since the Restoration, several developments tended to bring the burghs under the influence of the court. The re-establishment of episcopacy in 1661–2 led to renewed supervision of the ecclesiastical burghs by bishops chosen by the king. In Brechin, the bishop picked one of the three bailies; the others were selected by the earl of Panmure and the burgh community. Even so, James did not feel the need himself to name magistrates for Brechin.[22] The provost and bailies of Glasgow were chosen by the archbishop. Here James nominated in 1686 only, at a time when Archbishop Alexander Cairncross had been marginalised for his reluctance to act against anti-Catholic preaching.[23] The king appointed magistrates for St Andrews in 1686, and later removed one of his chosen bailies. But he otherwise allowed the election of 1687 to proceed as normal, under the guidance of the archbishop.[24]

The Restoration period also saw a growth in direct royal scrutiny of town councils. This was driven by the need to ensure that office-holders were loyal, that they conformed to the established Church, and that they had sworn the increasingly complicated state oaths designed to test these qualifications. Importantly, enforcement was in the hands of the privy council, rather than the more autonomous convention of royal burghs. The controversial Test oath of 1681 increased the council's interventions in towns, especially those where the magistrates were reluctant to swear the oath and thus delayed the elections due around Michaelmas (29 September) 1681.[25] The most prominent case was Ayr, where the previous year's councillors resigned, protesting that 'there was to be no more government in that place'. Their successors were named by the privy council.[26] In Lanark, local government was in disarray in the early 1680s, partly as a result of a fine of 6,000 merks imposed by the privy council on the burgh after radical presbyterians staged a protest there in January 1682. Though an election was held as normal at Michaelmas 1682, its results were overturned after Cromwell Lockhart of Lee, a local landowner, obtained the privy council's nomination to be provost of Lanark. Lockhart then proceeded to appoint as bailies and councillors men he considered loyal to the king.[27] Thus the western towns of Ayr and Lanark, where sympathy for presbyterianism was widespread, saw considerable central intervention before James became king.

In these cases, the privy council reacted to specific local problems. But in the wake of the disrupted elections of 1681, the council sought to acquire a copy of the setts of all the royal burghs, making it better prepared to take the initiative in any future involvement.[28] Indeed, the crown also asserted the right to impose men as magistrates, even when no civic uncertainty required this. In 1683, Charles II revived the practice, periodically exercised by his predecessors, of choosing the provost of Edinburgh.[29] In 1685, James's first invasion of a burgh's electoral privileges was a letter instructing the privy council to suspend Edinburgh's Michaelmas election. He followed this order with another recommending the council to choose Bailie Thomas Kennedy as their new provost, and otherwise allowing the election to continue as normal.[30] Perhaps this two-stage procedure was adopted to give James time to take advice before naming a provost. Certainly, the two letters served to assert the royal prerogative with respect to council elections; they also set a precedent for James's approach in the years 1686–8. In 1686, James continued in office the existing provost and dean of guild, but in 1687 he chose only the provost and otherwise allowed the capital's magistrates and council to be elected as normal.[31] In 1685, James also imposed a provost on Aberdeen. In this case, he did so through a letter from the secretary of state, the viscount of Melfort, to the burgh council, issued sufficiently early not to require the suspension of the election. The letter reveals how James understood his prerogative: 'The King having in himselfe the power of naming the Magistrates of all his Burghs Royall so oft as may be for the good of his Service, does recommend to you ... to Elect & Nominate George Lesly Baily to be Provest'. Though couched as a recommendation, James asserted his right to choose burgh magistrates. Aberdeen council's swift obedience probably encouraged the king's blanket intervention in the royal burghs in 1686.[32]

* * *

Building on these experiments of 1685, King James developed his policy in the royal burghs with the explicit aim of avenging his parliamentary failure in 1686. Many were responsible for parliament's reluctance to repeal the penal laws, but contemporaries judged that the burgh commissioners were particularly obstructive to the king's will. The burghs were, in John Lauder of Fountainhall's memorable phrase, the 'brazen wall the Papists found hardest'.[33] This impression is borne out by a surviving record of the vote in the Articles on the proposed act in favour of Catholics, which indicates that, of the seven burgh commissioners present, six voted against the measure.[34] The court was evidently inclined to blame the burgh commissioners. Before parliament was adjourned, Melfort began to think that James should name magistrates and councillors for 'all touns' that year.[35] In early September, James instructed his other secretary of state, the earl of Moray, to write to the chancellor, the earl of Perth, announcing the new strategy for bringing the burghs to heel. '[T]he miscarriage of the Kings affaires' in parliament, Moray wrote, was 'in a great measure to be ascribed to the Com[missione]rs of the Royall Burroughs'. In response, James had 'resolved for the future to take such care as that [e]state may intirely depend upon himselfe'. At this stage, it was proposed that burghs whose commissioners had been willing to support the king's parliamentary agenda would continue to elect their councils, while the magistrates and councillors of other towns would be nominated by the king from lists supplied by the privy council. Moray envisaged that it might be necessary to suspend some burghs' Michaelmas elections.[36] It was clearly impossible for officers of state in Scotland to communicate suggestions of nominees to the king at such short notice, and on 12 September James wrote to the privy council ordering the suspension of elections in all royal burghs. The king justified this action with reference to 'some undutifull Acts done by their Com[missione]rs in some of their Meetings at Edinburgh', perhaps a reference to the convention of royal burghs' opposition to an extension of the excise proposed in the parliament of 1686.[37]

The privy council received the king's letter on 16 September, and dispatched missives to the burghs suspending their elections (see Figure 4.1).[38] Royal orders suspending elections – and privy council letters putting these into effect – were also issued in the September of 1687 and 1688.[39] In seventeen towns, the magistrates and councils elected at Michaelmas 1685 remained in office until 1689.[40] But from September 1686 to November 1688, James nominated some or all of the magistrates and councillors of forty-eight burghs. Starting with the most important towns, the crown made forty sets of nominations in the year 1686–7, sent down twenty-five further lists of nominees in 1687–8, and twelve more from July to November 1688. There were a few additional orders naming clerks for specific burghs. As we shall see, not quite all of the king's nominations were implemented. But there was general obedience to his will. Unsurprisingly, James took the opportunity to remove leading opponents of his policy in the parliament of 1686. Whether those he selected in their place would have been more compliant was never put to the test.

There is little information about how James selected suitable magistrates and councillors. But it is likely that members of the privy council provided advice about the choice of nominees, in line with Moray's proposal. Among Moray's surviving papers are two lists of towns, one annotated with the names of privy councillors and other officials who were presumably thought able to make suggestions.[41] In December 1687, when the council election in Glasgow took place in the normal manner, Archbishop John Paterson selected Walter Gibson as provost, apparently on the recommendation of Perth and George Drummond of Blair Drummond, keeper of the signet.[42] Drummond of Blair Drummond, a man of some influence during James's reign, may also have been responsible for the imposition of a new joint clerk on Aberdeen council two months later.[43] But there was not a Scottish body comparable to the regulators employed in England to investigate the circumstances of local communities and make recommendations for the purging and appointing of members of borough corporations.[44] Nor was the crown accurately advised about every burgh. At first, too few councillors and officers were nominated for Aberdeen and Linlithgow;[45] in February 1688, Dumfries's councillors took the liberty of admitting Martin Newall as a bailie, instead of the 'Walter Newall' specified by

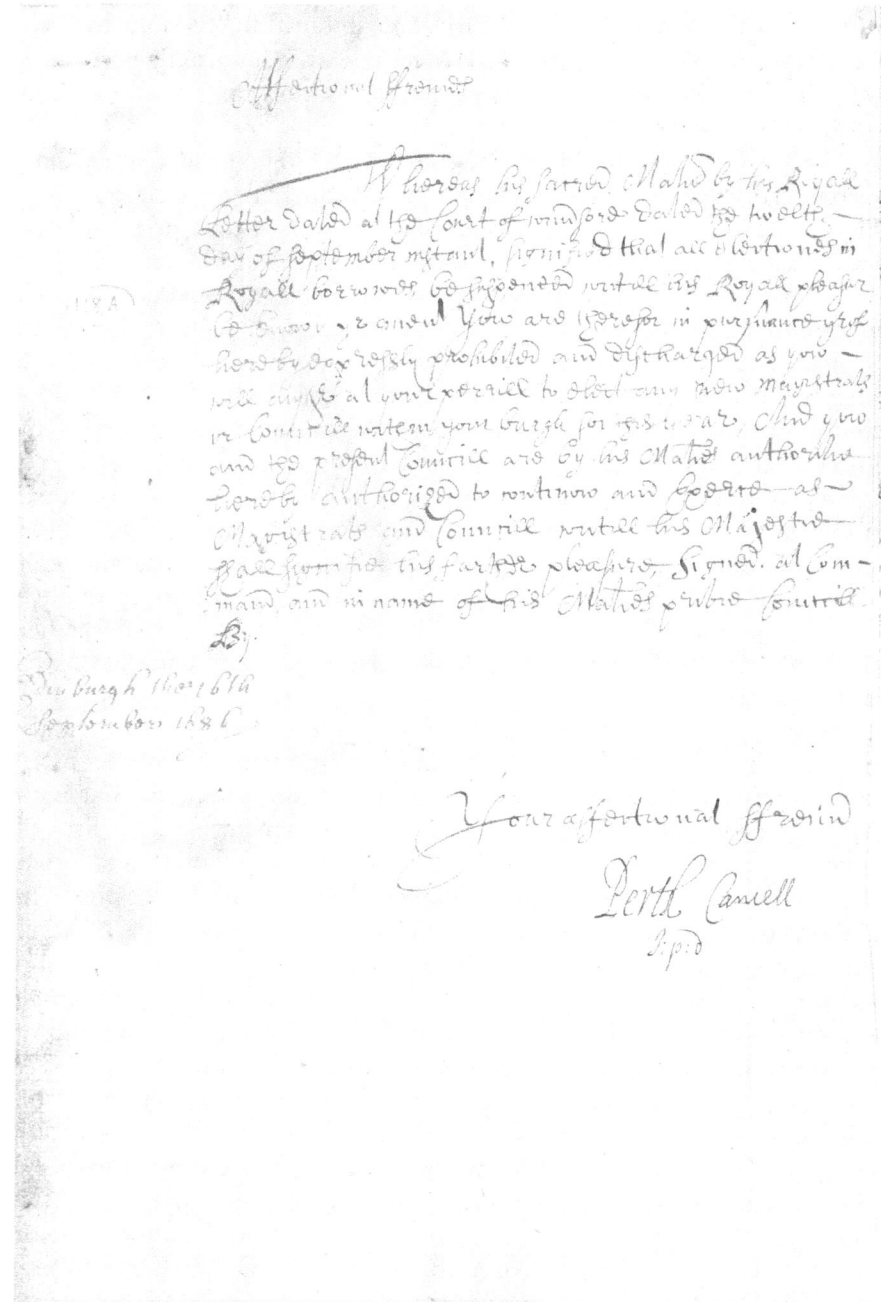

Figure 4.1 Earl of Perth to the magistrates and council of Kirkwall, 16 Sep. 1686, OLA, K1/1/3, fo. 118Ar. Reproduced by permission of Orkney Library and Archive.

the king, '[the]r[e] being none of [tha]t name in toune except walter newall who is appoynted deacon of the smiths'.⁴⁶ In spite of these small errors, the crown possessed enough information to issue a large number of nominations within months of first suspending the burghs' elections.

In some towns, there were particular individuals or groups among the residents who served as sources of intelligence and intermediaries between the court and the burgh council. In May 1689, the convention of estates heard evidence that David Auchterlonie of Montrose 'was the only persone that did procure a letter from the late King James ... nominateing and appoynting the magistrats and councill' of the burgh.⁴⁷ Even if the petition against Auchterlonie exaggerated his importance, he was part of a wider pattern. At the revolution, Patrick Hay and George Oliphant, imposed in 1686 as provost and eldest bailie of Perth, were singled out for criticism for 'their soliciting for and injoying [thei]r places as magistrats' by the king's nomination.⁴⁸ The career of one well-connected local figure gives an indication of how some of the crown's nominations may have been coordinated. David Eadie, a former bailie of Aberdeen, was close to the court, and had lobbied for the king's agenda in the parliament of 1686.⁴⁹ Though he was described as a protestant in October 1688, he converted to Catholicism in the following decade and was banished from Scotland for his apostasy.⁵⁰ When in November 1688 the privy council allowed Aberdeen to conduct an election as normal, it was rumoured that the results were determined by a list sent from Edinburgh, supplied by Eadie. He was present in the capital for a meeting of the convention of royal burghs, and perhaps procured the privy council's order for the election to take place.⁵¹ If there was not a figure like Eadie in every town, there was nevertheless some degree of local involvement in James's interventions in the royal burghs.

Some townsmen put themselves forward for nomination unsuccessfully. In January 1688, following the deaths of the two bailies of Dingwall, a resident of the town wrote to a contact in Edinburgh, expressing the hope that, if the privy council were to appoint replacement magistrates, his name would be suggested by George Mackenzie, Viscount Tarbat, the lord clerk register and a local nobleman. New bailies were nominated that summer, but our correspondent was not one of them.⁵² Paisley, though it was a burgh of regality and not covered by James's order to suspend elections, decided not to elect councillors and bailies at Michaelmas 1686. A group of three burgesses, pretending to have a commission from the town council, then went to Edinburgh and asked the privy council to nominate magistrates from a list they supplied. What was probably an attempt by the three to promote themselves to office was averted by the existing bailies and the privy council.[53] But the burgesses' strategy, if unusually duplicitous, was perhaps not dissimilar to that of powerbrokers in other towns.

There was little or no open suggestion that the king's actions were illegal. Indeed, sitting councillors were willing to override local regulations that stood in the way of obeying the king's orders. In Edinburgh, there was a minor obstacle arising from an act of the town council prohibiting magistrates from serving more than two consecutive years in office, and requiring them to uphold this restriction on oath. James's letters thus required some to break their oaths, and they entered protests explaining that they acted under royal commands.[54] In Linlithgow, the king's nomination of James Smith as bailie and Alexander Smith as dean of guild led the town council to suspend an act preventing a father and son from holding office concurrently.[55] Neither council tried to qualify its compliance with James's instructions.

In order to draw conclusions about the nature of royal power, we need to assess how efficiently the king's policy was implemented. As well as obedience by the burghs, James's approach depended on prompt action by the privy council and its clerks. In most cases, towns received the council's order to suspend their elections before they were due to take place. In 1686, however, the council's letter came late to a few towns. Elections were held before the letter arrived in Pittenweem, Fortrose and Kirkcudbright (where the first of two stages of voting had taken place).[56] Each town duly rescinded its election. On the other hand, there is no record of the suspension of elections in the fragmentary records of Wick. There George Sinclair, earl of Caithness served as hereditary provost, and seems to have chosen bailies as usual at Michaelmas 1686.[57] In Kirkwall on Orkney, two of the four bailies were replaced in the election on 29 September 1686. When the king's instructions came on 4 October, it apparently did not occur to the magistrates and councillors to cancel the election, and the provost instead wrote to Edinburgh justifying the 'verie Litle alteratione' to the magistracy that had been made.[58]

Though the suspension of elections was generally successful, James's nominations were implemented with less efficiency. As with the royal instructions not to hold elections, the king's nominations were conveyed by letters to the privy council, which then issued its own orders to the burghs concerned. Sometimes there was a delay of several months between the royal letter and the admission to office of the king's nominees. In the cases of Cupar and Dunbar, to take two of the longest delays, royal letters of nomination were issued on 16 and 31 December 1686 respectively. Details of the letter concerning Cupar were known there by 14 January, when the council, to 'tack off all suspition of contempt and disobedience to his Ma[jes]ties authority', resolved to invite the royal nominees to assume their offices. This decision was not acted on, and in spite of the burgh's willingness to comply, the privy council did not make its order to Cupar until 11 April, on which date it also produced instructions to Dunbar. It was as late as 13 June and 5 October 1687 that the appointees were installed, in Dunbar and then Cupar.[59]

Winter weather might have contributed to the slow implementation of some of James's orders, but there were also administrative reasons. In several instances, it appears that a royal nomination of burgh magistrates was not put into effect by the privy council – and possibly that the king's letter was not even opened – until a fee was paid by the burgh in question to the secretary of state. Typically the charge was £7.10s. sterling; some burghs sent their own officers to collect the privy council's orders.[60] Selkirk – not a place remarkable for its accurate record-keeping or the honesty of its officials – apparently paid £17.10s. sterling to 'the secretaries & o[the]rs the Clerks of Counsell & ther servants' for 'procuring of the Commissione from His Ma[jes]tie & his Counsell'. In spite of the expense, Selkirk's magistrates were installed within a month of the royal letter.[61] In December 1687, it seems that the Edinburgh law agent for Dumbarton town council paid the secretary's fees on the burgh's behalf, ensuring that the time between the royal nomination and the new magistrates' assumption of office in Dumbarton was under six weeks.[62] But while many of James's nominations were implemented quickly, the inability or reluctance of some towns to make what were substantial payments probably accounts for delays in the settling of their nominated councils. As we have seen, the Claim of Right specifically complained about the fee levied.

Partly because of this dilatory response to the king's orders, some nominations were not effected at all.[63] As might be expected, this was true of several of the lists sent to Scotland in the final months of the reign. The royal letters of 25 September 1688 naming the magistrates and councils of Arbroath, Wigtown and Renfrew were not implemented, though one of the same date concerning Stirling was.[64] We do not know if the last royal letter, dated 12 November 1688 and appointing the magistrates and councillors of Selkirk, was executed.[65] A few of the earlier letters were not acted on. James gave warrant to the specified magistrates and councillors to serve until the following Michaelmas, and the delays we noted above meant that some orders were out of date before they could be implemented. A royal order giving magistrates and councillors for Rutherglen, dated 20 April 1688, never took effect. In this case, it is possible that the local laird specified as provost was reluctant to serve.[66] Royal nominations to Wigtown, Kirkwall and Peebles of July and August 1687 were not realised; James issued identical orders to Wigtown and Peebles in the following January, and another nomination for Kirkwall in July 1688.[67] An order of 15 August 1687 to Rothesay had not been executed by the time of James's letter of 8 September suspending all council elections. In recognition of this, the September letter specifically required that the earlier nomination for Rothesay be implemented, which finally happened in December.[68] In February 1688, there was a new order concerning Wigtown, which would have restored the provost removed in January. But neither this, nor the previously mentioned fourth nomination of September 1688, came into force.[69] On the face of it, Wigtown was the Scottish burgh to receive most central interference under James VII. In reality, the Galloway town exposes one of the limitations of James's policy.

* * *

What difference did James's meddling make to the governing class of Scotland's royal burghs? To what extent did he give authority to men who had not previously held power in the towns? These questions have two dimensions. First, to test the Claim of Right's allegation, it is important to consider whether the king imposed on town councils Catholics and protestant dissenters who would formerly have been barred from office. Second, we can examine the relationship of the nominees to the burghs for which they were chosen: did James promote landowners and officials of the central government in place of resident merchants and craftsmen?

Starting with the religious persuasions of James's chosen men, we should note that only in the period before the king's suspension of the Test oath in the first indulgence of February 1687 is it easy to recognise Catholics and presbyterian dissenters among the nominees. Since 1681, burgh magistrates and councillors had been required to swear the Test. Thirty-three lists of nominations were sent to Scotland during the period of the oath's enforcement. From these, it has been possible to identify only one nominee who did not swear because he was a presbyterian: Thomas Main, named a councillor in Linlithgow in 1686. He at first refused to serve because he would not swear, and though he was fined £100 and imprisoned, he began to attend meetings only after the Test was abrogated. We know that he was a protestant because he was elected as a bailie in April 1689, when Catholics were excluded from the election.[70]

In its first phase at least, royal policy differed from that in England, which came to depend on ejecting members of the established Church in favour of protestant dissenters. The context changed after James's second indulgence and the resulting presbyterian revival. In the period of multi-confessional choice, there was little to stop holders of burgh office from attending presbyterian services, at least in places where presbyterian ministers were active. But as we saw in Chapter 2, the Ayrshire burgh of Irvine was the only town where we know that the council gave corporate support to a new presbyterian congregation. Some former magistrates of towns including Dumfries and Ayr raised financial support for presbyterian ministers.[71] As far as we can tell, however, most councillors and magistrates continued to attend the established Church's services. James does not seem deliberately to have appointed presbyterian sympathisers to local office.

Did the king impose numerous Catholics, as the Claim of Right later asserted? Among the thirty-three sets of men appointed while the Test was in force, we can easily recognise the Catholics, because James explicitly dispensed them from swearing. In fact, there were only two Catholics named before February 1687: John Maxwell of Barncleuch, provost of Dumfries, and William Broun of Nuntoun, provost of Kirkcudbright.[72] Among later nominees, a few other Catholics can be identified. Sir William Wallace of Craigie, a Catholic landowner and soldier, was appointed provost of Ayr in November 1687.[73] Gavin Dunbar was in the same month named one of the bailies of Kirkcudbright, where he was commissary clerk. In December 1688, 'In respect of the present circumstances of affairs', custody of the town's charter chest was transferred from him to another bailie, suggesting that Dunbar was one of the Catholic office-holders complained about in a letter received from the privy council a few days later.[74] Sir Godfrey McCulloch of Myrton, a Catholic convert mentioned in Chapter 3, seems to have been named to the council of Wigtown in September 1688, though this nomination was not put into effect.[75]

If there were few Catholics among James's nominees, some protestant magistrates may have been selected because they were judged likely to convert. In January 1688, a priest claimed that the nominated provost of Arbroath, John Kidd, 'wants nothing of a catholike but reception'.[76] After the collapse of James's regime, a few more of his nominees were accused of popery. James Stewart, dean of guild in Perth, had allegedly attended mass in London sixteen years before the revolution, and had more recently joined Catholic worship at Stobhall, one of the earl of Perth's houses, and at Holyrood Abbey.[77] When Perth's burgesses met to elect a commissioner to the convention of estates, Stewart, the former provost Patrick Hay and the erstwhile bailie George Oliphant were also accused of going to Catholic services.[78] In January 1689, a petition from some of the residents of Culross complained that James Mackie and Daniel MacDonald, nominated merchant bailies, 'are truelie and actuallie papists and have been severall tymes at Mass in the Abbay'.[79] It is difficult to tell whether these were convenient allegations to hurl at rivals in 1689, or whether the magistrates had become active supporters of Catholicism.

Even the long-standing Catholics were not, their religion aside, unusual holders of local office. Maxwell of Barncleuch, Broun of Nuntoun and Wallace of Craigie all owned land close to the towns of which they were placed in charge.[80] Barncleuch was a former town clerk of Dumfries and son-in-law of John Irving, a late provost. That provost's son, also John Irving, was named as a bailie, as was another John Irving, perhaps also related to Barncleuch. In Dumfries, then, the king's nomination brought into the magistracy an extra member of a family already prominent in the town.[81] Barncleuch's Catholicism ensured that he lost office at the revolution, but otherwise his nomination brought only two significant changes in the administration of Dumfries, both reversed after the revolution. The first was a 400 per cent increase in the provost's salary, to which was added a wine allowance, 'It being customary in o[the]r burrowes of note to lay in provisione of wynes yearly to [thei]r proveist out of [thei]r Comon good'.[82] The other innovation was the removal of a religious test from the oath sworn by new burgesses, justified as being in accordance with the royal indulgence. Though we might expect a Catholic provost to have promoted this reform, the protestant magistrates of Aberdeen made a similar change in March 1686.[83] As in Dumfries, so in Ayr, the imposition of a Catholic provost made few obvious differences. Sir William Wallace's Catholicism had hitherto excluded him from the magistracy, but he was prominent locally as hereditary provost of Newton-on-Ayr, a neighbouring burgh of barony. He had frequently borrowed money from Ayr merchants.[84] He seems to have left day-to-day government to the bailies. Wallace's relationship to the town was that of a landed patron, not an unusual role in early modern Scotland.

This brings us to the second theme: were gentlemen and servants of the central government imposed on the royal burghs? In a few cases, James nominated men who did not have civic privileges, and were thus obvious outsiders who would not normally have been considered eligible for office. These individuals were promptly made burgesses and guild brethren, allowing them to take up their positions.[85] More generally, a large number – up to 45 per cent – of the royal orders named at least one gentleman or nobleman whose interests were not primarily related to trade.[86] Lauder of Fountainhall noted that such nominations contravened a law of 1609 limiting urban office-holding to merchants living in the towns.[87] Though others presumably recalled this statute, it was quite widely disregarded by towns themselves before 1686. Prior to James's intervention in urban government, James Douglas, earl of Drumlanrig, a soldier aged in his twenties, was provost of Dumfries, while nearby Annan had chosen the still younger William Johnstone, second earl of Annandale as its provost.[88] At the same time, the earl of Balcarres was provost of Cupar.[89] The long-standing tradition of noble and gentry provosts was not extinct in the Restoration period, though James gave the phenomenon new encouragement.[90] There was a more serious obstacle in the path of the king's landed nominees: an act of the convention of royal burghs, passed in 1675, which required commissioners to parliament and meetings of the convention to be resident merchants. In July 1687, the convention suspended this act, also dropping the customary qualification that commissioners should be protestant.[91]

It is hard to generalise about the impact made by James's landed provosts. On becoming provost of Selkirk, the local laird John Riddell of Hayning seems to have pressed for greater administrative efficiency – or at least regular minutes of meetings – in the town. But the fact that in the late 1660s and early 1670s he had been at dispute with the burgh council may have limited the effectiveness of his civic career.[92] After Sir William Paterson, clerk to the privy council, became provost of Haddington, its council passed an act allowing the bailies 'to call counsells in absence of the provost'. Sure enough, Paterson attended meetings very infrequently, though he represented Haddington in the convention of royal burghs. Council business continued as usual.[93] Sir Adam Blair of Carberry seems to have been absent from all council meetings during his tenure as provost of Dunbar. Nevertheless, he sat for the town in the convention of royal burghs and involved himself in Dunbar's negotiations with the earl of Tweeddale about the watercourse serving its mills.[94]

If the merchants of Haddington and Dunbar had little to complain about following the introduction of these genteel figureheads, some residents of Elgin claimed that the king's nomination of two gentlemen to the magistracy brought a tangible change for the worse in the town's government. In April 1687, in accordance with a royal letter of the previous December, Sir Alexander Innes of Coxton became provost. Joined with him as bailies were three former councillors, who were therefore conventional holders of office, and another new man, Mr Alexander Grant, probably the sheriff clerk of that name with whom the burgh had recently been in dispute.[95] Though there are few signs that the conduct of the council changed, the collapse of James's authority exposed discontent among part of the population. In December 1688, a merchant claiming to represent 'manie of the nighbouris' petitioned the privy council against the nominated magistrates and council. The petition described them as 'for the most pairt straingers to and wnconcernid with the affaires of the brughe', which had suffered 'great prejudice' and 'decay' under their leadership.[96] The following year, Elgin reported to the convention of royal burghs that the nominated magistrates, because they were 'Countrey Gentlemen', had neglected the town's concerns. Responding to the burgh's economic difficulties, the convention had in July 1687 ordered a visitation of Elgin by representatives of other local towns. Yet the opponents of the king's magistrates alleged that they attempted to prevent any action arising from the visitors' report. These petitions probably exaggerated the adverse impact that two landed magistrates had on Elgin's fortunes. But the argument that gentlemen 'hade nothing to lose or Gaine by the standing or falling' of a royal burgh – a mercantile and artisanal community – was a powerful case against James's interference.[97]

Whatever the influence of the Elgin gentlemen, the traditional burgh elite was not marginalised. A similar point can be made about Kirkcaldy, where the provost's and bailies' offices were given to landowners. The nominated provost of Kirkcaldy was the earl of Balcarres, regional magnate and sheriff of Fife. The bailies were two Fife lairds, James Crawford of Mountquhannie and James Lundie of Strathairlie. Though resident magistrates had been displaced by a nobleman and lairds, the royal instructions allowed Balcarres, Crawford and Lundie to select the council, and they chose one of the previous bailies as dean of guild and the other bailie and former provost as councillors. Even in a town where superficially it appears that outsiders were put into power, significant residents remained in positions of influence. The fact that in April 1689 Crawford and Lundie were chosen provost and bailie by the burgesses suggests that their administration as royal nominees had been generally acceptable.[98]

The magistrates of Kirkcaldy illustrate another aspect of James's policy: the infiltration of servants of the central government into the royal burghs. As well as being a local landowner, Balcarres was at the heart of the king's administration in Scotland, serving as a treasury commissioner, privy councillor and a member of the council's secret committee. His *Memoirs touching the Revolution* (1690) demonstrate his loyalty to the king.[99] In total, at least fifteen current or recent officials of the royal administration and military establishment were nominated to office in thirteen burghs. Aside from Balcarres, the privy councillors imposed on towns were George Livingstone, third earl of Linlithgow, who became provost of Queensferry, his son George, Lord Livingstone, who presided over Linlithgow, and John Graham of Claverhouse, named provost of Dundee in February 1688. Each man also served in the army, and Linlithgow was justice-general.[100] Wallace of Craigie was a captain in the regiment of horse and was added to the privy council in September 1688.[101] Charles Maitland, named bailie of North Berwick in November 1686, was governor of the garrison on the Bass Rock.[102] As we saw above, the clerk of the council, Sir William Paterson, became provost of Haddington.

Six or seven of the nominees had served as collectors of the inland excise while it was under direct collection in 1686.[103] Crawford and Lundie, the bailies of Kirkcaldy, were collectors and then, from November 1686, farmers of the excise in the counties of Fife, Kinross and Forfar.[104] Sir Patrick Threipland of Fingask, who was appointed provost of Perth in September 1687, Alexander Grant, bailie of Elgin, and William Williamson, town clerk of Peebles, also made the transition from collector to farmer.[105] William Duff, named a bailie of Inverness in August 1688, had previously been a collector; Broun of Nuntoun perhaps also served in this role.[106] Though he may not have continued to hold office under James, Blair of Carberry was formerly part of the central government as a receiver of taxes. He was still owed over £21,000 by the crown in May 1686.[107] Sir William Sharp of Scotscraig, master of the mint and James's choice as provost of St Andrews, had become financially dependent on the crown for the same reason. Scotscraig was the son of the assassinated archbishop of St Andrews, and nephew of Sir William Sharp of Stoneyhill, Charles II's cashkeeper, who had borrowed on his own credit to finance the crown's suppression of presbyterian nonconformity. In May 1686, Scotscraig petitioned the privy council, expressing his reluctance to enter heir to his uncle, who had died in debt.[108] That autumn, shortly before he was nominated as provost, Scotscraig received a gift from the tack duty and rents of crown lands in Orkney, to repay his uncle's debts.[109] If not all of the crown servants promoted to office in the burghs were as beholden to James as Scotscraig, his case suggests how the king's policy compromised the independence of at least some towns.

There is plentiful evidence, then, of the crown's deployment of landowners in urban government, and of the promotion of figures more aligned to the interests of the court than to those of the burghs. But while these developments might have influenced the leadership of the burgess estate in a future meeting of parliament, the changes affected only a minority of the royal burghs. As we noted above, perhaps 45 per cent of royal nominations included gentlemen who could be judged outsiders to the towns they were to govern. Excluding two orders that were not implemented, these nominations related to at most twenty-five towns. Of the remaining forty parliamentary burghs, seventeen received no royal orders to admit magistrates or councillors. There were thus at least twenty-three towns to which James nominated magistrates, and in many cases councillors as well, without presenting any men who were obviously not merchants, craftsmen or otherwise ordinarily resident burgesses. It should be stressed that these counts of towns with and without gentry magistrates and councillors are approximate. Nevertheless, they suggest that James did not attempt systematically to supplant resident urban governors.

In many of Scotland's towns, the chief difference between the magistrates and councils in office before and after Michaelmas 1686 was simply that the former held power by virtue of election, the latter by royal command. Most of the men running the royal burghs remained in place. In the burghs that received no nomination from the crown, all those elected in 1685 stayed in post, barring a few deaths and extraordinary changes allowed by the privy council.[110] Twenty-one of James's orders appointed magistrates only, leaving it to them to choose councillors. Very often, they picked individuals who had served before. Even in cases where the crown named the full council, many nominees had formerly been councillors. The council of twenty specified for Dunbar in December 1686 included only five who had not served in 1684–6.[111] When a nomination of Montrose's council took effect in 1687, three of the four magistrates had not held their offices in the previous year. But only five or six of the former councillors were replaced.[112] In Lanark, on the other hand, eleven of the nineteen named in 1686 had not been elected in 1684 or 1685, though the provost (Cromwell Lockhart) and one of the two bailies remained unaltered.[113] If the changes made by James's nominations were rarely negligible, they were scarcely sweeping either. In the less well-documented burghs, shifts in the composition of the councils may have made more difference than we can detect.

But overall it seems that James did not attempt – and probably would not have been able – to dislodge the oligarchies that controlled urban affairs.

* * *

The king's interference made little practical difference in many of the small and middle-ranking burghs. This helps to explain why opposition to James's policy was largely invisible until December 1688. But while no one questioned the legality of the reconfigured relationship between central and local government, it nevertheless fostered discontent, especially in the bigger, more socially complex towns. By the 1680s, we might argue, some larger burghs exhibited 'partisan politics' on the model proposed for England by Paul Halliday: a type of factious behaviour, in which rival groups tried to dish their opponents by persuading central authorities to purge town councils.[114] In burghs where James's intervention gave one pre-existing faction victory over its opponents, it is particularly likely that there was local cooperation with the crown's nominations. And there was a further reason for urban unrest in James's reign. Developing a policy begun under Oliver Cromwell and Charles II, the crown granted warrants allowing a number of towns to levy local excise taxes, on beer and other alcoholic drinks, to raise extra revenue. Though these imposts should have put the burghs concerned in a stronger position, they tended to alienate townsfolk, who were typically reluctant to pay, from the magistrates and councillors set over them by the king. While negotiating for the royal warrants, moreover, town councils became dependent on a number of shadowy middlemen and servants of the central government.

Whether deliberately or otherwise, James promoted to office several men who were deeply unpopular in their communities. This was especially evident in Ayr, where local politics was characterised by a factionalism of bewildering complexity. William Cunningham, the provost who refused to hold elections in 1681, had thereafter endeavoured to regain power. On two occasions, serving magistrates complained to the privy council that Cunningham was using underhand means to influence elections. In February 1686, however, Cunningham finally achieved victory over his rival Robert Hunter, whose removal from office by the privy council allowed Cunningham to return as provost.[115] He was continued provost by the king's first nomination, and though in December 1687 he made way for the Catholic Wallace of Craigie, Cunningham's allies retained other positions.[116] In December 1688, when the fall of the regime was under way, the town council dispatched its treasurer to Edinburgh, instructing him to inform the privy council of the 'great oppression and designed Arbitrary Government of William Cun[n]ygham'.[117] In Ayr, it seems, the most unpopular consequence of James VII's policy was not the introduction of a Catholic into office, but the revived influence of a loathed protestant.

Factional struggles also determined the impact of the king's policy in Stirling. Here there was a long-standing confrontation between a group centred on Robert Russell, who had monopolised power for much of the Restoration period, and rivals who accused him of corruption. In 1679 and 1680, the council introduced term limits, in an attempt to stop men from holding office for long periods. In 1683, councillors adopted measures designed to ensure that the town's properties were rented at competitive rates. In spite of these reforms, arguments about the management of the common good continued, and probably lay behind the council's decision to strip Hugh Kennedy of Shalloch, a former provost, of his privileges as burgess and guild brother.[118] In September 1686, however, Kennedy was nominated as provost.[119] One of his first actions in office was to overturn the act that had removed his rights, which was attributed to the 'malicious and unwarrantable proceedings' of Russell and his 'relationes'. The new council also resolved to refund John Dick, the promoter of reforms in 1680, a fine of £100 unfairly imposed by the former magistrates in their 'splen and malice'.[120]

In several other towns, the king's nominations gave one faction a temporary victory over another. Linlithgow's nominated provost, Lord Livingstone, took the place of Alexander Milne, a man prominently associated with opposition to the king in the parliament of 1686.[121] Livingstone had been provost in 1684, when he faced criticism from a party including Milne and the town clerk William Bell. At that stage, Milne was prosecuted before the privy council. In May 1687, the nominated magistrates engineered the removal of Bell from the office of clerk, alleging that, in 1684, he had petitioned the convention of royal burghs complaining of the 'arbitrarie Goverment of my Lord Livingstoun'.[122] In Glasgow, Archbishop's Cairncross's choice as provost, John Johnston, had already lost out to his rivals before the king nominated the town's magistrates. In June 1686, soon after the end of the parliamentary session, the privy council deposed Johnston from office and in his place installed John Barnes, one of his predecessors. Johnston was accused of having said that Archbishop Ross of St Andrews, formerly archbishop of Glasgow, had accepted a bribe from John Bell, another past provost. But Johnston's fall was perhaps made more likely by his decision to vote in the Articles against the act in favour of Catholics.[123] In October 1686, the king confirmed Barnes as provost.[124] This was only the latest skirmish in a continuing struggle for control of a burgh that was, partly because it had a resident feudal superior in the person of the archbishop, at least as corrupt as any in Scotland.[125]

Perhaps the most provocative of James's nominations was that of John Graham of Claverhouse, commanding officer of the regiment of horse and later viscount of Dundee. His lands of Claverhouse were a few miles from Dundee, and in 1683 he was granted the nearby estate of Dudhope, once the possession of his relatives the Scrymgeour family.[126] With Dudhope came the office of constable of the former royal castle of Dundee, for long a bone of contention in the burgh because of the rights of jurisdiction claimed by successive constables.[127] In March 1686, before his systematic interference in the royal burghs, King James ordered Dundee's council to recognise Claverhouse as first magistrate, with precedence over the provost.[128] Though the council had protested against Claverhouse's claim to judge violent crimes in the town, legal advice sought in Edinburgh confirmed that the constable had jurisdiction in capital and many lesser crimes, as well as a sole right to decide civil cases on the eight days surrounding the annual fair in August.[129] In Dundee, therefore, the crown's nomination of magistrates served two purposes: to humble a provost who had voted in the Articles against relieving Catholics of the penal laws,[130] and to make compliant a council that had resisted the authority of one of the king's staunch allies. After first appointing Alexander Rait as provost, in February 1688 the king chose Claverhouse himself to lead the town, naming among the bailies two Grahams who may have been related to the new provost.[131]

The overstretched finances of the royal burghs, and their search for new revenues, often contributed to civic tension under James. A particularly significant source of grievance, which found expression in the Claim of Right, was the collection of local excises, chiefly on beer and other alcoholic drinks.[132] Some burgh councils attempted to make voluntary agreements with local brewers, under which the latter would pay a specified sum for every boll of malt used, or a smaller levy on each pint of beer or ale sold. But brewers were rarely happy to see their costs increase, and in most cases town councils sought the king's permission to impose a compulsory local excise. This tax was charged on top of the countrywide excise on beers and spirits, first introduced under the Covenanters in 1644 and a major part of the crown's income in the Restoration period.[133] In the towns that levied a local excise on beer and other beverages, therefore, brewers and drinkers were required to shoulder an additional burden, intended chiefly to pay off debts contracted by the burgh council.

There was of course nothing new in the crown's granting fiscal privileges to burghs. The excise on malt and brewing was in most respects similar to the customs and tolls traditionally collected in towns by virtue of their charters. Nevertheless, this new form of local tax was especially lucrative. In 1690, Edinburgh's duty on ale and beer was by far the largest source of municipal revenue, accounting for almost 38 per cent of annual income. The local levy on wine, which in some towns was granted with the excise on beer, contributed a further 18 per cent of Edinburgh's funds.[134] Indeed, Edinburgh was one of the first towns to collect its own excise taxes, receiving parliamentary approval for an imposition on wine, spirits and tobacco in 1649, and warrant for levying beer duty from Lord Protector Oliver Cromwell in 1654.[135] There followed new gifts of impositions on beer and wine in 1660, 1662, 1671 and 1680.[136] In the Restoration period, it was common for the crown to make this sort of gift on its own authority, though at least in the 1660s and early 1670s parliament was sometimes involved in granting or ratifying local excises.[137]

In keeping with his view of the royal prerogative, James issued gifts warranting local excises without reference to parliament. Indeed, the frequency of grants increased, and ten burghs received the right to levy duties, or had it renewed, during the king's reign.[138] One reason for the proliferation of these taxes may have been that towns were encouraged to negotiate for a royal gift by various officials of the central government, who in turn hoped to profit from the transaction. When Edinburgh secured its renewal of the impost on beer in 1671, the council arranged to pay 60,000 merks (£3,333.6s.8d. sterling) to the secretary of state, John Maitland, earl of Lauderdale. In 1680, the burgh offered Lauderdale £6,000 sterling for his role in procuring that year's gift.[139] In 1687, Glasgow's council paid £1,000 sterling to Melfort, secretary of state, and other 'procureris' of a royal gift of an imposition on beer, wine and spirits.[140]

Smaller burghs would not have been able to afford these large sums, but they were required to make payments nonetheless. When in February 1688 one of Burntisland's bailies took advice in Edinburgh about clearing his town's debts, he was advised that receiving a gift from the king to impose a local excise would be the best solution, but that it would 'be very chargeable to this toune to procure the same'. The burgh seems to have offered £50 sterling each to Drummond of Blair Drummond, keeper of the signet, and James Hay, a writer to the signet.[141] Montrose agreed to give Blair Drummond £4,722.6s. (£393.10s.6d. sterling) for arranging its gift, received in March 1688.[142] To receive a royal grant for excise on beer and wine, Dundee paid 5,000 merks (£3,333.6s.8d. Scots) to Blair Drummond, 500 merks to Hay, a further £873.6s.8d. to officials in the chancellery, as well as a small sum to a clerk who wrote grateful letters to the king and Melfort.[143]

The evidence suggests that the two keepers of the signet, especially Blair Drummond but also his colleague Sir Hugh Paterson of Bannockburn, were the key intermediaries for towns trying to obtain a royal gift. As we have seen, Blair Drummond regularly collaborated with the writer James Hay; the two men took part in discussions leading to a renewed grant of Edinburgh's beer duty in 1688.[144] Blair Drummond and Bannockburn were close administrative colleagues and clients of the joint secretaries of state, Melfort and Moray, and we can presume that the latter used their proximity to the king to secure his agreement.[145] That the process of receiving a gift depended on informal lobbying conducted by avaricious middlemen explains why such large, if varied, sums of money changed hands. A possible exception to this pattern was the negotiation of Elgin's excise, which was meant to fund the development of a harbour at Lossiemouth. Elgin's council commissioned the German engineer Peter Bruce, later the king's Catholic printer, to design the harbour and procure the right to levy a local tax. Bruce approached the privy council, which wrote to the secretaries of state on Elgin's behalf. Bruce was paid 20 rix dollars (worth about £60 Scots or £5 sterling) for his design; it is unclear whether there was a further fee for his advocacy.[146] But if Elgin's magistrates secured their royal gift on the cheap, other councils contracted new debts in pursuit of the right to collect an excise. The nominated magistrates and council of Irvine borrowed 5,000 merks from merchants in Glasgow and Dublin for the purpose of arranging the town's gift of an impost on beer and wine.[147] While the strongest objections to local imposts were expressed after the collapse of James's regime, before 1688 there was nevertheless discontent at the way these taxes were negotiated and the fiscal burden they created.

Unsurprisingly, the main indicator that local excises were unpopular was the reluctance of residents to pay. Recognising that a new levy on malt and wines for which warrant had been granted might be disliked, Ayr town council convened a mass meeting of the 'community' and offered to forgo the tax if the inhabitants would collectively defray Ayr's debts. No agreement was reached and the excise was put into effect. Soon after contracting to uplift the excise for the council, the tacksmen sought royal letters charging the millers of malt, on whom the levy was imposed, to cooperate with its collection.[148] This suggests that a new excise was, at the very least, difficult to implement. In 1700, Elgin's councillors claimed that there had never been an attempt to collect the malt duty allowed in 1686, perhaps because of local opposition.[149] As we shall see in Chapter 6, the upheaval of the revolution made it still more challenging to exact local taxes granted by James. Though it was not until the Claim of Right in 1689 that critics of local excises argued that they were illegally levied, the introduction of so many such taxes under James VII contributed to dissatisfaction with his interference in the royal burghs.

* * *

We can conclude by distinguishing three ways in which King James's approach to the royal burghs might be evaluated. The first is in terms of legality. By suspending their annual elections and requiring the admission of his own choice of magistrates and councillors, the king invaded the burghs' established privileges. Before the end of 1688, however, no one refused to implement the king's orders. Nor did anyone openly criticise the policy by arguing that it was illegal. There was widespread acceptance that James acted within his royal prerogative. The second way of assessing the crown's interventions is to ask how efficiently they were implemented. Did the central government in James's Scotland have the administrative capacity to replace local elections with direct appointments to the councils of sixty-five burghs? In this respect, there were clearly practical limits to the king's absolute authority. If the Michaelmas elections were mostly suspended without difficulty, there were long delays in the execution of some of the king's nominations, and at least ten of the seventy-seven were not put into effect.

The limits on royal power are still more evident when we consider a third criterion for judging James's policy: the difference it made in the towns themselves. There was some change to the governing class of urban Scotland, in the promotion to office of four Catholics, significant numbers of landowners and fifteen or more men dependent on the central government. But in most towns, existing oligarchies were scarcely challenged. This was perhaps because James and his advisers considered it sufficient to ensure that magistrates and councils owed their authority to the king. If in these circumstances the traditional urban governors would support the court in parliament, the objective of royal policy would have been met. In fact, it is likely that James had little choice but to retain so many magistrates and councillors whose commissioners had opposed

Catholic relief in 1686. The king probably had too little information about many towns, and there were often few credible alternatives to the existing councillors. Nevertheless, the crown's interventions in burghs prompted unease, though not yet outspoken criticism. If the economy seemed to suffer in Elgin and elsewhere, and factional strife was exacerbated in several large towns, and if the introduction of unpopular taxes seemed to be the fault of the king's magistrates – or of James himself – then the sudden reaction against the royal policy in the Claim of Right is easier to explain. As we shall see in the next chapter, the royal burghs started to turn against their enforced supervision by the king as soon as his government began to collapse.

5

The Revolution in the Localities

THE REVOLUTION IN SCOTLAND was neither glorious nor bloodless, though probably no more than twelve deaths can be attributed to disturbances in the interval from early December 1688 to mid-March 1689.[1] This chapter reconstructs the events of that period. It argues that James VII's downfall triggered major disruption in localities across Scotland. Indeed, the transformation of political realities that we call the 'revolution of 1688–9' in Scotland was, more than in England, a patchwork of local crises and contests for particular offices and positions of influence. It is important to underline the differences between the course of events in each kingdom. In swift succession, England experienced an invasion, a resignation of authority by the king and the assumption of political control by William of Orange. William had gained London by 18 December 1688; on Christmas Day, an assembly of peers at Westminster invited him to take over the kingdom's civil and military administration, pending the meeting of a convention on 22 January.[2] In Scotland, the pace of change was slower. Though the earl of Perth's position crumbled rapidly in early December, the power of the central government ebbed away gradually over the remainder of the month. There followed more than two months of uncertainty and disorder, even though William assumed responsibility for the country's administration on 10 January. In early February, William ordered elections to the planned convention of estates, and issued a declaration to keep the peace. But thereafter he seems to have been reluctant to intervene in Scotland, perhaps fearing that he would lose support if he did so.[3] The political vacuum began to be filled only after the meeting of the convention of estates in March 1689.

Beginning in November 1688, many individuals and Scottish communities enthusiastically seized the opportunity to reject James's personnel and policies and to express support for William. But in contrast to England, where William's progress was assisted by an organised body of landed conspirators and defectors, the revolution in Scotland lacked clear leadership. As we argued in the Introduction, Scotland did not exhibit the classic 'revolutionary situation' described by Charles Tilly, in which rival groups of the political elite struggle for control. The chief reason why the Scotland of 1688–9 is difficult to understand in these terms is that events unfolded in reaction to developments elsewhere, especially England. From the start of the crisis, Scottish nobles and gentlemen took their decisions in light of the shifting balance of power in the southern kingdom. Meanwhile, Scots who participated in revolutionary actions in local communities were not coordinated by any coherent Williamite party, and nor were they following scripts dictated from Edinburgh. The revolutionaries in the Scottish localities had an eye to events in England and elsewhere in Scotland, but most of the upheavals of 1688–9 have to be understood in the context of local tensions and rivalries. We should not conclude that Scots were generally reluctant to act, nor that events in Scotland were a sideshow to the real revolution happening in England.[4] Rather, we should recognise that it was the cumulative effect of numerous local protests and shifts of power that gave the revolution in Scotland its character.

We begin by describing the government's preparations to defend Scotland from Dutch invasion. The chapter then distinguishes four types of revolutionary activity taking place over the winter of 1688–9. The first saw violent crowds reject James's multiconfessional experiment, attacking Catholic chapels and the houses in which priests had been harboured, before turning on the episcopalian clergy of the south and west. Though they repudiated a central aspect of James's rule, members of the crowds did not necessarily favour making William king. In the second form of action, moreover, residents of royal burghs complained about their nominated magistrates and demanded fresh elections, again without declaring for the prince of Orange. It was only in a third type of revolutionary participation that Scots explicitly expressed support for William, by publicly reading his *Declaration of Reasons* for the invasion, and sending addresses to the prince. The fourth activity, the election of commissioners to the convention of estates, took place in late February and early March. Participants in the elections recognised William's interim authority in Scotland – he had ordered the elections – but it does not seem that the succession was the overriding concern for voters. Some of the most divisive contests pitted loyal servants of James against critics of his regime. But the electoral battles were also driven by local rivalries, and a significant number of commissioners were returned unanimously or at least with overwhelming support. Though the outcome of Scotland's crisis remained unclear on the eve of the convention, we shall see in Chapter 6 that the estates moved quickly to resolve the uncertainty.

* * *

The collapse of James's Scottish government can be attributed in part to failings in its response to the Dutch invasion in the autumn of 1688. News that a hostile expedition from the Netherlands was planned had probably reached Scottish ministers by 4 September. On that day, the privy council ordered sheriffs to assemble their counties' heritors (landowners), wadsetters (mortgagees) and life-renters, and to return lists to Edinburgh. From these county meetings, the council received encouraging reports of the armed preparedness of the country's leading men.[5] This was the prelude to a proclamation of 18 September, appointing a rendezvous of the militia in nine eastern shires from Forfar to Berwick, also including the town of Edinburgh. There were conflicting rumours about where the Dutch hoped to land, and some claimed that the east of Scotland was the target.[6] James had received more certain information about the intended invasion by 24 September; he seems to have assumed that the Dutch would aim for England. Thus on 24th he wrote to the Scottish privy council, calling for the army to be assembled on the border with England.[7] According to the earl of Balcarres, the council's secret committee advised that a force made up of militiamen, mounted gentry and highlanders could be sent to defend northern England, allowing the Scottish army to maintain order at home. This suggestion came to nothing, and on 27 September, in a letter confirming his expectation that the Dutch would invade England, James ordered the entire Scottish army (apart from the troops in garrisons) to march south over the border.[8]

Having received the king's letter, the council began issuing directions to raise militiamen across Scotland.[9] The act of parliament of 1663 regulating the militia defined it as a force of 20,000 foot and 2,000 horse. At first the council hoped to ready a third of these numbers with twenty-eight days' maintenance; later in October, councillors decided that a quarter with provision for forty days would be 'sufficient ... in the present circumstances'.[10] Remembering the contribution of irregular highland forces against the earl of Argyll, the council also ordered levies of clansmen to assemble at Stirling.[11]

Some of the men chosen for the militia refused to serve. Though the council instructed that bodies of local heritors should take the place of the militia in the south-west, there were specific reports that the forces in Nithsdale and Renfrewshire were unreliable.[12] By mid-November, the militia, highlanders and the company of regular troops remaining at Holyroodhouse together numbered 5,573, excluding officers. This was a large force, but the militiamen were less experienced than the standing army, their discipline was inferior and their leadership ineffectual. In Balcarres's view, the newly raised men 'signified little to keep up the face of authority', and the militia's perceived weakness gave encouragement to supporters of William.[13]

There was no military organisation on the Williamite side, however, and the militia was not required to engage in an armed confrontation. When it was clear that there would be no battle between James and William in England either, the prince's sympathisers on the privy council argued for the disbanding of the Scottish militia. The council stood the militia down on 7 December, though four companies of 120 infantry and some horsemen were retained.[14] Hearing on 22 December that Irish Catholics were invading the south-west, the marquis of Atholl wrote, in terms strangely distancing himself from the decision, that 'I beleeue designedly they in the governm[en]t disbanded all the millitia' so that there would be 'nothing to opose' the Irish with.[15] He summoned the privy council, which ordered new rendezvous of the heritors, to take place in January.[16] In Edinburgh, the lords of session organised an armed guard, which helped to keep order and to prevent violence against episcopalian clergy, before being disbanded in February.[17] But elsewhere in southern Scotland, we shall see, little was done to restrain the epidemic of crowd violence.

The winter's most significant outbreaks of violence started in mid-December, when there was no militia to deter riots. But already in late November, Scots had begun to stage crowd protests against the royal policy of multiconfessionalism. A wave of disturbances began with anti-Catholic demonstrations, which intimidated priests and their congregations, putting a stop to Catholic proselytising in much of the country. By late December, after some attacks on Quakers in Lanarkshire, episcopalian ministers were bearing the brunt of the violent reaction against the multiconfessional experiment. Through the forced eviction of the established Church's ministers from over 200 southern parishes – a phenomenon known as 'rabbling' – crowds of radical presbyterians ensured that competition between religious groups would cease in most of the areas where it had flourished since July 1687.

The earliest anti-Catholic protests took place in late November, after it was known that William had landed at Torbay, but before the outcome of his invasion became clear. In Edinburgh, the town college's students, some of whom had probably participated in the anti-Catholic riots of 31 January and 1 February 1686, planned a symbolic renunciation of the king's religion: a ceremony in which they would burn the pope in effigy. According to a newsletter printed in London, the students overcame opposition to their idea, and duly incinerated an effigy at the mercat cross, perhaps on 23 or 24 November. Two days after this display, the same source reports, students occupied the parliament house to stage a mock trial of the pope. His sentence – to be burned at the cross – was to be effected on 25 December.[18] On 26 November, possibly before the protest at parliament house, Edinburgh's provost warned the town council 'that there was ane tumult like to rise within the Cittie by the convocation of some idle persones ... who had seduced and perswaded severall of the students of the Colledge to joyne with them'. Some of the potential rioters had been imprisoned, and the council revived an act passed after the 1686 disturbances requiring the burgh's guilds to bind their members not to take part in tumults.[19] There seems to have been no further unrest in Edinburgh until 9 December. Despite the students' demonstrations, one resident reported on 1 December that 'wee be all in peace & quiet heir & not as yet trobled'.[20] Nevertheless, Catholics found the atmosphere intimidating. On 27 November, a priest wrote that he expected to leave the capital shortly, 'not being secure from the rable of whom we feare euery houre a tumult'. Teaching in the Jesuits' college ceased on 28 November; services in the chapel royal ended two days later.[21] Relatively peaceful and small-scale protests had shaken the priests' resolve and fatally set back the cause of Catholic revival.

Pope-burning displays were soon planned by the students of Scotland's other universities. They may have heard reports of the events in Edinburgh, but it is also likely that pope-burning was a familiar practice, known from visual representations of the protests in London during the exclusion crisis of 1679–81, and from a similar demonstration during James's stay in Edinburgh in 1680.[22] In Glasgow on 30 November 1688, students took part in a procession and burning of the pope, an event in which Scotland's protestant archbishops and episcopalian clergy were also impersonated and condemned. There was an attempt, apparently frustrated by the university's masters, to hold a similar demonstration in Glasgow on 8 December.[23] 'Thousands of Spectators', including members of the privy and burgh councils, observed the Edinburgh students' pope-burning at the capital's mercat cross on 25 December, the day on which the town council resolved to address William.[24] As Alexander Monro, then principal of the town college, admitted, the presence of the college mace was proof that at least some members of the faculty approved of the protest.[25] In contrast to the essentially presbyterian demonstration in Glasgow, the procession, trial and burning of the pope that was staged in Aberdeen on 11 January lacked any obvious criticism of the episcopalian Church. But the proceedings made reference to two other ways in which Aberdeen had repudiated James's rule: the election of new magistrates and councillors, and the ringing of the bells of Trinity Church, recently used for Catholic worship, and now back in protestant hands.[26] Of the university towns, only St Andrews did without a pope-burning display. There some of the students attempted to hold such a protest, but they were prevented by supporters of James among the university's staff.[27] In Edinburgh, Glasgow and Aberdeen, but not St Andrews, pope-burning constituted a rejection of the king's religion, and a sign that his authority had largely evaporated.

If the pope-burnings were symbolic and peaceful, they took place alongside more violent and destructive anti-Catholic demonstrations. The most spectacular, and best-known, episode happened in Edinburgh on 10 December.[28] On the previous evening, crowds of boys walked the streets chanting anti-Catholic slogans. They smashed windows in the houses of a few Catholics; more ominously, they shouted against the earls of Perth and Melfort, allegedly offering 'Two Thousand Pounds for *Melfort's* Head'.[29] The disturbances on 9 December were sufficiently serious to inspire on the following day a proclamation of the privy council for securing the peace.[30] Nevertheless, on the 9th the locked town gates prevented the crowds from reaching the Canongate and Holyrood, the centre of the Catholic revival. On the evening of 10 December, however, a body of students left Edinburgh and approached Holyrood, then guarded by 120 soldiers led by the Roman Catholic Captain John Wallace. Wallace fired on the crowd, killing several. Hearing reports of the violence, the privy council ordered the town to raise its trained bands and apprehend Wallace and his men.[31] This led to an exchange of fire between the bands and Wallace's troops, before the latter were surprised from the rear and dispersed. The crowd then took the opportunity to attack the chancellor's apartments in Holyroodhouse, the chapel and residences of the Jesuits and the refurbished chapel royal in the Abbey. They carried off Catholic books and devotional items, burning them together with furniture from the houses of other leading Catholics. The riot continued until the early hours of 11 December, and there was probably some further pillaging of Catholic property on the following days.[32]

The explosion of violence in Edinburgh was significant in numerous ways. It was an expression of anti-Catholic feeling, a response to rumours of a Catholic plot against the city and a successful operation to enforce the laws against the mass. At the same time, the riot ruptured multiconfessional coexistence in the Canongate, putting an end to the king's promotion of a vital Catholic presence in Scotland. As well as scattering the priests resident at Holyrood,[33] the crowd targeted Peter Bruce, the king's Catholic printer. His house was plundered; Bruce fled, and the privy council soon had him in prison. The press was seized, apparently by a creditor of one of its former owners, and some of Bruce's stock was destroyed.[34] There would be no imminent resumption of Catholic proselytising, through preaching or print. Moreover, the rioting was encouraged by leading presbyterian figures in Edinburgh. Episcopalian witnesses claimed that the crowd was egged on by a merchant named Menzies (either John or William) and George Stirling, a surgeon who became one of Edinburgh's commissioners to the convention of estates.[35] Members of the United Societies were probably involved.[36] Perhaps the presence of radical presbyterians made episcopalians worry that their property would soon be attacked. Certainly the episcopalian Alexander Monro believed that presbyterian politicians had manipulated the crowd to advance their own positions.[37]

The Edinburgh riots struck at the leaders of James's regime in Scotland. Balcarres understood the disturbances as part of a coup against Perth, engineered by Atholl and the chancellor's other rivals on the privy council. Having secured the council's agreement to disband the militia, Atholl's group persuaded Perth to withdraw from Edinburgh to the country for his own safety.[38] Perth's departure, on 10 December, was one of the triggers for the violence.[39] When he learned that James intended to go to France, Perth became convinced that he was in danger anywhere in Scotland and sought to follow his master. Intercepted in the Firth of Forth by seamen from Kirkcaldy, Perth was committed to prison in Stirling Castle.[40] As well as ending the chancellor's career in Scotland, the riot directly targeted some of his allies. The Drummond brothers' client and servant George Drummond of Blair Drummond had his house 'rifild'.[41] Captain Wallace, one of the chancellor's loyal military supporters, was soon captured and incarcerated on the Bass Rock.[42] Crowds attacked the homes of Catholic privy councillors; the duke of Gordon, earl of Traquair and others retreated to Edinburgh Castle for their safety.[43] The protestant councillors continued to meet, and on 12 December they resolved to send John Campbell, earl of Breadalbane to the king to give an account of the riot.[44] Two days later, the council decided that it was now necessary to ask James to call a 'frie Parliament ... for further secureing the Protestant Religion and for Establishing the Lawes'.[45] It is unclear whether this plea reached the king. Within days, as we shall see, the councillors were directing such requests to the prince of Orange.

A series of violent attacks on Catholic properties took place over the following month. There is some evidence of raids on Roslin and Niddrie, two houses belonging to Catholics in Edinburghshire, perhaps by members of the crowd that attacked Holyroodhouse.[46] Elsewhere in southern Scotland, Cameronians took the lead in anti-Catholic violence. According to Patrick Walker, one of their number, the group 'thought it some way belonged to us, in the *Inter-regnum*, to go to all Popish Houses, and destroy their Monuments of Idolatry'.[47] The most detailed testimony we have of this relates to Traquair House, whose vestments and objects of devotion were carefully inventoried before being burned at the cross of nearby Peebles.[48] But the centre of this activity was Nithsdale and Galloway, where armed members of the United Societies seem to have visited numerous properties. The countess of Nithsdale's house at Terregles was 'much Riffled', and an altar and other pieces of furniture were removed. These items were probably added to a bonfire of Catholic effects, on which an effigy of the pope was burned at Dumfries on 25 December.[49] It is unclear how much effort local magistrates made to prevent the destruction of property. On 24 December, the town council of Dumfries instructed some of its members to negotiate with the gentlemen of the shire 'for preventing trouble in the toune & for disperseing of the Countrey people now in armes'.[50] This initiative came too late to avert the incineration of Catholic property on the following day.

With the pope-burning displays, as with the attacks on Catholic houses, it is possible to argue that Edinburgh inspired the provinces, establishing a pattern for the Scottish revolution. In a proclamation of 13 December, the privy council condemned the 'late Execrable Tumults' in Edinburgh, whose effects were felt 'not only within this City'. Rioting, the council claimed, had 'spread it self over the Countrey'.[51] But the participants in anti-Catholic violence were responding to a number of developments, and seem to have been motivated chiefly by news originating in places other than Edinburgh. Most obviously, the failure of James to resist William's invasion gave encouragement to Scottish crowds. Moreover, many reports attributed the outbreaks of violence partly to fears of Catholic insurrection. According to their history of events, the Cameronians acted primarily on 'the alarming noise of the

Papists burning Kirkcudbright which did run through the country'.[52] These reports, the Cameronian minister Alexander Shields recalled, prompted the Societies to organise themselves in armed companies.[53]

Rumours of Catholic attacks had been spread deliberately in England, especially through a spurious declaration of William of Orange, dated 28 November and warning of 'great Numbers of Armed Papists' in London and Westminster. Because the stories emphasised the danger from Irish Catholic soldiers, historians have called this interval of panic the 'Irish Alarms' or 'Irish fright'.[54] In Scotland, fears of Catholic violence focused on Galloway, partly because of the small indigenous Catholic population, but also because of its proximity to Ireland.[55] The panic probably reached its height after the middle of December. Alexander Shields had heard of the burning of Kirkcudbright by 18 December; reports reached Edinburgh on 22 December.[56] Episcopalian writers later claimed that news of an attack on Kirkcudbright was spread deliberately from place to place by their presbyterian rivals, who hoped to gain an advantage from the turmoil. Thus the story reached Stranraer on 22 December, in a letter from John Muir, a leading lay presbyterian in Ayr who was soon to be that burgh's provost.[57] But in other cases the message passed between serving magistrates, who presumably had less to gain from fomenting popular anxiety. On 22 December, the council of Linlithgow received a letter from the magistrates of Glasgow, reporting 'That the papeists out of severall p[ar]ts of the kingdom has met togither at Kirkcoubright in Galloway In armes'.[58] On 24 December, the privy council referred to the

> Apprehensions His *Majesties* Leidges generally have, of the Papists being in Arms in *Galloway* and other places, and the Suspitions there may be of the *Irishes*, and other Papists from *England* and *Ireland*, in this dangerous Conjuncture, their joyning with them.[59]

Reports of threatening Catholics spread north of the Forth valley. The minister of Kinglassie, Fife, cancelled his sermon on 23 December, 'by reason of ane alarme of Papests'.[60] Five days later, the council of Brechin, recording that the 'wholl Kingdome is alaramed by the noyse of Invasione by papists From France and Ireland and of assaults and insurrections by papists within this Kingdome', ordered the fencible men to be ready to defend the town.[61]

Anti-Catholic anxieties, though fuelled by rumours, were probably exacerbated by the central government's responses to the perceived threat. On 14 December, the privy council called for the prevention and punishment of violence against Catholics and their property, and ordered magistrates to search Catholics' houses and secure arms and ammunition.[62] Two days later, perhaps prompted by the publication of the council's act, 'se[ver]all of the minor Inhabitants' of Dumfries 'did goe throw streits in a seiming tumultous maner'. The burgh council's first reaction was to expand the town guard, and to order the fencible inhabitants to be ready in the event of further tumults.[63] But it was soon clear that the Dumfries crowd was pushing an anti-Catholic agenda beyond what was authorised by the privy council in Edinburgh. John Maxwell of Barncleuch, Dumfries's Catholic provost, stopped attending the town council's meetings after the protest. Within days, he had been arrested and imprisoned. The council ordered two officers of the town guard to liaise with Sir Christopher Musgrave, governor of Carlisle, about men – probably Catholic soldiers – who were reportedly crossing the border from England. It was only on 31 December that the magistrates received a letter from the privy council approving the arrest of Barncleuch and other Catholics, and applauding the burgh's efforts to prevent them 'from Joyening with any who may be in armes'.[64]

Dumfries's magistrates may not have been fully in control of the disarming of Catholics in and around the town. When on 15 January the council compiled a list of arms in Dumfries, it was found that by no means all of the weapons taken from Catholics were in the hands of local office-holders. John Arthur, a councillor, possessed two bayonets and a pistol acquired during a search of Dumfries, presumably after the privy council's act of 14 December. Thomas Irving, a captain of the town's guard, had 'a pair of litle pistolls belonging to my Lo[rd] nithsdale', a Catholic.[65] But the investigation also revealed that residents without office had taken part in disarming raids into the surrounding country. James Johnston, who was not then a councillor or other officer but may have been on the council in 1685–6, had been part of a group that visited the Catholic house of Carruchan, a few miles outside of Dumfries. There he found three swords in the 'priests bed'. Johnston also kept a pistol taken from John Maxwell of Lochfoot, while another party had seized weapons from the largely Catholic village of Cargen.[66] This evidence suggests that there was considerable popular enthusiasm for disarming Catholics around Dumfries, a district with an unusually high Catholic population.

The riots in Edinburgh, the collapse of James's authority and rumours of Catholic violence had stimulated a dramatic reaction against Catholicism, which the privy council's attempts to keep order could not restrain. By late December, southern Scotland was witnessing a still more decisive rejection of multiconfessionalism. As we shall see, the rabbling of episcopalian clergy was the most important aspect of this revolutionary action. But the attacks on episcopalians were preceded by violence against the Quakers of Lanarkshire. According to the Friends' own records, five raids on Quakers' homes and meetings took place over a period of about a week, beginning on 20 December 1688. Groups of men, perhaps Cameronians, appeared at the houses of James Gray, John Hart in Heads, Glassford, and George Weir, in the parish of Dalserf. On each occasion, the visitors pretended to search for arms, but in fact removed other items, especially books and papers. Burning some of the papers seized from Hart's house at the cross of Hamilton, the attackers said 'they would extirpate all quakerism out of [th]e land'. The armed disturbers of a Quaker meeting at Hugh Wood's house in Hamilton also stole some of the group's records, and inflicted violence on the worshippers present.[67] These events did not necessarily shake the commitment of the small community of Quakers in Lanarkshire. But the violence indicated that the most intolerant of local presbyterians hoped to sabotage all multiconfessional coexistence.

The rabbling of episcopalian clergy had a far greater impact, probably removing at least 200 parish ministers from their churches. It took place in south-western counties as far north as Dunbartonshire, as well as in Linlithgowshire, Peeblesshire and Edinburghshire further to the east.[68] Typically, rabblings involved coordinated demonstrations at the manses and churches of episcopalian ministers, who were persuaded by threats and mild violence to cease preaching. Most rabblings were orchestrated by members of the United Societies, some of whom, as we have seen, were already in arms. The Societies brought a degree of military discipline, and also common practices and rhetoric, to the violence. In a few cases, crowds of rabblers made use of a standard paper, drawn up by the Societies, warning episcopalian ministers to leave their parishes. In general, rabbling was effected by intimidation and the destruction of symbolic items of property such as clerical gowns, more than by serious assault. Apologists for the rabblings claimed that the episcopalians had connived at the persecution of lay presbyterians, that they had no legitimate claim to their churches, and that Scots were bound by the Solemn League and Covenant to uproot episcopacy.[69]

The rabbling began on 25 December, and carried on sporadically through the winter and spring of 1689. Though some clergy agreed to stop preaching within days or weeks of the start of the campaign, others endured months of intimidation.[70] In at least a few cases, an attempted rabbling did not lead the episcopalian targeted to flee his parish. On 27 January, the episcopalian incumbent of Spott, Haddingtonshire, complained that 'Three Fanaticks armed w[i]t[h] swords & guns assaulted his house' at night, led him to the church, seized its Bible and keys, and discharged him from serving as minister. It is unknown whether these opportunistic rabblers were members of the Societies; they were more likely from Dunbar than Spott itself. The minister ignored their threats and continued to preach.[71] A more typical report concerns Thomas Douglas, minister of Skirling, Peeblesshire. According to an episcopalian pamphlet, he was threatened by a large crowd of Cameronians in early February 1689. Having left the manse for his safety, he preached on the several following Sundays, before the rumour of another visit from his adversaries prompted him to flee for Edinburgh.[72]

Episcopalian ministers in the synod of Glasgow responded to the rabbling by sending Dr Robert Scott, dean of Glasgow, to London with a petition to William and accounts of the violence.[73] On 6 February, Scott's lobbying encouraged William to issue a declaration requiring protestants to 'live Peaceably together'. Indeed, the declaration sought, at least temporarily, to restore the multiconfessional coexistence promoted by James. Thus William exhorted protestants to

> Enjoy their several Opinions and Forms of Worship, whether according to Law, or otherways, with the same Freedom, and in the same manner, in which they did Enjoy them in the Moneth of *October* last, till such time, as by Regular and Legal Methods a due Temper may be fallen on, for Composing and Settling those Differences.[74]

The declaration, though widely distributed, had little impact on anti-episcopalian violence. In at least two cases, at Glasgow and Tinwald and Trailflat, Dumfriesshire, ejected clergy tried to regain their churches after the declaration, but were obstructed by hostile crowds.[75] William was unable to turn back the tide. Cumulatively across 200 or more parishes, rabbling shattered the episcopalian Church in areas where it was already weak. In large parts of the south and south-west, the multiconfessional experiment was over.

* * *

In the second type of revolutionary action, Scots rejected James's policy in the royal burghs. In the months before the king fell from power, as we saw in Chapter 4, the efficiency of the crown's direct appointment of councils declined. Most of the nominations issued in late September 1688 were not implemented. In November and December, moreover, the privy council allowed elections to take place as normal in Aberdeen, Montrose and Forfar, apparently anticipating that men loyal to the king would be chosen. We saw in Chapter 4 that the outcome of Aberdeen's election seems to have been dictated by the court's agent David Eadie. The election in Montrose did not make major changes: magistrates active before the royal interventions replaced James's choice of provost and senior bailie, but the second bailie retained office and James's nominated treasurer became third bailie.[76] Forfar was one of the smaller royal burghs that had not received a royal nomination; though its provost was re-elected, the long-standing bailies were perhaps grateful to be replaced.[77] By allowing these elections to go ahead, the privy council seems to have recognised that directly appointing magistrates and councils could do little to make the royalist towns of the north-east more loyal. The elections should not be seen as evidence that a more general reversal of James's policy in the royal burghs was under way before the revolution.

Once James's authority had collapsed, however, the panic sweeping Scotland prompted the privy council to remove the few Catholic provosts and bailies who had gained office since 1686. As we saw above, Dumfries's council imprisoned Maxwell of Barncleuch, the town's Catholic provost, on its own initiative. It may have been news of the disturbances in Dumfries on 16 December that persuaded the privy council itself to act against Catholic magistrates. On 20 December, Dumfries council sent representatives to Edinburgh to report on the state of the town. It was presumably as a result of this mission that, on 22 December, Atholl wrote instructing the councillors who were in office before James's nominations to choose new office-holders for the ensuing year. By displacing the Catholic provost, the letter claimed, this measure would avert the 'fears and Jealousies' that were threatening the town's 'peace & quiet'.[78] Around the same time, the privy council sent a similar letter to Kirkcudbright, where the provost, William Broun of Nuntoun, and probably also the bailie Gavin Dunbar were Catholics.[79] There were differences of opinion within the privy council about the legitimacy of this approach. When the council of Ayr met on 1 January to choose 'ane new proveist in place of Sir William Wallace of Craigy In regaird he is ane papist', they did so on the authority of an act of the privy council dated 24 December. After the meeting had begun, however, a councillor produced a second order from Edinburgh, of 29 December, 'stoping and recalling the foirs[ai]d act of Counsell untill the maiter be reconsidered in ane full quorum of Counsell or the [secret] Committy'. It may be that the second privy council act was issued after lobbying by George Anderson, the burgh treasurer nominated by James, whom the town council sent to Edinburgh on 26 December.[80] No new council election took place in Ayr until April. Nevertheless, Craigie was absent serving with James's army in Ireland (he later fought at Killiecrankie), and did not attempt to exercise authority in Ayr.[81] Even if Wallace remained the burgh's provost in early 1689, it was unlikely that Catholics would benefit from his nominal power.

With respect to Dumfries and Ayr, then, the weak and vacillating remnant of James's privy council did not lead the process of revolution, but instead reacted to demands originating in the localities. The same conclusion emerges when we examine a group of other towns, numbering at least six, from which petitions were sent to the privy council against James's nominated magistrates and councillors. The first such address, drawn up by a merchant in Elgin, probably predated the attempts by Dumfries council to gain the central government's support for its local revolution. As we noted in Chapter 4, the petition alleged that the king's nominees for Elgin were mostly non-residents who had mismanaged the local economy. The privy council responded to the petition on 22 December, instructing the burgh council that was in place before the royal nomination to elect new magistrates and councillors, and to restore the former town clerk. This order was put into effect on 7 January. As Chapter 4 suggests, probably only the nominated provost and one of the four bailies of Elgin were unqualified for office in a royal burgh. Though the election removed the provost and three of the four bailies from office, the dean of guild chosen by the king became a bailie and the nominated treasurer remained in post.[82] In all likelihood, the government of Elgin was little altered in 1688–9. Significantly, however, such change as the town experienced was a result of local initiative more than central direction.

Other towns followed where Elgin led. A petition calling for a new election of the magistrates of Haddington was drawn up by the burgh's nominated provost, Sir William Paterson, who as clerk to the privy council was presumably aware of its response to the address from Elgin. On the privy council's order, the magistrates and councillors who were in place before James's intervention chose new officials for Haddington in early January, not before thanking Paterson formally 'for his good service' to the town while provost.[83] At the same time, a new council election took place in Lanark, after an address to the privy council – made by the appointed magistrates themselves – reported that some of the royal nominees were dead or had ceased to exercise their offices.[84]

In Haddington and Lanark, when local elites regained their control of elections, there was no obvious expression of hostility towards the men chosen by James. This was equally true in Kirkcaldy. Here the nominated bailies, Crawford of Mountquhannie and Lundie of Strathairlie, petitioned the privy council for a new election in the town, perhaps doubting that their authority could endure when the king's had evaporated. The council granted the request on 4 January. But the burgh council attempted unsuccessfully to persuade the two bailies to remain in office without the formality of a new election. When legal advice was received confirming that the last freely chosen councillors should indeed elect their successors according to the burgh's sett, the council duly returned Crawford and Lundie as provost and bailie. It might have been true, as Perth wrote after his capture at Kirkcaldy, that it was the former bailie John Boswell, now made dean of guild, who had real popular authority in the town. Nevertheless, Crawford and Lundie were clearly acceptable magistrates in spite of their association with King James.[85]

As we saw in Chapter 4, however, royal intervention had inflamed local enmities in several burghs. A petition from some of the inhabitants of Culross, heard by the privy council on 3 January, made specific allegations against James's nominees. Asserting that the magistrates were 'illegallie elected contrair to Law and the constitution of the burgh', the petition claimed that they had 'misapplyed the Common good', and that the merchant bailies James Mackie and Daniel MacDonald were Catholics.[86] In the case of Inverness, where no nomination had been made until August 1688, and the men chosen can have served for little more than two months,[87] the petitioners were strategic, if not cynical, in their manipulation of rhetoric. Noting that the town had been 'depryved of the benefit of a frie election conform to the constitution', the petition complained that James's nominees 'wer fitt for such designes as wer proposed to them at ther Ingadgeing in ther offices', and that their 'governement in ane arbitrarie way' threatened to provoke tumults. As with Culross and the other towns to petition the privy council, Inverness was allowed to have a new election. The result was the return to office of a provost, John Cuthbert of Drakies, who was in fact the leading beneficiary of James's policy, having served continuously throughout the reign until the autumn of 1688. The provost who had temporarily displaced Cuthbert, Finlay Fraser, protested against the privy council's act, but the newly elected burgh council included several of the men chosen by James.[88] Thus even the petitions that complained of the king's nominees aimed primarily to restore local electoral control, and did not seek any punishment of unpopular magistrates aside from their removal from office.

In the first weeks of 1689, several other towns brought the royal intervention in their affairs to an end by holding new council elections, with or without the privy council's approval. There was probably an election in Aberdeen on 11 January, though the only evidence that it took place is in a pamphlet describing the pope-burning procession of that date, dedicated by the authors to the 'new Elected Council' on 'this day of your Election'.[89] On 21 January, the council of Burntisland, 'being certainly informed Th[at] ther are se[ver]all of the royall burrowes of this Kingdom that have ellected new baillies and Councill', resolved to hold a fresh election. There was apparently no order to do so from the central government. As with most other towns, the resulting vote constituted a rejection of James's policy, but did not overthrow the men he had nominated. One of the appointed bailies remained in post; the other two stayed on the council.[90] Annan, a town in which it is unclear if James's nomination of magistrates and councillors was ever implemented, followed suit with a new election on 8 February. The earl of Annandale, who had been excluded from the royal nomination of February 1688, and was quick to support William's invasion, was unanimously chosen provost.[91] If this was a return to politics as usual in the small southern town, the same was true in nearby Lochmaben, where on 14 February 'the councell all in one voce nemine contradicente continowed the magistrats till Michelmas as formerly'.[92] A more unusual response to the interregnum was apparent in Irvine, where the magistrates seem to have resigned and vital council business – the setting of leases to the burgh's property – was carried out by the community as a whole, probably coordinated by the town clerk.[93]

In some of the towns that did not see new council elections in late December or the first two months of 1689, the continuing presence of James's magistrates was a source of tension. As well as trying to restrain violence against episcopalian ministers, William of Orange's declaration of 6 February ordered Catholics remaining in public office to resign, to be replaced by protestants.[94] The arrival of this declaration in Perth brought animosities among the nominated council to a head. On 18 February, Bailie Henry Deas intervened in a council meeting to demand that his colleagues purge themselves of popery, asserting that 'non may continou in [thei]r Statione but such as ar trew protestants conforme to the Prince of Orange declaration'. The nominated provost, Sir Patrick Threipland of Fingask, promptly declared himself a 'trew protestant', but James Stewart, dean of guild, refused either to do likewise or to resign his office. Deas claimed that Stewart had attended mass in London sixteen years before, and more recently participated in Catholic worship at Holyrood and Stobhall, a property of the earl of Perth. Stewart had allegedly been introduced to the king by the Jesuit courtier Sir Edward Petre, and helped to bring two priests to Scotland.[95] If Deas and other councillors had known these things for some time, it was presumably the prince's declaration that allowed him to speak out so dramatically. A dean of guild created trouble in Inverkeithing, too, where 'in publict and privat conferences' he questioned the council's power to meet, even though William's declaration allowed protestants to continue in office. In this case, the dean's attitude was founded not so much on constitutional principles, as on personal antagonisms and his own alleged mismanagement of the harbour. But as the other councillors deposed him from office, it must have seemed that their own grip on power was increasingly tenuous.[96]

* * *

If the protests and upheavals discussed so far served primarily to repudiate James's rule, a third form of action gave explicit approval to William of Orange's intervention in British politics. The distribution of the Scottish *Declaration of Reasons* for William's invasion probably began after he landed at Torbay; it is unclear whether the privy council had seen a copy of the *Declaration* before issuing a proclamation against it on 10 November.[97] The Scottish *Declaration* shared some passages (concerning the advance of Catholicism and the allegedly fraudulent birth of the prince of Wales) with the simultaneous *Declaration* relating primarily to England. But the Scottish document, which was probably composed by presbyterian exiles at William's court in The Hague, addressed developments in the northern kingdom in some detail. The *Declaration*'s objections to the advance of Catholicism and Catholics, to the king's absolutist pretensions and misgovernment, may have helped to stimulate the violent protests of late November and December.[98] From December, the *Declaration* was put to a more peaceable, but highly significant, use: public reading. Readings of the document disseminated the prince's message, and allowed for a clear statement of support for his cause. The readings of which we have detailed information took place in royal burghs at the mercat cross, the place where royal proclamations were published. In most cases, reading was ordered by the town council, and was accompanied by at least some of the formalities attending important public announcements.

The first known public reading of the *Declaration* took place in Glasgow, on or around 25 December. It lacked the town council's approval, and was apparently the initiative of presbyterians, including the Cameronian preacher William Boyd.[99] Boyd's participation exacerbated a dispute within the United Societies about the extent to which the group should support William's invasion and send an address to the prince.[100] Nevertheless, other burghs followed Glasgow's example. By appointment of the town council, the *Declaration* was read at the cross of Ayr during the market on 29 December.[101] On 1 January, a meeting in Edinburgh of what was described as a 'great Councell' (a larger body than the councillors elected at the previous Michaelmas) heard reports that armed men from the west – perhaps including some who had accompanied Boyd in Glasgow – 'were approaching this cittie upon pretence of publishing his highnes the prince of Orange his declaration'. Fearing that they also planned to rob the town's inhabitants, the council attempted to prevent the men's approach by having the *Declaration* publicly read. According to the council minutes, 'the solemnitie was performed in the usuall method with ringing of bells and bonfyres'.[102] On 8 January, the *Declaration* was read at a town council meeting in Burntisland; the councillors appointed it to be published at the cross on 10 January, with 'all solemnities requisit'. The burgh's inhabitants were instructed to light bonfires in front of their houses.[103] On the previous day, the *Declaration* was proclaimed in Dumfries, probably at the town council's order, and St Andrews, where the students protested their opposition.[104] There are suggestions that the *Declaration* was publicly read in other towns. As well as mentioning its proclamation at Glasgow and Ayr, Robert Wodrow claimed that it was read in Irvine 'and most other burghs'.[105] The treasurer of Banff paid for bell-ringing at the 'declara[tio]n of the Prince of Orange declaratione', probably referring to the *Declaration of Reasons* rather than to any of the other papers issued in his name before he became king.[106] And at Arbroath on 5 January, John Kidd, the provost who was reportedly close to adopting Catholicism, was accused of drinking a toast to the prince of Orange's confusion. Perhaps this indiscretion, which Kidd denied, took place after a reading of the *Declaration*.[107]

As well as deciding what, if anything, to do with the *Declaration of Reasons*, local magistrates considered whether to make their own representations to William, who by late December was in control of London. Having resolved on 14 December to ask James for a free meeting of parliament, the privy council renewed its request on the 24th, this time in an address to William.[108] The general meeting of presbyterian ministers and elders produced at least two, and possibly as many as four, draft petitions to the prince; though one was adopted on 3 January, it may not have been presented until the following month.[109] Several other addresses were made to the prince from royal burghs and other local jurisdictions. On 25 December, Edinburgh's town council drafted a petition to William emphasising its fears of Catholicism, and asking him to summon a free parliament. All magistrates and councillors, except for the dean of guild, were prepared to sign.[110] Before the end of the year, various noblemen and gentlemen from Haddingtonshire were joined by magistrates and councillors of Dunbar and Haddington in another address to William.[111]

If the councillors of Edinburgh and the landowners and leading burgesses of Haddingtonshire were generally united in their willingness to address William, other communities were less sure. Some potential signatories may have thought that supplications would be unwelcome or ill-timed, especially if made after the Scottish noblemen and gentlemen addressed William on 10 January. John Hay, Lord Yester took this view, and discouraged a planned address from Fife, remarking that 'such compliments are not much card [i.e. cared] for or regarded they having been too common thes years by past', during the reigns of Charles II and James VII.[112] Other communities disagreed about the wisdom of addressing William. Glasgow, where the council had not countenanced the reading of the prince's *Declaration*, was divided. In October, the burgh's offer to raise ten companies of 120 militiamen was so welcome to James's government that it was reported in the *London Gazette* as a sign of Scottish support for the king.[113] But by mid-November, the town council complained that some inhabitants failed to take their turn at guarding Glasgow. Though this might have resulted from laziness rather than political sentiment, in January the burgh disbanded its regiment, which 'refuises to obey the magistrats'.[114] Meanwhile, an address to William had been drawn up, supported by unidentified members of the 'Nobilitie Gentry Majestrats and inhabitants' of Glasgow, together with 'others nou in armess in the west of Scotland', possibly Cameronians.[115] The surviving copy of this hearty endorsement of William's intervention is dated 1688; if it was indeed signed before the end of the year, its promoters committed themselves to the prince's cause earlier than others in the burgh. The town council did not consider the text of an address – perhaps a new document – until 24 January; even then it was signed by only 'the most pairt' of the councillors, and the meeting left the provost to decide whether to send it to London.[116] There was probably a split in Glasgow between enthusiastic Williamites and loyal but cautious supporters of James, who were a significant presence on the council. A similar division may have existed in Aberdeen, though the evidence from that town is more difficult to interpret. At a council meeting on 8 January, James Reid, councillor and hospital master, protested against sending George Garden as commissioner to William, and another councillor also indicated his opposition. As an envoy, Garden was either an odd choice or a very deliberate one. As an episcopalian minister, who in later years was a prominent Jacobite, it is unlikely that he could have persuaded William that Aberdeen was fully behind the revolution.[117]

* * *

The final focus of our analysis of the revolution in the localities is on the elections to the convention of estates. This body was summoned to meet at Edinburgh on 14 March by William of Orange, acting on the request of 10 January from the Scottish noblemen and gentlemen present in London. Though some eligible voters boycotted the elections, large numbers took part, suggesting that there was widespread acceptance that William had the right to summon the estates. But it is by no means clear what motivated the voters. Derek Patrick, in two detailed studies of the elections, argues that the succession played a key role in determining electoral outcomes, and that large numbers of 'revolutioner' or Williamite candidates can be identified.[118] Yet in most contests there is too little evidence to draw these conclusions. Rather, we should recognise that national questions were entwined with a range of local struggles, and that some voters sought to overthrow nominated magistrates, not necessarily to depose the king himself. Moreover, in the considerable number of elections that were unanimous or nearly so, we seem to observe a solidarity born not from agreement on the national issues, but from a desire to protect local interests. Rather than a simple competition between revolutionaries and loyalists, then, the elections reflected a complex mixture of concerns, varying much from place to place. Indeed, the elections are further evidence that the upheavals of 1688–9 were a patchwork of local events, each shaped by its own dynamics.

From the perspective of William's Scottish sympathisers, of course, it was important to minimise the support for James in the convention. This was clearly the aim of the meeting of gentlemen and nobles in London. In its address to the prince, the meeting advised that the normal property qualifications for voters should be observed, but that otherwise electors and members of the convention should 'be *Protestants*, without any other Exception, or Limitation whatsoever'. Thus the Test oath, which the law of 1681 required electors to swear, was discharged; presbyterians and others who objected to the oath's definition of royal authority would be entitled to vote and sit in the convention. The nobles and gentlemen also recommended a change to the franchise in the royal burghs. Whereas a burgh's commissioner would normally have been chosen solely by the town council, the meeting persuaded William to give all protestant burgesses a vote.[119] Politicians remaining loyal to James opposed these innovations. Balcarres complained that the omission of the Test gave Williamites an advantage.[120] An anonymous paper objected to the extension of the franchise in burghs, seeing it as a new invasion of the rights of town councils, following that committed by James.[121] The duke of Queensberry argued that the participation of all burgesses would lead to tumults.[122] Edinburgh's council also opposed the arrangements, noting that council elections in the capital had continued (almost) as normal under James.[123] While the provost of Edinburgh probably feared that he would not be elected by a vote of all protestant burgesses, another observer thought that the continuing power of many magistrates nominated by James would turn the elections against the Williamite cause.[124] In the absence of any coordinated management of the elections, it was not clear that widening the franchise alone would secure a Williamite result.

In a few localities, there were attempts to protest against the holding of an election, or otherwise to frustrate the voting. After William's instruction to elect commissioners was publicly read in Culross, Alexander and James Mackie, sons of one of the bailies suspected of Catholicism, 'did without the least provocation most insolentlie ... fall upon the Clerk and called him rascall and villain'.[125] Even though the prince's order was sent to town clerks, apparently to prevent nominated magistrates and councillors from obstructing the process, some members of Fortrose's council tried to prevent the document from being published.[126] At the election for Kincardineshire on 1 March, one of the barons sought to delay the vote, arguing that the 'tempestuousness of the weather' had prevented many electors from attending. There were indeed more absentees than participants among the eligible electorate in Kincardineshire, and this might have resulted from doubts about the legitimacy of the election, rather than stormy conditions.[127] Balcarres claimed that some supporters of James scrupled to take part in the elections, though we cannot determine how much effect this had on the outcome.[128]

In some better documented elections, especially those taking place in large towns, we can recognise how national debates over the succession and Church government interacted with arguments about the conduct of local government. Edinburgh's vote took place over three days; nearly 1,400 citizens took part. After the first day, the earl of Tweeddale reported of the four candidates that 'the prowost & Jhon Bayly ar on[e] party &

Sr Jhon Hal & Georg Stirling Another'. When the contest was decided in favour of Hall and Stirling, Tweeddale explained that 'the presbeterians haue caryed it'.[129] The presbyterian surgeon George Stirling, as we have seen, was implicated in the riot of 10 December. Sir John Hall had been chosen as a bailie in 1668 and 1672, but was excluded from the council in 1675 after his party in the convention of royal burghs came into conflict with the duke of Lauderdale.[130] Stirling had been removed from office as deacon of the surgeons after declining to swear the declaration of 1662 against the Covenants.[131] Presumably Stirling and Hall were obvious candidates to oppose the provost Sir Magnus Prince, and to advance a Williamite and presbyterian agenda. In April 1689, Hall became the burgh's provost and Stirling re-joined the council.[132]

In Dundee, likewise, it must have been obvious to voters that the outcome of the local struggle would have significant implications for the national settlement. After the burgh's election was announced, recently created burgesses attempted to secure their right to vote by having their names entered in the town's official record, the 'Lockit Book'. Because they declined to swear the burgess oath, claiming that it had been discharged by the king (presumably by the indulgence of February 1687), the viscount of Dundee and the nominated council refused to register their privileges. But if the viscount hoped that this would exclude enough voters to ensure the election of one of his allies, he was disappointed. The burgh instead chose as its commissioner James Fletcher, its former provost and member of the 1686 parliament, who had opposed the granting of toleration to Catholics.[133]

The election in Perth, where the nominated magistrates were holding on to power, showed how a contest for local eminence could reflect the tensions caused by James's government and William's invasion. On 28 February, the election began in the East Kirk with James's choice of provost, Threipland of Fingask, casting his vote. Three former magistrates then entered a protest against the anticipated election of Fingask as commissioner, alleging that he had promised the king to support the repeal of the penal laws, had given burgess rights to a Jesuit and, since William's landing in England, had spoken 'belyinglie, approbriouslie and irreverentlie' about the prince.[134] Fingask responded by producing a minute of the recent council meeting in which he had abjured popery. Matthew Gibson, a nominated councillor, then entered another protest, seeking to deny three magistrates their right to vote, as the burgesses 'heir present most suspect to be of the popish faith'. The men in question included James Stewart, the dean of guild who had refused to disown popery, and the provost and senior bailie nominated in 1686, who had apparently solicited their places. The votes of other burgesses were then recorded, giving a narrow majority to Fingask over the former bailie Robert Smith, but with ballots cast for seven other candidates. Though the meeting was then dissolved, additional votes were later taken at the church, in favour of Smith, and at Gibson's house, for Fingask. The wrangling continued on the following day, when Smith's supporters alleged that some of the weavers who voted for Fingask were not burgesses. Unable to resolve the disagreement, Perth sent two commissioners to Edinburgh, where the convention decided in favour of Smith.[135]

Perth's was one of eight disputed elections that had to be adjudicated by the convention.[136] These cases reflect the high level of political disagreement present in some constituencies. Jedburgh's election could not be decided in the town itself, and rival commissions were given to Robert Ainslie and Adam Ainslie. The convention found that the magistrates had used threats and manipulation to carry the election for the former candidate. The commission to his rival narrated that the majority of burgesses had protested against the council's 'sinistrous & unlawfull wayes', before withdrawing from the election and unanimously choosing Adam Ainslie as their representative.[137] It is unclear what role the big questions facing the convention played in this election. But in the case of Linlithgow, which produced commissions in favour of the nominated provost, Lord Livingstone, and William Higgins, we can see that both local and national matters were at stake.[138] Higgins, whose election the convention approved, certainly supported the revolution settlement; he was later ordained as a presbyterian minister.[139] At the local level, as became clear when he was made a bailie in April, Higgins aimed to overturn Livingstone's influence, in part by ejecting the former provost's choice of clerk and restoring his old enemy William Bell.[140]

While some elections were fiercely competitive, others were concluded unanimously. The documents recording commissions to the convention often do not specify how the votes were divided, but they give evidence of at least eleven unanimous polls, mostly in small towns.[141] Six other urban contests, including those in the larger burghs of Glasgow and Haddington, were decided with very little contradiction.[142] The pattern was probably repeated in many shires, in which tiny numbers were qualified to vote. Thus in Peeblesshire, fifteen landowners voted to elect two commissioners. All agreed on Sir Archibald Murray of Blackbarony, and thirteen also supported the other successful candidate, David Murray, younger of Stanhope.[143] It is difficult to interpret these elections. In some, the obvious social or political eminence of a candidate (or pair of candidates) must have stifled the expression of ideological disagreement at the polls. But perhaps in other cases solidarity itself was prized above all else. In these circumstances, voters put aside their disagreements about national issues, preserved communal harmony and prioritised the defence of local interests.

Some constituencies instructed their commissioners how to act in the convention. Unfortunately, the scanty evidence we have of these instructions tells us little about how voters wanted Scotland's constitutional crisis to be resolved. One of the more specific instructions, agreed to by a majority of the voters in Wigtownshire, warned the commissioners to 'do nothing prejudicial to moderate Presbyterian Government'. They were also told to contribute to the settlement of Scotland's grievances, not condoning 'arbitrary government or absolute power', and to attempt to reduce the country's tax burden.[144] Most commissioners were allowed a good deal of discretion. Haddington's council directed its commissioner to 'vot for the preserving the protestant religione', but 'recommended all other things to be proposed in the meetting to his owne prudence'.[145] The council of Culross requested only that its commissioner try to restore the royal burghs' trading privileges and reduce the burden of cess.[146] Irvine seems to have done no more than to empower its commissioner to act 'for secureing the Protestant Religion, Redressing the greivances in Church & State, and restoreing the Lawes and Liberties'.[147] Whereas in 1690 some towns told their representatives to vote for the re-establishment of presbyterianism, there is no evidence in 1689 of similarly precise instructions concerning the succession or constitutional reform.[148] It is possible that the views of some commissioners were well known to the voters, and it was thought unnecessary to prescribe how they should act in the convention. Alternatively, we might argue that commissioners were left to their own judgement because their constituents were divided or undecided on the major questions.

* * *

In this chapter, we have seen that the collapse of James's authority in December 1688 led to three months of political uncertainty at the centre and an often violent activism in Scottish localities. To the most radical participants in the protests and disorder, the revolutionary interval was an interregnum, in which government was dissolved and change was to be effected by ordinary Scots.[149] If the country's urban elites took a different view, they nevertheless seized the opportunity of James's fall to secure their positions and reassert local autonomy. Scots in each locality responded to, and frequently emulated, events elsewhere in the country.

But while we might date the revolution's outbreak to the riots against Holyroodhouse of 10 December 1688, Edinburgh did not figure as the crucible of the revolution in the period from December to the opening of the convention in the following March. Local powerbrokers sought to adjust political realities in their towns and districts; the elections of late February and early March were at least as much about influence over small communities as about the succession to the throne. Meanwhile, the noblemen and other political luminaries who might have taken control of the state apparatus for William, or sought to regain it for James, did little, and awaited the meeting of the convention of estates. It is to the convention, and the resolution of the crisis, that we must now turn.

6

The Revolution Settlement of 1689–1690

IN EARLY MARCH 1689, Scotland remained unstable. The anti-Catholic panic of December 1688 had abated, but violence against episcopalian ministers continued. Six towns, and probably more, had endorsed William of Orange's *Declaration* in public readings. Yet in many parts of the country local elites were cautious about how far to recognise the prince. The elections to the convention of estates revealed pockets of clear commitment to a Williamite outcome, and showed that parts of Scotland were deeply divided. Yet in other elections, voters prioritised local unity and returned candidates whose attitudes towards the succession may well have been undecided. On the eve of the convention, it seemed probable that the estates would repudiate James's policies and style of government, thereby vindicating the country's protests. In spite of the uncertainty evident in the election results, moreover, various developments made it likely that the convention would settle the crown on the prince and princess of Orange. James's authority had collapsed, a range of leading figures had defected to William, and a larger body of the political elite had agreed to give William responsibility for Scottish government. Most importantly, the English convention had resolved in favour of William and Mary, proclaiming them king and queen of England on 13 February.

This chapter begins by recounting the circumstances in which crisis and uncertainty gave way to a decisive victory to William's monarchical ambitions. In the convention, the tactical successes of the prince's supporters, and the indecision and blunders of his opponents, secured an overwhelming vote in favour of offering the throne to William and Mary. This was followed, in the Claim of Right and Articles of Grievances, by a thoroughgoing rejection of James's rule, and also of many of the institutions and assumptions that had characterised Scottish politics since the Restoration. The revolution settlement – a series of political and religious reforms – began to take shape after the convention had reconvened as a parliament in June 1689. But the appearance of an assertive political opposition ensured that it was not until the following summer that agreement was reached on the main issues. Though the transfer of power to William was achieved peacefully, and the settlement was the product of parliamentary negotiation, Scotland's revolution nevertheless brought about a civil war. The chapter concludes by analysing that conflict, and explaining why it had little impact on the revolution's outcome.

* * *

The first job of the convention of estates was to decide who should occupy the throne. That Scotland faced a stark choice was underlined in several pamphlets published in early March to influence the convention. Williamite writers argued that the fall of James and the rise of William were the work of divine providence. '*Heaven it self has very fully loos'd the Nation from their Allegiance*' to James, one pamphleteer averred.[1] Another declared that 'Almighty God hath raised up the Prince of *Orange*', and 'blessed his great and good Designs with suitable success'.[2] In these circumstances, the argument went on, there was no real alternative to settling the crown on the prince and princess of Orange. 'God from Heaven, presents to us, and the Highest Necessity determines us, to embrace their Highnesses as the only Persons that can, and ought' to possess the throne.[3] By contrast, a writer loyal to James called on Scots to set an example of loyalty to their erring southern neighbours, by restoring the rightful monarch as in 1660.[4] But others pointed out that such an endeavour would ally Scotland with Catholic France in a war against protestant England. James 'cannot now be Re established but upon the Ruines of the whole Reformed Interest in *Christendom*', one pamphlet urged.[5] Supporters of William could argue that it would have been immoral and disastrous to fight for James's restoration. Allies of the dispossessed king were constrained to appeal to loyalty rather than practicality.

As we saw in Chapter 5, two changes to electoral procedure – the suspension of the Test oath and the participation of all burgesses – seemed likely to advantage candidates who were sympathetic towards William. And yet we should be wary of assuming that such men could be readily identified in all of Scotland's communities in February and March 1689. Of course, some leading Scots had declared their support for the prince by the time of the elections. But while observers pointed to a body of 'presbyterians' and former exiles who were expected to advance William's claim to the throne, we should not assume that this group amounted to a pro-revolution party with candidates in each constituency.[6] Indeed, we do not know how many of the elected commissioners favoured making William king prior to hearing the debates in the convention. After the matter was decided, a large majority of members accepted the settlement of the throne and swore allegiance to William and Mary. Around 30 per cent of shire commissioners and under 15 per cent of burgh commissioners refused to do so, and most were ultimately expelled from the convention.[7] But it is unlikely that these data reflect the balance between Williamites and Jacobites in the spring of 1689. It seems probable that many members remained undecided when the convention assembled on 14 March. If this is true of commissioners from small communities, it is all the more evident in the case of Scotland's leading magnates. Some, notably the duke of Queensberry and the marquis of Atholl, remained flexible in their allegiances for long after the throne was settled.[8]

Nevertheless, the effectiveness of William's supporters, combined with the errors of James and his allies, ensured a swift Williamite outcome. Jacobite commissioners complained that Edinburgh was swarming with armed men sympathetic to the prince of Orange, some of whom were certainly Cameronians. John Graham, viscount of Dundee, who soon left the convention in disgust, claimed that it was unsafe for him to remain in a town apparently at the mercy of his presbyterian foes.[9] Moreover, the leading advocates of William, even if they were at first unsure of the extent of their support, acted resolutely to gain influence over the convention. The duke of Hamilton, perceived as a pro-revolution figure, defeated Atholl by forty votes in the competition to be president of the convention. According to the earl of Balcarres, this outcome led over twenty members to give up their support for James's cause.[10] Observers on both sides agreed that the majority of the committee named to resolve controverted elections supported William. The committee generally seems to have decided against the candidates more likely to favour James.[11] On 16 March, in a dramatic episode, letters were read to the convention from the rival claimants of the throne. Committing a tactical mistake, James's sympathisers agreed to a resolution that the convention should continue to sit, regardless of the content of his letter. When the missive was read, the king's threatening tone and uncompromising language dismayed his supporters, prompting Dundee and others to withdraw from the convention.[12] On 27 March, a committee of twenty-four was appointed to prepare a measure settling the government; half or more of its members were known presbyterians and Williamites.[13] It was this committee that, on 3 April, brought to the full convention a resolution that King James had forfeited the throne. On the following day, a large majority of those present voted in favour of this motion, giving their approval to what was a first draft of the Claim of Right. Whatever their views on 14 March, all but twelve of those still attending the convention were willing to agree that James, by his actions as king, had 'forefaulted the right to the croune and the thron is become vacant'.[14]

This resolution was ambiguous, and it inspired much discussion. For some, the convention intended to make clear that James had lost his Scottish throne by his own actions, and the estates were simply declaring that this had taken place. Sir John Dalrymple made this case in the convention. Unlike in England, he argued, where James had 'abdicated' his executive responsibilities by leaving the kingdom, the justification for his loss of the Scottish crown was to rest entirely on his misgovernment.[15] Dalrymple's father Sir James, observing the convention from England, thought that 'the terme of forfating' was potentially misleading. It should not be understood to assert that the convention had jurisdiction superior to the monarch, he maintained, but rather that James's breach of 'his pairt of the mutuall engagments' between ruler and the ruled had liberated Scots from their allegiance.[16] But we should not conclude that the convention's resolution was in essence conservative, as Bruce Lenman argues.[17] The very obscurity of the convention's language allowed contemporaries to invest the resolution with a range of meanings, some more radical than others.[18]

After agreeing on 4 April that the throne was vacant, on 11 April the estates approved an expanded declaration, containing fuller justifications for James's forfeiture: the Claim of Right. Some members, notably Queensberry and Atholl, avoided casting a vote on the Claim, but returned to the meeting to support a separate resolution offering the throne to William and Mary. If they disliked some of what was said about their former master, these politicians nevertheless recognised that the Williamite cause had triumphed.[19] The shape of the constitutional settlement that would result from this victory became clearer on 13 April, when the convention adopted, in addition to the Claim of Right, a second declaration of intent: the Articles of Grievances.

* * *

We now need to examine in some detail the convention's critique of James and his rule, as well as its prospectus for settling Scotland.[20] We can classify most of the matters complained about in the Claim of Right and Articles of Grievances under four headings. The first and fundamental issue concerns the magnification of royal power. The Claim began by lamenting that James VII assumed royal authority without swearing the coronation oath. Thereafter he 'did, by the advyce of wicked and evill counsellers, invade the fundamentall constitution of this kingdome and altered it from a legall limited monarchy, to ane arbitrary despotick power'. The most obvious sign of this invasion and alteration, the Claim pointed out, was the 'publick proclamation' – the first declaration of indulgence – in which James asserted his right to suspend laws. According to the Claim, James had never been entitled to rule. No Roman Catholic could be monarch, the document argued, and not even a protestant could exercise regal powers without swearing the coronation oath. The marriage of a king or queen to a Catholic, the Grievances added, was 'dangerous to the Protestant religion and ought to be provyded against'. Moreover, 'all proclamationes asserting ane absolute power to cass, annull and dissable lawes', the Claim asserted, 'are contrair to law'. These statements flew in the face of recent thinking about the succession and the royal prerogative. We saw in Chapter 1 that the succession act of 1681 had allowed James to take the throne despite his Catholicism and unwillingness to swear the oath.[21] Even if James's indulgences had stretched earlier understandings of the prerogative, there was no explicit criticism of the suspending power before 1689. The Grievances made it still clearer that the convention sought to change the laws defining the monarch's powers. Not only had parliament in 1663 given the king too much discretion over customs on foreign imports, the Grievances maintained, but the act of 1669 asserting the royal ecclesiastical supremacy should be repealed, and the act of 1681 granting the king cumulative jurisdiction, or the right to take cognisance of any case he chose, was a 'greivance'.[22]

Having denounced James's arbitrary power, the Claim went on to list some of the ways in which the king 'did exerce that power to the subversion of the Protestant religion'. In doing so, the Claim introduced a second theme: the promotion of Catholicism. Enumerating the key features of the Catholic revival, the Claim noted that Catholics had worshipped publicly, sometimes in formerly protestant venues, the Jesuits had opened a college in Holyroodhouse, Catholic books were printed and dispersed with royal support, there was state funding for Catholic institutions and the king employed Catholics in public offices and the army. But the Claim was not simply an anti-Catholic document. As the text was expanded between the vote of 4 April that the throne was vacant and the adoption of the final version on 11 April, the estates added to the Claim a clause asserting that 'prelacy' – government of the Church by bishops – was a 'great and insupportable greivance' that 'ought to be abolished'. This clause, allegedly introduced at the suggestion of Sir James Montgomery of Skelmorlie, one of the members for Ayrshire, was approved by at least three quarters of the commissioners present in the convention of 10 April.[23] The anti-episcopalian agenda was reflected in the Grievances, with its call for the repeal of the act of supremacy, as 'inconsistant with the establishment of the church government now desyred'.

A third type of complaint drew attention to other ways in which the king had abused his authority. James, the convention objected, had repeatedly acted without parliamentary consent in spheres where that was necessary. These included the imposition of oaths – perhaps the new test of allegiance in the first indulgence was particularly intended – and authorising the exaction of money. This latter criticism was probably inspired by the local excises collected in royal burghs by the king's gift; we shall see that the modification of these taxes formed part of the towns' struggle for a settlement in 1689–90. The convention also expressed its opposition to the keeping of a standing army in peacetime without parliamentary approval. This important facet of the Restoration state was mentioned in the Claim, but it was not there declared contrary to law. The fact that the standing army was referred to again among the Grievances suggests that, though it was widely disliked, it was not generally considered illegal.

There was also a series of objections to abuses in the exercise of justice. The Claim condemned 'exorbitant fines' and 'extravagant baile', unexplained imprisonment and defective prosecutions, particularly mentioning the ninth earl of Argyll's conviction in 1681. It was complained that the king interfered in the business of the courts, suspending their cases and 'commanding them how to proceed'. The terms of the royal commissions appointing men to judicial office had been changed from the traditional '*ad vitam aut culpam*' (for life unless a fault was committed) to '*durante beneplacito*' (during the king's pleasure). Some judges had been removed from office for offending the king.[24] The crown had granted personal protections to debtors 'contrair to law'. The Claim mentioned more specific injustices, including attempts to make suspects incriminate themselves, and the use of torture in interrogation when there was no strong evidence against suspects or 'in ordinary crymes'. The Claim also identified two judgements in which the court of session interpreted treason too broadly. The imposing of bonds to keep the peace without parliamentary authority, the government's policy in 1674 and 1677, and the serving at the king's instance of lawburrows – a further surety of the peace invoked in 1678 – were also 'contrary to law'. These clauses were inspired primarily by the suppression of presbyterian dissent under Charles II.[25] The same was true of the Claim's objection to the fining of men for their wives' nonconformity, at dispute in the early 1680s and allowed by a statute of 1685.[26] The Grievances also complained of assize of error, the procedure by which members of a jury were tried for bringing an incorrect (or unwelcome) verdict. This referred to a case of 1681, which led to the conviction of seven jurors whose verdict had acquitted presbyterians accused of treason. There had been several prosecutions for assize of error in the sixteenth century, but the procedure's revival under Charles II caused misgivings.[27] Especially in their most specific articles, the Claim and Grievances exposed the perceived unfairness of the state's campaign against dissent, under both James and Charles. What went unmentioned was that James also recognised the difficulty of enforcing the penal laws and had abandoned them in the multiconfessional experiment.

Several of the alleged abuses of royal power highlighted by the convention had allowed the crown to increase its involvement in local communities, a fourth theme in the Claim and Grievances. This was especially the case with complaints relating to the standing army. The Claim protested against the crown's use of soldiers as judges, a strategy used in the suppression of dissent under Charles and James. The practice was obnoxious, the Claim remarked, not only because it had resulted in the summary execution of suspects, but also because it invaded the jurisdiction of heritable magistrates, the normal sources of justice in their districts. As we noted above, the Grievances referred to the 1681 act recognising the king's cumulative jurisdiction, which had provided legal backing to the crown's use of special judicial commissions. The Claim also declared that the 'sending of ane army in ane hostile manner' into part of the kingdom was unlawful. Here the convention referred to the so-called Highland Host, a force of highland recruits and other militiamen and soldiers sent to suppress nonconformity in the south-west in 1678. The garrisoning of private houses without their owners' consent was likewise branded illegal. Relating specifically to James's reign, the Claim condemned the king's policy of suspending elections in the royal burghs and nominating magistrates and councillors.

Most of the abuses of royal power had been carried out under Charles II, and both Restoration monarchs had interfered unlawfully in local communities. If the promotion of Catholicism was a feature of James's reign itself, the restoration of episcopacy had taken place in 1661–2. Thus the political and religious settlement envisaged by the Claim and Grievances was conceived in rejection of the constitutional realities of the Restoration period as a whole. First Charles and then James had given answers to the core questions concerning the government of Scotland. The settlement of 1689–90 offered alternative responses to the same problems. There were three main dimensions to the proposed settlement: religious uniformity; a reconfigured relationship between the crown, parliament and the privy council; and a revival of local autonomy. But before these emerged as the signature notes of the settlement, there was some pressure for a still more radical constitutional reform: greater union with England. This idea was included in neither the Claim nor the Articles, and it lacked widespread support in England. It nonetheless reflects one of the possibilities for political settlement that was seriously canvassed by some Scots in 1689.

* * *

For those who attributed at least some of Scotland's difficulties to its relationship with England, the crisis of 1688–9 seemed an ideal opportunity for negotiating a new partnership with the southern kingdom. Andrew Fletcher, the Haddingtonshire gentleman, participant in Monmouth's rising and recent Dutch exile, was one supporter of this agenda. 'For my owen part I thinck we can never come to any new setelment but by uniting with England in Parliaments, and Traid', he wrote in January 1689.[28] But if the prospect of economic amelioration was a good reason to redefine the Anglo-Scottish union, there was a similarly strong political case. Numerous contemporaries had observed the tendency of Charles II and James VII to use one kingdom to set an example for the other; this had been especially apparent in James's assertion of absolute power, first in Scotland, then in England.[29] The earl of Tweeddale had been a leading advocate of union when it was proposed in 1670, and he now claimed that the collapse of those negotiations had helped our 'comon enimys' in their endeavours 'to introduce popery by arbitrary gouernment'. Thus he argued that 'the flourishing & security of both kingdoms' depended on union.[30] In late December 1688, an address was signed by the noblemen, gentry and burgesses of Haddingtonshire (East Lothian), probably acting under Tweeddale's influence, in which a 'more strict and inseperable union' of Scotland and England was proposed. This, the address argued, would prevent the infringement of liberty in both kingdoms, as it would no longer be possible for monarchs to raise a standing army in one and deploy it in the other (see Figure 6.1).[31] Union also had its supporters among the Scottish noblemen and gentry in London in early 1689, and William seemed to favour the policy.[32]

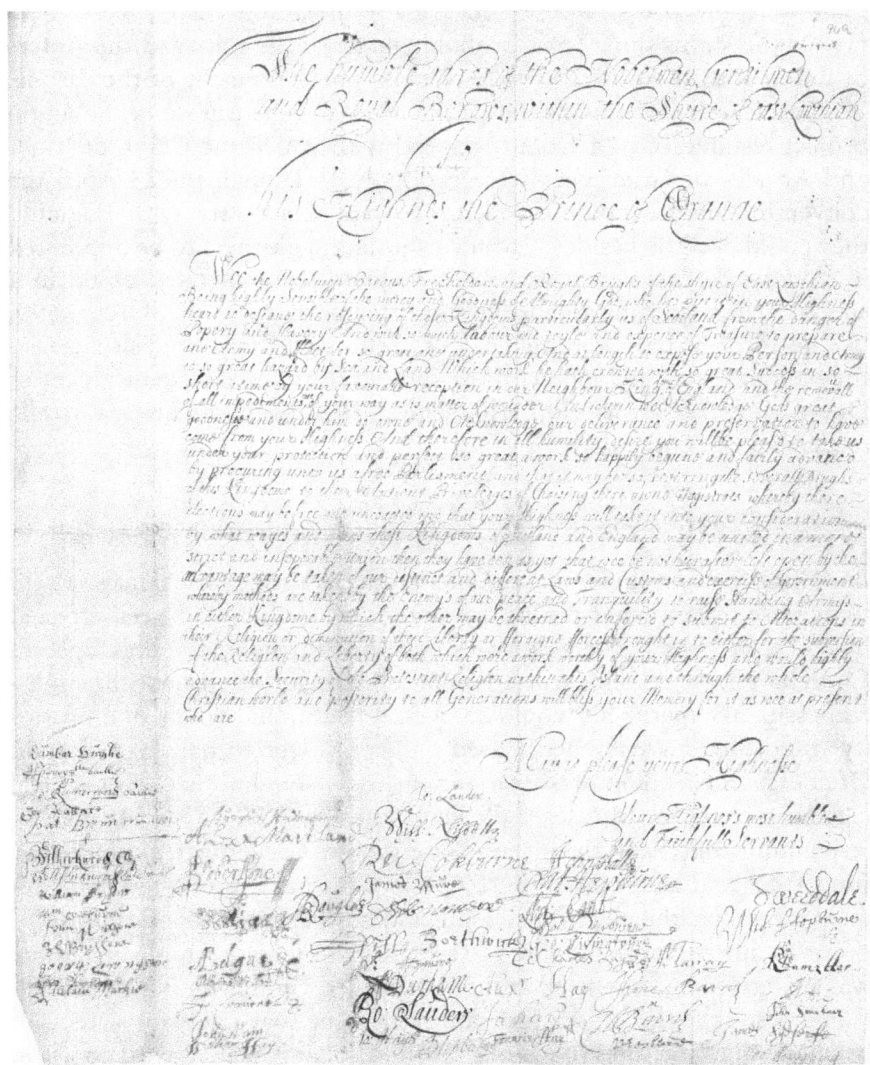

Figure 6.1 'The humble adres of the Nobelmen, Gentilmen and Royal Borows, within the Shyre of east Lowthian', NLS, MS. 7026, fo. 94ar. Reproduced by permission of the National Library of Scotland.

By the opening of the convention, then, union seemed to be high on the agenda. William's letter to the meeting explained the 'usefulnes' of greater union, and the estates' response expressed hope that the prince would encourage English support for such a scheme.[33] Tweeddale placed faith in the presence of so many elected commissioners, thinking that these members of the convention were more likely to support union than were the peers, whose concern for titles and rights made them favour the status quo.[34] But probably some of the outward supporters of union sought to use the issue to delay the settlement of the throne. William feared that this would be the case, and the eclipse of the union project resulted in part from the speed with which the Claim of Right and Articles of Grievances were produced.[35] Though on 23 April the convention named commissioners to prepare a treaty with England, they could do little besides wait for negotiating partners to be appointed in London.[36] This never happened: William recommended union in a speech at the opening of the Westminster parliament in March 1690, but no further steps were taken.[37] With no significant English interest, the plan never gained momentum. Only in the altered circumstances of Queen Anne's reign would parliamentary union become integral to the settlement of Scotland.[38]

* * *

By calling for a presbyterian settlement, the Claim and Grievances sought to achieve in law what during the winter of 1688–9 had been effected by force, at least in the south-west: the overthrow of the episcopalian Church. With Catholics scattered and episcopacy abolished, the multi-confessional experiment would be over. A traditional policy of uniformity could then be fashioned, based on a presbyterian national Church. Of course, the leading presbyterians earnestly sought this outcome. The general meeting's addresses to William in early 1689 hoped for presbyterian uniformity, and the meeting's petition to parliament, submitted in June 1689 and again in April 1690, claimed that a presbyterian settlement would be 'the mean of quieting and uniting the whole Countrey'.[39] But even among those prepared to see presbyterianism established, there was no agreement about what the refurbished Church should look like. William sought the most moderate settlement that could be achieved, believing that 'the rules of disiplen' should be 'adjusted, and all occasion of complaint for rigour' removed. Probably he also wanted to maintain some sort of royal supremacy and the right of lay patrons to present ministers to vacant parishes.[40] A crucial matter was the fate of the episcopalian clergy. Many of the ministers who remained loyal to James quickly fell foul of a proclamation of the convention, dated 13 April, requiring clergy to acknowledge and pray for William and Mary as monarchs. By November 1689, some 193 ministers had been deprived by the estates or privy council for failing to comply.[41] Nevertheless, a substantial body of episcopalian ministers professed themselves willing to accept the new monarchs. On 2 July, parliament received an address from the Williamite clergy in the synod of Aberdeen, which called for 'ane union with all our Protestant brethren who differ ... only in matters of church government'.[42] Several pamphlets published to coincide with the meeting of the convention promoted the same agenda.[43] A minority of presbyterians hoped that numerous episcopalian ministers could be integrated into the re-established Church, but the leading presbyterians were uncompromising in their distrust of the episcopalians.[44]

Further complicating matters, the future character of the Church was soon central to the struggle between the crown and the formidable parliamentary opposition that had come to be called the Club. Though supporters of the Club favoured a presbyterian Church, the group's leadership sought to delay the ecclesiastical settlement while it pushed for reforms to the powers of the crown.[45] When on 17 July Hamilton introduced an act settling the Church on the basis of the presbyterian system recognised by parliament in 1592, other members tabled rival proposals less likely to be acceptable to episcopalian clergy.[46] The prospects for a Church settlement able to comprehend presbyterians and episcopalians were receding. The abolition of episcopacy was secured on 22 July, but no act determining the government of the Church had been agreed by the time of parliament's adjournment on 2 August.[47]

When parliament met again in the spring of 1690, the royal commissioner, now George, earl of Melville, found himself obliged to accept most of the Club's demands. We shall shortly examine the consequences of this for the crown's relationship with parliament. As far as the Church settlement was concerned, the success of the Club ensured that, in addition to an act establishing presbyterianism as it was settled in 1592 and approving the Westminster confession of faith, parliament repealed the act of supremacy of 1669. It also abolished the right of lay patrons to present ministers to vacant churches, introducing instead a system that gave the nomination to parish elders and all owners of heritable property. Ministers who had been deposed for nonconformity to episcopacy since 1661 were restored to their former churches. Several provisions in this package of legislation made clear that episcopalian ministers would have little role in the re-established Church. The ministers rabbled before 13 April 1689 were deemed to have fled their churches, and the parish stipends for 1689 were given to presbyterians. The re-established Church was to be governed by the clergy ejected for presbyterian nonconformity, together with ministers and elders acceptable to them. These presbyterians were given warrant 'to try and purge out all insufficient, negligent, scandalous and erroneous ministers' who continued to possess churches.[48] This gave presbyterian church courts an excuse to deprive episcopalians of their parishes on grounds other than Jacobitism. Meanwhile, the reformed system of choosing ministers would prevent episcopalian patrons from frustrating the advance of presbyterian control over Scotland's many vacant churches.[49]

The legislation implied that the Church was to be a presbyterian, uniform and national institution. Reflecting this expectation, parliament refused to consider a proposal offered in early June 1690 for the toleration of episcopalian worship.[50] From the start, however, it seemed unlikely that religious uniformity would be achieved. When in July 1690 parliament repealed 'all acts enjoyneing civil paines upon sentences of excommunication', it presumably recognised that episcopalian nonconformity, and thus the excommunication of dissenters by the Church, would be widespread.[51] Many episcopalian ministers retained their parishes, especially in northern Scotland, where there were at first few presbyterians and patchy demand for their preaching. In the south, the supply of presbyterian ministers could not meet demand, and some parishes remained vacant for years after 1690. In some southern communities, as in the north, landowners frustrated the advance of presbyterian influence. In Newton (Dalkeith presbytery), where the episcopalian minister had been deprived in 1689, locals refused to cooperate with the presbytery and the parish remained vacant until 1696.[52] William Lindsay, episcopalian minister of Alva in the presbytery of Stirling, lost his legal right to the parish on the return of the presbyterian incumbent of 1661. But when the presbyterian moved elsewhere, Alva's landowners and householders 'called and Intreatted' Lindsay to serve the church. He did so until 1696, apparently without the approval of the presbyterian authorities, and was regarded by the establishment as an unlawful intruder.[53]

Two solutions were proposed to the existence of several hundred unreconciled episcopalian ministers and their congregations. The first, favoured by the crown, was a form of comprehension or accommodation. Under schemes introduced at the general assembly of 1692 and adopted by parliament in the following year, episcopalian clergy who had sworn allegiance to William and Mary and continued to hold churches would be integrated into the government of the re-established Church. In the short term, this policy failed, though by the end of the decade around sixty episcopalians had been received into the Church.[54] If the crown sought to assimilate episcopalians to the Church, the presbyterian courts pursued a second approach. This we might call a monoconfessional agenda: an aggressive, if only gradually successful, policy of ejecting their rivals and gaining control over churches. In response, parliament passed an act in 1695 protecting loyal episcopalian ministers who retained the parishes they held before the revolution, but not giving them a role in the Kirk's government. One hundred and sixteen ministers swore allegiance to qualify, becoming an anomalous group – part of the Church's parish structure, but not involved in its government in presbyteries, synods or general assemblies.[55] Unlike the presbyterians in 1687, however, the episcopalians who benefited from the act of 1695 had no authority to operate beyond their parishes or to organise congregations parallel to those of the established Church. Aside from the 116 protected ministers, there was no legal recognition of episcopalian worship. In 1703, Queen Anne instructed the privy council to protect episcopalians, including those who had set up meeting houses, from prosecution. Yet Anne lacked her father's suspending power, and her letter to the council was of questionable legal status. Lay dissenters escaped prosecution, but magistrates at both central and local levels continued periodically to cooperate with the presbyterians' agenda by suppressing episcopalian meeting houses, especially where the preachers refused to pray for William and Mary or Anne.[56]

The mistrust that prevented a fuller accommodation of episcopalians in the re-established Church was based on more than a struggle for churches and stipends. In the two decades after the revolution, the doctrinal distance between the two groups grew, as more episcopalians became convinced of the divine right of bishops and accepted a broadly Arminian theology. The groups' differences in piety and worship expanded, especially in the late 1700s, when a growing number of episcopalian congregations adopted the English Book of Common Prayer.[57] If the consolidation of a distinct episcopalian culture is one reason why large numbers of Scots did not accept the re-established Kirk, the close relationship between episcopalianism and Jacobite sympathy is another. The commitment of many episcopalian ministers to the cause of the exiled Stuarts helped to ensure that episcopalian dissent remained widely popular, especially in the north-east and the highlands. By drawing attention to the security threat posed by Jacobite episcopalians, on the other hand, presbyterians could lobby the government for action against their rivals. But before the setback of the Jacobite rising of 1715, the link between episcopalian dissent and Jacobitism benefited both.

* * *

A second feature of the revolution settlement of 1689–90 was the altered relationship between the crown, parliament and the privy council. This new configuration of central government had three aspects. The first was frequent parliaments. The Claim of Right asserted that, 'for redress of all greivances and for the amending, strenthneing and preserveing of the lawes, parliaments ought to be frequently called and allowed to sit'. Freedom of speech and debate in parliament should be 'secured'. As well as asserting parliament's legislative function, the Claim sought to guarantee its judicial role, declaring the right of subjects to protest in parliament 'for remeed of law' (that is, to appeal) against sentences of the court of session.[58] The Grievances called for a second change: the abolition of the Articles, the parliamentary committee that prepared legislation for consideration by the full parliament. Critics of the committee saw it as a tool of the crown, its membership under ministerial control and its function to force through unwanted acts. In 1686, of course, the Articles' support for a measure relieving Catholics from the penal laws was not reproduced in parliament, which stood firm against the proposal. Nevertheless, in 1689 the estates declared the committee a 'great greiveance to the nation'.[59] As well as pressing for a reduction of the crown's parliamentary influence through the abolition of the Articles, members of the convention made specific criticisms of William's initial choice of ministers. Thus a third aspect of the new relationship between crown and parliament was a greater resolution on the part of commissioners to hold the government to account. The three innovations were to influence the conduct of Scottish politics until the union.

Like its English counterpart, the Scottish parliament met frequently under William, Mary and Anne. After 1689, thirteen parliamentary sessions were held before the union. The longest interval between meetings was the thirty-one months from September 1690 to April 1693. By contrast, significantly bigger periods separated parliamentary sessions before the revolution. Six years elapsed between the sessions of 1663 and 1669, and there was a space of nearly seven years and ten months between the adjournment of parliament in December 1673 and the next session in September 1681, though a convention of estates met in 1678 to vote taxation. In the 1690s and 1700s, frequent parliaments were ensured as much by the government's need for grants of taxation as by sincere commitment on its part to constitutional reform. At first, Scottish taxpayers shouldered the burden of suppressing Jacobite unrest. From August 1689, the country was engaged in an expensive war with France. The two parliamentary sessions in 1690 agreed cess to cover a period of thirty-one months and an additional tax on hearths.[60] This allowed the crown to avoid holding a parliament in 1691 and 1692, but thereafter it sought further supply, including cess, additional grants of excise and poll taxes, in 1693, 1695 and 1696. None of the grants of cess extended to a period longer than eighteen months, helping to ensure that the crown continued to assemble parliament.[61] Of the thirteen sessions in the period 1690–1707, only those of May 1700 and 1703 failed to approve taxation. We shall return to the circumstances of these sessions in the Conclusion.

The abolition of the Articles threatened to make it much more difficult for the government to manage parliament and to achieve its fiscal and legislative objectives. In 1689, William and his ministers hoped that a compromise could be reached and that some committee resembling the Articles could be preserved.[62] This seemed plausible: the Grievances implied that the creation of committees to prepare legislation would be acceptable, as long as their members were 'freely chosen by the estates' and proposals for acts were first tabled in full parliament. On 17 June, Hamilton moved that the three estates should each elect members to sit as the Articles, and to prepare legislation 'in the usuall manner', albeit that acts not approved by the committee could also be tabled in parliament. The proposal was derailed by the Club, which adopted a radical position, going beyond that of the Grievances, against all standing committees.[63] On 25 June, parliament passed an act asserting its right to choose members of committees and to exclude officers of state from them. For the Club, Lord Ross argued that the Claim and Grievances had to be treated as fundamental laws, and that an act preserving the Articles could not be 'obtruded against the solemn determination of the States of the Kingdom'.[64] Hamilton withheld the royal assent from the act of 25 June, and on 9 July the court again tried to procure a compromise by proposing a larger standing committee.[65] But the question of the Articles remained unresolved when parliament was adjourned on 2 August. Rather than try again in the next session to reach a deal preserving a standing committee, on 8 May 1690 Melville accepted an act abolishing the Articles.[66]

Not only would the crown have to manage the estates without exercising influence through a committee of Articles, but the Club set a precedent for more vigorous parliamentary criticism of government ministers than had been possible before the revolution. In May 1689, William made appointments to his first Scottish privy council. In an attempt to secure support for the regime, the council's membership encompassed a large spectrum of the political elite, ranging from committed Williamites to men whose support for the revolution was manifestly lukewarm. Figures close to the king, notably Hamilton, questioned the wisdom of including peers who had opposed William's desires in the convention.[67] The appointment to the council of some key politicians from the previous reign, including Atholl, also provoked dismay. The leaders of the Club seized the opportunity to criticise the lord advocate, Sir John Dalrymple, who had allegedly suggested the membership of the council. Dalrymple's enemies hated him as a former opponent of the Restoration regime who had come to terms with James and served as his lord advocate. Moreover, Dalrymple had been one of the three commissioners who presented the estates' offer of the crown to William and Mary.[68] Some members of the convention insisted that the offer was conditional on William's promising to resolve the estates' grievances, and Dalrymple was accused of not making this clear to the prince.[69] Now it appeared that Dalrymple was making way for his widely despised former colleagues Queensberry and Viscount Tarbat to return to office. In the most extreme reading of events, William's regime threatened to be as arbitrary as its predecessor. The pamphleteer Robert Ferguson wrote that 'Whosoever Counsels His Majesty to employ those that were the Instruments of the former Tyranny, must intend to bring him under a Suspicion, both of approving that, and of designing the like'.[70] Responding to this concern, members of the Club brought forward an act incapacitating from office those who were to blame for the actions condemned in the Claim of Right. Though the act did not receive the royal assent, and William retained control over ministerial appointments, the development was symbolic of a new resolve on the part of opposition politicians.[71]

By the summer of 1689, then, it seemed that the revolution had created a new political context, in which parliamentarians were more assertive and the king's decisions were called into question. These circumstances, together with his position as a novice in Scottish politics, ensured that William's style of executive government contrasted starkly with that of James. Whereas James had employed a small secret committee within the privy council to direct his affairs, William set a quorum of nine for the council and did not reappoint a secret committee.[72] In a further effort to broaden his government, he entrusted several of the major offices of state to commissions.[73] At times, particularly in his relationship with the Church, William was almost as high-handed a ruler as James.[74] But the crown abandoned its former pretensions to absolutism, whatever the fears of Ferguson and the Club. In some ways, the crown became more powerful after 1689. Royal income grew and the outbreak of war required a larger standing army than ever before. Already in January 1691, the army (excluding garrisons and artillery) was expected to number 4,077, a 25 per cent increase on James's forces in 1685.[75] Even in 1701, amid vigorous criticism of the maintenance of a standing army in peacetime, parliament agreed to continue funding a force of 3,000 men.[76] Yet William, unlike James, could pose as the protector of European protestantism. Critics of the regime would soon argue that the Glencoe massacre of 1692 bore an ominous resemblance to the policies of the Restoration regime.[77] Even so, William's exercise of power was less aggressive, and more accountable, than that of his royal predecessor.

* * *

The third function of the settlement of 1689–90 was to restore a traditional balance between central and local power by reviving the autonomy of the royal burghs. As we noted in Chapter 4 and in the present chapter, both William of Orange's Scottish *Declaration of Reasons* and the Claim of Right condemned the interference of the crown in the burghs' elections. After the collapse of James's authority, we saw in Chapter 5, several burghs held new council elections, on the instruction of the privy council or at their own initiative. These elections ejected a few of James's most loyal nominees, but generally did not result in wholesale changes in local government. In the elections to the convention of estates, the influence of the nominated magistrates and councillors in the other royal burghs was diluted by the extension of the franchise to all burgesses. After the convention had begun, several burgh commissioners who might have proved faithful to James were removed by the committee for deciding controverted elections. Thereafter, the convention prioritised restoring the accountability of burgh councils to their communities, by ordering new elections in the towns. This was the first step towards reasserting the burghs' privileges. There was also a reaction against the local excises established under royal warrant, and criticism of the financial management of James's nominees. In 1690, the convention of royal burghs finally succeeded in its campaign to restore the towns' exclusive trading privileges, partially overturning the reform of 1672.

An early indication that members of the convention were concerned about the continuing authority of James's burgh magistrates came on 28 March 1689, when the provost, bailies and councillors of Edinburgh were ordered to swear an oath of fidelity to the estates. If they refused, it was threatened, the convention would 'proceed to name other magistrats and counsellors in their place'. It is unclear whether members of the council were removed from office after declining to swear, as one source suggests.[78] Nevertheless, the estates soon decided that a clean sweep of the council was required. On 5 April, the convention ordered a new council election in Edinburgh, in which all burgesses were to have a vote. This was justified with reference to the 'great invasiones ... upon the priviledges of the royall burrowes ... in the election of their magistrats, by recomendationes and nominationes made by the late king in ane arbitrary and despotick way'. James's interference had been 'contrair to the lawes and liberties of the kingdome', and thus the men presently holding sway over Edinburgh's citizens were 'not ther true magistrats and councill by them freely elected' (of course, this was less true of Edinburgh than of other towns). The election removed the magistrates and all but one of the councillors chosen in the previous October. The burgh's Williamite commissioners to the convention, Sir John Hall and George Stirling, became respectively provost and a trades councillor.[79]

The day after Edinburgh's election was concluded, the estates called for a new council election in Dundee, the burgh of which the viscount of Dundee, who had now withdrawn from the convention, was provost. This order followed a petition from some of Dundee's residents, who probably feared that the nominated council would entangle their town in the viscount's Jacobite resistance. The ensuing election removed from office those chosen by the crown in February 1688, but restored three of James's nominees of 1686.[80] The convention also ordered a new council election in Rothesay, perhaps because the burgh's commissioner was thought to be loyal to James.[81] Then on 18 April, the convention passed a measure for new elections by the poll of burgesses in the other royal burghs. Again the justification was that James's policy had encroached on the burghs' liberties, denying burgesses the right 'to elect and be elected'. Warrants for elections in thirty-four towns were soon issued, but by no means all burghs chose new councils before Michaelmas.[82]

The elections demonstrate that, in reacting against James's interference in their communities, urban Scots did not necessarily cast out of office those who had benefited from the king's policy. Certainly, there were towns in which James's appointees were swept from power. Ayr's election was a particularly striking reaction against the council nominated by James: only the dean of guild remained in post, and one former bailie became a councillor.[83] Most of the men now chosen had signed a letter to Montgomery of Skelmorlie on 31 December 1688, professing their support for the revolution and the desire of most in Ayr to see a presbyterian settlement.[84] In Peebles, only the nominated treasurer and one other councillor (who became a bailie) survived the election of 27 April.[85] But other towns saw less change. In Aberdeen, the provost and three of four bailies elected in November were returned to office, as were the treasurer and several councillors.[86] Inverkeithing's election gave the two men chosen as bailies by James seats on the council.[87] At Stranraer, one of James's bailies retained office; the other bailie now elected had been an appointed councillor. Here, as happened elsewhere, the nominated provost was succeeded by a man who had not recently sat on the council. But this probably did not represent the victory of an anti-Jacobite faction in the town, and instead was a mundane rotation of office-holders.[88] Many of the results are difficult to interpret. At Burntisland, the election by the burgesses in May, like the January election by the council discussed in Chapter 5, apparently circulated men between positions, and did not reduce the number of royal nominees who remained in office. In October, however, Alexander Gedd, one of James's chosen bailies, told the privy council that several of his erstwhile colleagues, who retained power, were not entitled to hold office, being mere sellers of ale and other tradesmen. The result of this complaint was yet another election, with careful scrutiny by the privy council of the winners' qualifications.[89] In Burntisland, the process of reasserting control by the urban elites was unusually convoluted. Elsewhere, local autonomy was in most cases regained without much upheaval. Just as James had done little to disturb the ruling oligarchies of many towns, so the elections by the burgesses in 1689 confirmed the authority of these elite groups.

A few elections exposed local divisions appearing to pit Williamites against Jacobites. After the election at Montrose on 2 May, the goldsmith David Auchterlonie went south to complain to the convention about the conduct of the poll. Auchterlonie asserted that ineligible men had been allowed to vote, with the effect that one group of candidates carried the election against the will of a majority of qualified burgesses. The elected magistrates responded by blaming Auchterlonie for the encroachments on the burgh's privileges under James, and by reporting that he had uttered 'severall expressions derogatory to' King William. Deciding in favour of the magistrates, the estates contrasted

Auchterlonie's disloyalty with the provost's 'diligence and forward zeall to the present government'.[90] In September 1689, the privy council received a complaint from Stirling, where most of James's former nominees had retained office in the election held in June. Hoping to be re-elected at Michaelmas, it was claimed, Provost Hugh Kennedy and his associates had required several of the burgh's deacons to 'promise not to vote for any Presbyterian', but instead to choose Kennedy's allies. These 'methods of arbitrary power', Kennedy's critics asserted, had been 'discharged as contirare to the Kings proclamatione'. After the election had taken place, and Kennedy's faction had triumphed, a further petition persuaded the privy council to declare the poll invalid.[91] Though this struggle was essentially a continuation of the political strife in Stirling of the Restoration period, the magistrates' Jacobite sympathies added a further complication, prolonging the central authorities' oversight of the burgh. Nevertheless, like the other burghs, Stirling was in the process of regaining its autonomy.

In line with this general trend, the crown granted the former ecclesiastical burghs fuller control over their own elections. In May 1689, William instructed the duke of Hamilton to pass through parliament an act asserting the royal burghs' electoral rights, and also to allow Glasgow and St Andrews to choose their own magistrates.[92] With the abolition of episcopacy, the control of these towns' councils by the archbishops would cease. In the case of Glasgow, the privy council investigated whether the duke of Lennox had a right to select the magistrates, and ordered that William should be offered a choice of candidates for provost. But the king waived this power, issuing a new charter to confirm the town's right to elect its magistrates and council.[93] The burgh of St Andrews seems to have assumed the same privilege with less complication; in Brechin, where one bailie continued to be chosen by the earl of Panmure, William also declined to assert any control.[94] Paisley, the one burgh of regality brought under the privy council's control in 1686, was also allowed a free election by the burgesses.[95] In each case, then, there was an unwinding of the central government's supervision of local centres of power. The privy council retained the right to intervene when burgh elections were disputed or maladministration was alleged, but this authority was not used for systematic interference in local government.[96] In 1691, during debates in the privy council over a disputed election in Edinburgh, one councillor remarked that because 'the late king was put from the throne for streaches to that thrid estate' – that is, for exaggerating his authority over the burghs – King William was all the less likely to invade urban rights.[97]

At the same time, townspeople reacted against some of the policies and practices of James's chosen urban governors. The revolution triggered a backlash against the local excise taxes levied under royal warrant that, as we saw in Chapter 4, had proliferated under James VII. Residents proved reluctant to pay these taxes, provoking local disputes and prompting the Claim of Right's condemnation of taxes granted without parliamentary approval. By May 1689, there seems to have been a general boycott of Burntisland's excise, perhaps connived at by the maltmen and ale-sellers alleged to be on the council.[98] In Montrose, the brewers petitioned against the duty on malt, and the town council agreed to halve the sum payable on each boll.[99] There were petitions to parliament or the privy council against the local excises of Dundee and Linlithgow.[100] In May 1690, an address from the magistrates, council and community of Irvine called for parliament to declare the burgh's tax on ale void, as an imposition ruled illegal by the Claim of Right. The address drew attention to another controversial habit of the magistrates named by James, complaining that Irvine's governors had contracted large debts to procure the right to levy the excise. The petitioners argued that the burgh should be free of the debts contracted by James's nominees.[101] Unsurprisingly, this did not satisfy the town's creditors, who continued to pursue the magistrates for repayment.[102] In 1695, parliament granted Irvine the right to levy a new excise on malt, to fund repairs to the harbour and bridge, and to pay off the debts incurred during James's reign.[103] As this case suggests, burgh councils would in future seek to charge local imposts, despite the controversy they caused in 1689–90. But because of the Claim of Right, towns now applied to parliament for permission, and it appears that the estates gave fuller consideration to the arguments against these taxes than James VII's courtiers had.[104] Presumably, less money now changed hands to secure the privilege of local taxation.

From an economic point of view, the crucial demand of the burghs in 1689–90 was for the restoration of their exclusive trading privileges. As we saw in Chapter 4, this had been sought by the convention of royal burghs since 1672, when parliament extended the right to trade overseas to unfree burghs. On 24 April 1689, the convention voted to add to the Grievances the demand that 'the greivances of the burrowes be considered and redressed in the first parliament'. This was unspecific, but referred especially to trading privileges rather than to James's electoral manipulation, which was highlighted in the Claim.[105] By mid-July, the convention of royal burghs had drafted an act asserting the burghs' monopoly of all imports, and of exports apart from corn, cattle, coal, salt, lime and stone. The convention compiled a list of twenty-five further grievances and suggestions for reform, to be pursued in parliament. Among other things, these called for greater scrutiny of magistrates' financial management, for the monopoly of the manufacture of playing cards held by James's Catholic printer Peter Bruce to be declared invalid, and for the other burghs to concur in a petition of the Edinburgh merchants against the policy of restricting imports introduced in 1681.[106] But as the convention made clear in an address to William in August, repealing the law of 1672 – which the convention blamed on the 'creiping in' of 'arbitrary government' – was the top priority.[107] When parliament granted this demand, in June 1690, the convention's draft act was amended to add horses, sheep, metals and minerals to the list of exemptions from the monopoly of exports, and to allow Scots resident outwith the royal burghs to import livestock.[108] Though the act of 1690 was a symbolic victory for the royal burghs, the unfree towns continued to evade the restrictions on their involvement in foreign trade. In response, the royal burghs conceded that their competitors could take part, but tried to ensure that, in exchange, the other towns would shoulder some of the burgess estate's tax burden. In the long term, however, the economic privileges of the royal burghs seemed increasingly antiquated.[109]

* * *

The Williamite victory in the convention of estates triggered a civil war. For the first time in Scotland, there was an armed confrontation between supporters of the revolution and individuals remaining loyal to James. Two of the main reasons why no conflict occurred prior to the summer of 1689 were the removal of James's Scottish army to England in September 1688 and the disbanding of most of the militia in December. The standing army, had it remained in Scotland, might well have resisted the new regime. In March 1689, a large portion of the earl of Dumbarton's regiment, then at Ipswich, refused William's commands, declared for James and set out with their cannon to march north. The mutineers were forced to surrender within a few days, but they had by this point travelled about a hundred miles towards Scotland.[110] Though suppressed without violence, the mutiny was a harbinger of subsequent events in Scotland.

At the opening of the convention, the clearest indication that William would not gain military mastery of Scotland without opposition was the continuing occupation of Edinburgh Castle by the Catholic duke of

Gordon. After James's flight to France, Gordon had been ready to surrender the garrison, but Balcarres and Dundee persuaded him to hold out.[111] During its first nine days, the convention conducted two sets of negotiations with Gordon for his departure; no agreement could be reached and a siege of the castle began.[112] Gordon was again encouraged by Dundee: on his departure from Edinburgh to take up arms for King James, the viscount spoke to Gordon, apparently promising to relieve the castle within twenty days. This assistance was not forthcoming, and Gordon's resolve, probably always limited, ebbed away, as did his support in the garrison. Gordon renewed talks on 11 June, and the soldiers left the castle three days later.[113] While Edinburgh was the last major castle to fall into Williamite hands, Charles Maitland, lieutenant governor of the small garrison on the Bass Rock in the Firth of Forth, refused to surrender until 15 August.[114] A few soldiers died during the siege of Edinburgh Castle, nearby houses were damaged and the Nor' Loch was partially drained.[115] North Berwick delayed its new council election until the return of Maitland, a nominated bailie of the burgh.[116] But neither garrison's resistance did much to obstruct the formulation of a settlement in 1689–90.

A more serious obstacle to the settling of Scottish politics was the Jacobite rising led by Dundee. After he abandoned Edinburgh and parliamentary politics on 18 March, Dundee journeyed extensively in Perthshire, Angus, the north-east and western highlands, gaining supporters and generating concern among politicians further south. The convention responded by making its own preparations for war, in effect levying a new Scottish army to replace the forces that had marched south in September 1688.[117] In an audacious and widely reported raid on Perth in May, Dundee captured the Williamite soldiers William Blair of Blair, whom the estates had recently commissioned to command a troop of horse, and Sir John Maxwell of Pollok.[118] In early July, there was a brief panic in Edinburgh, after Hamilton received information of a Jacobite conspiracy. Its leaders allegedly planned to assassinate the royal commissioner and other members of parliament, before joining Dundee.[119] In reality, perhaps only the defeat by the Irish Jacobites of their protestant opponents in Derry and Enniskillen, allowing forces to be transferred to Scotland, would have given Dundee the initiative in the south. In the absence of Jacobite victory in Ulster, the decisive Scottish battles of 1689 were fought in highland Perthshire, not least because Patrick Steuart of Ballechin, the marquis of Atholl's bailie, held the strategically important Blair Castle for Dundee.[120] On 27 July, the Jacobites gained victory over their enemies at Killiecrankie, but saw their commander die on the field. Dundee was replaced by Alexander Cannon, who led the Jacobites to defeat at Dunkeld on 21 August 1689. There was renewed campaigning in 1690, culminating in a second defeat at Cromdale on 1 May 1690. Meanwhile, the course of the war in Ireland made it increasingly unlikely that the efforts of the highland Jacobites, though many remained willing to fight, would contribute to the restoration of their king.[121]

Dundee's campaign compromised Williamite control of Scotland north of the Tay, at least until the battle of Dunkeld. Nevertheless, while Dundee gained considerable backing, especially from clan chiefs in Lochaber and the isles, he lacked the support of the greater magnates of northern Scotland. He made Steuart of Ballechin colonel of 'all men of Atholl, Vassalls, Tennants, neighbours, who have been in use to serve under the Marquess of Atholl'. This was an admission of weakness, since Atholl himself avoided all involvement by going to Bath for his health, while his eldest son, Lord John Murray, discouraged his father's tenants from joining the rising.[122] Viscount Tarbat claimed credit for persuading many of the Mackenzies to stay at home, though their chief, the Catholic earl of Seaforth, showed his loyalty by accompanying King James. Most of Dundee's Lochaber and Kintyre followers were vassals or tenants of the forfeited ninth earl of Argyll, Tarbat argued, and they fought to oppose the likely restoration of the earldom.[123] Dundee himself complained that most of the nobility had defected to William, were under arrest, or remained quietly in their houses.[124] If Dundee had 2,000 men under his command at Killiecrankie, this was a far smaller number than he and his supporters had anticipated.[125] Though some reinforcements were sent from the Jacobite forces in Ireland, they did not fulfil Dundee's repeated promises that such assistance would transform the situation in Scotland.[126]

The effects of the war in local communities were considerable. People living in the path of one or both armies risked having their money, livestock or horses seized, and their crops consumed or spoilt. Farmers around Forfar, through which the Williamite army passed before and immediately after the battle of Dunkeld, reckoned that they had lost £972 worth of corns, 'Cutt, eattin and distroyed, Be ther majesties forces'.[127] Urban dwellers worried about having to accommodate potentially unruly soldiers. When the magistrates of Elgin received a letter from Dundee ordering them to quarter 900 or 1,000 highlanders, they sent it on to General Hugh Mackay, the Williamite commander, predicting (correctly) that he could prevent the Jacobites from coming to the town.[128] In September, Perth's burgh council dispatched a bailie and the town clerk to Edinburgh to lobby Mackay and the privy council, in the hope that 'als small ane number of the forces as possable' would be quartered in Perth.[129] Communities further south were also inconvenienced. Cupar's magistrates resolved to address the estates about the vast expense of quartering soldiers.[130] Haddington's council heard that the 'poore of this burgh suffered much damadge' when two regiments passed through bound for Edinburgh.[131] In September, Dumfries quartered at least 600 English troops, some of whom refused to 'give present money for [th]air intertainment'. Their colonel allegedly assaulted the provost.[132]

Burghs and shires were also required to raise militiamen and supply horses for the Williamite campaign. On 30 March 1689, the convention issued a proclamation calling out the militia across the country to the south of the Tay. Further orders initiated levies of horsemen and made arrangements for specific counties.[133] Some burgh councils complained of the cost of contributing men.[134] Others registered concerns about the burden of supplying baggage horses for Mackay's army, especially after the major push in the summer of 1689.[135] And while in many burghs, especially in the south, the nightly guard was reorganised in response to panics in December or January, others were threatened by continuing instability later in 1689. In August, Cullen's council ordered that the town's guard be kept 'exactly and nightlie'.[136] Inverness bore the costs of fire and candle for its garrison, and felt vulnerable to raids from its highland neighbours. In December, appointing a rendezvous of men aged sixteen to sixty, the council lamented the 'fear and danger the town is exsposed to by the frequent threatnings of the hielanders Incursiones upon them who are convocated in ane armie of great numbers in a warlyk posture'.[137] The civil war over William's accession continued to destabilise some Scottish communities for months after the possession of the throne had been decided in Edinburgh.

In hindsight, the highland war was not much of a threat to the Williamite regime. Most magnates failed to give Dundee their support, and his army was correspondingly small. His death was a major blow to the campaign. Moreover, the timing of Dundee's action ensured that only a victory far more decisive than that at Killiecrankie could have reversed the outcome of the revolution. The conflict, like the upheavals of the winter of 1688–9, illustrates the diversity of Scottish experiences of revolution, and shows that many developments were experienced not in the capital, but in other localities the length and breadth of Scotland. Furthermore, Dundee's campaign helps us to recognise an essential characteristic of the revolution. William lacked full military control of Scotland in 1689, but this did not prevent him from assuming a position of political pre-eminence. Civil war broke out after the transition of power and was not integral to the overthrow of the former regime. The revolution settlement was far from complete at the time of the main battles of the summer of 1689. And yet it was parliamentary opposition, not military conflict, that delayed the settling of Scotland.

Conclusion: Revolutions, Settlements and Scotland's Political Development

THE REVOLUTION SETTLEMENT OF 1689–90 repudiated many of the principles and policies of royal government in the Restoration period. But while their responses were different, James VII and the makers of the settlement sought solutions to the same fundamental problems. By studying the upheavals of the 1685–90 period, we have focused on two sets of challenges confronting the rulers of seventeenth-century Scotland. The first concerned the character of the established Church. How was it to be constituted and what was the appropriate role for the monarch in its government? How should the civil magistrate deal with religious dissent? A second cluster of problems involved the crown's power and authority. Was the king 'absolute' and what did this mean in practice? To what extent was local government in Scotland autonomous, and how far was it amenable to central direction?

These questions had been answered in various ways by seventeenth-century Scotland's earlier 'settlements'. The Covenanting revolution of 1638–41 addressed the country's religious disagreements by imposing a rigorous presbyterianism, founded on a national oath in defence of protestant principles. The Covenanters reduced the crown's power over parliament and conciliar institutions within Scotland, while setting out to exercise greater central control in the localities.[1] The Restoration settlement of 1661–2 re-established episcopacy, but endorsed the Covenanters' belief that the Kirk should be a uniform institution comprehending all Scots. The settlement gave rise to the problems of nonconformity that King James, in his most experimental policy, attempted to resolve. Moreover, we saw in Chapter 1 that the royalist statutes and rhetoric of the Restoration enabled the king's absolutist approach.

James, at least in theoretical terms, was an absolute king of Scotland. But in his northern kingdom, he was not the systematic moderniser of the state's civil and military capacity depicted by Steve Pincus.[2] Instead, he was a radical experimentalist, who lacked the foresight – and adequate advice from his councillors – to anticipate the effects of his policies. By granting toleration, James broke with the traditional assumptions on which the settlements of 1638–41 and 1661–2 were based. Yet his religious policy compromised the established Church in the performance of its social functions. By asserting his dispensing and suspending powers and interfering in the burghs, James made greater demands on his subjects' obedience than his predecessors had done. If the Scots' opposition became clear in 1689, there was at first a general acquiescence in his commands. James did not need to stimulate the sort of popular campaign in support of toleration reconstructed in Scott Sowerby's study of England.[3] Partly, this was because printed debate was less crucial in the northern kingdom, though James made a large investment in his Catholic printing press. More fundamentally, the widespread compliance with James's will reflected the lack of serious challenge to his absolutist rhetoric before late 1688.

Until it became clear that he had lost control of England, James enjoyed the loyalty of national and local elites in Scotland. This loyalty did not translate into very significant support for his continuing claim to the throne in 1689, either in the convention of estates, or in the country at large. Jacobitism was a greater threat to governments in the eighteenth century than it was to William of Orange's accession. Of course, the revolution settlement itself gave some Scots reasons to prefer the exiled Stuarts. The settlement arrived at solutions to Scotland's problems quite distinct from those proposed by James. As we saw in Chapter 6, parliament sought to revive religious uniformity on a presbyterian foundation. The settlement also aimed to limit the king's powers while increasing the significance of parliament and political opposition, and to restore the traditional freedoms and privileges of the royal burghs.

This concluding chapter argues that, while the revolution settlement was meant to tackle the problems of governing Scotland, it was not until the 'union settlement' of 1707–12 that lasting solutions were put in place. The settlement of 1689–90, we saw in Chapter 6, was itself a source of political instability. On the one hand, the restoration of autonomous urban government proved to be an enduring reform. Even if the economy of many royal burghs remained fragile, the towns' grievances had been substantially addressed. But by recalibrating the balance between crown and parliament, the revolution settlement gave rise to a style of politics in which the government's agenda was often frustrated by organised opposition. It is conventionally – and convincingly –

argued that the executive's repeated failure to command a majority in parliament persuaded Queen Anne's Scottish and English ministers to embrace the most radical option suggested at the revolution: Anglo-Scottish parliamentary union.

Two particularly fraught parliamentary sessions illustrate the difficulties the crown faced in managing Scottish politics after the revolution. The first took place in May 1700, a time of widespread popular anger at the failure of the short-lived Scottish colony at Darien on the isthmus of Panama. Inflamed by the reluctance of English officials to assist the settlers, as well as by more general economic decline, concerns about the Church and the crown's desire to maintain a standing army in peacetime, there was significant backing for the critics of the government. On 24 May, in a reprise of the tactics of the Club, the opposition forced through a motion demanding that parliament prioritise the discussion of Darien and acts to secure presbyterianism. Parliament soon became a platform for hard-line presbyterians and supporters of the Scottish colony, and it looked unlikely that the king's request for supply would be heeded. In response, the royal commissioner adjourned parliament without securing new taxation, and before any other acts could be passed.[4] Though the government's strategy was more successful in the next session, when parliament agreed to a grant of twelve months' cess, King William revived his former support for union.[5]

In the turbulent session of 1703 – crucial to the standard narrative of the making of the union – the opposition steered a still more provocative course. Its greatest achievement was the act of security, a measure providing for the continuation of government after Queen Anne's death. Insisting that the next monarch swear the coronation oath and agree to govern 'in the terms' of the Claim of Right, the act aggressively reasserted the principles of the revolution.[6] Furthermore, the act made it seem likely that Scotland would not follow England's decision of 1701 to settle the succession to the throne on the house of Hanover.[7] This raised the possibility of a future Jacobite restoration and Anglo-Scottish war. The crown refused to sanction the act in 1703, but gave reluctant assent in the following year in order to secure a grant of taxation. Most importantly, the act shocked English politicians into pressing for a fuller union between the kingdoms. In September 1705, the Scottish parliament agreed to begin negotiations.[8] The parliamentary opposition in May 1700 and 1703, by adopting the attitudes and practices of the Club, showed the potential for political stalemate in post-revolution Scotland. A new problem of government had arisen, and it could not, unlike in 1686–7, be overcome by the use of the royal prerogative. The abolition of the Scottish parliament, the chief arena of political dissent under William and Anne, seemed to be the solution.

The union settlement consisted of the Anglo-Scottish parliamentary union finalised in 1707 and a body of statutes following from it, the most significant of which abolished the separate Scottish privy council (1708) and granted toleration for episcopalian worship (1712).[9] By uniting England and Scotland into the new kingdom of Great Britain and securing the Hanoverian succession to the throne, the union solved the political crisis that had erupted in 1703. Offering Scots free trade with England and participation in the imperial economy, union also addressed the economic difficulties voiced in Scotland in the 1680s and, with greater urgency, since the collapse of the Darien scheme. More fundamentally, the union settlement had a transformative impact on the problems of Scottish government identified at the start of this chapter. The first elements of the union settlement affected royal power, the distribution of authority among central institutions, and the balance between central and local government. In 1712, furthermore, it became apparent that the settlement was also a milestone in Scottish religious life.

The union settlement changed the relationships between the crown and political opposition, and between the centre and the localities. Most obviously, union replaced a vigorous and sometimes obstructive parliament in Edinburgh with a small Scottish representation in the Westminster parliament, which remained preoccupied with English and international affairs. In a separate development in 1708, parliament phased out the Scottish privy council, and Scots were added to a single British council. Though presented as a measure to make the union 'more intire and compleat', the reform had not been intended by the leading promoters of union among the court party. Rather, it was the product of pressure from the Squadrone Volante, a smaller unionist party that hoped to gain from the council's abolition.[10] The result of the change was to centralise executive responsibility for Scotland around the monarch, and the removal of the privy council left a large administrative and judicial void. Royal government was further away from the people and from Scottish institutions, and there were fewer ministers of state with the time and expertise to address Scottish concerns. At first, more work fell to the lord advocate. In 1711, the government tried to compensate for the council's loss with a commission reviving the traditional powers of the lord chamberlain. This abortive experiment was followed in 1714 by a more enduring but largely ineffectual commission of police.[11] In the longer term, however, Scotland became subject to 'management'. This style of politics sought stability through the use of patronage: administration relied on networks of patrons and clients made possible by the increasing number of civil and military offices in the British state and the crown's growing influence in the Church and universities. In some ways as informal as seventeenth-century government, the system was overseen by a series of unofficial viceroys, from Archibald Campbell, earl of Ilay in the 1720s and 1730s to Henry Dundas at the century's end.[12]

As this suggests, the union settlement had considerable implications for the government of Scotland's communities. In its respect for the functions of local magistrates, the treaty of union echoed the revolution settlement. By articles twenty and twenty-one, the union preserved unchanged all heritable jurisdictions and the rights of the royal burghs.[13] The abolition of the privy council might well have had the effect of increasing the workload and influence of local magistrates. On the other hand, the legislation of 1708 gave greater powers to JPs, who were crown appointees. The act also appointed twice-yearly circuits of the court of justiciary.[14] Further research would be required to judge whether these changes gave central government more influence in Scottish communities. It is significant, however, that there was in the early eighteenth century no radical attempt to rebalance central and local government. It was not until the abolition of heritable jurisdictions in 1747 that a reform as sweeping as James VII's intervention in the royal burghs was implemented.[15] By this time, Scottish localities – especially the royal burghs – had become entangled in more subtle webs of control than those spun by James. Whatever their formal autonomy, local magistrates were subject to the new politics of management, receiving both directions and favours from the country's leading men.[16]

The union settlement transformed the regulation of religious diversity. Many ministers and lay presbyterians worried that by subjecting the Church of Scotland to a largely Anglican British parliament, the union would put the presbyterianism re-established in 1690 at risk. To allay these fears, parliament passed with the union an act promising that presbyterian government would 'remain and continue unalterable' after 1707, and would 'be the only government of the church within the kingdom of Scotland'.[17] In spite of this measure, the new institutional frameworks, and the sympathy of many English politicians for the Scottish episcopalian cause, made it likely that the union would bring the episcopalians some relief from the occasional disruption they had experienced since 1690. In 1711, the episcopalian minister James Greenshields, who had been imprisoned in Edinburgh for worshipping using the English Prayer Book, realised this potential. The court of session upheld the legality of Greenshields's incarceration by the magistrates of Edinburgh, but Greenshields took advantage of the newly established right to appeal against the session's decisions to the House of Lords. By winning his appeal there, Greenshields built an overwhelming case for a toleration bill.[18] The resulting legislation, passed in 1712, protected episcopalian services conducted by ministers who abjured the Stuart pretender and swore allegiance to, and prayed for, Queen Anne. As well as allowing episcopalian ministers to conduct worship and solemnise marriages and baptisms, the toleration act exempted the episcopalian laity from the discipline of the established Church. We saw in Chapter 3 that during James's multiconfessional experiment, some episcopalian courts had called on the civil authorities to help them exercise discipline. The act of 1712 explicitly forbade magistrates from providing such assistance.[19]

The toleration act formally recognised the existence of religious pluralism in Scotland. No longer were magistrates entitled to uphold a monopolistic established Church and nor could presbyterian courts expect compliance from all members of the community. It was now clear that, while presbyterianism would remain the government of the established Church, the uniformity assumed by the Church settlement of 1690 was an idea of the past. But while episcopalian dissent grew in scale as well as confidence under Anne, the Jacobite beliefs of most ministers would later prompt renewed restrictions on their worship, especially after the risings of 1715 and 1745. The result was that the episcopalian population shrank over the century.[20] The chief beneficiaries of the new approach to religious diversity adopted in 1712 were in fact the presbyterian dissenters who, from the 1730s onwards, began to abandon the established Church in large numbers.[21]

Unlike the settlement of 1689–90, the various reforms of 1707–12 were not at the time conceived as a package. Nevertheless, we can now see that the union settlement provided a more durable and decisive set of responses to Scotland's problems than emerged at the revolution. If Scotland was 'in revolution' from 1685 to 1690, it was not quite 'settled' during William's reign, nor for much of Anne's. After 1712, however, the country faced neither the sort of experimental rule practised by James, nor the governmental instability and religious uncertainty characteristic of the 1690s and 1700s. Rather, Scottish politics and society were subject to gradual change, with the rise of management and the fragmentation of presbyterianism. Aside from the abolition of the heritable jurisdictions, there was no major constitutional reform before the nineteenth century. Given the Jacobite risings and the patterns of protest evident after 1712, it would be misleading to say that Scotland was tranquil in the wake of the union.[22] But it became clear that religious uniformity, royal absolutism and even political revolution had been consigned to the past. They would play no further role in Scotland's political development.

Notes on the Sources

CHURCH RECORDS

The analysis in Chapters 2 and 3 is based on the following sources:

1. All surviving records of the presbyteries and synods established by presbyterians from 1687 to 1690. These are listed in the bibliography.
2. All surviving records of episcopalian presbyteries, and selected synod records, covering any part of the period 1687–90. These are listed in the bibliography.
3. Presbyterian kirk session registers from the period 1687–90, of which not many survive. To these I added a selection of presbyterian kirk session registers beginning after 1690. The registers cited in the book are listed in the bibliography.
4. A small sample of Old Parish Registers (recording births, marriages and deaths). Records were chosen on the basis of information derived from other sources. The registers cited in the book are listed in the bibliography.
5. A large sample of episcopalian kirk session registers from the period 1687–90. Because I examined these records to explore the effects of multiconfessionalism, I focused on the parishes of southern and central Scotland. I consulted all the available kirk session minutes of parishes in the synods of Lothian and Tweeddale (58 parishes), the Merse and Teviotdale (18), Dumfries (1), Galloway (0) and, with the exception of one parish,[1] Glasgow and Ayr (27). I also consulted all surviving kirk session minutes for the presbytery of Kirkcaldy (9), and sampled less systematically from presbyteries elsewhere in Fife, Kinross-shire, Stirlingshire and Perthshire.

Only the kirk session registers cited in the book are listed in the bibliography.

ROYAL BURGHS

I endeavoured to consult all the council minutes surviving from James VII's reign. As with other scholars of this material, I began with the printed editions published in the nineteenth and twentieth centuries. Except in the cases of Rothesay and Lochmaben, where full transcriptions of the minutes have been published, I also read the manuscript minutes. When a printed edition offers an accurate and reliable transcription, I have usually cited it in preference to the manuscript, to make it easier for readers to judge the context of the evidence I discuss. Some printed editions of burgh minutes are too erroneous[2] or selective to be of much use. On the other hand, in at least two cases nineteenth-century printed works offer the only evidence of council minutes that now appear to be lost.[3] Often, I supplemented the council minutes with other burgh records, including court books, records of incorporations and miscellaneous papers. Only the manuscripts cited in the book are listed in the bibliography. Of the royal burghs not mentioned in the book, I read records relating to three.[4] These sources were unrevealing for my purposes. At least seventeen royal burghs have no minutes, or no records at all, for this period.

Notes

INTRODUCTION: SCOTLAND IN REVOLUTION, 1685–1690

1. Among numerous accounts of events in England, see esp. Jones, *Revolution of 1688*, chs 10–11; Beddard, 'The unexpected whig revolution of 1688'; Harris, *Revolution*, ch. 7; Gibson, *James II and the Trial of the Seven Bishops*.
2. Balcarres, *Memoirs*, pp. 18–19; NLS, Earl of Tweeddale to Lord Yester, 11 Dec. 1688, MS. 7026, fo. 81r.; Same to same, 15 Dec. 1688, MS. 7026, fo. 84r.; Same to same, 18 Dec. 1688, MS. 7026, fo. 87r.
3. NRS, Secretary's warrant book, SP4/13, pp. 243–4, 284–5; *Proclamation, taking off the Stop of Execution against Heretors*.
4. NRS, Treasury register, 13 Sep. 1688–4 Aug. 1690, E7/5, pp. 69–71, 77–8 [pages numbered from back of book]. No meetings of the treasury are recorded between 7 Jan. and 21 March 1689. The privy council register was not written up for most of James's reign. *Proclamation, for Payment of His Majesties Cess and Excise*; *Act, for Inbringing of His Majesties Excise and Supply*; NLS, Earl of Tweeddale to Lord Yester, 31 Jan. 1689, MS. 7026, fo. 119r.; Same to same, 2 Feb. 1689, MS. 7026, fo. 122.
5. Harris, *Revolution*, p. 313.
6. *Collection of Papers relating to the Calling and Holding the Convention of Estates of England*, pp. 13–17. Signatories to the address to William are listed in NRS, Transcripts of proceedings of the convention of estates and parliament and other state papers, 1667–1693, RH13/20, second pagination series, pp. 85–6.
7. NLS, Tweeddale to Yester, 2 Feb. 1689, MS. 7026, fo. 122r.
8. NLS, Lord David Hay to earl of Tweeddale, ?16 Jan. 1689, MS. 7011, fo. 160r.
9. SCA, Placid Fleming to Lewis Innes, 25 Jan. 1689, BL/1/121/7; see also Placid Fleming to William Leslie, 9 May 1689, BL/1/121/9.
10. Balcarres, *Memoirs*, p. 2.

11. NLS, Sir Patrick Murray to the earl of Tweeddale, 6 Nov. 1689, MS. 7011, fo. 245r.
12. *Munimenta Alme Universitatis Glasguensis*, III, p. 591.
13. For the claim that the cyclical sense of revolution predominated in the seventeenth century, see esp. Snow, 'The concept of revolution'; Cohen, 'The eighteenth-century origins of the concept of scientific revolution', pp. 264–5; Koselleck, 'Historical criteria of the modern concept of revolution', pp. 41–4; Niggemann, 'Some remarks on the origins of the term "Glorious Revolution"'. For evidence that a more modern sense of revolutionary change was emerging, see Hill, 'The word "revolution"'; Rachum, 'The meaning of "revolution"'; Harris, 'Did the English have a script for revolution?'.
14. For a recent attempt to define revolution with reference to mid seventeenth-century Scotland, see Goodare, 'The Scottish revolution'.
15. Baker, 'Revolution 1.0'; Baker and Edelstein (eds), *Scripting Revolution*.
16. Goldstone, *Revolution and Rebellion in the Early Modern World*, esp. p. xxiii.
17. Huntington, *Political Order in Changing Societies*, pp. 270–1.
18. Moore, *Social Origins of Dictatorship and Democracy*; Huntington, *Political Order in Changing Societies*, ch. 5; Skocpol, *States and Social Revolutions*; Goodwin and Rojas, 'Revolutions and regime change'.
19. Pincus, *1688*. The argument in Davidson, *Discovering the Scottish Revolution*, places little emphasis on 1688–9; cf. Goodare, 'The Scottish revolution', pp. 92–3.
20. Tilly, *European Revolutions*, ch. 1; Tilly, *From Mobilization to Revolution*, pp. 190–4. See also Hobsbawm, 'Revolution', pp. 19–20.
21. Cowan, 'The reluctant revolutionaries'. See also Cowan, 'Church and state reformed?'.
22. Lenman, 'The Scottish nobility and the revolution'.
23. Harris, 'The people, the law, and the constitution'; Harris, 'Reluctant revolutionaries?'; Harris, *Revolution*, ch. 9.
24. Gardner, *Scottish Exile Community*, pp. 178–96; Jackson, *Restoration Scotland*, ch. 8; Jackson, 'Revolution principles, *ius naturae* and *ius gentium* in early-enlightenment Scotland'. Recent interpretations of political thought in and after the Scottish revolution have reacted against Lenman, 'The poverty of political theory'.
25. For recent guides to these events, see Goodare, 'The rise of the Covenanters'; Cust, 'The collapse of royal power'; Harris, *Rebellion*.
26. Dickinson and Donaldson (eds), *Source Book of Scottish History: Volume Three*, pp. 199–200. Criticising this perspective is Glassey, 'The revolution of 1688'.
27. Balcarres, *Memoirs*, pp. 12–13; SCA, David Burnet to Charles Whytford, 1 Nov. 1688, BL/1/109/22; Alexander Dunbar to Lewis Innes, 30 Oct. and 1 Nov. 1688, BL/1/111/8; NLS, Sir Patrick Murray to the earl of Tweeddale, 1 Nov. 1688, MS. 7011, fo. 136r.; BL, Earl of Perth to Sir

Thomas Haggerston, 20 Nov. 1688, Egerton 3335, fo. 57r.; *RPC*, 3rd ser., XIII, pp. 348–9, 351.
28. NRS, Various magistrates, councillors and residents of Ayr to Sir James Montgomery, 31 Dec. 1688, GD3/5/784; Nine Ayrshire gentlemen to Sir James Montgomery, 14 Jan. 1689, GD3/5/786.
29. Of the seven stages of revolutionary change discussed in Tilly, *From Mobilization to Revolution*, pp. 216–17, Scotland in 1688–9 lacked the third ('unsuccessful efforts by the government ... to suppress the alternative coalition') and probably also the fourth ('establishment by the alternative coalition of effective control over some portion of the government' before the resolution of the crisis).
30. See e.g. Hosford, *Nottingham, Nobles and the North*; Speck, 'The revolution of 1688 in the north of England'; Miller, 'The militia and the army in the reign of James II'; Farguson, 'Dynastic politics, international protestantism and royal rebellion'.
31. Beddard, 'The unexpected whig revolution of 1688'; Levillain, 'London besieged?'.
32. Due to the survival and distribution of the sources used in Chapters 2–4, much of the discussion concerns lowland Scotland. For an analysis of the central government's impact in the highlands, using different sources, see Kennedy, *Governing Gaeldom*, esp. ch. 6.
33. Safley, 'Multiconfessionalism: a brief introduction', p. 7.
34. For a useful overview, see Headley et al. (eds), *Confessionalization in Europe*.
35. Recent studies include Glaser (ed.), *Religious Tolerance in the Atlantic World*; Shagan, *Rule of Moderation*, ch. 8; Marshall, *John Locke, Toleration and Early Enlightenment Culture*; Coffey, *Persecution and Toleration in Protestant England*.
36. In addition to the essays in Safley (ed.), *Companion to Multiconfessionalism*, see the review article by Walsham, 'Cultures of coexistence in early modern England', and e.g. Dixon et al. (eds), *Living with Religious Diversity in Early-Modern Europe*; Kaplan, *Divided by Faith*; Walsham, *Charitable Hatred*; Hanlon, *Confession and Community in Seventeenth-Century France*.
37. On England, see Sowerby, *Making Toleration*.

CHAPTER 1 KING JAMES'S SCOTLAND

1. For a range of perspectives on this subject, see Raffe, 'The Restoration, the revolution and the failure of episcopacy'; Hyman, 'Church militant'; Cowan, *Scottish Covenanters*.
2. On the ideal of religious uniformity, see e.g. Walsham, *Charitable Hatred*, esp. ch. 2; Coffey, *Persecution and Toleration in Protestant England*, ch. 2; Goldie, 'The theory of religious intolerance in Restoration England'.

3. Raffe, *Culture of Controversy*, pp. 53–4.
4. *RPC*, 3rd ser., III, pp. 38–40, 47, 586–90.
5. *RPS*, 1661/1/24.
6. Ibid., 1661/1/16 (quotation), 1661/1/17, 1661/1/23, 1661/1/24.
7. Ibid., 1662/5/9, 1669/10/13.
8. Jackson, *Restoration Scotland*, ch. 3.
9. *RPC*, 3rd ser., VI, pp. 264–5, 459–62. See also Chapter 2, p. 36.
10. Clarke (ed.), *Collection of Letters*, pp. 23, 26, 51–2, 57 (quotation).
11. *RPS*, 1681/7/17, 1681/7/29 (quotation). On the Test and its relationship to the period's other state oaths, see Raffe, 'Scottish state oaths and the revolution'.
12. Clarke (ed.), *Collection of Letters*, pp. 48–9.
13. *RPC*, 3rd ser., VI, pp. 567–8, quotation at p. 568. The council's missive was printed as *Letter directed from the Council of Scotland, to the King*.
14. *RPS*, 1681/7/18; Harris, *Restoration*, pp. 375–6.
15. *RPS*, 1681/7/42.
16. *RPC*, 3rd ser., VII, pp. xix–xx, 25, 45–6, 97–105, 651–84; *RPS*, 1681/7/36; Macinnes, *Union and Empire*, pp. 85, 206. See also Graham, *Maritime History of Scotland*, pp. 51–5.
17. *RPC*, 3rd ser., VII, pp. 599–600, 664–5, 671–2; Macinnes, *Union and Empire*, pp. 165–9; Landsman, *Scotland and its First American Colony*, pt 2.
18. *RPC*, 3rd ser., VII, p. 653.
19. *RPS*, 1672/6/13. See Chapter 4, pp. 82–3.
20. Ouston, 'York in Edinburgh'; Mann, *James VII*, pp. 138–9, 140.
21. See esp. Mann, *James VII*, ch. 4; MacIntosh, *Scottish Parliament under Charles II*, ch. 7; McAlister, 'James VII and the Conduct of Scottish Politics', chs 2–4.
22. Paterson, *No Tragic Story*, ch. 4; Willcock, *Scots Earl in Covenanting Times*, chs 13–14.
23. *RPC*, 3rd ser., X, pp. 133–6, quotation at p. 136. In another part of the proclamation, James was styled 'King of Great Brittain, France and Ireland'. See also Lauder, *Historical Notices*, II, p. 615.
24. For a basic introduction, see Cowan, *Scottish Covenanters*, chs 7–8. For more detail, see Jardine, 'United Societies'.
25. *RPC*, 3rd ser., VIII, pp. 318–19.
26. Cowan, *Scottish Covenanters*, p. 118.
27. *RPC*, 3rd ser., IX, pp. 154–9, 345–8, 349–52, 383–4, X, pp. 80–2, 106–8. In January, the commission for the area between the Rivers Spey and Ness was extended to cover Inverness-shire, Ross, Cromarty and Sutherland: ibid., X, pp. 101–2.
28. *Letters of Intercommuning against Mr. James Rennick*.
29. [Renwick, Shields et al.,] *Informatory Vindication*, pp. 185–91.
30. *RPC*, 3rd ser., X, pp. 84–6.

31. The label 'killing time' was current by 1687: [Shields,] *Hind Let Loose*, p. 200.
32. For the best introductions to these cases, see Adams, 'Brown, John' and 'Wilson, Margaret'. The latter article tends towards the view that the executions at Wigtown took place, which has been questioned.
33. *RPC*, 3rd ser., X, pp. 204–6, quotation at p. 204, XI, pp. 25–6.
34. Ibid., X, pp. 28–9.
35. Ibid., X, pp. 155–6, quotation at p. 155.
36. *RPS*, 1685/4/14 (quotation), 1685/4/16, 1685/4/33; cf. NRS, Secretary's warrant book, SP4/9, p. 228; Mann, '"James VII, King of the Articles"', esp. p. 198.
37. *RPS*, 1685/4/28.
38. *RPC*, 3rd ser., XI, pp. 29–31; Paterson, *No Tragic Story*, chs 7–9; Willcock, *Scots Earl in Covenanting Times*, chs 18–20; Hopkins, *Glencoe and the End of the Highland War*, pp. 95–101; Greaves, *Secrets of the Kingdom*, pp. 278–84.
39. Kennedy, 'Rebellion, government and the Scottish response to Argyll's rising'; Jardine, 'United Societies', pp. 132–42.
40. *RPS*, 1685/4/69, 1685/4/39, 1685/4/79, 1685/4/77.
41. Fraser, *Chiefs of Grant*, II, p. 26; Fraser, *Sutherland Book*, II, pp. 41–2; *RPC*, 3rd ser., XI, p. 85; NRS, ? to the earl of Arran, 1 July 1685, GD406/1/3225.
42. NRS, Secretary's warrant book, SP4/9, p. 230; *RPS*, 1685/4/34.
43. NRS, Secretary's warrant book, SP4/9, pp. 496–7, quotation at p. 496.
44. *RPC*, 3rd ser., XI, p. 59; NRS, Secretary's warrant book, SP4/9, p. 491.
45. *RPC*, 3rd ser., XI, pp. 212–13; *RPS*, 1685/4/33.
46. NRS, Secretary's warrant book, SP4/10, pp. 282–3.
47. Ibid., SP4/10, pp. 340–1; *RPC*, 3rd ser., XI, pp. 514–15.
48. Clarke (ed.), *Collection of Letters*, pp. 96–8.
49. NRS, Secretary's warrant book, SP4/10, pp. 509–11.
50. Ibid., SP4/11, p. 57; NRS, Viscount of Melfort to the duke of Hamilton, 8 May 168[6], GD406/1/9187; Duke of Hamilton to the earl of Arran, 1 May 1686, GD406/1/7179; NRAS217, Viscount of Melfort to the earl of Moray, 20 Apr. 1686, Box 7, no. 591 (quotation); Same to same, 22 Apr. 1686, Box 7, no. 592; Same to same, 1 May 1686, Box 7, no. 600.
51. *RPS*, 1686/4/6 (quotation); Wodrow, *History*, IV, pp. 361–2; NRS, Secretary's warrant book, SP4/10, pp. 12–17.
52. Lauder, *Historical Notices*, II, pp. 720–1; NRAS217, Viscount of Melfort to the earl of Moray, 15 May 1686, Box 7, no. 609.
53. HMC, *Mar and Kellie*, I, pp. 218–19; Wodrow, *History*, IV, p. 366.
54. Wodrow, *History*, IV, pp. 366–7; HMC, *Laing*, I, pp. 446–7.
55. NRAS217, Viscount of Melfort to the earl of Moray, 3 June 1686, Box 7, no. 624; Same to same, 3 June 1686, Box 7, no. 625; HMC, *Hamilton*, p. 173.

56. NRAS217, Viscount of Melfort to the earl of Moray, undated, Box 7, no. 594 (quotation); Same to same, 20 May 1686, Box 7, no. 616.
57. NRAS217, Viscount of Melfort to the earl of Moray, undated, Box 7, no. 596; Same to same, 12 May 1686, Box 7, no. 610.
58. *RPS*, 1685/4/119. For a fuller account of the parliament, see McAlister, 'James VII and the Conduct of Scottish Politics', pp. 280–307.
59. Among many sources, see esp. *RPC*, 3rd ser., XII, pp. 92–7. Houston, *Social Change in the Age of Enlightenment*, pp. 305–6; Harris, *Revolution*, pp. 151–3.
60. Canaries, *Rome's Additions to Christianity*; Clarke, 'Canaries, James'; Harris, *Revolution*, pp. 149–51; Lauder, *Historical Notices*, II, pp. 775–6.
61. NRS, Secretary's warrant books, SP4/10, p. 527 (quotation), SP4/12, p. 270.
62. *Proclamation against Slanderers and Leesing-makers* (quotation); *Proclamation Reviving and Renuing a former Proclamation against Slanderers*; *RPS*, 1584/5/14. For evidence that the proclamation was repeatedly read in churches, see e.g. SBA, Presbytery of Jedburgh minutes, 1682–1688, CH2/198/5, pp. 58, 60, 63; NRS, Presbytery of Fordyce minutes, 1674–1688, CH2/158/4, fos 146r., 148r., 153r., 155r., 162r.
63. *RPC*, 3rd ser., XII, pp. 221, 237, 238; NRS, Secretary's warrant book, SP4/11, pp. 126–7; Lauder, *Historical Notices*, II, pp. 723, 728.
64. NRS, Secretary's warrant book, SP4/10, pp. 439–51; *RPC*, 3rd ser., XII, pp. 275, 278.
65. Macaulay, *History of England*, II, p. 768; Speck, *James II*, p. 93.
66. McAlister, 'James VII and the Conduct of Scottish Politics', pp. 243–55, 275–6. See also Miller, *James II*, pp. 213–14.
67. NRS, Secretary's warrant book, SP4/11, pp. 265, 312–14, 436–7.
68. Ibid., SP4/8, pp. 177–8.
69. E.g. Lenman, *Jacobite Risings in Britain*, pp. 28–9; Hopkins, *Glencoe and the End of the Highland War*, p. 108.
70. See the bishops' address to James of 3 Nov. 1688: *Letter from the Arch-Bishops and Bishops to the King's most excellent Majesty*.
71. Goldie et al. (eds), *Entring Book of Roger Morrice*, IV, p. 366. See also Miller, *James II*, p. 210.
72. NRS, Secretary's warrant book, SP4/11, pp. 257–60, quotation at pp. 257–8; printed in Wodrow, *History*, IV, pp. 389–90; *RPC*, 3rd ser., XII, p. 435.
73. For a discussion of the penal laws, see Chapter 2, p. 34.
74. *By the King. A Proclamation*, Wing J249. The proclamation was published on 18 Feb.: *RPC*, 3rd ser., XIII, pp. 123–4.
75. NRS, Secretary's warrant book, SP4/12, pp. 3–4, quotation at p. 3; printed with verbal changes in Wodrow, *History*, IV, p. 423.
76. NRS, Secretary's warrant book, SP4/12, pp. 65–6; *His Majesties Royal Letter to his Privy Council of Scotland concerning His Indulgence*. This

was printed by the Catholic printer James Watson at Holyroodhouse. Robert Wodrow referred to the letter as the 'second toleration': *History*, IV, p. 424.

77. *RPC*, 3rd ser., XII, p. 454; HMC, *Mar and Kellie*, I, p. 219. See Mar's attempt to justify his position: NRS, Earl of Mar to King James, June 1686 (copy), GD124/15/184.
78. Lauder, *Historical Notices*, II, p. 751.
79. *RPC*, 3rd ser., XIII, p. 124; NRS, Secretary's warrant book, SP4/12, pp. 3–4; Wodrow, *History*, IV, p. 423.
80. *By the King. A Proclamation*, Wing J252. By Wodrow's count, this was the king's 'third toleration': *History*, IV, p. 426.
81. NUL, James Johnston to ?Hans Willem Bentinck, 21 Dec. 1687 (copy), Pw A 2120; James Johnston to John Hutton, 23 May 1688, Pw A 2161.
82. *By the King. A Proclamation*, Wing J255 (quotation). This was published on 16 May 1688. Wodrow, *History*, IV, p. 440 (which calls this the 'fourth indulgence'); NRS, Duke of Hamilton to the earl of Arran, 8 May 1688, GD406/1/7593. On the English policy, see Harris, *Revolution*, p. 259.
83. NRS, Secretary's warrant book, SP4/9, pp. 230, 464 (quotation), 490; *RPS*, 1685/4/61, cf. 1669/10/4. James's understanding of his power probably accorded with the act of 1661 asserting the royal prerogative over the militia: *RPS*, 1661/1/24.
84. NRS, Secretary's warrant book, SP4/10, pp. 509–11, quotation at p. 510.
85. On *Godden v. Hales*, see Harris, *Revolution*, pp. 192–4. In June 1687, the lords of session met under a new commission not requiring them to swear the Test. Lauder of Fountainhall interpreted their acceptance of this change as a recognition of the royal suspending power: *Historical Notices*, II, p. 796.
86. *By the King. A Proclamation*, Wing J249.
87. Burnet, 'Some reflections on his majesty's proclamation', pp. 10, 11. On France's reputation for tyranny, see Miller, 'The potential for "absolutism"', p. 188.
88. *RPS*, 1685/4/16 (quotation); *His Majesties Gracious Letter to the Parliament of Scotland*, p. 7; Dalrymple, *Memoirs of Great Britain and Ireland*, I, pp. 134–5.
89. NRAS217, Viscount of Melfort to the earl of Moray, 20 May 1686, Box 7, no. 616 (quotation); Same to same, 22 May 1686, Box 7, no. 618. See also NLS, James Steuart to William Carstares, 29 July 1687, Wod. Oct. XXX, fo. 46r.
90. *By the King. A Proclamation*, Wing J255.
91. NRS, Secretary's warrant book, SP4/12, p. 314.
92. *Addres of the University of St Andrews*, esp. pp. 7–9. See Goldie, 'Absolutism', pp. 283–4.
93. Goodare, *State and Society in Early Modern Scotland*; Goodare, *Government of Scotland*, esp. ch. 12.

94. Stewart, *Rethinking the Scottish Revolution*, esp. chs 4–5; Stevenson (ed.), *Government of Scotland under the Covenanters*.
95. Lee, 'Government and Politics in Scotland', p. 137; Stewart, 'The "rise" of the state?', pp. 230–5.
96. Western, *Monarchy and Revolution*, esp. chs 3–5.
97. Pincus, *1688*, esp. ch. 6.
98. NRS, Accounts of the lord treasurer and treasury commission, 1682–1692, E26/12, pp. 143–9, 196.
99. See Chandaman, *English Public Revenue*, p. 260.
100. Goodare, *State and Society in Early Modern Scotland*, p. 319; *RPS*, 1706/10/257.
101. NRS, Accounts of the treasury commission, 1667–1682, E26/11, pp. 213–16.
102. Ibid., p. 355; Accounts, E26/12, pp. 8, 74–5, 148.
103. NRS, Accounts, E26/12, pp. 138–9, 196.
104. NRS, Secretary's warrant books, SP4/10, pp. 399–400, SP4/11, pp. 51–2; NRS, Treasury register, 5 March 1686–11 Sep. 1688, E7/4, pp. 73–4, 213; NRS, Accounts, E26/12, pp. 75, 148; Chandaman, *English Public Revenue*, pp. 71–6.
105. NRS, Treasury register, E7/4, p. 96; NRS, Warrants of the exchequer register, May–Dec. 1686, E8/38 [unnumbered], Proclamation appointing a roup of the farms of customs, foreign excise and inland excise, 15 Sep. 1686, Tacks of inland excise, 3, 8, 11 Dec. 1686; Lauder, *Historical Notices*, II, p. 763.
106. NRS, Accounts, E26/12, pp. 69–78, 143–9, 196.
107. For a general discussion, see McLay, 'The Restoration and the glorious revolution'.
108. Lee, 'Government and Politics in Scotland', pp. 130–3; NRS, Accounts, E26/12, pp. 81–7, cf. pp. 13–21.
109. 'Establishment for the pay of his majesty's standing forces'; NRS, Secretary's warrant book, SP4/10, pp. 188–93. See also HMC, *Tenth Report*, pp. 135–7; Childs, *The Army, James II, and the Glorious Revolution*, p. 2, which overlooked the 1685 figures.
110. Lenman, 'Militia, fencible men, and home defence', p. 184; Miller, 'The militia and the army in the reign of James II'.
111. NRS, Secretary's warrant books, SP4/10, pp. 568–9, SP4/12, p. 220.
112. *Proclamation commanding the Return of all His Majesties Subjects*; HMC, *Laing*, I, p. 460; NRS, Secretary's warrant book, SP4/12, pp. 622–3, 678–9; Dalton, *Scots Army*, pt 2, pp. 159–61; Childs, *The Army, James II, and the Glorious Revolution*, p. 4. For the background and consequences of the decision to recall men serving in the Netherlands, see e.g. Kenyon, *Robert Spencer, Earl of Sunderland*, pp. 177–9, 182–5, 217; Carswell, *Descent on England*, ch. 9.
113. NRS, Accounts, E26/12, pp. 81–7, 151–4, 156–7.

114. Calculated from the figures in Childs, *The Army, James II, and the Glorious Revolution*, pp. 1, 4.
115. Munck, *Seventeenth-Century Europe*, p. 352; Rowlands, *Dynastic State and the Army under Louis XIV*, p. 171.
116. 'Lists of fees and pensions granted to the officers of state', pp. 149–52, 156–8, 163–7; NRS, Accounts, E26/12, pp. 162–4, 167–9.
117. Aylmer, *The Crown's Servants*, pp. 142–3.
118. Goodare, *Government of Scotland*, ch. 8; Brown, *Noble Power in Scotland*, ch. 4.
119. *RPC*, 3rd ser., VII, pp. 304–6, cf. p. 471. See also Agnew, *Agnews of Lochnaw*, pp. 387–9.
120. NRS, Register of the Great Seal, 1685–1688, C3/12, nos 107, 120, 202, 207, 270, 271, 388; NRS, Secretary's warrant books, SP4/9, pp. 116–19, 466–8, 530–2, SP4/10, pp. 467–9, SP4/11, pp. 181–2, 369–70, 425–6, 625–7, SP4/12, pp. 42–3, 96–7, 222–3, SP4/13, pp. 65–6, 294–6, 353–4; *RPC*, 3rd ser., XI, pp. 62–3.
121. NRS, Register of the Great Seal, C3/12, nos 94, 98, 108, 121, 122, 209, 245, 249, 432, 433; NRS, Secretary's warrant books, SP4/9, pp. 206–8, 441, 488–90, 532–4, 542–4, SP4/10, pp. 8–10, 28–30, SP4/11, pp. 400–2, 499–500, SP4/13, pp. 321–3, 356–7; *RPC*, 3rd ser., X, pp. 204–6, XI, pp. 25–6, 31–2, 48–9; Fraser, *Scotts of Buccleuch*, II, pp. 321–2.
122. *RPC*, 3rd ser., XI, pp. 103–4; Kennedy, *Governing Gaeldom*, pp. 237–49.
123. See esp. Jones, *Revolution of 1688*, ch. 6; Glassey, *Politics and the Appointment of Justices of the Peace*, ch. 3; Walker, *James II and the Three Questions*.
124. See e.g. Beik, *Absolutism and Society in Seventeenth-Century France*, ch. 5; Bonney, *Political Change in France under Richelieu and Mazarin*.
125. See Miller, 'Britain', pp. 211–14.

CHAPTER 2 JAMES'S RELIGIOUS EXPERIMENT

1. Wodrow, *History*, I, p. xxxviii, IV, p. 199; Brown, *History of Scotland*, II, pp. 433, 435; Brown, *Surveys of Scottish History*, pp. 70–1.
2. Ashley, *James II*, p. 293; Speck, 'James II and VII'; cf. Speck, *Reluctant Revolutionaries*, ch. 8.
3. Miller, 'James II and toleration'; Sowerby, *Making Toleration*, pp. 24–8.
4. NRS, Secretary's warrant book, SP4/11, pp. 257–60, quotations at p. 260; Wodrow, *History*, IV, p. 390.
5. *By the King. A Proclamation*, Wing J249.
6. Wodrow, *History*, IV, pp. 416–37.
7. For further information, see 'Notes on the Sources'.
8. *RPS*, A1560/8/6, A1567/12/4, 1594/4/14.
9. Ibid., 1581/10/27, 1587/7/13, 1592/4/32, 1593/4/30, 1600/11/40, 1607/3/13, 1609/4/19.

10. Ibid., 1579/10/24, 1609/4/15.
11. Ibid., 1661/1/56.
12. Ibid., 1681/7/17; Macinnes, 'Catholic recusancy and the penal laws', pp. 54–6.
13. *RPS*, 1685/4/15.
14. Macinnes, 'Catholic recusancy and the penal laws', pp. 56–7.
15. Mackenzie, *Memoirs of the Affairs of Scotland*, p. 62.
16. *RPS*, 1661/1/7, 1661/1/88.
17. Ibid., 1681/7/29. The first indulgence also discharged three further acts that clarified or extended the range of persons required to swear the Test: ibid., 1681/7/45, 1681/7/49, 1685/4/34.
18. Spurlock, *Cromwell and Scotland*. But by English standards, the competition between these groups was limited: Capp, 'The religious marketplace', p. 53.
19. E.g. Langley, *Worship, Civil War and Community*, p. 81. On the controversy more generally, see Holfelder, 'Factionalism in the Kirk'.
20. E.g. *Fasti*, I, p. 222, a case discussed by Chris Langley at the conference of the Scottish Church History Society on 22 Oct. 2016.
21. *RPC*, 3rd ser., III, pp. 38–40, 47, 586–90; Cowan, *Scottish Covenanters*, pp. 76–80; Raffe, *Culture of Controversy*, pp. 75–6.
22. *RPC*, 3rd ser., VI, pp. 264–5.
23. Ibid., VI, pp. 459–62; Clarke (ed.), *Collection of Letters*, pp. 13, 21–3.
24. *RPC*, 3rd ser., VIII, pp. 319–20, 355–8. A fifth minister reportedly had his licence cancelled in March: Lauder, *Historical Notices*, II, p. 532. Three more licences were revoked in November: *RPC*, 3rd ser., X, pp. 36–8. On the 1683 thanksgiving, see Mears et al. (eds), *National Prayers*, pp. 738–40.
25. *RPC*, 3rd ser., X, p. 43.
26. *By the King. A Proclamation*, Wing J252.
27. NRS, South Leith presbyterian kirk session minutes, 1687–1691, CH2/716/9, pp. 1–2; Robertson, *South Leith Records*, p. 154.
28. NRS, Duke of Hamilton to the earl of Arran, 20 Aug. 1687, GD406/1/6208; cf. Lauder, *Historical Notices*, II, p. 816.
29. *Proclamation, anent Field Conventicles and House Meetings*. There was apparently another act to this effect on 1 March 1688: NRS, Duke of Hamilton to the earl of Arran, 1 March 1688, GD406/1/7555.
30. *RPC*, 3rd ser., XIII, pp. lxi, 192–6, 203–12, 226–7, 274, 288; McNeill and MacQueen (eds), *Atlas of Scottish History*, p. 399.
31. Fraser-Mackintosh (ed.), *Letters of Two Centuries*, p. 118; Cramond (ed.), *Records of Elgin*, I, p. 344.
32. *RPC*, 3rd ser., XIII, p. 195.
33. Mears et al. (eds), *National Prayers*, pp. 756–7, 762–3; Lauder, *Historical Notices*, II, p. 846.
34. Raffe, 'Presbyterianism, secularization, and Scottish politics', pp. 332–3.

35. See e.g. Wood (ed.), *Edinburgh Extracts, 1681 to 1689*, pp. 229–30; ELA, Haddington town council minutes, 1682–1692, HAD/2/1/2/8, fo. 70r.; *Extracts from the Council Register of the Burgh of Aberdeen*, p. 309; FCAC, Culross town council minutes, 1682–1712, B/Cul/1/1/3, pp. 213–14: Culross's council threatened to fine inhabitants who did not attend the town's festivities on the June thanksgiving day in arms.
36. Anson, *Underground Catholicism*, pp. 80, 82; SCA, Copy of David Burnet and Alexander Dunbar to William Leslie, 22 Nov. 1687, BL/1/100/15; Meeting of clergy to William Leslie, 6 Apr. 1688, BL/1/109/28.
37. SCA, David Burnet to Walter Leslie, 30 Aug. 1688, BL/1/118/16 (1). See also Dilworth, 'The Scottish mission in 1688–1689'.
38. SCA, Burnet and Dunbar to Leslie, 22 Nov. 1687, BL/1/100/15; see also William Leslie to Lewis Innes, 8 Aug. 1687, BL/1/105/17.
39. SCA, David Burnet to ?, 22 Feb. 1687, BL/1/98/5.
40. SCA, Lewis Innes to William Leslie, 8 Feb. 1688, BL/1/113/10.
41. SCA, Walter Leslie to ?Charles Whytford, 2 Sep. 1687, BL/1/105/10; Anson, *Underground Catholicism*, pp. 85–7, 90–1.
42. Hay, *Genealogie of the Hayes of Tweeddale*, p. 56; SCA, Placid Fleming to Lewis Innes, 21 Aug. 1687, BL/1/101/6; Lewis Innes to Charles Whytford, 9 Nov. 1687, BL/1/103/7.
43. SCA, Burnet and Dunbar to Leslie, 22 Nov. 1687, BL/1/100/15; Clergy to Leslie, 6 Apr. 1688, BL/1/109/28; John Irvine to William Leslie, 6 Sep. 1688, BL/1/114/2. Hay, *Architecture of Scottish Post-Reformation Churches*, pp. 153–4, describes a Catholic chapel, also dedicated to St Ninian, built nearby in 1755.
44. NRS, Secretary's warrant book, SP4/13, pp. 59–60; SCA, Clergy to Leslie, 6 Apr. 1688, BL/1/109/28; Robert Strachan to Charles Whytford, 18 Feb. 1688, BL/1/118/5; Same to ?same, 29 March 1688, BL/1/118/6; Same to same, 3 July 1688, BL/1/118/11.
45. NRS, Secretary's warrant book, SP4/11, pp. 348–9. The letter is printed in Rogers, *History of the Chapel Royal*, pp. ccxix–ccxx.
46. Lauder, *Historical Notices*, II, pp. 763, 764–5.
47. NRS, Secretary's warrant book, SP4/11, pp. 577–8; Rogers, *History of the Chapel Royal*, pp. ccxx–ccxxi.
48. NRS, Secretary's warrant book, SP4/12, pp. 218–20; Wood (ed.), *Edinburgh Extracts, 1681 to 1689*, p. 211; Lauder, *Historical Notices*, II, pp. 808–9. The French protestants had arranged for repairs in Lady Yester's Church in Dec. 1686, perhaps indicating their recent arrival there: Wood (ed.), *Edinburgh Extracts, 1681 to 1689*, pp. 192–3. On the new Canongate Kirk, see Raffe, 'Worship and devotion in multiconfessional Scotland'.
49. Glozier, 'The earl of Melfort'.
50. NRS, Secretary's warrant books, SP4/12, pp. 323–4, 415, 524–6, SP4/13, p. 63.

51. SCA, John Jameson to Charles Whytford, 12 Dec. 1687, BL/1/104/9.
52. HMC, *Stuart Papers*, I, p. 30; Lauder, *Historical Notices*, II, p. 860.
53. *Rules of the Schools of the Royal Colledge*; *Rules of the Schools at the Savoy*; *Rules of the Schools at the Jesuits in Fanchurch-Street*.
54. DesBrisay, 'Catholics, Quakers and religious persecution', pp. 164–5; *Reliquiae Barclaianae*, p. 51.
55. Miller, 'Gleanings from the records of the yearly meeting of Aberdeen', pp. 62–4. I am grateful to Gordon DesBrisay for this reference. The meeting had read the London Quakers' address published in *London Gazette*, no. 2238, 28 Apr.–2 May 1687. Barclay's address was published in *London Gazette*, no. 2252, 16–20 June 1687.
56. *London Gazette*, no. 2270, 18–22 Aug. 1687. For Heads, see Burnet, *Story of Quakerism*, pp. 13, 156–7.
57. See NRS, Edinburgh quarterly meeting records, 1669–1737, CH10/1/1, pp. 49–59; NRS, Edinburgh monthly meeting records, 1669–1713, CH10/1/2, pp. 50–9; NRS, Kinmuck/Lethendy monthly meeting records, 1679–1782, CH10/3/37; Miller, 'Gleanings from the records of the yearly meeting of Aberdeen', pp. 62–4.
58. NRS, 'Remembrance, or Record of the Sufferings of some Freinds', CH10/1/65 [unpaginated]. See Chapter 5, p. 116.
59. E.g. *RPC*, 3rd ser., XII, pp. 367–70, XIII, pp. 124–31.
60. *Proclamation, offering a Reward*; *Proclamation, against Field Conventicles, and offering a Revvard*; Jardine, 'United Societies', pp. 180–2, 184, 190.
61. [Renwick et al.,] *Testimony of some Persecuted Presbyterian Ministers*, pp. 16–17; Raffe, *Culture of Controversy*, pp. 52–7.
62. [Renwick et al.,] *Testimony of some Persecuted Presbyterian Ministers*, p. 22.
63. Renwick, *January 24. 1688. Some Notes or Heads of a Sermon*, p. 9.
64. Renwick, *January 22. 1688. Some Notes or Heads of a Sermon*, p. 15.
65. [Renwick et al.,] *Testimony of some Persecuted Presbyterian Ministers*, pp. 7–9, 25–8; [Shields,] *Hind Let Loose*, pp. 173–80.
66. *By the King. A Proclamation*, Wing J252 (quotation); [Renwick et al.,] *Testimony of some Persecuted Presbyterian Ministers*, pp. 22–3.
67. [Renwick et al.,] *Testimony of some Persecuted Presbyterian Ministers*, pp. 23–4; Renwick, *January 22. 1688. Some Notes or Heads of a Sermon*, p. 14 (quotation).
68. Raffe, *Culture of Controversy*, pp. 75–6.
69. [Shields,] *Hind Let Loose*, pp. 544–5, 569 (quotation), 570–5.
70. *Cloud of Witnesses*, pp. 252–6, at p. 255; Raffe, *Culture of Controversy*, pp. 25–6, 105–7.
71. Wodrow, *History*, IV, p. 428; NRS, Synod of Lothian and Tweeddale minutes, 1687–1690, CH2/252/5, p. 1, suggests that the meeting took place on 5 July, the date of the second indulgence's publication in Edinburgh.

72. To the King's most excellent Majesty, the Humble Address of the Presbyterian Ministers; Wodrow, History, IV, p. 428.
73. London Gazette, no. 2280, 22–6 Sep. 1687. There was apparently another address from the presbyterian ministers and lay people in and around Glasgow: [Sage,] Case of the Present Afflicted Clergy, app., p. 80.
74. Carruthers (ed.), Confession of Faith of the Assembly of Divines at Westminster, pp. 19 (ch. 23), 20 (ch. 25, art. 6). When the general assembly approved the confession in 1647, it asserted a presbyterian interpretation of the document: Acts of the General Assembly, pp. 158–9.
75. Fragmentary minutes of the general meetings are in NLS, Wod. Fol. XXXVIII, fos 80r.–81v., 91r.–92v. Though those present at the first meeting attended without commissions from local courts, subsequently the membership was appointed by presbyteries: Wodrow, History, IV, p. 429; e.g. NRS, Presbytery of Ayr minutes, 1687–1705, CH2/532/2, p. 2.
76. Wodrow, History, IV, pp. 432–3. There are copies of the overtures at NLS, Wod. Fol. XXVII, fo. 199; Wod. Fol. XXXVIII, fos 80v.–81.
77. NRS, Presbytery of Dunfermline minutes, 1689–1691, CH2/105/2, p. 1.
78. NRS, Presbytery of Irvine minutes, 1687–1699, CH2/197/2, p. 1; NRS, Presbytery of Ayr, CH2/532/2, p. 1; NRS, Presbytery of Glasgow minutes, 1687–1694, CH2/171/7, p. 2; NRS, Presbytery of Paisley minutes, 1660, 1687–1699, CH2/294/4, p. 17.
79. NRS, Presbytery of Hamilton minutes, 1687–1695, CH2/393/1, p. 1; NRS, Presbytery of Kintyre minutes, 1655–1707, CH2/1153/1, fo. 34r.; NRS, Presbytery of Dumfries minutes, 1687–1695, CH2/1284/2, p. 2; NRS, Presbytery of Linlithgow minutes, 1687–1694, CH2/242/7, p. 1.
80. 'Register of the provincial synod of Glasgow and Ayr', p. 215; NRS, Synod of Argyll minutes, 1687–1700, CH2/557/3, p. 1.
81. NRS, Synod of Lothian and Tweeddale, CH2/252/5, p. 1. Minutes of the presbytery of Edinburgh itself are missing. The presbytery of Dalkeith met from Apr. 1688, but the register for 1688–92 is missing: Fasti, I, p. 301. The synod of Fife was operating by Oct. 1689, but its minutes begin in 1690: NRS, Presbytery of Kirkcaldy minutes, 1688–1693, CH2/224/2, pp. 17–18; NRS, Synod of Fife minutes, 1690–1696, CH2/154/4.
82. See e.g. NRS, Presbytery of Linlithgow, CH2/242/7, p. 1; NRS, Presbytery of Dunfermline, CH2/105/2, p. 1.
83. Wodrow, History, IV, p. 432; NRS, Synod of Lothian and Tweeddale, CH2/252/5, pp. 1–2.
84. Wodrow, History, IV, p. 433.
85. RPC, 3rd ser., XIII, p. 296.
86. NRS, Renfrew kirk session minutes, 1653, 1691–1700, CH2/1596/1/1, p. 41; Fasti, III, p. 186.
87. Fasti, V, pp. 29, 71; NRS, Presbytery of Kirkcaldy, CH2/224/2, pp. 2–6; NRS, Presbytery of Dunfermline, CH2/105/2, p. 1.

88. Lauder, *Historical Notices*, II, p. 819; *Fasti*, II, p. 159; NRS, United presbyteries of Chirnside and Duns minutes, 1690–1702, CH2/516/1, p. 2a.
89. NRS, Synod of Argyll, CH2/557/3, pp. 1, 3, 11, 13, 15–16; NRS, Presbytery of Dunoon minutes, 1690–1707, CH2/111/3, p. 2.
90. NRS, John Inglis to the duchess of Hamilton, 6 Sep. 1687, GD406/1/3455; Duchess of Hamilton to John Inglis, 8 Sep. 1687, GD406/1/3457; Same to same, 15 July ?1690, GD406/1/3456/2; 'Register of the provincial synod of Glasgow and Ayr', pp. 216–17; NRS, Presbytery of Hamilton, CH2/393/1, pp. 2–3.
91. *Fasti*, I, p. 302; NRS, Borthwick kirk session minutes, 1690–1731, 1769–1811, CH2/38/1, p. 1.
92. Landsman, *Scotland and its First American Colony*, p. 145; *RPC*, 3rd ser., XIV, pp. 337–8, 427, 584. The privy council agreed to exchange a prisoner in Dunnottar Castle, probably the Catholic priest Alexander Christie, for Riddell and Charles Gordon, the minister of Veere in the Netherlands, who had been captured while travelling to Scotland and imprisoned at Dunkirk for seven months: *Fasti*, VII, p. 541.
93. NLS, Sarah Carstares to William Dunlop, 24 Feb., 29 June, 20 July, 5 Aug., 30 Dec. 1686, 19 Feb., 3 Apr., 20 Apr., 30 Apr. 1687, MS. 9250, fos 21, 25r., 27r.–28r., 29r., 34, 38r.–39r., 42, 45, 46; William Moncrieff, Ralph Rogers, William Crichton to William Dunlop, 29 June 1687, MS. 9250, fo. 50r.
94. NLS, Sarah Carstares to William Dunlop, 23 July, ?July 1687, 25 Feb. 1688, MS. 9250, fos 52r., 54, 65r.; Margaret Dunlop to William Dunlop, 1687, MS. 9250, fo. 60r.; William Dunlop to Sarah Carstares, 5 May 1688, MS. 9250, fo. 67r.
95. NRS, William Dunlop to Sir James Montgomery, 26 March 1688, GD3/5/778; NLS, William Dunlop to Lady Hartwood, 24 May 1688, MS. 9250, fo. 69r.; James Dunlop to William Dunlop, 20 Sep. 1689, MS. 9250, fo. 89av.
96. Gordon (ed.), *Freedom after Ejection*, pp. 80, 348; *Fasti*, II, pp. 126–7, 285; NRS, Presbytery of Dumfries, CH2/1284/2, pp. 7, 19, 22, 28, 29, 36, 37, 40, 56.
97. *Fasti*, I, p. 39.
98. Gardner, *Scottish Exile Community*, pp. 12, 213–15; Wodrow, *History*, IV, pp. 435–7; NRS, Presbytery of Irvine, CH2/197/2, p. 5; *Fasti*, V, pp. 63, 66.
99. *Calendar of State Papers Domestic*, p. 44 (quotation). In the letter quoted, of 2 Aug. 1687 (n.s.), Carstares told Hans Willem Bentinck that he was reluctant to accept the call, but a later letter to his sister suggests that he was undecided: NLS, William Carstares to Sarah Carstares, 6 Oct. 1687, MS. 9250, fo. 61r. See also NLS, James Steuart to William Carstares, 24 Sep. 1687, Wod. Oct. XXX, fo. 50r.; Story, *William Carstares*, p. 150.

100. Dunlop, *William Carstares and the Kirk by Law Established*, esp. pp. 53–4, 59–61. Esther Mijers is at work on a new biography.
101. Gardner, *Scottish Exile Community*, pp. 205–6; 'Register of the provincial synod of Glasgow and Ayr', p. 220; NRS, Presbytery of Hamilton, CH2/393/1, pp. 7, 9.
102. NRS, South Leith presbyterian kirk session, CH2/716/9, pp. 1–2; Robertson, *South Leith Records*, p. 154.
103. NRS, Queensferry kirk session minutes, 1687–1718, CH2/689/2, p. 1.
104. NRS, South Leith presbyterian kirk session, CH2/716/9, pp. 12–13, 14–16, 18, 19–20; Robertson, *South Leith Records*, pp. 156–7; NRS, Synod of Lothian and Tweeddale, CH2/252/5, p. 29; NRS, Queensferry kirk session, CH2/689/2, pp. 2–3, 4; NRS, Presbytery of Linlithgow, CH2/242/7, p. 4.
105. NRS, Presbytery of Irvine, CH2/197/2, p. 1.
106. *Acts of the General Assembly*, pp. 212–13.
107. This was true of South Leith and Queensferry. See also the case of Robert Livingstone at Libberton (Biggar): NRS, Presbytery of Peebles and Biggar minutes, 1688–1694, CH2/35/3, pp. 3, 5, 9–10, 11–12, 16–17, 21. The general meeting recommended that presbyteries should create elderships where they were lacking, so as to allow for an orderly call: Wodrow, *History*, IV, p. 432.
108. E.g. NRS, Presbytery of Ayr, CH2/532/2, p. 2; NRS, Synod of Galloway minutes, 1689–1712, CH2/165/2, p. 1.
109. NRS, Presbytery of Hamilton, CH2/393/1, pp. 22–3, 28 (quotation), 29; [Sage,] *Case of the Present Afflicted Clergy*, app., pp. 36–7; *Fasti*, III, p. 223; Jardine, 'United Societies', ch. 4.
110. Foster, *Bishop and Presbytery*, pp. 95–101. Institution in the episcopalian Church closely resembled presbyterian ordination: see e.g. NRS, Presbytery of Forres minutes, 1651–1688, CH2/162/1, p. 522.
111. NRS, Presbytery of Hamilton, CH2/393/1, pp. 8 (quotation), 9.
112. NRS, Presbytery of Dumfries, CH2/1284/2, p. 5.
113. NRS, Presbytery of Linlithgow, CH2/242/7, p. 2; NRS, Presbytery of Peebles and Biggar, CH2/35/3, p. 1.
114. NRS, Presbytery of Irvine, CH2/197/2, pp. 3 (quotation), 4.
115. 'Register of the provincial synod of Glasgow and Ayr', p. 229.
116. Wodrow, *History*, IV, p. 432.
117. 'Register of the provincial synod of Glasgow and Ayr', pp. 237, 246; NRS, Presbytery of Irvine, CH2/197/2, p. 17.
118. Jardine, 'United Societies', pp. 189–90.
119. 'Register of the provincial synod of Glasgow and Ayr', p. 229; NRS, Presbytery of Hamilton, CH2/393/1, p. 17; NRS, Presbytery of Dumfries, CH2/1284/2, pp. 32–3.
120. NRS, Presbytery of Ayr, CH2/532/2, pp. 1–3, 8.

121. NRS, Presbytery of Peebles and Biggar, CH2/35/3, pp. 11 (quotation), 12. See also NRS, Synod of Lothian and Tweeddale, CH2/252/5, p. 15.
122. NLS, 'List of Presbiterian Ministers in Ireland and come from it May 20 1689', Wod. Oct. XII, fos 1–4, quotation at fo. 1r. The list was printed in Reid, *History of the Presbyterian Church in Ireland*, II, pp. 589–91.
123. NRS, Presbytery of Dumbarton minutes, 1689–1695, CH2/546/4, p. 5.
124. NRS, Presbytery of Dumfries, CH2/1284/2, pp. 37, 39, 41.
125. NRS, Presbytery of Hamilton, CH2/393/1, pp. 12–13, 21; NRS, Presbytery of Paisley, CH2/294/4, pp. 28, 30; NRS, Presbytery of Ayr, CH2/532/2, pp. 20–1, 25, 28.
126. NLS, Letter from the general session of Glasgow, 1689, Wod. Qu. XXVIII, fo. 77r.; *Fasti*, III, pp. 398, 453, 454; Killen, *History of Congregations of the Presbyterian Church in Ireland*, pp. 75, 118, 137, 182.
127. NRS, Renfrew kirk session, CH2/1596/1/1, pp. 41–2.
128. NRS, Cambuslang kirk session minutes, 1658–1788, CH2/415/1, p. 58.
129. NRS, Presbytery of Irvine, CH2/197/2, p. 5.
130. NRS, Dumfries St Michael's kirk session minutes and accounts, 1689–1712, CH2/537/15, pp. 1–4, quotation at p. 1. For a similar case in 1691, see NRS, New Abbey kirk session minutes, 1691–1725, CH2/1042/1, pp. 2–3.
131. 'Register of the provincial synod of Glasgow and Ayr', p. 262. See also NRS, Presbytery of Dumbarton, CH2/546/4, p. 11.
132. Wykes, 'James II's religious indulgence', pp. 92–3.
133. Fraser-Mackintosh (ed.), *Letters of Two Centuries*, p. 118; Mackay (ed.), *Records of the Presbyteries of Inverness and Dingwall*, p. 129.
134. PKCA, 'Informatione for the Ministers of Perth', c. 1691, B59/28/58/1.
135. NLS, General meeting minutes, 1687–1690, Wod. Fol. XXXVIII, fo. 91r.
136. *Extracts from the Records of the Burgh of Glasgow*, p. 405; M'Ure, *View of the City of Glasgow*, pp. 70–1, 249; *RPC*, 3rd ser., XIII, p. 226.
137. NRS, Secretary's warrant book, SP4/12, pp. 446–7, quotation at p. 446.
138. Ibid., SP4/12, pp. 608–9, quotation at p. 608.
139. ECA, Edinburgh dean of guild court minute book, 1687–1695, SL144/1/7, pp. 119–21. I am grateful to Leona Skelton for this reference.
140. NLS, Diary of Thomas Kincaid, 1687–1688, Adv. 32.7.7, fos 44v., 45v., 46v., 59v., 93v.; Paul (ed.), 'The diary of the Rev. George Turnbull', pp. 330, 331, 332, 333, 335; NRS, Synod of Lothian and Tweeddale, CH2/252/5, p. 13; *RPC*, 3rd ser., XIII, p. 296. The places in Edinburgh mentioned are Anderson's printing house, the Magdalen Chapel, Skinners' Hall, Tailors' Hall, the Castlehill meeting house, St Mary's Chapel and Glovers' Hall. The two meeting houses authorised in 1688 seem to have been additional, though the nine venues were perhaps not used simultaneously.
141. NRS, Secretary's warrant book, SP4/12, pp. 333–4; *Fasti*, III, pp. 87, 88.
142. Strawhorn, *History of Ayr*, p. 66; NRS, Presbytery of Ayr, CH2/532/2, p. 2.

143. NLS, Diary of Kincaid, Adv. 32.7.7, fo. 55r.
144. NRS, Queensferry kirk session, CH2/689/2, pp. 1, 2.
145. DGA, Maintenance roll for George Campbell, *c.* 1687–1690, BH5/2/9.
146. NRS, Presbytery of Peebles and Biggar, CH2/35/3, pp. 2, 3 (quotation), 4.
147. NRS, Presbytery of Ayr, CH2/532/2, p. 1.
148. Foster, *Bishop and Presbytery*, pp. 109–10.
149. NRS, Presbytery of Dumfries, CH2/1284/2, pp. 9–10 (quotation), 27, 28–9.
150. 'Register of the provincial synod of Glasgow and Ayr', p. 248.
151. NRS, Presbytery of Kintyre, CH2/1153/1, fo. 35r.
152. NRS, Presbytery of Dumfries, CH2/1284/2, pp. 28, 33, 37, 43, 49 (quotation).
153. *RPS*, 1690/4/13.
154. *Fasti*, II, pp. 326–7.
155. [Morer, Sage, Monro,] *Account of the Present Persecution*, p. 11.
156. *Late Letter Concerning the Sufferings of the Episcopal Clergy*, pp. 4–7; [Sage,] *Case of the Present Afflicted Clergy*, first pagination sequence, pp. 3–4. Secondary works citing these sources include Maxwell, 'Presbyterian and episcopalian in 1688'; Harris, *Revolution*, p. 173; Raffe, *Culture of Controversy*, p. 191.
157. *RPC*, 3rd ser., XIV, p. 170 (quotation); *Fasti*, I, p. 290.
158. *APS*, IX, app., p. 17; Easson, 'A Scottish parish in Covenanting times', p. 125; Cowan, *Scottish Covenanters*, p. 134.
159. Maxwell, 'Presbyterian and episcopalian in 1688', pp. 33–7.
160. Cowan, *Scottish Covenanters*, p. 134.
161. NRS, Synod of Galloway, CH2/165/2, p. 1.
162. NRS, Lenzie Easter kirk session minutes, 1666–1688, CH2/237/1, pp. 220–33.
163. NRS, West Kirk kirk session accounts and minutes, 1686–1688, CH2/718/10, pp. 4–5, 6–7 (in most cases, it is impossible to read the number of pennies collected); NRS, South Leith kirk session accounts, 1684–1690, CH2/716/221, pp. 77, 79, 81, 83, 85, 87, 101, 103, 105, 107, 109, 111.
164. NRS, Edinburgh Trinity College kirk session minutes, 1685–1690, CH2/141/5, pp. 59–74, 91–104. The averages (calculated by omitting special collections and the unusually large communion collections) were £12.19s.4½d. for Jan.–June 1687 and £10.14s.5d. for the same period in 1688.
165. NRS, Dysart kirk session accounts, 1686–1706, CH2/390/11, fos 6v., 7v., 8v., 9v., 14v., 15v., 15Av.; NRS, Presbytery of Kirkcaldy, CH2/224/2, p. 1. For Dysart's poverty, see e.g. ECA, Convention of Royal Burghs [Moses] Bundles, Bundle 211 [unfoliated], Petition of Dysart, 1688.
166. NRS, Penicuik kirk session accounts and minutes, 1674–1744, CH2/297/2, pp. 231–2, 233–4 (a fall from 10s.11½d. to 3s.6d.).

167. NRS, Dumfries St Michael's kirk session minutes and accounts, 1616–1688, CH2/537/14, pp. 354–66, 376–84. The average collections were £5.0s.0d. for Jan.–June 1687 (excluding one abnormally large collection) and £2.15s.7d. for the same period in 1688.
168. NRS, Queensferry kirk session, CH2/689/2, pp. 4 (quotation), 9.
169. *Fasti*, III, p. 99; NRS, Irvine town council minutes, 1674–1680, 1687–1700, B37/12/4, pp. 7, 11, 62 [from back of book].
170. *Late Letter Concerning the Sufferings of the Episcopal Clergy*, pp. 6–7.
171. E.g. NRS, Synod of Lothian and Tweeddale, CH2/252/5, pp. 23–4; NRS, Presbytery of Hamilton, CH2/393/1, pp. 2, 6; NRS, South Leith presbyterian kirk session, CH2/716/9, p. 2; Robertson, *South Leith Records*, pp. 154–5.
172. Wodrow, *History*, IV, p. 437.
173. NRS, Earl of Arran to the duchess of Hamilton, 1 Oct. 1687, GD406/1/7684; Duke of Hamilton to the duchess of Hamilton, 4 Oct. 1687, GD406/1/6236. BC, NRAS234, Sermons by William Tullideff and James Rymer, May 1688, Bundle 1630, a manuscript record of two presbyterian sermons, is in the hand of Lord John Murray.

CHAPTER 3 MULTICONFESSIONAL SCOTLAND

1. See esp. Finke and Stark, 'Religious economies and sacred canopies'; Finke, 'Religious deregulation', esp. pp. 622–4; Stark and Iannaccone, 'A supply-side reinterpretation of the "secularization" of Europe'. I would not, however, wish to endorse these theorists' critique of the secularisation thesis or their characterisation of individuals' religious motivations in terms of instrumental rationality. See Bruce, *Choice and Religion*; Jerolmack and Porpora, 'Religion, rationality, and experience'.
2. Hopkins, *Glencoe and the End of the Highland War*, pp. 105–6, 118.
3. Shaw, 'Campbell, Archibald'; Gardner, *Scottish Exile Community*, p. 191.
4. *RPC*, 3rd ser., XIII, p. 484. In Feb. 1685, McCulloch received a protection from captions for two years: NRS, Secretary's warrant book, SP4/9, p. 169. See Chapter 4, p. 93.
5. *Publick Occurrences Truly Stated*, no. 3, 6 March 1688; SCA, Thomas Nicolson to Charles Whytford, 23 Feb. 1688, BL/1/117/7 (quotation); Fraser, *Red Book of Grandtully*, II, p. 286. Wodrow, *History*, IV, pp. 437–8, has another anecdote about Stanfield.
6. [Con?,] *An Answer, to a little Book call'd Protestancy to be Embrac'd*, sigs. [**3]v.–[**4]r. This work was published by James Watson at Holyroodhouse: Lauder, *Historical Notices*, II, p. 764.
7. Grant (ed.), *Seafield Correspondence*, pp. 42–3, 147.
8. *RPC*, 3rd ser., XI, p. 213; Hopkins, 'Mackenzie, Kenneth'.
9. Henderson, 'Stewart, Alexander'.

10. SCA, Earl of Perth to Charles Whytford, 19 July 1687, BL/1/106/16; De Sales, *Introduction to a Devout Life*, sig. *3. I am grateful to Mary Hardy for informing me of this book, which was evidently a production of the Holyroodhouse printing press.
11. Joly, *Un Converti de Bossuet*, ch. 6.
12. Hett (ed.), *Memoirs of Sir Robert Sibbald*, pp. 86–94, quotations at pp. 86, 94; Lauder, *Historical Notices*, II, pp. 671, 694, 725–6, 734; Grant (ed.), *Seafield Correspondence*, pp. 25, 29; Goldie et al. (eds), *Entring Book of Roger Morrice*, III, p. 136. On the riots, see Houston, *Social Change in the Age of Enlightenment*, pp. 305–6.
13. SCA, Nicolson to Whytford, 23 Feb. 1688, BL/1/117/7; John Jameson to William Leslie, 4 Apr. 1688, BL/1/114/7; David Burnet to ?, 9 July 1688, BL/1/109/7. See also Harris, *Revolution*, p. 180.
14. SCA, Burnet to ?, 9 July 1688, BL/1/109/7. Burnet explained that, prior to the indulgences, priests had refused to baptise illegitimate children, fearing prosecution for allowing protestants to evade the established Kirk's discipline.
15. *Extracts from the Council Register of the Burgh of Aberdeen*, p. 307.
16. SCA, Robert Strachan to Lewis Innes, 7 Jan. 1687 [?or 1688], BL/1/107/8.
17. NRS, Synod of Aberdeen minutes, 1662–1688, CH2/840/10, p. 400; NRS, Presbytery of Aberdeen minutes, 1673–1688, CH2/1/2, p. 529; NRS, Presbytery of Ellon minutes, 1672–1689, CH2/146/5, pp. 443, 451; NRS, Presbytery of Fordyce, CH2/158/4, fos 149v.–150v., 153v.; NRS, Synod of Brechin minutes, 1681–1688, CH2/40/19, p. 55.
18. ACAA, Aberdeen incoming letters book, 1682–1699, CA/8/1/7, no. 100, Earl of Perth to council, 29 June 1687, no. 102, James Leslie to the lord provost and bailies, 30 July 1687, no. 103, Council to Andrew Burnet, 5 Aug. 1687, no. 104, James Leslie to council, 13 Aug. 1687, no. 106, Information for James Boyes and James Leslie, 26 Oct. 1687, no. 108, Council to the earl of Perth, 1687, no. 112, Instructions for George Seton, 4 Jan. 1688, no. 115, Andrew Burnet to council, 8 Feb. 1688. The entries in *Fasti*, VI, pp. 15, 38, give no indication of the dispute, and the dates there seem incorrect.
19. SCA, Robert Strachan to Charles Whytford, 29 March 1688, BL/1/118/6; Same to same, 31 March 1688, BL/1/118/7; David Burnet to Walter Leslie, 30 Aug. 1688, BL/1/118/16 (1); Dilworth, 'The Scottish mission in 1688–1689', pp. 72, 74.
20. [Reid,] *Account of the Popes Procession*. See Chapter 5, p. 111.
21. On the relationship between Edinburgh and the Canongate, see Allen, 'Conquering the suburbs'. More generally, see Dennison, *Holyrood and Canongate*, ch. 5.
22. NLS, Memoirs of John Brand, minister of Bo'ness, MS. 1668, fo. 5r.
23. NLS, Diary of Kincaid, Adv. 32.7.7, fos 18v., 33v., 55r., 62v., 97v.; Meikle (ed.), 'An Edinburgh diary', pp. 139, 144.

24. Dilworth, 'The Scottish mission in 1688–1689', p. 71.
25. Lauder, *Historical Notices*, II, p. 794.
26. NRS, Parliamentary visitation of Edinburgh's town college, 1690–1702, PA10/4 [unfoliated], Libel against Alexander Cunningham, 1690; EUL, Account of Edinburgh's town college after the revolution, by David Gregory, Dk.1.2², item 23; [Monro,] *Presbyterian Inquisition*, pp. 102–3; Hannay, 'The visitation of the college of Edinburgh', pp. 93–5.
27. Lauder, *Historical Notices*, II, p. 823; [Gordon,] *Request to Roman Catholicks*, p. 1. The author is misleadingly described on the title page as a 'Moderate Son of the Church of *England*'. Gordon again used this sobriquet in 1706: [Gordon,] *Some Charitable Observations on a late Treatise*.
28. Lauder, *Historical Notices*, II, p. 816.
29. Mann, *Scottish Book Trade*, pp. 119, 127–8; Cowan, 'The Holyrood press'; NRS, Secretary's warrant books, SP4/11, pp. 277–8, SP4/12, pp. 541–2.
30. NRS, Secretary's warrant book, SP4/12, pp. 142 (quotation), 143, 522.
31. Lauder, *Historical Notices*, II, p. 784.
32. There is an incomplete bibliography in Cowan, 'The Holyrood press', pp. 92–100, and a fuller discussion in Raffe, 'Worship and devotion in multiconfessional Scotland'.
33. Raffe, 'The Restoration, the revolution and the failure of episcopacy', pp. 103–5.
34. NLS, Diary of Kincaid, Adv. 32.7.7, fos 91r., 94r.; Meikle (ed.), 'An Edinburgh diary', p. 154.
35. Raffe, 'The Restoration, the revolution and the failure of episcopacy', p. 97. See Chapter 1, p. 17.
36. Lauder, *Historical Notices*, II, pp. 717, 725; NLS, Memoirs of Brand, MS. 1668, fo. 5v. (quotation).
37. See Chapter 1, pp. 18–19.
38. Lauder, *Historical Notices*, II, pp. 669–70, 680.
39. *Fasti*, II, pp. 244, 255, 348.
40. Burnet, *Theses Philosophicae*, pp. 10–11; NRS, Secretary's warrant book, SP4/11, p. 211; Lauder, *Historical Notices*, II, pp. 726, 754; Wood (ed.), *Edinburgh Extracts, 1681 to 1689*, p. 186; NRS, Visitation of Edinburgh's town college, PA10/4, Libel against Thomas Burnet, 28 Aug. 1690; [Monro,] *Presbyterian Inquisition*, pp. 27, 30–1, 53–8; Hannay, 'The visitation of the college of Edinburgh', p. 82.
41. NRS, Presbytery of Ellon, CH2/146/5, pp. 344, 404, 415, 440 (quotation), 450, 465.
42. Cramond (ed.), *Annals of Banff*, II, pp. 42–3; NRS, Presbytery of Fordyce, CH2/158/4, fo. 161r. (quotation).
43. NRS, Presbytery of Forres, CH2/162/1, pp. 524, 526; NRS, Presbytery of Fordoun minutes, 1684–1688, CH2/157/2, p. 24; NRS, Presbytery of Elgin minutes, 1673–1688, CH2/144/4, p. 184.

44. *By the King. A Proclamation*, Wing J252.
45. [Cunningham,] *Some Questions Resolved concerning Episcopal and Presbyterian Government*, p. 24.
46. NUL, Johnston to ? Bentinck, 21 Dec. 1687, Pw A 2120.
47. [Rule,] *A Vindication of the Church of Scotland*, p. 31.
48. BC, NRAS234, Sermons by William Tullideff and James Rymer, May 1688, Bundle 1630, p. 5.
49. NLS, Sermons, 1688, MS. 5770, p. 262.
50. NLS, Sermons by Patrick Warner, 1688, MS. 2788, p. 92. Here Warner referred to Deut. 32: 17.
51. Lauder, *Historical Notices*, II, p. 863; Wodrow, *History*, IV, p. 455; Harris, *Revolution*, p. 176.
52. Lauder, *Historical Notices*, II, pp. 819–22; NUL, Copy of intelligence letter, 8 Dec. 1687, Pw A 2112; Harris, *Revolution*, pp. 175–6.
53. GCA, Sermons by Matthew Crawford, 1688–1689, T-PM 114/15, fo. [16]v. See also NLS, Sermons, MS. 5770, p. 167; NLS, Sermons by Warner, MS. 2788, pp. 65, 73, 74, 120.
54. GUL, Late seventeenth-century sermons, MS. Murray 221, p. 94.
55. NLS, Sermons by Warner, MS. 2788, p. 282.
56. Ibid., pp. 289, 409.
57. Wodrow, *History*, IV, p. 433.
58. Raffe, *Culture of Controversy*, p. 198.
59. GCA, Sermons by Crawford, T-PM 114/15, fos [16]v.–[17]r.
60. Wodrow, *Analecta*, I, p. 178; *RPC*, 3rd ser., XIII, pp. 271, 275–6, 279–80, 287, quotation at p. 276; Fraser, *Annandale Family Book*, II, pp. 41–4; Jardine, 'United Societies', pp. 190–1.
61. [Shields,] *Faithful Contendings Displayed*, first pagination sequence, p. 355.
62. Raffe, 'Presbyterians and episcopalians', pp. 581–6.
63. [Morer, Sage, Monro,] *Account of the Present Persecution*, p. 11; *Scotch Presbyterian Eloquence*, p. 14; [Ridpath,] *Answer to the Scotch Presbyterian Eloquence*, p. 44; NRS, Earl of Perth to the duke of Hamilton, 20 Aug. 1687, GD406/1/9217.
64. Raffe, 'Presbyterians and episcopalians', pp. 587–8.
65. *RPS*, 1690/4/43, 1661/1/158, rescinding (among other acts) 1649/1/78a.
66. Raffe, 'Presbyterians and episcopalians', pp. 592–3.
67. Wodrow, *History*, IV, p. 432.
68. This passage summarises Raffe, 'Preaching, reading and publishing the Word'. See also Donaldson, 'Covenant to revolution'; Cowan, 'Worship and dissent in Restoration Scotland'.
69. Wodrow, *History*, II, p. 148; *RPC*, 3rd ser., III, p. 123 (quotation).
70. NLS, Earl of Tweeddale to Sir Robert Moray, 3 Feb. 1670, MS. 7025, fo. 10r. (quotation); NLS, Earl of Kincardine to the earl of Tweeddale, 27 Apr. 1670, MS. 7004, fo. 33.

71. NRS, Ormiston kirk session accounts and minutes, 1661–1689, CH2/292/2, p. 87 (quotation); *Fasti*, I, p. 340.
72. NLS, Sermons by Warner, MS. 2788, pp. 47–78, 86–122, 129–62, quotations at pp. 116, 118.
73. *RPS*, 1685/4/22; [Renwick, Shields et al.,] *Informatory Vindication*, pp. 192–204.
74. For a longer discussion of attitudes towards the Covenants after 1660, see Raffe, *Culture of Controversy*, ch. 3.
75. GCA, Sermons by Crawford, T-PM 114/15, fo. [143]v.
76. NLS, Reasons for a fast, 1689, Wod. Qu. XXVIII, fo. 78r.
77. *Acts of the General Assembly*, pp. 227–30. The debate generated by this fast is summarised in Raffe, *Culture of Controversy*, pp. 82–3.
78. NRS, Presbytery of Linlithgow minutes, 1687–1694, CH2/242/7, pp. 3 (quotations), 4; NRS, Queensferry kirk session, CH2/689/2, pp. 1, 2–3, 4; *Fasti*, I, p. 225, II, p. 87, V, p. 320.
79. NRS, Presbytery of Peebles and Biggar minutes, 1688–1694, CH2/35/3, pp. 12, 16. It is unclear whether Thomson swore the Test: NRS, Manor kirk session minutes, 1663–1732, CH2/257/1, p. 63 suggests that there were no services in the church until Thomson's successor was installed in Apr. 1683. *Fasti*, I, pp. 281–2 suggests that Thomson was temporarily restored to his church in Oct. 1682.
80. *Fasti*, I, p. 139, VI, p. 2; ACAA, Aberdeen incoming letters book, CA/8/1/7, no. 102, James Leslie to the lord provost and baillies, 30 July 1687; NRS, Presbytery of Irvine, CH2/197/2, p. 7; NRS, Kilwinning kirk session minutes, 1688–1698, CH2/591/2, p. 1; Wodrow, *Analecta*, I, p. 176; Henderson, 'Meldrum, George'.
81. NRS, Presbytery of Inverness minutes, 1670–1688, CH2/553/2, pp. 232–7, quotation at p. 236; Mackay (ed.), *Records of the Presbyteries of Inverness and Dingwall*, pp. 124–7; *Fasti*, VI, pp. 456–7.
82. NRS, Presbytery of Inverness, CH2/553/2, pp. 239–42, quotations at pp. 240, 242; Mackay (ed.), *Records of the Presbyteries of Inverness and Dingwall*, pp. 128–30.
83. Lauder, *Historical Notices*, II, pp. 834, 855; Warrand (ed.), *More Culloden Papers*, I, pp. 201–4; Fraser-Mackintosh (ed.), *Letters of Two Centuries*, p. 118; NRS, Presbytery of Inverness, CH2/553/2, pp. 244–5; Mackay (ed.), *Records of the Presbyteries of Inverness and Dingwall*, pp. 131–2.
84. *Fasti*, VI, pp. 456–7.
85. NRS, General assembly committee of the north papers concerning John Murray, 1694, CH1/2/2/2, fos 131r.–132r. The language of Murray, one of his episcopalian critics, is discussed in Raffe, 'Presbyterians and episcopalians', p. 591.
86. NRS, Presbytery of Dalkeith minutes, 1673–1688, CH2/424/5, p. 328.
87. *By the King. A Proclamation*, Wing J249; *By the King. A Proclamation*, Wing J252.

88. SP, Barony marriages register, 1672–1777, OPR 622/6, fo. 10v.
89. *Act of Privy Council in Favours of the Clerks of Kirk-Sessions* (quotation); SCA, David Burnet to Lewis Innes, 12 March 1688, BL/1/108/10. For the distribution of the act, see e.g. NRS, Presbytery of Lanark minutes, 1664–1688, CH2/234/2, p. 236; NRS, Presbytery of Dunkeld minutes, 1681–1689, CH2/106/1, p. 51.
90. NRS, Dalkeith kirk session minutes and accounts, 1687–1690, 1714–1721, CH2/84/7, fo. 11v.
91. NRS, Bathgate kirk session minutes, 1672–1856, CH2/30/2, p. 60.
92. *RPC*, 3rd ser., XIII, pp. 296–7, quotation at p. 296.
93. NRS, Spott kirk session minutes, 1683–1703, CH2/333/2, p. 35.
94. Gunn and Gunn (eds), *Records of the Baron Court of Stitchill*, p. 103.
95. NRS, Kirkliston kirk session minutes, 1659–1688, CH2/229/1, p. 404 (quotation); SP, Kirkliston register of baptisms and marriages, 1675–1731, OPR 667/1, fos 59r., 189r.
96. Wodrow, *History*, IV, p. 432; e.g. SP, Irvine baptisms register, 1687–1788, OPR 595/1; SP, Kilmarnock baptisms register, 1640–1740, OPR 597/1, fo. 81r.; SP, Kilwinning register of baptisms and marriages, 1669–1727, OPR 599/1, fo. 25v.
97. *Extracts from the Records of the Burgh of Glasgow*, pp. 404–5; SP, Glasgow baptisms register, 1670–1688, OPR 644¹/6; SP, Glasgow baptisms register, 1687–1698, OPR 644¹/7.
98. Armet (ed.), *Edinburgh Extracts, 1689 to 1701*, pp. 6–7; SP, Edinburgh baptisms register, 1684–1687, OPR 685¹/10, fos 124r., 128r., 133v.; SP, Edinburgh baptisms register, 1688–1692, OPR 685¹/11, e.g. fos 1v., 5v., 8v., 15v., 20r.
99. NRS, Renfrew kirk session, CH2/1596/1/1, p. 42.
100. See esp. McCallum, 'Charity and conflict'; Stewart, 'Poor relief in Edinburgh'. The older view can be found in Mitchison, *Old Poor Law in Scotland*, chs 1–2.
101. NRS, Ratho kirk session minutes, 1682–1689, CH2/309/1, p. 68.
102. On the principles and practices of accountability in the kirk session, see Mutch, *Religion and National Identity*.
103. NRS, Kelso kirk session minutes, 1677–1689, CH2/1173/6, p. 137.
104. NRS, Lenzie Easter kirk session, CH2/237/1, pp. 220–1.
105. NRS, Dron kirk session minutes, 1683–1717, CH2/93/2, pp. 40–1 (quotations); *Fasti*, IV, p. 202.
106. NRS, Spott kirk session, CH2/333/2, p. 32 (quotation); Mitchison, *Old Poor Law in Scotland*, pp. 29–30; *RPS*, 1672/6/69.
107. NRS, Spott kirk session, CH2/333/2, pp. 33, 38 (quotation).
108. NRS, Bathgate kirk session, CH2/30/2, pp. 58, 60.
109. NRS, Barony kirk session minutes and accounts, 1637–1698, CH2/173/1, p. 89.
110. Wodrow, *History*, IV, p. 432.

111. NRS, West Kirk kirk session, CH2/718/10, p. 37.
112. NRS, South Leith presbyterian kirk session, CH2/716/9, pp. 11, 25, which suggest an average weekly collection of £10.2s.11d. for 10 July–1 Nov. 1687, and of £7.14s.9½d. for Nov. 1687–Feb. 1688. As noted in Chapter 2, the episcopalians' average collection fell from £16.17s.1d. in the first half of 1687 to £11.6s.6d. in the same period of 1688.
113. NRS, Presbytery of Duns minutes, 1659–1688, CH2/113/1, p. 307.
114. NRS, Presbytery of Linlithgow minutes, 1676–1688, CH2/242/6, pp. 189 (quotation), 191.
115. See Moir, '"Some Godlie, Wyse and Vertious Gentilmen"', pp. 223–41.
116. *RPS*, 1661/1/423.
117. NRS, Presbytery of Lanark, CH2/234/2, p. 239; NRS, Archbishop John Paterson to Sir William Fleming, James Hamilton and Gabriel Hamilton, 9 Apr. 1688, GD3/10/3/8.
118. NRS, Cramond kirk session accounts, 1687–1709, CH2/426/22, p. 23.
119. Wood (ed.), *Edinburgh Extracts, 1681 to 1689*, p. 262.
120. Armet (ed.), *Edinburgh Extracts, 1689 to 1701*, pp. 17, 25.
121. NRS, Spott kirk session, CH2/333/2, p. 42.
122. Cullen, *Famine in Scotland*, pp. 105–10.
123. Some examples are discussed in Leneman and Mitchison, *Sin in the City*, pp. 84–5.
124. Mackay (ed.), *Records of the Presbyteries of Inverness and Dingwall*, p. 364.
125. NRS, Rutherglen kirk session minutes, marriages, baptisms, testimonials and accounts, 1658–1780, CH2/315/1, p. 91.
126. NRS, Edinburgh Trinity College kirk session, CH2/141/5, pp. 89, 94 (quotation).
127. NRS, Presbytery of Dalkeith, CH2/424/5, pp. 290–2, 295, 298–300, 310, 312, 314, 316, 318, 332, 333 (quotation).
128. Ibid., pp. 333 (quotation), 334, 337.
129. Ibid., pp. 334–7; NRS, Dalkeith kirk session, CH2/84/7, fos 15v., 16r.
130. Mackay (ed.), *Records of the Presbyteries of Inverness and Dingwall*, pp. 363, 366 (quotation).
131. NRS, Presbytery of Paisley minutes, 1663–1687, CH2/294/5, fos 145r. (quotations), 145v., 146, 147r.
132. NRS, Presbytery of Dumbarton minutes, 1684–1688, CH2/546/3, pp. 14, 19, 21–2, 24 (quotation).
133. Ibid., pp. 25 (quotation), 27–8.
134. SBA, Presbytery of Jedburgh, CH2/198/5, pp. 62, 64–5 (first quotation), 67 (second quotation), 68–9 (further quotations). The digital surrogate in the NRS is partially illegible.
135. NRS, Bathgate kirk session, CH2/30/2, p. 59.
136. NRS, Presbytery of Peebles minutes, 1649–1688, CH2/295/4, pp. 340–2.
137. NRS, Presbytery of Peebles and Biggar, CH2/35/3, p. 2 (quotation); NRS, Presbytery of Peebles, CH2/295/4, p. 342a.

138. Wodrow, *History*, IV, p. 432.
139. NRS, Presbytery of Peebles and Biggar, CH2/35/3, pp. 2–3; NRS, Presbytery of Peebles, CH2/295/4, pp. 341, 342.
140. NRS, Presbytery of Kintyre, CH2/1153/1, fo. 34r.; NRS, Presbytery of Peebles and Biggar, CH2/35/3, pp. 14, 16–17, 21.
141. NRS, Dalkeith kirk session, CH2/84/7, fo. 13r.
142. NRS, Newbattle kirk session minutes, 1673–1702, CH2/276/5, pp. 129–33, 137 (quotation).
143. NRS, Presbytery of Kintyre, CH2/1153/1, fo. 37v.
144. Stark and Bainbridge, *Theory of Religion*, pp. 131–3, discusses some of these considerations in abstract and schematic terms.
145. Raffe, *Culture of Controversy*, p. 191.

CHAPTER 4 JAMES AND THE ROYAL BURGHS

1. *Declaration of His Highness William Henry ... of the Reasons Inducing Him to Appear in Arms for Preserving of the Protestant Religion*, sig. [A]v.
2. *RPS*, 1689/3/108.
3. Ibid., 1689/3/97, 1689/3/113, 1689/3/134. See Chapter 6, pp. 148–50.
4. For a contemporary discussion of these matters, see [Skene,] *Memorialls for the Government of the Royall-Burghs*, esp. pp. 18, 81, 106–7.
5. Rait, *Parliaments of Scotland*, pp. 250, 255–7; MacDonald, *Burghs and Parliament*, pp. 12–13, 27.
6. *RPS*, 1686/4/2, 1689/3/2, 1690/4/2. The 1690 figure included all the parliamentary burghs at the time of the 1707 union, with the exception of Campbeltown, which first sat in parliament in 1700: Rait, *Parliaments of Scotland*, p. 275; MacDonald, *Burghs and Parliament*, p. 195.
7. Pagan, *Convention of the Royal Burghs*; MacDonald, *Burghs and Parliament*, ch. 3; Toller, '"Now of little significancy"'.
8. *RPS*, 1672/6/13.
9. See e.g. [Skene,] *Memorialls for the Government of the Royall-Burghs*, pp. 106–7.
10. MacIntosh, *Scottish Parliament under Charles II*, p. 202; cf. Mackenzie, *Scottish Burghs*, p. 149, which implies that an act was passed in 1681, probably misled by *Ancient Laws and Customs of the Burghs*, pp. 157–8, which prints a draft act.
11. Lauder, *Historical Notices*, I, pp. 323–4.
12. *Records of the Convention of the Royal Burghs*, IV, pp. 59–61, 63–4.
13. 'Register containeing the state and condition of every burgh'; Toller, '"Now of little significancy"', pp. 114–18.
14. Rait, *Parliaments of Scotland*, pp. 260–1; ECA, Convention of Royal Burghs [Moses] Bundles, Bundle 211, Petition of Anstruther-Wester, 1688, Petition of Kilrenny, 1688, Bundle 212 [unfoliated], Petition of Anstruther-Wester, 1689.

15. ECA, Convention of Royal Burghs [Moses] Bundles, Bundle 211, Petition of Dysart, 1688; FCAC, Dysart town council minutes, 1674–1761, B/DY/1/1/2, has no minutes between 28 Sep. 1682 and 12 Nov. 1690; NRS, Dysart kirk session minutes, 1654–1695, CH2/390/3, p. 215.
16. See e.g. ECA, Convention of Royal Burghs [Moses] Bundles, Bundle 211, Petition of Tain, 1688, Petition of Sanquhar, 1688.
17. 'Setts of the royal burghs', pp. 161–4.
18. Lynch, 'The crown and the burghs', esp. pp. 58–9; MacDonald, *Burghs and Parliament*, pp. 39–40.
19. Brown, 'Toward political participation and capacity', p. 18; Bain et al. (eds), *Calendar of the State Papers relating to Scotland*, XI, p. 189; Wood (ed.), *Edinburgh Extracts, 1589 to 1603*, pp. 96–8; Lynch, *Edinburgh and the Reformation*, esp. p. 6; MacDonald, *Burghs and Parliament*, pp. 40–1.
20. Stewart, 'Politics and government in the Scottish burghs'; Stewart, *Urban Politics and the British Civil Wars*, pp. 165–6.
21. Stevenson, 'Burghs and the Scottish revolution', pp. 185–6; MacDonald, *Burghs and Parliament*, pp. 41–2.
22. AA, Brechin town council minutes, 1672–1712, B1/1/1, e.g. fos 89v.–90r.
23. NRS, Secretary's warrant books, SP4/11, pp. 382–3, SP4/12, p. 505, SP4/13, pp. 349–50; *RPC*, 3rd ser., XII, pp. 511, 513–14, 552–3; *Extracts from the Records of the Burgh of Glasgow*, pp. 391–2, 407–9, 417–19; Jackson, 'Glasgow in transition', p. 65. See Chapter 1, p. 18.
24. NRS, Secretary's warrant books, SP4/11, pp. 476–7, SP4/12, pp. 353–4; SAUL, St Andrews town council minutes, 1673–1707, B65/11/2, pp. 151, 159–60.
25. Pagan, *Convention of the Royal Burghs*, pp. 82–3; Toller, '"Now of little significancy"', ch. 1; *RPC*, 3rd ser., VII, pp. 203–4, 234, 235, 249–50, 251–2, 273–4, 421.
26. *RPC*, 3rd ser., VII, pp. 255–7, quotation at p. 255; Strawhorn, *History of Ayr*, pp. 66, 80.
27. LL, Lanark town council minutes, 1650–1694 [unfoliated], 29 Sep. 1682, 29 March 1683; *Extracts from the Records of the Royal Burgh of Lanark*, pp. 212–15; *RPC*, 3rd ser., VIII, pp. 66–7; Robertson, *Lanark*, pp. 117–23.
28. *RPC*, 3rd ser., VII, pp. 330–1.
29. Wood (ed.), *Edinburgh Extracts, 1681 to 1689*, pp. 83–4.
30. NRS, Secretary's warrant book, SP4/10, pp. 69, 72–3; *RPC*, 3rd ser., XI, pp. 188, 194; Wood (ed.), *Edinburgh Extracts, 1681 to 1689*, pp. 151, 153; HMC, *Buccleuch & Queensberry*, II, pp. 93–4.
31. NRS, Secretary's warrant books, SP4/11, pp. 406–7, SP4/12, p. 396; *RPC*, 3rd ser., XII, pp. 511, 514, 524, 526; Wood (ed.), *Edinburgh Extracts, 1681 to 1689*, pp. 188–9, 226.
32. NRS, Secretary's warrant book, SP4/10, p. 70 (quotation); ACAA, Aberdeen town council minutes, 1682–1704, CA/1/1/57, pp. 185–9.

Leslie's long-serving predecessor as provost, Sir George Skene of Fintry, had enemies in Aberdeen, but it is unclear whether they influenced the crown's decision to nominate: NLS, William Cochrane to John, Lord Cochrane, 25 Nov. 1684, MS. 14407, fo. 99r.
33. Lauder, *Historical Notices*, II, p. 727.
34. HMC, *Mar and Kellie*, I, pp. 218–19.
35. NRAS217, Melfort to Moray, undated, Box 7, no. 594.
36. NRS, Secretary's warrant book, SP4/11, pp. 311 (quotations), 312.
37. Ibid., SP4/11, p. 324 (quotation); *Records of the Convention of the Royal Burghs*, IV, p. 64. The king had earlier expressed his objections to unspecified acts in the convention of 1685: NRS, Secretary's warrant book, SP4/11, p. 147.
38. *RPC*, 3rd ser., XII, p. 454; Lauder, *Historical Notices*, II, p. 752.
39. NRS, Secretary's warrant books, SP4/12, pp. 352–4, SP4/13, pp. 233–4.
40. As noted above, some of these towns may have lacked magistrates in the period.
41. NRAS217, Lists of towns, undated, Box 7, nos 319, 320.
42. NRS, Secretary's warrant book, SP4/12, p. 505; *Extracts from the Records of the Burgh of Glasgow*, pp. 407–8; Lauder, *Historical Notices*, II, p. 843.
43. Lauder, *Historical Notices*, II, p. 864; NRS, Secretary's warrant book, SP4/12, pp. 610–11.
44. Sowerby, *Making Toleration*, esp. pp. 136–42; Miller, *Cities Divided*, pp. 228–37; Halliday, *Dismembering the Body Politic*, esp. pp. 244–50.
45. NRS, Secretary's warrant book, SP4/11, pp. 407–8; *RPC*, 3rd ser., XII, pp. 514–15; ACAA, Aberdeen council minutes, CA/1/1/57, pp. 239–40; NRS, Linlithgow town council minutes, 1673–1694, B48/9/4, p. 724.
46. DGA, Dumfries town council minutes, 1680–1694, WA2/5, pp. 254–5.
47. *RPS*, 1689/3/222. Auchterlonie was named the burgh's dean of guild in Nov. 1686, but this nomination seems not to have taken effect: NRS, Secretary's warrant book, SP4/11, pp. 460–1; AA, Montrose town council minutes, 1673–1702, M1/1/3, pp. 85, 106, 107, showing that the council of 1685 was still in office when the nomination of 1687, which Auchterlonie was accused of procuring, was implemented. The latter nomination, which excluded Auchterlonie, is at NRS, Secretary's warrant book, SP4/12, pp. 398–9.
48. *RPC*, 3rd ser., XII, pp. 542–3; PKCA, Account of the election of commissioners from Perth to the convention of estates, 28 Feb. 1689, B59/34/6 (quotation).
49. Lauder, *Historical Notices*, II, pp. 735, 737.
50. ECA, Convention of Royal Burghs [Moses] Bundles, Bundle 211, Commission to David Eadie, 30 Oct. 1688; NRS, Privy council acta, 4 Sep. 1696–11 July 1699, PC1/51, pp. 588, 593; Privy council acta, 13

July 1699–5 May 1703, PC1/52, pp. 6, 36–8; Bellesheim, *History of the Catholic Church*, IV, p. 143.
51. *Extracts from the Council Register of the Burgh of Aberdeen*, p. 310; ACAA, Aberdeen council minutes, CA/1/1/57, pp. 296, 297; 'The Erroll papers', p. 295; Young (ed.), *Parliaments of Scotland*, I, pp. 5–6.
52. NLS, John Tuach to John Mackenzie of Delvine, 21 Jan. 1688, MS. 1102, fo. 103r.; NRS, Secretary's warrant book, SP4/13, pp. 79–80.
53. PCL, Paisley burgh court book, 1682–1698, P1/1/15, pp. 179–80, 182; *RPC*, 3rd ser., XII, pp. 503, 505–6.
54. Wood (ed.), *Edinburgh Extracts, 1665 to 1680*, pp. 139–42; Wood (ed.), *Edinburgh Extracts, 1681 to 1689*, pp. 185, 220, 226; Lauder, *Historical Notices*, II, p. 752.
55. NRS, Linlithgow council minutes, B48/9/4, p. 725, cf. p. 485.
56. SAUL, Pittenweem town council minutes, 1629–1727, B60/6/1, fo. 105; NRS, Fortrose burgh court and council records, 1674–1690, B28/7/3 [unpaginated], 27 Sep. 1686, 4 Oct. 1686; SM, Kirkcudbright town council minutes, 1683–1700, G1/1/6, fos 27v.–28r.
57. CAC, Wick council and burgh court minutes, 1660–1711, BW/1/1, fo. 46r.
58. OLA, Kirkwall town council minutes, 1673–1691, K1/1/3, fos 118v., 118Ar., 119r., 119v. (quotation).
59. NRS, Secretary's warrant book, SP4/11, pp. 478–9, 511–12; SAUL, Cupar town council minutes, 1685–1698, B13/14/1, fos 19v. (quotation), 22r.; ELA, Dunbar town council minutes, 1671–1687, DUN/2/1/1/1 [unpaginated], 13 June 1687.
60. FCAC, Kirkcaldy town council minutes, 1680–1717, B/KDY/1/2, fo. 68r.; NRS, Irvine council minutes, B37/12/4, p. 10 [from back of book]; ELA, Haddington council minutes, HAD/2/1/2/8, fo. 55v. (where the fee quoted is £7). See also Lauder, *Historical Notices*, II, p. 755. Rutherglen apparently received its nomination in 1687 at the knock-down price of £24 Scots (£2 sterling): GCA, Rutherglen town council minutes, 1681–1692, RU3/1/7, p. 214.
61. SBA, Selkirk court record and council minutes, 1635–1704, BS1/1/1, fo. 500r. (quotation); cf. NRS, Copy of Selkirk town council minutes, 1687–1688, GD123/183, fo. 4r.; NRS, Secretary's warrant book, SP4/12, pp. 407–8.
62. DL, Dumbarton town council minutes, 1673–1693, DB1/1/4, pp. 561, 574, 577; NRS, Secretary's warrant book, SP4/12, pp. 411–12.
63. See also n. 47 above.
64. NRS, Secretary's warrant book, SP4/13, pp. 254–60; AA, Arbroath burgh court minute book, 1681–1704, A1/1A/4, fo. 34r.; StrM, Wigtown town council minutes, 1680–1694, WN1/1/1, fos 125v.–128v.; PCL, Renfrew town council minutes, 1684–1695 [unpaginated], see 25 Dec. 1688;

SCAS, Stirling town council minutes, 1680–1703, B66/20/6, fo. 236r.; *Extracts from the Records of the Royal Burgh of Stirling*, p. 54.
65. NRS, Secretary's warrant book, SP4/13, pp. 350–2; SBA, Selkirk court record and council minutes, BS1/1/1, fo. [507]v., peters out in July 1688.
66. NRS, Secretary's warrant book, SP4/12, pp. 670–1; GCA, Rutherglen council minutes, RU3/1/7, pp. 237–9, shows the previous council still in office at Michaelmas 1688. Sir James Hamilton of Manor Eliston, James's choice of provost, had in 1685 refused to sit for the burgh in parliament: GCA, Rutherglen council minutes, RU3/1/7, pp. 132, 136, 137–8.
67. NRS, Secretary's warrant books, SP4/12, pp. 259–60, 274–5, 306–7, 546–8, SP4/13, pp. 167–8; StrM, Wigtown council minutes, WN1/1/1, fo. 111v.; SBA, Peebles burgh court book, 1678–1704, B58/9/3 [unpaginated], 5 Feb. 1688; OLA, Kirkwall council minutes, K1/1/3, fos 124r.–125v., 130Ar., 130. Kirkwall council began choosing magistrates and deacons as normal at Michaelmas 1687, but suspended the election on 30 Sep., before the royal order to do so was received: see fos 124B, 124A, 124v., 125B, 125v.
68. NRS, Secretary's warrant book, SP4/12, pp. 326–7, 353; Johnston (trans.), *Rothesay Town Council Records*, I, pp. 435–6.
69. NRS, Secretary's warrant books, SP4/12, pp. 589–90, SP4/13, pp. 257–9; StrM, Wigtown council minutes, WN1/1/1, fos 111v.–128v.
70. NRS, Linlithgow council minutes, B48/9/4, pp. 721, 744, 786. The William Cockburn who refused the Test in Dunbar after being chosen as a councillor in Sep. 1685 was probably not the man of the same name nominated in Dec. 1686, though (as noted above) this nomination was put into effect after the first indulgence: ELA, Dunbar council minutes, DUN/2/1/1/1, 21 Sep. 1685, 13 June 1687.
71. See Chapter 2, pp. 50–1, 54–5.
72. NRS, Secretary's warrant book, SP4/11, pp. 462–4; *RPC*, 3rd ser., XIII, pp. 42–3.
73. NRS, Secretary's warrant book, SP4/12, pp. 402–3; AyA, Ayr town council minutes, 1669–1694, B6/18/4, fo. 306r.
74. NRS, Secretary's warrant book, SP4/12, pp. 410–11; SM, Kirkcudbright council minutes, G1/1/6, fo. 50r.
75. NRS, Secretary's warrant book, SP4/13, p. 258. See Chapter 3, p. 58.
76. SCA, John Jameson to Charles Whytford, 16 Jan. 1688, BL/1/114/5; NRS, Secretary's warrant book, SP4/11, p. 488. Perhaps Kidd was influenced by the promise of large payments from the king, awarded in Dec. 1687 and May 1688: NRS, Secretary's warrant books, SP4/12, p. 528, SP4/13, p. 76.
77. PKCA, Perth town council minutes, 1680–1693, B59/16/10, fos 111v.–112r.
78. PKCA, Account of the election of commissioners from Perth, B59/34/6.
79. FCAC, Culross council minutes, B/Cul/1/1/3, p. 250. A James Mackie, bailie of Culross and probably the same man, swore the Test in Oct. 1683: *RPC*, 3rd ser., VIII, p. 625.

80. On Broun of Nuntoun, see Armet (ed.), *Kirkcudbright Sheriff Court Deeds*, I, p. 294.
81. DGA, Dumfries council minutes, WA2/5, pp. 210–11; McDowall, *History of the Burgh of Dumfries*, pp. 472–4; Fraser, *Book of Carlaverock*, I, p. 602.
82. DGA, Dumfries council minutes, WA2/5, pp. 260 (quotation), 261, 287.
83. Ibid., pp. 248, 299; *Extracts from the Council Register of the Burgh of Aberdeen*, p. 307.
84. Strawhorn, *History of Ayr*, p. 81; e.g. NRS, Bonds detailing loans to Sir William Wallace of Craigie, RH15/112/2/45–6.
85. NRS, Linlithgow council minutes, B48/9/4, p. 719; ELA, Dunbar council minutes, DUN/2/1/1/1, 10 Jan. 1687; NRS, Inverkeithing guildry minutes, 1590–1742, B34/11/1, p. 76; SM, Kirkcudbright council minutes, G1/1/6, fo. 35v.
86. This is necessarily a rough approximation. The count on which it is based excludes men such as Sir Patrick Threipland of Fingask who owned land but had formerly been involved in the government of their towns and may have been active merchants: see Young (ed.), *Parliaments of Scotland*, II, pp. 696–7. The count includes several individuals who were probably landowners but about whom we lack the information to exclude on these grounds.
87. Lauder, *Historical Notices*, II, p. 755; *RPS*, 1609/4/27.
88. DGA, Dumfries council minutes, WA2/5, p. 164; McDowall, *History of the Burgh of Dumfries*, p. 472; AM, Annan town council minutes, 1678–1712, AB1/1/1, p. 41; Steel (ed.), *Records of Annan*, p. 38.
89. SAUL, Cupar council minutes, B13/14/1, fos 5r., 17r.
90. MacDonald, *Burghs and Parliament*, pp. 36–9.
91. *Records of the Convention of the Royal Burghs*, IV, p. 71, cf. p. 91; Lauder, *Historical Notices*, II, p. 806. The convention declared that the king's nominees would not be affected by the act of 1675, which amounted to its suspension. Lauder implied that the act was renewed, and his statement misled Rait, *Parliaments of Scotland*, p. 306, and Harris, *Revolution*, p. 178.
92. SBA, Selkirk court record and council minutes, BS1/1/1, fos 497r.–[507]v. On the earlier disputes, see e.g. NRS, Information for John Riddell of Hayning against Selkirk, 1672, GD123/184/2.
93. ELA, Haddington council minutes, HAD/2/1/2/8, fos 56r. (quotation), 60r., 60v., 74v., 75r.; *Records of the Convention of the Royal Burghs*, IV, pp. 68, 73, 81.
94. ELA, Dunbar council minutes, DUN/2/1/1/1, esp. 14 Oct. 1687; ELA, Dunbar town council minutes, 1688–1712, DUN/2/1/1/2, fos 8v., 9v.; *Records of the Convention of the Royal Burghs*, IV, pp. 69, 74.
95. NRS, Secretary's warrant book, SP4/11, pp. 509–10; MHC, Elgin town council minutes, 1670–1705, ZBEl A2/10 [unfoliated], 25 Aug. 1685, 25 Apr. 1687; Cramond (ed.), *Records of Elgin*, I, p. 339.

96. Cramond (ed.), *Records of Elgin*, I, p. 346. See Chapter 5, p. 119.
97. ECA, Convention of Royal Burghs [Moses] Bundles, Bundle 212, Petition of Elgin, 1689 (quotation); *Records of the Convention of the Royal Burghs*, IV, p. 70.
98. NRS, Secretary's warrant book, SP4/11, pp. 479–80; FCAC, Kirkcaldy council minutes, B/KDY/1/2, fos 68v.–69r., 88v.; Macbean, *Kirkcaldy Burgh Records*, p. 212.
99. NRS, Secretary's warrant books, SP4/11, pp. 438–9, SP4/12, pp. 180–7, SP4/13, p. 299; *RPC*, 3rd ser., XI, p. 12, XIII, p. 140; Balcarres, *Memoirs*.
100. *RPC*, 3rd ser., XI, p. 12, XII, pp. 491–2, XIII, p. 140; NRS, Secretary's warrant books, SP4/11, pp. 360–1, 583–4, SP4/12, pp. 588–9; Furgol, 'Livingstone, George'.
101. NRS, Secretary's warrant books, SP4/11, p. 189, SP4/13, pp. 248–9.
102. Ibid., SP4/11, pp. 444–5; *RPC*, 3rd ser., XII, p. 125.
103. See Chapter 1, p. 27.
104. NRS, Treasury register, E7/4, p. 21; NRS, Warrants of the exchequer register, E8/38, Tack of inland excise of Forfarshire, Fife, Kinross-shire and Clackmannanshire, 16 Dec. 1686.
105. NRS, Secretary's warrant book, SP4/12, pp. 306–7, 351–2; NRS, Treasury register, E7/4, pp. 19, 20, 125–6; NRS, Warrants of the exchequer register, E8/38, Tacks of inland excise, 3, 8 Dec. 1686.
106. NRS, Secretary's warrant book, SP4/13, pp. 224–5; NRS, Treasury register, E7/4, pp. 19, 21 (which refers to John Broun of Nunland), 125–6.
107. NRS, Secretary's warrant book, SP4/11, pp. 106–7.
108. NRS, Secretary's warrant books, SP4/10, pp. 314–18, SP4/11, pp. 476–7; *RPC*, 3rd ser., XII, pp. 211–12, 257, 260–1; Murray, 'The Scottish treasury', pp. 98–9.
109. Lauder, *Historical Notices*, II, p. 764.
110. In Feb. 1688, the earl of Perth allowed Forfar to elect a new treasurer in place of George Wood, who had served since Apr. 1686, the office being financially burdensome: AA, Forfar town council minutes, 1685–1723, F1/1/2, p. 49.
111. ELA, Dunbar council minutes, DUN/2/1/1/1, e.g. 23 Feb. 1685, 21 Sep. 1685, 13 June 1687.
112. NRS, Secretary's warrant book, SP4/12, pp. 398–9; AA, Montrose council minutes, M1/1/3, p. 85.
113. NRS, Secretary's warrant book, SP4/11, pp. 443–4; LL, Lanark council minutes, 29 Sep. 1684, 8 Oct. 1685.
114. Halliday, *Dismembering the Body Politic*, esp. pp. 5–7, 15.
115. *RPC*, 3rd ser., VIII, pp. 245–50, XI, pp. 180, 193–4, 339–42, 456–8, 472–5, 548–50, 573–84; Strawhorn, *History of Ayr*, pp. 66, 79–81.
116. NRS, Secretary's warrant books, SP4/11, p. 487, SP4/12, pp. 402–3, SP4/13, pp. 166–7; AyA, Ayr council minutes, B6/18/4, fos 287r., 306r., 324v.–325r.

117. AyA, Ayr council minutes, B6/18/4, fo. 334r.
118. *RPC*, 3rd ser., IX, pp. 112–14; *Extracts from the Records of the Royal Burgh of Stirling*, pp. 27–31, 38–40, 41–2.
119. NRS, Secretary's warrant book, SP4/11, pp. 361–2; *RPC*, 3rd ser., XII, pp. 493–4; *Extracts from the Records of the Royal Burgh of Stirling*, pp. 49–50.
120. *Extracts from the Records of the Royal Burgh of Stirling*, pp. 50–1, 52.
121. Lauder, *Historical Notices*, II, pp. 725, 735; HMC, *Mar and Kellie*, I, p. 219; Mann, '"James VII, King of the Articles"', p. 202.
122. *RPC*, 3rd ser., VIII, pp. 517–18, 527; NRS, Linlithgow council minutes, B48/9/4, pp. 741–5, quotation at p. 743.
123. *RPC*, 3rd ser., XII, pp. 256–7, 259–60, 265–6, 299–300, 311; *Extracts from the Records of the Burgh of Glasgow*, pp. 386–7, 388–9; Lauder, *Historical Notices*, II, pp. 737, 740, 741.
124. NRS, Secretary's warrant book, SP4/11, pp. 382–3; *RPC*, 3rd ser., XII, pp. 511, 513–14.
125. See e.g. the dispute recorded at *Extracts from the Records of the Burgh of Glasgow*, pp. 339–41; Jackson, 'Glasgow in transition', p. 66.
126. Terry, *John Graham of Claverhouse*, ch. 7.
127. MacDonald, 'Dundee and the crown', p. 42; *Charters, Writs, and Public Documents of the Royal Burgh of Dundee*, pp. 105–8.
128. DCA, Dundee town council minutes, vol. 6, 1669–1707, fos 202v.–203r.; *RPC*, 3rd ser., XII, p. 256.
129. *Charters, Writs, and Public Documents of the Royal Burgh of Dundee*, pp. 103–5; DCA, Dundee council minutes, vol. 6, fos 203v.–205v.
130. HMC, *Mar and Kellie*, I, p. 219.
131. NRS, Secretary's warrant books, SP4/11, pp. 417–18, SP4/12, pp. 588–9; DCA, Dundee council minutes, vol. 6, fos 209v.–210r., 226.
132. This subject has not attracted much scholarly attention. There is a starting point in Turner, *History of Local Taxation*, pp. 137–43.
133. *RPS*, 1644/6/282, 1644/6/283, 1661/1/160, 1681/7/32, 1685/4/16. For discussions of the excise, see Stewart, *Rethinking the Scottish Revolution*, pp. 201–5; Lennox, 'Lauderdale and Scotland', pp. 308–13; Lee, 'Government and Politics in Scotland', ch. 3.
134. Maitland, *History of Edinburgh*, p. 109.
135. *RPS*, 1649/1/232; Wood (ed.), *Edinburgh Extracts, 1642 to 1655*, pp. 334, 342. Montrose had a grant for a malt levy in 1653: Toller, '"Now of little significancy"', p. 26.
136. Wood (ed.), *Edinburgh Extracts, 1655 to 1665*, pp. 219, 223, 225, 301, 305; *RPS*, 1662/5/60; Wood (ed.), *Edinburgh Extracts, 1665 to 1680*, pp. 82, 100–1, 104, 404, 411.
137. Mooney (ed.), *Charters and Other Records of Kirkwall*, pp. 76–9; Anderson (ed.), *Charters and Other Writs of Aberdeen*, pp. 207–11. These and other references are given in Toller, '"Now of little significancy"', p. 26

n. 40. *RPS*, 1661/1/332, 1662/5/60, 1662/5/72, 1669/10/138, 1670/7/20, 1670/7/63, 1672/6/136.
138. In addition to those discussed in the following paragraphs, there were gifts in favour of Kirkcaldy and Culross (with the parishes of Torryburn and Kincardine): NRS, Secretary's warrant books, SP4/12, pp. 510–11, 616–17, SP4/13, pp. 217–18.
139. Wood (ed.), *Edinburgh Extracts, 1665 to 1680*, pp. 101, 104, 112, 411.
140. *Extracts from the Records of the Burgh of Glasgow*, pp. 400–1; NRS, Secretary's warrant book, SP4/11, pp. 551–2.
141. NRS, Burntisland town council minutes, 1680–1688, B9/12/14, fos 119r., 135v., 136r. (quotation), 136v.
142. AA, Montrose council minutes, M1/1/3, pp. 101, 122; NRS, Secretary's warrant book, SP4/12, p. 654.
143. NRS, Secretary's warrant book, SP4/11, pp. 614–16; DCA, Dundee council minutes, vol. 6, fos 213v., 215v., 216.
144. NRS, ?Sir Thomas Kennedy to George Drummond, 10 Sep. 1687, GD24/1/463/50; NRS, Secretary's warrant book, SP4/13, pp. 275–6. Hay was involved in the registration with the great seal of at least two grants: *Charters of the Royal Burgh of Ayr*, p. 68; *Muniments of the Royal Burgh of Irvine*, I, p. 113.
145. *RPC*, 3rd ser., XI, pp. 161–2; Lauder, *Historical Notices*, II, p. 663. Burntisland first approached Bannockburn: NRS, Burntisland council minutes, B9/12/14, fos 119r., 135v.–136r.
146. MHC, Elgin council minutes, ZBEl A2/10, 19 Oct. 1685, 22 Oct. 1685, 4 Oct. 1686 (recording a payment of 3 guineas to Mr Andrew Foster, which might have related to the scheme), 10 Jan. 1687; *RPC*, 3rd ser., XI, pp. 355–6, 448, 450–1; NRS, Secretary's warrant book, SP4/11, p. 236.
147. *RPS*, A1690/4/4; *Muniments of the Royal Burgh of Irvine*, I, pp. 112–15; NRS, Secretary's warrant book, SP4/13, pp. 312–13. See Chapter 6, p. 151.
148. NRS, Secretary's warrant book, SP4/11, pp. 552–3; AyA, Ayr council minutes, B6/18/4, fos 288r.–290r.; *Charters of the Royal Burgh of Ayr*, pp. 66–72.
149. *To his Grace His Majesties High Commissioner ... The Petition of the Magistrats and Town Council of Elgin*; cf. *RPS*, 1700/10/124.

CHAPTER 5 THE REVOLUTION IN THE LOCALITIES

1. Balcarres, *Memoirs*, p. 15, claimed that a dozen died as a result of firing on the crowd outside Holyroodhouse on 10 Dec. For lower estimates, compare the other sources cited in n. 28 below.
2. *London Gazette*, nos 2411, 2414, 17–20 Dec., 27–31 Dec. 1688.
3. NLS, Lord Yester to the earl of Tweeddale, 9 Feb. 1689, MS. 14404, fo. 17r; cf. Beddard, 'The unexpected whig revolution of 1688', p. 65.

4. Cowan, 'The reluctant revolutionaries'; Barnes, 'Scotland and the glorious revolution'.
5. *RPC*, 3rd ser., XIII, pp. 305–7, 310–11, 311–13; Fraser, *Melvilles*, III, p. 192.
6. *Proclamation, appointing a Rendezvous of the Militia-Regiments*; Luttrell, *Brief Historical Relation of State Affairs*, I, p. 465.
7. Jones, *Revolution of 1688*, p. 258; NRS, Secretary's warrant book, SP4/13, pp. 243–4.
8. Balcarres, *Memoirs*, pp. 11–12; NRS, Secretary's warrant book, SP4/13, pp. 284–5.
9. *RPC*, 3rd ser., XIII, pp. 319–23; *Proclamation, for calling out Heretors &c.*
10. *RPS*, 1663/6/64; Murray, *Chronicles of the Atholl and Tullibardine Families*, I, pp. 269–70; *RPC*, 3rd ser., XIII, p. 338 (quotation); Lenman, 'Militia, fencible men, and home defence', p. 184.
11. NRS, Earl of Perth to the earl of Mar, 1 Oct. 1688, GD124/15/189/3; Same to same, 31 Oct. 1688, GD124/15/189/6; Fraser, *Chiefs of Colquhoun*, I, p. 300; Fraser, *Red Book of Grandtully*, I, pp. cxlvii–viii; Fraser, *Chiefs of Grant*, II, p. 27.
12. *Act of Privy Council, Anent the Punishment of these who refuse to Serve*; *Act of Privy Council, Anent the Shires of Dumfreis, Air, &c.*; *RPC*, 3rd ser., XIII, pp. 346, 348.
13. *RPC*, 3rd ser., XIII, p. 349; Balcarres, *Memoirs*, p. 12.
14. Balcarres, *Memoirs*, p. 14; *Proclamation, taking off the Stop of Execution against Heretors*; Fraser, *Melvilles*, III, p. 192.
15. BC, NRAS234, Marquis of Atholl to Lord Murray, 22 Dec. 1688, Box 29, 1/5/82.
16. *Act of Privy Council, for calling out the Heretors*.
17. Balcarres, *Memoirs*, p. 23; *Declaration by His Highness the Prince of Orange; for the Keeping of the Peace*; NLS, Earl of Tweeddale to Lord Yester, 16 Feb. 1689, MS. 7026, fo. 137v.; Same to same, 22 Feb. 1689, MS. 7026, fo. 143r.
18. *Five Letters from a Gentleman in Scotland*, p. 1. For the earlier riots, see Chapter 1, p. 18 and Chapter 3, p. 59.
19. Wood (ed.), *Edinburgh Extracts, 1681 to 1689*, pp. 250–1 (quotation at p. 250), 166.
20. NRS, Alexander Baird to Andrew Russell, 1 Dec. 1688, RH15/106/659/17.
21. SCA, David Burnet to Charles Whytford, 27 Nov. 1688, BL/1/109/24; Same to same, [29] Nov. 1688, BL/1/109/25. The college's closure had been anticipated since at least the start of October: NLS, Sir Patrick Murray to the earl of Tweeddale, 4 Oct. 1688, MS. 7011, fo. 75r.
22. Harris, *London Crowds in the Reign of Charles II*, esp. pp. 93, 103–6; Harris, *Restoration*, pp. 187–8.
23. Raffe, *Culture of Controversy*, pp. 218–19.

24. *Five Letters from a Gentleman in Scotland*, p. 4 (quotation); Wood (ed.), *Edinburgh Extracts, 1681 to 1689*, p. 254.
25. [Monro,] *Apology for the Clergy of Scotland*, p. 8.
26. [Reid,] *Account of the Popes Procession*.
27. Hannay, 'The visitation of St Andrews University', p. 10.
28. The following account is based on the contemporary and near-contemporary reports in: Fraser, *Melvilles*, II, pp. 102–3; NLS, Earl of Tweeddale to Lord Yester, 11 Dec. 1688, MS. 7026, fos 81–2; NLS, Letter, 12 Dec. 1688, Wod. Fol. XXVI, fo. 267; *Five Letters from a Gentleman in Scotland*, pp. 1–3; *London Mercury*, no. 3, 18–22 Dec. 1688; *Universal Intelligence*, no. 4, 18–22 Dec. 1688; Balcarres, *Memoirs*, pp. 15–17. For secondary accounts, see Wodrow, *History*, IV, pp. 473–5; Houston, *Social Change in the Age of Enlightenment*, pp. 306–9; Harris, *Revolution*, pp. 372–3.
29. *Five Letters from a Gentleman in Scotland*, pp. 1–2 (quotation at p. 2); Wood (ed.), *Edinburgh Extracts, 1681 to 1689*, pp. 251–2.
30. *Proclamation of Privy Council, for Securing the Peace of the City of Edinburgh*. The only known copies are in NRS, RH14/268.
31. Wood (ed.), *Edinburgh Extracts, 1681 to 1689*, pp. 252–3.
32. Balcarres, *Memoirs*, p. 17; Wood (ed.), *Edinburgh Extracts, 1681 to 1689*, pp. 253–4. Some sources suggest that there was no anti-Catholic action after the early morning of 11 Dec. But on 13 Dec. the privy council thought fit to issue a proclamation against disturbances in Edinburgh, and on 14 Dec. ordered the restoration of stolen goods: *Proclamation, for Suppressing of Tumults in Edinburgh*; *Proclamation, for Restoring the Goods of such Persons as were Robbed*.
33. Dilworth, 'The Scottish mission in 1688–1689', esp. pp. 72, 74.
34. NLS, Tweeddale to Yester, 11 Dec. 1688, MS. 7026, fo. 82v.; *RPC*, 3rd ser., XIII, p. 427; Cowan, 'The Holyrood press', p. 90; Watson, 'The publisher's preface', p. 17.
35. Balcarres, *Memoirs*, p. 15; [Monro,] *Apology for the Clergy of Scotland*, pp. 9–10. See also Speke, *Secret History of the Happy Revolution*, pp. 45–6.
36. [Shields,] *Faithful Contendings Displayed*, first pagination sequence, p. 367.
37. [Monro,] *Apology for the Clergy of Scotland*, pp. 8–9.
38. Balcarres, *Memoirs*, pp. 13–15.
39. NLS, Tweeddale to Yester, 11 Dec. 1688, MS. 7026, fo. 81r.
40. Jerdan (ed.), *Letters from James, Earl of Perth*, pp. 1–7; NLS, Earl of Tweeddale to Lord Yester, 22 Dec. 1688, MS. 7026, fo. 89r.
41. NLS, Tweeddale to Yester, 11 Dec. 1688, MS. 7026, fo. 82v.
42. Rogers, *History of the Chapel Royal*, p. ccxliii, app., pp. 107–13; Wood (ed.), *Edinburgh Extracts, 1681 to 1689*, p. 258.
43. Fraser, *Melvilles*, II, p. 103; *Five Letters from a Gentleman in Scotland*, p. 2.

44. NRS, The privy council to King James, 12 Dec. 1688 (copy), GD112/39/144/14.
45. NRS, Act of the privy council, 14 Dec. 1688, GD112/39/144/15.
46. *APS*, IX, app., p. 3; Forbes (ed.), *Curiosities of a Scots Charta Chest*, p. 42; Paterson, *History and Genealogy of the Family of Wauchope*, p. 34.
47. Walker, *Biographia Presbyteriana*, I, p. 280.
48. HMC, *Laing*, I, pp. 460–2.
49. [Shields,] *Faithful Contendings Displayed*, first pagination sequence, pp. 367–8; Walker, *Biographia Presbyteriana*, I, p. 280; GCA, Hugh Maxwell to Sir John Maxwell, 14 Jan. 1689, T-PM 113/810 (quotation); McDowall, *History of the Burgh of Dumfries*, pp. 476–7. In April 1689, the convention heard that the countess and her family were again troubled by a disorderly 'rable': *RPS*, 1689/3/89.
50. DGA, Dumfries council minutes, WA2/5, p. 280.
51. *Proclamation, for Suppressing of Tumults in Edinburgh*.
52. [Shields,] *Faithful Contendings Displayed*, first pagination sequence, p. 367.
53. [Shields,] *Short Memorial of the Sufferings and Grievances*, p. 40.
54. *Collection of Papers relating to the Present Juncture of Affairs*, pp. 31–4, quotation at p. 33; Jones, *Revolution of 1688*, pp. 301–3; Pincus, *1688*, pp. 247–9. See also Greaves, *Secrets of the Kingdom*, pp. 324–6.
55. GCA, Maxwell to Maxwell, 14 Jan. 1689, T-PM 113/810; *Five Letters from a Gentleman in Scotland*, p. 4.
56. Wodrow, *Analecta*, I, p. 187; NLS, Tweeddale to Yester, 22 Dec. 1688, MS. 7026, fo. 89; BC, NRAS234, Atholl to Murray, 22 Dec. 1688, Box 29, 1/5/82. Scots in London were more sceptical of the reports: BC, NRAS234, Earl of Breadalbane to the marquis of Atholl, 27 Dec. 1688, Box 29, 1/5/84.
57. [Morer, Sage, Monro,] *Account of the Present Persecution*, p. 15; *Late Letter Concerning the Sufferings of the Episcopal Clergy*, pp. 7–8.
58. NRS, Linlithgow council minutes, B48/9/4, p. 783.
59. *Act of Privy Council, for calling out the Heretors*.
60. NRS, Kinglassie kirk session minutes and accounts, 1666–1694, CH2/406/2, p. 160.
61. AA, Brechin council minutes, B1/1/1, fos 104r.–105r., quotation at fo. 104r.
62. *Act of Council, anent Papists*.
63. DGA, Dumfries council minutes, WA2/5, pp. 278–9, quotation at p. 278.
64. Ibid., pp. 280, 284 (quotation); Harrison, 'Musgrave, Sir Christopher'. For the circumstances of one Scottish Catholic soldier, who was imprisoned in Dumfries after returning from England in Dec. 1688, see *RPC*, 3rd ser., XIII, p. 372.
65. DGA, Dumfries council minutes, WA2/5, pp. 278, 287; DGA, List of arms held in Dumfries, 15 Jan. 1689, RB2/5/32, fo. 8, quotation at fo. 8v.

66. DGA, List of arms, RB2/5/32, fo. 4r. (quotation); DGA, Dumfries council minutes, WA2/5, p. 199; Dilworth, 'The Scottish mission in 1688–1689', p. 70.
67. NRS, 'Remembrance, or Record of the Sufferings of some Freinds', CH10/1/65.
68. NLS, Lists of ministers in 1662, 1689 and 1701, Adv. 32.3.6, fos 13r.–46v., specifies 108 ministers who were rabbled, and a further 67 who deserted or demitted office at the time of the violence, but is an incomplete record.
69. For more detailed accounts, see Raffe, *Culture of Controversy*, pp. 219–23; Harris, *Revolution*, pp. 376–8; Shukman, *Bishops and Covenanters*, ch. 3.
70. [Sage,] *Case of the Present Afflicted Clergy*, second pagination sequence, pp. 1, 4; [Monro,] *Letter to a Friend*, pp. 17–19.
71. NRS, Spott kirk session, CH2/333/2, p. 37; cf. Jardine, 'United Societies', app. 7.7.
72. *Late Letter Concerning the Sufferings of the Episcopal Clergy*, pp. 21–2; *RPC*, 3rd ser., XVI, pp. 457–8. The presbyterian Gilbert Rule claimed that Douglas fled the parish because of his debts: [Rule,] *Second Vindication of the Church of Scotland*, pp. 124–5.
73. [Morer, Sage, Monro,] *Account of the Present Persecution*, p. 20; NRS, Commission to Robert Scott, 22 Jan. 1689, CH12/12/773.
74. *Declaration by His Highness the Prince of Orange; for the Keeping of the Peace.*
75. [Morer, Sage, Monro,] *Account of the Present Persecution*, pp. 20–1; [Sage,] *Case of the Present Afflicted Clergy*, pp. 50–3; NLS, Account of the 'carriage of the people of Glasgow to the curats anno 1689', Wod. Qu. LXXIII, fo. 10; Edwards, *Love & Loyalty*, pp. 15–19, 21.
76. AA, Montrose council minutes, M1/1/3, pp. 131, 132–3.
77. AA, Forfar council minutes, F1/1/2, pp. 64–8.
78. DGA, Dumfries council minutes, WA2/5, pp. 279, 281 (quotation).
79. SM, Kirkcudbright council minutes, G1/1/6, fo. 50.
80. AyA, Ayr council minutes, B6/18/4, fos 335r. (quotation), 334r.
81. Dalton, *Scots Army*, pt 2, p. 143.
82. Cramond (ed.), *Records of Elgin*, I, pp. 346–7; MHC, Elgin council minutes, ZBEl A2/10, 7 Jan. 1689.
83. ELA, Haddington council minutes, HAD/2/1/2/8, fos 87r. (quotation), 87v.–88r.
84. *Extracts from the Records of the Royal Burgh of Lanark*, pp. 226–7.
85. FCAC, Kirkcaldy council minutes, B/KDY/1/2, fos 83v.–85r.; Jerdan (ed.), *Letters from James, Earl of Perth*, p. 4.
86. FCAC, Culross council minutes, B/Cul/1/1/3, p. 250.
87. NRS, Secretary's warrant book, SP4/13, pp. 224–5. The previous provost and bailies (apart from one who seems to have died) were still in office on 22 Oct. 1688: Mackay et al. (eds), *Records of Inverness*, II, p. 357.

88. HAC, Inverness town council minutes, 1689–1702, BI/1/1/7, pp. 1–3, quotations at p. 1; Mackay et al. (eds), *Records of Inverness*, II, p. 358. On Inverness burgh politics in the Restoration period, see esp. Kennedy, 'The urban community in Restoration Scotland'; Miller, *Inverness*, ch. 6.
89. [Reid,] *Account of the Popes Procession*, p. 2. There is no record of the election in ACAA, Aberdeen council minutes, CA/1/1/57.
90. NRS, Burntisland town council minutes, 1688–1701, B9/12/15, fos 10r. (quotation), 11v.
91. AM, Annan council minutes, AB1/1/1, p. 55; Steel (ed.), *Records of Annan*, p. 40; NRS, Secretary's warrant book, SP4/12, pp. 591–2; Balcarres, *Memoirs*, p. 10.
92. Wilson (ed.), *Lochmaben Court and Council Book*, p. 189.
93. NRS, Irvine council minutes, B37/12/4, pp. 31–3 [from back of book].
94. *Declaration by His Highness the Prince of Orange; for the Keeping of the Peace*.
95. PKCA, Perth council minutes, B59/16/10, fos 111v. (quotations), 112r.; *Memorabilia of the City of Perth*, pp. 191–2.
96. NRS, Additional libel and sentence against John Henderson, 23, 25 Feb. 1689, B34/20/169.
97. Japikse (ed.), *Correspondentie van Willem III en van Hans Willem Bentinck*, II, pp. 618–19; *Proclamation, against Spreading of False News*.
98. *Declaration of His Highness William Henry ... of the Reasons Inducing Him to Appear in Arms for Preserving of the Protestant Religion*; cf. *Declaration of His Highnes William Henry ... of the Reasons Inducing Him to Appear in Armes in the Kingdome of England*. Both *Declarations* are dated 10 Oct. 1688 (n.s.). See also Raffe, 'Propaganda, religious controversy and the Williamite revolution'.
99. [Shields,] *Faithful Contendings Displayed*, first pagination sequence, pp. 370, 373–4; *Five Letters from a Gentleman in Scotland*, p. 4.
100. [Shields,] *Faithful Contendings Displayed*, first pagination sequence, pp. 364–6, 369, 373–4; Wodrow, *Analecta*, I, pp. 182–4, 185–6.
101. NRS, Magistrates, councillors and residents of Ayr to Montgomery, 31 Dec. 1688, GD3/5/784.
102. Wood (ed.), *Edinburgh Extracts, 1681 to 1689*, pp. 256, 257–8 (quotations); NLS, Earl of Tweeddale to Lord Yester, 1 Jan. 1689, MS. 7026, fo. 98r. Tweeddale also reported that the *Declaration* was to be read in Haddington on 1 Jan. For Edinburgh's 'great council', see Stewart, *Urban Politics and the British Civil Wars*, pp. 42–4.
103. NRS, Burntisland council minutes, B9/12/15, fo. 9r. 'Scotlands fall' has been written in the margin in a hand other than the clerk's.
104. DGA, Dumfries council minutes, WA2/5, p. 286; NRS, Papers of the parliamentary visitation of the University of St Andrews, 1690s, PA10/6 [unfoliated], 27 Aug. 1690, 28 Aug. 1690; Hannay, 'The visitation of St Andrews University', p. 8.

105. Wodrow, *History*, IV, p. 472.
106. ACAA, Banff council account book and stent roll, 1684–1694, AS/Bbnf/11/1/1 [unpaginated].
107. AA, Arbroath burgh court minute book, A1/1A/4, fo. 34r.
108. Fraser, *Melvilles*, III, p. 193; NRS, Address of the privy council to William of Orange, GD157/1682.
109. Wodrow, *History*, IV, pp. 477–81; HMC, *Roxburghe; Campbell; Strathmore; and Seafield*, p. 117; BC, NRAS234, Lady Murray to Lord Murray, 14 Jan. 1689, Box 29, 1/5/96; Luttrell, *Brief Historical Relation*, I, p. 503. [Mackenzie and Mackenzie,] *Memorial for his Highness the Prince of Orange*, pp. 10–24, printed a different presbyterian address, which seems to be what Wodrow referred to as a 'maimed and false copy': *History*, IV, p. 482. Yet another address is NRS, 'The humble address of the M[i]n[iste]rs and Elders of the Church of Scotland who adhere to the way of the Reformed Churches in doctrine and discipline nou presently Conveened in their Gen[era]ll meeting', CH8/171.
110. Wood (ed.), *Edinburgh Extracts, 1681 to 1689*, pp. 254–6.
111. NLS, 'The humble adres of the Nobelmen, Gentilmen and Royal Borows, within the Shyre of east Lowthian', MS. 7026, fo. 94ar. NLS, Lord Yester to the earl of Tweeddale, 5 Jan. 1689, MS. 14404, fo. 3r. See also Chapter 6, pp. 138–9.
112. NLS, Lord Yester to the earl of Tweeddale, 19 Jan. 1689, MS. 14404, fo. 8v. Tweeddale had offered to send the Fife address to be presented by Yester, who was in London: NLS, Earl of Tweeddale to Lord Yester, 5 Jan. 1689, MS. 7026, fo. 78r. Tweeddale also referred to an address from Midlothian, which may not have been presented: Same to same, 28 Dec. 1688, MS. 7026, fo. 92r.
113. RPC, 3rd ser., XIII, p. 328; *Extracts from the Records of the Burgh of Glasgow*, pp. 414–15; *London Gazette*, no. 2392, 18–22 Oct. 1688; Harris, *Revolution*, p. 370.
114. *Extracts from the Records of the Burgh of Glasgow*, pp. 417, 419 (quotation).
115. NRS, Address from Glasgow to William of Orange, 1688, GD3/10/3/10; [Shields,] *Faithful Contendings Displayed*, first pagination sequence, p. 368.
116. *Extracts from the Records of the Burgh of Glasgow*, p. 420.
117. *Extracts from the Council Register of the Burgh of Aberdeen*, pp. 310–11; Findlay and Murdoch, 'Revolution to reform', pp. 267–8.
118. Patrick, 'People and Parliament in Scotland', chs 3–4; Patrick, 'Unconventional procedure'. See also Mann, 'Inglorious revolution', p. 128.
119. *His Highness the Prince of Orange his Speech to the Scots Lords and Gentlemen*, p. 2 (quotation); NRS, Andrew Fletcher to Andrew Russell, 8 Jan. 1689, RH15/106/690/7; Smout, 'The road to union', pp. 183–4. Patrick, 'Unconventional procedure', p. 213, reproduces the printed order to town clerks to organise elections.

120. Balcarres, *Memoirs*, p. 24.
121. NRS, 'Reasons humbly offered to his highnes the P. of Orange against the advice given in the address, relating to [th]e Election of Commissioners from the Burrowes', GD103/2/232.
122. NLS, Lord Yester to the earl of Tweeddale, 15 Jan. 1689, MS. 14404, fo. 5r.
123. Wood (ed.), *Edinburgh Extracts, 1681 to 1689*, pp. 260–1.
124. NLS, Earl of Tweeddale to Lord Yester, 5 Feb. 1689, MS. 7026, fo. 126v.; Same to same, 26 Feb. 1689, MS. 7026, fo. 145r.
125. FCAC, Culross council minutes, B/Cul/1/1/3, pp. 257–8.
126. NRS, Fortrose burgh court and council records, B28/7/3, 22 Feb. 1689.
127. NRS, Stonehaven (Kincardine) head court, freeholders and election papers, 1680–1689, SC5/70/8 [unfoliated], 1 March 1689.
128. Balcarres, *Memoirs*, p. 24.
129. NLS, Earl of Tweeddale to Lord Yester, 28 Feb. 1689, MS. 7026, fo. 147v.; Same to same, 2 March 1689, MS. 7026, fo. 149r.; Note of the Edinburgh election result, 2 March 1689, MS. 7026, fo. 153r.; NRS, Edinburgh parliamentary commission, 12 March 1689, PA7/25/59/14.
130. Wood (ed.), *Edinburgh Extracts, 1665 to 1680*, pp. 49, 131, 231–3; *RPC*, 3rd ser., IV, pp. 469–70, 471–2; Mackenzie, *Memoirs of the Affairs of Scotland*, pp. 274–6.
131. Wood (ed.), *Edinburgh Extracts, 1665 to 1680*, pp. 350, 355–6; *RPS*, 1662/5/70.
132. Armet (ed.), *Edinburgh Extracts, 1689 to 1701*, p. 1. See Chapter 6, p. 148.
133. DCA, Dundee council minutes, vol. 6, fo. 240r.; Millar, *Roll of Eminent Burgesses of Dundee*, pp. 206–7. No burgesses were entered in the book between 18 Sep. 1686 and 7 May 1689, when there was a backlog of sixty-five to be recorded: DCA, Dundee lockit book, fos 206r.–207r. It is unclear what was objected to in the burgess oath, which probably did not oblige its swearers to be members of the established Church. See DCA, Dundee lockit book, fos 17r. (where the oath's text is obliterated), 20v. (the oath as amended in 1708).
134. PKCA, Account of the election of commissioners from Perth, B59/34/6; PKCA, Protest by William Whyt, George Oliphant, David Murray and their adherents, 28 Feb. 1689, B59/34/5/2 (quotation).
135. PKCA, Account of the election of commissioners from Perth, B59/34/6; PKCA, Additional account of the election at Perth, 28 Feb. 1689, B59/34/7/1; PKCA, Perth council minutes, B59/16/10, fo. 112; *RPS*, 1689/3/14.
136. In addition to the three cases discussed here, the convention resolved disputed elections in Aberdeen (*RPS*, 1689/3/41), Berwickshire (1689/3/44), Kirkcaldy (1689/3/47), Anstruther-Easter (1689/3/49) and North Berwick (1689/3/66), and overturned the result in Ross-shire on a technicality (1689/3/225).

137. *RPS*, 1689/3/51; NRS, Jedburgh parliamentary commission, 25 Feb. 1689, PA7/25/71/9 (quotation).
138. NRS, Linlithgow parliamentary commissions in favour of George, Lord Livingstone, 21 Feb. 1689, PA7/25/80/10, and William Higgins, 12 March 1689, PA7/25/80/11.
139. *RPS*, 1689/3/23, 1700/5/26; *Fasti*, I, pp. 295–6; Patrick, 'People and Parliament in Scotland', p. 120.
140. NRS, Linlithgow council minutes, B48/9/4, pp. 784–6, 791.
141. NRS, Parliamentary commissions from Selkirkshire, 1 March 1689, PA7/25/31/9, Anstruther-Wester, 5 March 1689, PA7/25/38/6, Banff, 2 March 1689, PA7/25/41/10, Crail, 27 Feb. 1689, PA7/25/46/9/1, Cullen, 1 March 1689, PA7/25/48/7, Dumbarton, 4 March 1689, PA7/25/53/8, Forfar, 25 Feb. 1689, PA7/25/61/8, Kilrenny, 2 March 1689, PA7/25/72/5, Nairn, 4 March 1689, PA7/25/83/9, Pittenweem, 26 Feb. 1689, PA7/25/88/7; NRS, Execution of election, Arbroath, 25 Feb. 1689, PA7/25/39/8/2. The commission from Aberdeen also claimed unanimity, but was produced in a disputed election: NRS, Aberdeen parliamentary commission, 27 Feb. 1689, PA7/25/35/12.
142. NRS, Execution of election, Inverkeithing, 12 March 1689, PA7/25/67/9/2; NRS, Selkirk parliamentary commission, 27 Feb. 1689, PA7/25/95/11; NRS, Burntisland council minutes, B9/12/15, fo. 12r.; ELA, Haddington council minutes, HAD/2/1/2/8, fo. 90r.; Johnston (trans.), *Rothesay Town Council Records*, II, p. 457; NRS, John Stirling to Andrew Russell, ?26 Feb. 1689, RH15/106/688/4.
143. NRS, Peebles sheriff court diet and minute book, 1667–1689, SC42/1/2 [unpaginated], 1 March 1689.
144. Agnew, *Agnews of Lochnaw*, p. 438.
145. ELA, Haddington council minutes, HAD/2/1/2/8, fo. 90.
146. FCAC, Culross council minutes, B/Cul/1/1/3, p. 260.
147. NRS, Irvine council minutes, B37/12/4, p. 30. In addition to these examples, instructions were issued to the commissioner for Inverness, though no detail was recorded in the council minutes: HAC, Inverness council minutes, BI/1/1/7, p. 30.
148. ECA, Queensferry town council minutes, 1689–1703, SL59/1/1/3, pp. 33–4; NRS, Burntisland council minutes, B9/12/15, fo. 30v.
149. [Shields,] *Short Memorial of the Sufferings and Grievances*, pp. 49–50; *Brief and True Account of the Sufferings of the Church of Scotland*, pp. 19–20.

CHAPTER 6 THE REVOLUTION SETTLEMENT OF 1689–1690

1. *Allegiance and Prerogative Considered*, p. 4.
2. *Some Weighty Considerations, Humbly Proposed*, p. 7.

3. *Salus Populi Suprema Lex*, p. 3. One copy of this work, Henry E. Huntington Library, 434380 (available on Early English Books Online), is annotated on the title page 'By Iames Stewart'; Sir James Steuart of Goodtrees is a possible author.
4. *Address to the Nobility, Clergy and Gentlemen*, p. 3.
5. *Allegiance and Prerogative Considered*, pp. 5, 6 (quotation); *Letter to a Member of the Convention of States*, p. 6. The latter work has been incorrectly attributed to William Sherlock.
6. Balcarres, *Memoirs*, pp. 12–13; NLS, Lord Yester to the earl of Tweeddale, 5 Feb. 1689, MS. 14404, fo. 15r.; NLS, Earl of Tweeddale to Lord Yester, 7 Feb. 1689, MS. 7026, fo. 127r.; Same to same, 2 March 1689, MS. 7026, fo. 149r.
7. Seventeen shire commissioners and nine burgh commissioners (respectively 30.4 per cent and 13.8 per cent of those present on 14 March 1689) refused the tests of allegiance to William and Mary. These totals result from adding the twenty-three who had not sworn allegiance or subscribed the assurance and were unseated in Apr. 1693 (subtracting one subsequently re-elected), three members who had not subscribed the assurance by 25 Apr. 1693 and did not later attend parliament, and one additional nonsubscriber identified in May 1700. See *RPS*, 1689/3/2, 1693/4/21, 1693/4/22, 1693/4/28, 1700/5/17. Of the twenty-three removed in Apr. 1693, a few burgh commissioners may have failed to attend, not out of political principle, but because they lacked financial assistance from their towns to do so: Patrick, 'People and Parliament in Scotland', pp. 125–6.
8. Riley, *King William and the Scottish Politicians*, ch. 1.
9. Balcarres, *Memoirs*, p. 24; [Shields,] *Faithful Contendings Displayed*, first pagination sequence, pp. 387–8; Scott (ed.), 'Letters of Graham', p. 234.
10. *RPS*, 1689/3/4; *APES*, I, p. 1; Balcarres, *Memoirs*, pp. 24–5.
11. *RPS*, 1689/3/6; Balcarres, *Memoirs*, pp. 25–6; NRS, William Livingstone to Andrew Russell, 23 March 1689, RH15/106/685/12.
12. *RPS*, 1689/3/15–19; Balcarres, *Memoirs*, pp. 27–8, 30; *APES*, I, pp. 16–17, 20.
13. *RPS*, 1689/3/67. This statement is based on the list of Williamites in Balcarres, *Memoirs*, pp. 12–13.
14. *RPS*, 1689/3/93, 1689/3/94 (quotation); *APES*, I, p. 26.
15. Balcarres, *Memoirs*, p. 35; *APES*, I, p. 21.
16. *Leven and Melville Papers*, p. 9.
17. Lenman, 'The poverty of political theory', p. 255.
18. Harris, *Revolution*, p. 394.
19. *RPS*, 1689/3/108–9; Balcarres, *Memoirs*, pp. 35–6. In a letter to William, Atholl explained that he had failed to vote for the Claim because he refused to condemn episcopacy and impose new restrictions on the royal prerogative: *Leven and Melville Papers*, p. 12.

20. All quotations from the Claim of Right and Grievances are from the text in *RPS*, 1689/3/108, 1689/3/121.
21. Ibid., 1681/7/18.
22. Ibid., 1663/6/110, 1669/10/13, 1681/7/42.
23. NLS, Manuscript journal of the convention, 9–10 Apr. 1689, MS. 7026, fo. 195r.; NLS, 'Sir James Montgomerie of Skelmorly's representation and vindication of the presbyterians anent their carriage at the dissolution of the assembly 1692', Wod. Oct. XXX, fo. 60r. The claim that Montgomery had the clause inserted into the Claim rests on [Comber,] *Protestant Mask taken off from the Jesuited Englishman*, pp. 33–4; Hopkins, 'Sir James Montgomerie of Skelmorlie', p. 42.
24. The ordinary lords of session removed were Lord Tarbat in 1664, Lord President Stair, Lords Newbyth and Glendoick, in 1681, Lord Pitmedden in 1686, and Lords Harcarse and Edmonstone in 1688: see Lauder, *Historical Notices*, I, pp. 333–4, II, pp. 723, 856; Brunton and Haig, *Historical Account of the Senators of the College of Justice*, pp. 357, 369, 391, 403, 406–7, 415. See also Dalrymple, *Apology for Sir James Dalrymple of Stair*, sig. Av.; McNeill, 'The independence of the Scottish judiciary', pp. 145–6.
25. See Harris, *Revolution*, pp. 398–400; Levack, 'Judicial torture in Scotland'; Jackson, 'Judicial torture, the liberties of the subject, and Anglo-Scottish relations'.
26. Raffe, 'Female authority and lay activism', pp. 66–7; *RPS*, 1685/4/23.
27. Jackson, '"Assize of error" and the independence of the criminal jury'; Normand and Roberts (eds), *Witchcraft in Early Modern Scotland*, pp. 253–60.
28. NRS, Fletcher to Russell, 8 Jan. 1689, RH15/106/690/7.
29. See e.g. [Ferguson,] *Late Proceedings and Votes of the Parliament*, pp. 6–7; Harris, *Revolution*, pp. 184–5.
30. NLS, Earl of Tweeddale to Sir John Dalrymple, 29 Jan. 1689, MS. 7026, fo. 116r.
31. NLS, 'The humble adres of the Nobelmen, Gentilmen and Royal Borows, within the Shyre of east Lowthian', MS. 7026, fo. 94ar; cf. *RPS*, 1663/6/64.
32. *Leven and Melville Papers*, p. 10; NLS, Lord Yester to the earl of Tweeddale, 15 Jan. 1689, MS. 14404, fo. 5v. See also *Salus Populi Suprema Lex*, p. 8.
33. *RPS*, 1689/3/16 (quotation), 1689/3/58.
34. NLS, Earl of Tweeddale to Lord Yester, 5 Jan. 1689, MS. 7026, fos 77v.–78r.
35. Burnet, *History of his own Time*, IV, pp. 37–8; NLS, Earl of Tweeddale to Lord Yester, 12 March 1689, MS. 7026, fo. 156; *Leven and Melville Papers*, pp. 2–3.
36. *RPS*, 1689/3/158, 1689/3/159, see also M1689/3/27.
37. *Journals of the House of Lords*, XIV, p. 434.

38. For other perspectives, see Ferguson, *Scotland's Relations with England*, pp. 170–2; Whatley with Patrick, *Scots and the Union*, pp. 90–2.
39. *To His Grace, His Majesties High Commissioner ... the Humble Address of the Presbyterian Ministers*, p. 1 (quotation). The same petition was presented on both occasions: [Sage,] *Account of the Late Establishment of Presbyterian-Government*, pp. 6–10. See also *RPS*, M1689/6/16, M1690/4/3; *APES*, I, pp. 175, 210–14, II, 145. For the addresses to William, see Chapter 5, p. 123.
40. *Leven and Melville Papers*, p. 2 (quotation); Glassey, 'William II and the settlement of religion in Scotland'.
41. *RPS*, 1689/3/116; Clarke, 'Scottish Episcopalians', pp. 578–85.
42. *RPS*, M1689/6/8, A1689/6/8 (quotation); Clarke, 'The Williamite episcopalians and the glorious revolution', pp. 42–3.
43. *Letter to a Reverend Minister of the Gospel*; *Letter from the West to a Member of the Meeting of the Estates*. Also published was a reprint of Ussher, *Reduction of Episcopacy unto the Form of Synodical Government*.
44. *Leven and Melville Papers*, p. 258; NLS, Paper by Robert Wylie concerning the admission of episcopalian ministers into the Church, *c*. 1693, Wod. Qu. LXXIII, fos 15–20.
45. Halliday, 'The Club and the revolution'.
46. *RPS*, M1689/6/14; *APES*, I, p. 172; *Leven and Melville Papers*, pp. 136, 139, 174–6.
47. *RPS*, 1689/6/36, 1689/6/46.
48. Ibid., 1690/4/12, 1690/4/13, 1690/4/43 (quotation), 1690/4/114, cf. 1592/4/26. This was essentially the settlement sought by the general meeting, from whose address the adjectives quoted came: *To His Grace, His Majesties High Commissioner ... the Humble Address of the Presbyterian Ministers*, p. 2.
49. *Leven and Melville Papers*, p. 172. See also Whitley, *Great Grievance*, ch. 5.
50. *APES*, II, p. 191; *RPS*, M1690/4/21; [Sage,] *Account of the Late Establishment of Presbyterian-Government*, pp. 76–7.
51. *RPS*, 1690/4/119, which specifically mentioned acts of 1661 (1661/1/294) and 1663 (1663/6/105).
52. NRS, Newton kirk session minutes, 1651–1696, CH2/283/2, fos 108v.–110v.; *Fasti*, I, p. 337.
53. NRS, Privy council acta, 2 Feb. 1692–31 March 1693, PC1/48, pp. 297–8; *Fasti*, IV, p. 296.
54. Maxwell, 'The Church union attempt'; *RPS*, 1693/4/89. I am grateful to Ben Rogers, who is conducting doctoral research in this area at the University of Edinburgh, for advice.
55. *RPS*, 1695/5/186; Clarke, 'The Williamite episcopalians and the glorious revolution', p. 50.
56. NRS, Privy council acta, PC1/52, pp. 510–11; Raffe, *Culture of Controversy*, pp. 42–3, 51, 55. For more detail and other perspectives

on the subject of this paragraph, see Stephen, *Defending the Revolution*; Clarke, 'Scottish Episcopalians'.
57. Raffe, 'Presbyterians and episcopalians'.
58. Ford, 'Protestations to parliament for remeid of law'.
59. For a balanced assessment of the Articles in this period, see Mann, 'Inglorious revolution', pp. 123–6.
60. *RPS*, 1690/4/44, 1690/9/14. The second act, granting additional cess and the hearth tax, was in place of a proposed tax on annualrents (interest payments), which, it was decided, would be difficult to implement: *RPS*, 1690/4/59.
61. Ibid., 1693/4/34, 1693/4/37, 1693/4/56, 1693/4/74, 1695/5/93, 1695/5/111, 1695/5/187, 1695/5/188, 1696/9/53, 1696/9/54, 1696/9/148.
62. *Grievances Represented by the Estates of Scotland*, pp. 2, 4.
63. *RPS*, M1689/6/2 (quotation), M1689/6/3; *APES*, I, pp. 133–4, 135; NLS, Duke of Hamilton to the earl of Tweeddale, 20 June 1689, MS. 14407, fo. 138r.; *Leven and Melville Papers*, pp. 59, 62, 63–4, 67, 80; Fraser, *Melvilles*, II, p. 109.
64. *RPS*, M1689/6/5; *APES*, I, pp. 140–1; *Leven and Melville Papers*, pp. 93 (quotation), 99.
65. *RPS*, M1689/6/5, M1689/6/11; *Grievances Represented by the Estates of Scotland*, p. 4; *APES*, I, pp. 158–9.
66. *RPS*, 1690/4/22; Mann, 'Inglorious revolution', p. 129.
67. *RPC*, 3rd ser., XIV, pp. 378–81; *Leven and Melville Papers*, pp. 21, 23–4.
68. *RPS*, 1689/3/160, 168.
69. Raffe, 'Scottish state oaths and the revolution', pp. 177–8; *APES*, I, pp. 162–5.
70. [Ferguson,] *Late Proceedings and Votes of the Parliament*, p. 19; *Leven and Melville Papers*, pp. 23–4.
71. *Leven and Melville Papers*, pp. 87, 100–2, 105, 136; Fraser, *Melvilles*, II, pp. 110–11; *APES*, I, pp. 151–2; *RPS*, M1689/6/8.
72. *RPC*, 3rd ser., XIII, p. 379.
73. NRS, Secretary's warrant book, SP4/14, pp. 223, 226–36.
74. Raffe, 'Presbyterianism, secularization, and Scottish politics', pp. 328–31.
75. *RPC*, 3rd ser., XVI, pp. 10–13. The last set of audited treasury accounts, covering the period to 1 March 1692, appears to understate the level of military expenditure after March 1689: NRS, Accounts, E26/12, pp. 220–41.
76. *RPS*, 1700/10/244.
77. [Montgomery,] *Great Britain's Just Complaint for her Late Measures*, p. 32. See more generally Hopkins, *Glencoe and the End of the Highland War*, chs 10–12; Macinnes, 'William of Orange'.
78. *RPS*, 1689/3/73 (quotation); Wood (ed.), *Edinburgh Extracts, 1681 to 1689*, p. 270; *APES*, I, p. 20.
79. *RPS*, 1689/3/97 (quotations); Armet (ed.), *Edinburgh Extracts, 1689 to 1701*, pp. 1–2; Wood (ed.), *Edinburgh Extracts, 1681 to 1689*, pp. 246–7.

80. *RPS*, 1689/3/113, M1689/3/22; DCA, Dundee council minutes, vol. 6, fos 226, 240v.–241r.; NRS, Secretary's warrant books, SP4/11, pp. 417–18, SP4/12, pp. 588–9.
81. *RPS*, 1689/3/128, 1693/4/22.
82. Ibid., 1689/3/134, 1689/3/137.
83. AyA, Ayr council minutes, B6/18/4, fos 344v.–345r.; Strawhorn, *History of Ayr*, p. 84.
84. NRS, Magistrates, councillors and residents of Ayr to Montgomery, 31 Dec. 1688, GD3/5/784.
85. *Extracts from the Records of the Burgh of Peebles*, pp. 129–30; NRS, Secretary's warrant book, SP4/12, pp. 546–7.
86. ACAA, Aberdeen incoming letters book, CA/8/1/7, no. 130, Draft act of council, 1 May 1689; ACAA, Aberdeen council minutes, CA/1/1/57, pp. 297, 306. There seems to have been another election in January 1689: see Chapter 5, p. 121. The magistrates of Aberdeen and the earls of Erroll and Marischal had requested a delay to the election: *RPS*, M1689/3/26; cf. *APES*, I, p. 45. It was claimed in Sep. 1690 that the magistrates and council of Aberdeen, which then included three of the four bailies elected in May 1689, continued to support the 'popish interest': *RPC*, 3rd ser., XV, pp. 668–70.
87. NRS, Inverkeithing town council minutes, 1689–1745, B34/10/1, p. [1]; NRS, Secretary's warrant book, SP4/11, p. 484.
88. StrM, Stranraer burgh court book, 1684–1710, ST1/1/2 [unpaginated], 10 May 1689, 13 May 1689; NRS, Secretary's warrant book, SP4/12, pp. 666–7.
89. NRS, Burntisland council minutes, B9/12/15, fos 12v.–13r., 19v.–20r.; *RPC*, 3rd ser., XIV, pp. 413–14, 419–20, 455.
90. AA, Montrose council minutes, M1/1/3, pp. 147–8, 149; *RPS*, 1689/3/222 (quotations); cf. Chapter 4, p. 89.
91. *Extracts from the Records of the Royal Burgh of Stirling*, pp. 55–60, 61–2; SCAS, Stirling council minutes, B66/20/6, fo. 243v.; *RPC*, 3rd ser., XIV, pp. 334–6, 459–64, quotations at p. 335. On Stirling's factional politics before 1689, see Chapter 4, p. 100.
92. *Grievances Represented by the Estates of Scotland*, p. 3. The act did not materialise.
93. *RPC*, 3rd ser., XIII, pp. 452, 459–60; NRS, Secretary's warrant book, SP4/14, pp. 32, 178–9; Marwick and Renwick (eds), *Charters and Other Documents Relating to the City of Glasgow*, II, pp. 235–9; *RPS*, 1690/4/64.
94. SAUL, St Andrews council minutes, B65/11/2, pp. 197–8; *RPC*, 3rd ser., XIV, pp. 332–3, 338; AA, Brechin council minutes, B1/1/1, fos 109, 116r.–117r.
95. *RPC*, 3rd ser., XIV, p. 320.
96. E.g. ibid., XV, pp. 184–5, 447–8.

97. Fraser, *Melvilles*, II, p. 164 (quotation); *RPC*, 3rd ser., XVI, pp. 269, 294, 306–9.
98. NRS, Burntisland council minutes, B9/12/15, fos 15r., 17v.
99. AA, Montrose council minutes, M1/1/3, pp. 135, 137, 139–42.
100. *RPS*, M1690/4/18; *RPC*, 3rd ser., XVI, pp. 75, 224–5; NRS, Privy council decreta, 12 June 1689–31 Dec. 1691, PC2/23, fos 303r.–304r.
101. *RPS*, A1690/4/4; see also 1689/3/229, M1690/4/13, M1690/4/25, M1690/4/41.
102. *To His Grace, His Majesties High Commissioner ...The Petition of the Hospital of the Merchants, and Trades of Glasgow*; *RPS*, M1693/4/8, 1695/5/28, 1695/5/60, C1695/5/43.
103. *RPS*, 1695/5/196.
104. NRS, Printed petition to parliament and answers thereto from Dundee, 1700, PA7/17/1/55; NRS, Printed petition to parliament and answers thereto from Linlithgow, 1700, PA7/17/1/57; *RPS*, 1700/10/124.
105. *RPS*, 1689/3/161; cf. *Grievances Represented by the Estates of Scotland*, pp. 1, 3.
106. *Records of the Convention of the Royal Burghs*, IV, pp. 93–6; ECA, Convention of Royal Burghs [Moses] Bundles, Bundle 212, 'Acts in favours of the royal burghs', 1689, Petition of the merchant company of Edinburgh, 1689; cf. *RPS*, 1681/7/36; and Chapter 1, p. 12. Parliament later passed an act allowing the common good of towns to be audited: *RPS*, 1693/4/102; Riley, *English Ministers and Scotland*, pp. 174–5.
107. *Records of the Convention of the Royal Burghs*, IV, pp. 99–101, quotation at p. 100.
108. *RPS*, 1690/4/61.
109. Mackenzie, *Scottish Burghs*, pp. 150–1; Whyte, *Scotland before the Industrial Revolution*, pp. 184–5.
110. *Journals of the House of Commons*, X, pp. 49–50; *Journals of the House of Lords*, XIV, p. 149; *London Gazette*, no. 2438, 21–5 March 1689.
111. Balcarres, *Memoirs*, pp. 23–4; NLS, Earl of Tweeddale to Lord Yester, 3 Jan. 1689, MS. 7026, fo. 100r.; Same to same, 4 Jan. 168[9], MS. 7026, fo. 75v.
112. *RPS*, 1689/3/5, 1689/3/7, 1689/3/9–12, 1689/3/38–9, 1689/3/48, 1689/3/55; *APES*, I, pp. 1–4, 8, 9, 10–12; Bell (ed.), *Siege of the Castle of Edinburgh*, pp. 30–4, 37, 38–45.
113. Bell (ed.), *Siege of the Castle of Edinburgh*, pp. 38, 69–81; *RPC*, 3rd ser., XIII, pp. 431–2. See also Robertson, *Lordship and Power in the North of Scotland*, pp. 175–6.
114. *RPC*, 3rd ser., XIV, pp. 28, 63.
115. Bell (ed.), *Siege of the Castle of Edinburgh*, pp. 51, 53–4, 75; NRS, Alexander Brand to Andrew Russell, 11 May 1689, RH15/106/685/3; NRS, William Murray to William Murray, 26 Apr. 1689, GD219/282/20.

116. *RPC*, 3rd ser., XIV, pp. 318–19; ELA, North Berwick burgh court book, 1638–1720, NB/4/2/1, fos 101r.–102r.
117. E.g. *RPS*, 1689/3/138, 1689/3/142–9.
118. *APS*, IX, app., p. 19; Murray, *Chronicles of the Atholl and Tullibardine Families*, I, p. 277; Bell (ed.), *Siege of the Castle of Edinburgh*, pp. 52–3; Mackay, *Life of Lieut. General Hugh Mackay*, p. 25; *RPS*, 1689/3/142.
119. *APES*, I, pp. 157–62; NLS, Sir Francis Scott to the earl of Tweeddale, 9 July 1689, MS. 14407, fo. 149r.; Patrick Aikenhead to the earl of Tweeddale, 9 July 1689, MS. 14407, fo. 153r.
120. Scott (ed.), 'Letters of Graham', p. 256; HMC, *Athole and Home*, pp. 39–41.
121. For a detailed narrative of the war, see Hopkins, *Glencoe and the End of the Highland War*, esp. chs 4–6.
122. Scott (ed.), 'Letters of Graham', p. 260 (quotation); *Leven and Melville Papers*, pp. 40–1, 52, 54; Leneman, *Living in Atholl*, pp. 3, 215–16.
123. *Leven and Melville Papers*, pp. 37–9; Hopkins, *Glencoe and the End of the Highland War*, pp. 129–30.
124. Scott (ed.), 'Letters of Graham', pp. 243–4.
125. Hopkins, *Glencoe and the End of the Highland War*, p. 156; Scott (ed.), 'Letters of Graham', p. 249; SCA, Charles Whytford to Walter Leslie, 28 March 1689, BL/1/126/15; NLS, Sir Patrick Murray to the earl of Tweeddale, 30 May 1689, MS. 7011, fo. 188.
126. Hopkins, *Glencoe and the End of the Highland War*, pp. 134–5, 141–2, 154–5; Scott (ed.), 'Letters of Graham', pp. 237, 239, 246–7, 249, 251.
127. AA, Inventory of the corns cut and eaten by General Hugh Mackay's troops, 1689, F5/6, quotation at p. 1.
128. Mackay, *Memoirs of the War carried on in Scotland and Ireland*, pp. 13–15. Probably before this, Elgin's magistrates drank wine with Dundee, which act was reported to the convention: Cramond (ed.), *Records of Elgin*, I, p. 352; *RPS*, 1689/3/219–20; Hopkins, *Glencoe and the End of the Highland War*, p. 138.
129. PKCA, Perth council minutes, B59/16/10, fos 119v. (quotation), 120v.
130. SAUL, Cupar council minutes, B13/14/1, fos 32v.–33r.
131. ELA, Haddington council minutes, HAD/2/1/2/8, fo. 91r.
132. DGA, Dumfries council minutes, WA2/5, pp. 314–16, quotation at p. 315.
133. E.g. *RPS*, 1689/3/82, 1689/3/86, 1689/3/129, 1689/3/142, 1689/3/226.
134. AyA, Ayr council minutes, B6/18/4, fo. 340; GCA, Rutherglen council minutes, RU3/1/7, p. 250.
135. AA, Brechin council minutes, B1/1/1, fo. 106r.; FCAC, Kirkcaldy council minutes, B/KDY/1/2, fos 94v., 95v.; NRS, Burntisland council minutes, B9/12/15, fo. 17v. For the regulations about the pressing of horses, see *RPC*, 3rd ser., XIII, pp. 530–2, 553; *RPS*, 1689/6/38.

136. Cramond, *Annals of Cullen*, p. 52.
137. HCA, Inverness council minutes, BI/1/1/7, pp. 11, 15, 24–6, quotation at p. 26.

CONCLUSION: REVOLUTIONS, SETTLEMENTS AND SCOTLAND'S POLITICAL DEVELOPMENT

1. See e.g. Macinnes, *Charles I and the Making of the Covenanting Movement*, ch. 8; Stewart, *Rethinking the Scottish Revolution*.
2. Pincus, *1688*.
3. Sowerby, *Making Toleration*, esp. pp. 21–2, 23–4.
4. *RPS*, 1700/5/33, 1700/5/46; Hume, *Diary of the Proceedings in the Parliament and Privy Council*, pp. 3–6.
5. *RPS*, 1700/10/244; Bowie, 'Publicity, parties and patronage', pp. 82–3; Horwitz, *Parliament, Policy and Politics*, p. 303.
6. *RPS*, 1704/7/68.
7. The Claim of Right had not determined the succession beyond the heirs of Mary, Anne and William: ibid., 1689/3/108.
8. For detailed discussions, see Riley, *Union of England and Scotland*, chs 2–4; Whatley with Patrick, *Scots and the Union*, ch. 5.
9. Other changes included the imposition of English treason law on Scotland (1709) and the restoration of the right of lay patrons to present to vacant charges in the Church (1712). For other discussions, see Whatley with Patrick, *Scots and the Union*, ch. 9; Macinnes, *Union and Empire*, pp. 322–4; Raffe, *Culture of Controversy*, pp. 88–91.
10. 6 Ann. c. 6, in Ruffhead (ed.), *Statutes at Large*, IV, pp. 275–6; Riley, *English Ministers and Scotland*, pp. 90–5; Speck, *Birth of Britain*, pp. 126–9.
11. Riley, *English Ministers and Scotland*, pp. 96–102, 174–87.
12. Shaw, *Management of Scottish Society*; Sunter, *Patronage and Politics in Scotland*; Emerson, *Enlightened Duke*, esp. chs 12–14; Murdoch, 'The People Above'; Fry, *Dundas Despotism*.
13. *RPS*, 1706/10/257.
14. Further procedural reforms, including a reduction in the frequency of circuits to one per year, were made by 8 Ann. c. 16 and 10 Ann. c. 33: Ruffhead (ed.), *Statutes at Large*, IV, pp. 411–13, 595–6. See also Malcolm, 'Introduction', pp. xxvi–xxviii.
15. Whetstone, *Scottish County Government* focuses largely on the period after 1747. See also Murdoch, 'The People Above', pp. 22–7.
16. See esp. Murdoch, 'The importance of being Edinburgh'; Murdoch, 'Politics and the people in the burgh of Dumfries'.
17. *RPS*, 1706/10/257 (quotations); Stephen, *Scottish Presbyterians and the Act of Union*.
18. Tompson, 'James Greenshields and the House of Lords'; Clarke, 'Scottish Episcopalians', ch. 4.

19. 10 Ann. c. 7, in Ruffhead (ed.), *Statutes at Large*, IV, pp. 513–15.
20. See Raffe, 'Scotland'.
21. For an introduction, see Muirhead, *Reformation, Dissent and Diversity*, ch. 4.
22. See e.g. Macinnes, 'Jacobitism in Scotland'; Whatley, *Scottish Society*, chs 4–5.

NOTES ON THE SOURCES

1. The records of Dreghorn kirk session are held at the Burns Monument Centre, Kilmarnock; no digital surrogate is available in the NRS.
2. The published extracts of the Dumbarton and Annan council minutes are perhaps the worst.
3. There are quotations from the Banff burgh council minutes in Cramond (ed.), *Annals of Banff*, I. The records of Cullen, summarised in Cramond's *Annals of Cullen*, may survive in the poorly organised collection of the Moray Heritage Centre.
4. Crail, Kilrenny and Nairn.

Bibliography

MANUSCRIPT SOURCES

Aberdeen City and Aberdeenshire Archives

AS/Bbnf/11/1/1   Banff council account book and stent roll, 1684–1694
CA/1/1/57   Aberdeen town council minutes, 1682–1704
CA/8/1/7   Aberdeen incoming letters book, 1682–1699

Annan Museum

AB1/1/1   Annan town council minutes, 1678–1712

Angus Archives, by Forfar

A1/1A/4   Arbroath burgh court minute book, 1681–1704
B1/1/1   Brechin town council minutes, 1672–1712
F1/1/2   Forfar town council minutes, 1685–1723
F5/6   Inventory of the corns cut and eaten by General Hugh Mackay's troops, 1689
M1/1/3   Montrose town council minutes, 1673–1702

Ayrshire Archives, Ayr

B6/18/4   Ayr town council minutes, 1669–1694

Blair Castle, Blair Atholl

NRAS234   Papers of the dukes of Atholl

Bibliography

British Library, London
Egerton 3335　　Papers of the duke of Leeds

Caithness Archive Centre, Wick
BW/1/1　　Wick council and burgh court minutes, 1660–1711

Dumbarton Library
DB1/1/4　　Dumbarton town council minutes, 1673–1693

Dumfries and Galloway Archives, Dumfries
BH5/2/9　　Maintenance roll for George Campbell, *c.* 1687–1690
RB2/5/32　　List of arms held in Dumfries, 15 Jan. 1689
WA2/5　　Dumfries town council minutes, 1680–1694

Dundee City Archives
Dundee lockit book
Dundee town council minutes, vol. 6, 1669–1707

East Lothian Archives, Haddington
DUN/2/1/1/1　　Dunbar town council minutes, 1671–1687
DUN/2/1/1/2　　Dunbar town council minutes, 1688–1712
HAD/2/1/2/8　　Haddington town council minutes, 1682–1692
NB/4/2/1　　North Berwick burgh court book, 1638–1720

Edinburgh City Archives
Convention of Royal Burghs [Moses] Bundles 211–12
SL59/1/1/3　　Queensferry town council minutes, 1689–1703
SL144/1/7　　Edinburgh dean of guild court minute book, 1687–1695

Edinburgh University Library
Dk.1.2^2, item 23 Account of Edinburgh's town college after the revolution, by David Gregory

Fife Council Archive Centre, Kirkcaldy

B/Cul/1/1/3	Culross town council minutes, 1682–1712
B/DY/1/1/2	Dysart town council minutes, 1674–1761
B/KDY/1/2	Kirkcaldy town council minutes, 1680–1717

Glasgow City Archives

RU3/1/7	Rutherglen town council minutes, 1681–1692
T-PM	Maxwell of Nether Pollok papers

Glasgow University Library

MS. Murray 221 Late seventeenth-century sermons

Highland Archive Centre, Inverness

BI/1/1/7	Inverness town council minutes, 1689–1702

Lanark Library

Lanark town council minutes, 1650–1694

Moray Heritage Centre, Elgin

ZBEl A2/10	Elgin town council minutes, 1670–1705

National Library of Scotland, Edinburgh

Adv. 32.3.6	Lists of ministers in 1662, 1689 and 1701
Adv. 32.7.7	Diary of Thomas Kincaid, 1687–1688
MS. 1102	Correspondence of John Mackenzie of Delvine
MS. 1668	Memoirs of John Brand, minister of Bo'ness
MS. 2788	Sermons by Patrick Warner, 1688
MS. 5770	Sermons, 1688
MS. 7004	Letters to the earl of Tweeddale, 1670
MS. 7010–11	Letters to the earl of Tweeddale and Lord Yester, 1685–1689
MS. 7025–6	Letters from the earl of Tweeddale, 1670–1689
MS. 9250	Correspondence of William Dunlop
MS. 14404	Letters to the first marquis of Tweeddale, 1689–1696
MS. 14407	Tweeddale correspondence, 1675–1697
Wod. Oct. XII, XXX	Wodrow octavos (miscellaneous religious manuscripts)
Wod. Qu. XXVIII, LXXIII	Wodrow quartos (miscellaneous religious manuscripts)

Wod. Fol. XXVI, XXVII, XXXVIII   Wodrow folios (miscellaneous religious manuscripts)

National Records of Scotland, Edinburgh

Government and parliamentary records

C3/12	Register of the Great Seal, 1685–1688
E7/3–5	Treasury register, 15 May 1682–4 Aug. 1690
E8/38	Warrants of the exchequer register, May–Dec. 1686
E26/11–12	Accounts of the lord treasurer and treasury commission, 1667–1692
GD157/1682	Address of the privy council to William of Orange
PA7/17/1	Supplementary parliamentary papers, 1700–1701
PA7/25	Commissions to parliament
PA10/4	Parliamentary visitation of Edinburgh's town college, 1690–1702
PA10/6	Papers of the parliamentary visitation of the University of St Andrews, 1690s
PC1/48, 51–52	Privy council acta, 2 Feb. 1692–31 March 1693, 4 Sep. 1696–5 May 1703
PC2/23	Privy council decreta, 12 June 1689–31 Dec. 1691
RH14	Proclamations and other public announcements, 1599–1750
SP4/8–15	Warrant books of the secretary for Scotland, 5 April 1683–15 December 1691

Sheriff court records

SC5/70/8	Stonehaven (Kincardine) head court, freeholders and election papers, 1680–1689
SC42/1/2	Peebles sheriff court diet and minute book, 1667–1689

General assembly papers

CH1/2/2/2	General assembly papers, 1694
CH8/171	'The humble address of the M[i]n[iste]rs and Elders of the Church of Scotland who adhere to the way of the Reformed Churches in doctrine and discipline nou presently Conveened in their Gen[era]ll meeting'

Synod and presbytery records (episcopalian)

CH2/1/2	Presbytery of Aberdeen minutes, 1673–1688
CH2/6/1	Presbytery of Aberlour minutes, 1671–1688
CH2/8/22	Presbytery of Alford minutes, 1662–1688
CH2/15/1	Presbytery of Arbroath minutes, 1659–1689

CH2/40/19	Synod of Brechin minutes, 1681–1688
CH2/47/1	Presbytery of Caithness minutes, 1654–1677, 1682–1688
CH2/103/1	Presbytery of Dundee minutes, 1664–1689
CH2/106/1	Presbytery of Dunkeld minutes, 1681–1689
CH2/113/1	Presbytery of Duns minutes, 1659–1688
CH2/144/4	Presbytery of Elgin minutes, 1673–1688
CH2/146/5	Presbytery of Ellon minutes, 1672–1689
CH2/157/2	Presbytery of Fordoun minutes, 1684–1688
CH2/158/4	Presbytery of Fordyce minutes, 1674–1688
CH2/162/1	Presbytery of Forres minutes, 1651–1688
CH2/234/2	Presbytery of Lanark minutes, 1664–1688
CH2/242/6	Presbytery of Linlithgow minutes, 1676–1688
CH2/263/1	Presbytery of Meigle minutes, 1659–1689
CH2/294/5	Presbytery of Paisley minutes, 1663–1687
CH2/295/4	Presbytery of Peebles minutes, 1649–1688
CH2/424/5	Presbytery of Dalkeith minutes, 1673–1688
CH2/546/3	Presbytery of Dumbarton minutes, 1684–1688
CH2/553/2	Presbytery of Inverness minutes, 1670–1688
CH2/619/1	Presbytery of Auchterarder minutes, 1668–1687
CH2/722/7	Presbytery of Stirling minutes, 1662–1688
CH2/723/4	Presbytery of Dunblane minutes, 1671–1688
CH2/840/10	Synod of Aberdeen minutes, 1662–1688
CH2/1120/1	Presbytery of Turriff minutes, 1642–1664, 1670–1684, 1686, 1688
CH12/12/773	Commission to Robert Scott, 22 Jan. 1689

Synod and presbytery records (presbyterian)

CH2/35/3	Presbytery of Peebles and Biggar minutes, 1688–1694
CH2/105/2	Presbytery of Dunfermline minutes, 1689–1691
CH2/111/3	Presbytery of Dunoon minutes, 1690–1707
CH2/154/4	Synod of Fife minutes, 1690–1696
CH2/165/2	Synod of Galloway minutes, 1689–1712
CH2/171/7	Presbytery of Glasgow minutes, 1687–1694
CH2/197/2	Presbytery of Irvine minutes, 1687–1699
CH2/224/2	Presbytery of Kirkcaldy minutes, 1688–1693
CH2/242/7	Presbytery of Linlithgow minutes, 1687–1694
CH2/252/5	Synod of Lothian and Tweeddale minutes, 1687–1690
CH2/294/4	Presbytery of Paisley minutes, 1660, 1687–1699
CH2/298/1	Presbytery of Penpont minutes, 1690–1706
CH2/299/5	Presbytery of Perth minutes, 1690–1700
CH2/327/2	Presbytery of Selkirk minutes, 1690–1706
CH2/393/1	Presbytery of Hamilton minutes, 1687–1695
CH2/516/1	United presbyteries of Chirnside and Duns minutes, 1690–1702

CH2/532/2   Presbytery of Ayr minutes, 1687–1705
CH2/546/4   Presbytery of Dumbarton minutes, 1689–1695
CH2/557/3   Synod of Argyll minutes, 1687–1700
CH2/1153/1   Presbytery of Kintyre minutes, 1655–1707
CH2/1284/2   Presbytery of Dumfries minutes, 1687–1695

Kirk session records

CH2/30/2   Bathgate kirk session minutes, 1672–1856
CH2/38/1   Borthwick kirk session minutes, 1690–1731, 1769–1811
CH2/84/7   Dalkeith kirk session minutes and accounts, 1687–1690, 1714–1721
CH2/93/2   Dron kirk session minutes, 1683–1717
CH2/141/5   Edinburgh Trinity College kirk session minutes, 1685–1690
CH2/173/1   Barony kirk session minutes and accounts, 1637–1698
CH2/229/1   Kirkliston kirk session minutes, 1659–1688
CH2/237/1   Lenzie Easter kirk session minutes, 1666–1688
CH2/257/1   Manor kirk session minutes, 1663–1732
CH2/276/5   Newbattle kirk session minutes, 1673–1702
CH2/283/2   Newton kirk session minutes, 1651–1696
CH2/292/2   Ormiston kirk session accounts and minutes, 1661–1689
CH2/297/2   Penicuik kirk session accounts and minutes, 1674–1744
CH2/309/1   Ratho kirk session minutes, 1682–1689
CH2/315/1   Rutherglen kirk session minutes, marriages, baptisms, testimonials and accounts, 1658–1780
CH2/333/2   Spott kirk session minutes, 1683–1703
CH2/390/3   Dysart kirk session minutes, 1654–1695
CH2/390/11   Dysart kirk session accounts, 1686–1706
CH2/406/2   Kinglassie kirk session minutes and accounts, 1666–1694
CH2/415/1   Cambuslang kirk session minutes, 1658–1788
CH2/426/22   Cramond kirk session accounts, 1687–1709
CH2/537/14   Dumfries St Michael's kirk session minutes and accounts, 1616–1688
CH2/537/15   Dumfries St Michael's kirk session minutes and accounts, 1689–1712
CH2/591/2   Kilwinning kirk session minutes, 1688–1698
CH2/689/2   Queensferry kirk session minutes, 1687–1718
CH2/716/9   South Leith presbyterian kirk session minutes, 1687–1691
CH2/716/221   South Leith kirk session accounts, 1684–1690
CH2/718/10   West Kirk kirk session accounts and minutes, 1686–1688
CH2/1042/1   New Abbey kirk session minutes, 1691–1725
CH2/1173/6   Kelso kirk session minutes, 1677–1689
CH2/1596/1/1   Renfrew kirk session minutes, 1653, 1691–1700

Records of the Quakers

CH10/1/1	Edinburgh quarterly meeting records, 1669–1737
CH10/1/2	Edinburgh monthly meeting records, 1669–1713
CH10/1/65	'A Remembrance, or Record of the Sufferings of some Freinds of Truth in Scottland'
CH10/3/37	Kinmuck/Lethendy monthly meeting records, 1679–1782

Burgh records

B9/12/14	Burntisland town council minutes, 1680–1688
B9/12/15	Burntisland town council minutes, 1688–1701
B28/7/3	Fortrose burgh court and council records, 1674–1690
B34/10/1	Inverkeithing town council minutes, 1689–1745
B34/11/1	Inverkeithing guildry minutes, 1590–1742
B34/20/169	Additional libel and sentence against John Henderson, 23, 25 Feb. 1689
B37/12/4	Irvine town council minutes, 1674–1680, 1687–1700
B48/9/4	Linlithgow town council minutes, 1673–1694
GD123/183	Copy of Selkirk town council minutes, 1687–1688

Private papers

GD3	Papers of the Montgomerie family, earls of Eglinton
GD24/1/463	Papers connected with George Drummond of Blair Drummond
GD103/2/232	'Reasons humbly offered to his highnes the P. of Orange against the advice given in the address, relating to [th]e Election of Commissioners from the Burrowes'
GD112	Papers of the Campbell family, earls of Breadalbane
GD123/184/2	Information for John Riddell of Hayning against Selkirk, 1672
GD124	Papers of the earls of Mar
GD219	Papers of the Murray family of Murraythwaite, Dumfriesshire
GD406/1	Correspondence of the dukes of Hamilton
RH13/20	Transcripts of proceedings of the convention of estates and parliament and other state papers, 1667–1693
RH15/106	Papers of Andrew Russell, merchant in Rotterdam
RH15/112	Papers of Sir William Wallace of Craigie

National Register of Archives for Scotland

NRAS217	Papers of the earls of Moray

Nottingham University Library

Pw A   Papers of the first earl of Portland

Paisley Central Library

P1/1/15   Paisley burgh court book, 1682–1698
Renfrew town council minutes, 1684–1695

Perth and Kinross Council Archives, Perth

B59/16/10   Perth town council minutes, 1680–1693
B59/28/58/1   'Informatione for the Ministers of Perth', c. 1691
B59/34/5/2   Protest by William Whyt, George Oliphant, David Murray and their adherents, 28 Feb. 1689
B59/34/6   Account of the election of commissioners from Perth to the convention of estates, 28 Feb. 1689
B59/34/7/1   Additional account of the election at Perth, 28 Feb. 1689

St Andrews University Library

B13/14/1   Cupar town council minutes, 1685–1698
B60/6/1   Pittenweem town council minutes, 1629–1727
B65/11/2   St Andrews town council minutes, 1673–1707

ScotlandsPeople Centre, Edinburgh

OPR 595/1   Irvine baptisms register, 1687–1788
OPR 597/1   Kilmarnock baptisms register, 1640–1740
OPR 599/1   Kilwinning register of baptisms and marriages, 1669–1727
OPR 622/6   Barony marriages register, 1672–1777
OPR 644^1/6   Glasgow baptisms register, 1670–1688
OPR 644^1/7   Glasgow baptisms register, 1687–1698
OPR 667/1   Kirkliston register of baptisms and marriages, 1675–1731
OPR 685^1/10   Edinburgh baptisms register, 1684–1687
OPR 685^1/11   Edinburgh baptisms register, 1688–1692

Scottish Borders Archives, Hawick

B58/9/3   Peebles burgh court book, 1678–1704
BS1/1/1   Selkirk court record and council minutes, 1635–1704
CH2/198/5   Presbytery of Jedburgh minutes, 1682–1688

Scottish Catholic Archives, Aberdeen University Library

BL/1/97–128   Blairs Letters, 1687–1689

Stewartry Museum, Kirkcudbright

G1/1/6   Kirkcudbright town council minutes, 1683–1700

Stirling Council Archives Service, Stirling

B66/20/6   Stirling town council minutes, 1680–1703

Stranraer Museum

ST1/1/2   Stranraer burgh court book, 1684–1710
WN1/1/1   Wigtown town council minutes, 1680–1694

PRINTED PRIMARY SOURCES

Newspapers

London Gazette
London Mercury
Publick Occurrences Truly Stated
Universal Intelligence

Sources published before 1720

Act, for Inbringing of His Majesties Excise and Supply (Edinburgh, 1688).
Act of Council, anent Papists (Edinburgh, 1688).
Act of Privy Council, Anent the Punishment of these who refuse to Serve in the Foot-Militia (Edinburgh, 1688).
Act of Privy Council, Anent the Shires of Dumfreis, Air, &c. their Out-riek (Edinburgh, 1688).
Act of Privy Council, for calling out the Heretors, &c. (Edinburgh, 1688).
Act of Privy Council in Favours of the Clerks of Kirk-Sessions, and other Church-Officers of the Regular Established Clergie (Edinburgh, 1687).
The Addres of the University of St Andrews to the King (London, 1689).
An Address to the Nobility, Clergy and Gentlemen of Scotland ([Edinburgh?,] [1689]), Wing A567.
Allegiance and Prerogative Considered in a Letter from a Gentleman in the Country to his Friend upon his being Chosen a Member of the Meeting of States in Scotland ([Edinburgh?,] 1689).

A Brief and True Account of the Sufferings of the Church of Scotland Occasioned by the Episcopalians Since the Year 1660 (London, 1690).
Burnet, Gilbert, 'Some reflections on his majesty's proclamation of the twelfth of February 1686/7 for a toleration in Scotland', in Gilbert Burnet, *A Collection of Eighteen Papers, relating to Church & State, during the Reign of King James the Second* (London, 1689), pp. 10–24.
Burnet, Thomas, *Theses Philosophicae* (Aberdeen, 1686).
By the King. A Proclamation (Edinburgh, 1687), Wing J249.
By the King. A Proclamation (Edinburgh, 1687), Wing J252.
Canaries, James, *Rome's Additions to Christianity shewn to be Inconsistent with the True Design of so Spiritual a Religion* (Edinburgh, 1686).
A Cloud of Witnesses, for the Royal Prerogatives of Jesus Christ (Edinburgh, 1714), ESTC 006262106.
A Collection of Papers relating to the Calling and Holding the Convention of Estates of England (Edinburgh, 1689).
A Collection of Papers relating to the Present Juncture of Affairs in England, 3rd edn (London, 1689).
[Comber, Thomas,] *The Protestant Mask taken off from the Jesuited Englishman; being, an Answer to a Book, entituled, Great-Britain's Just Complaint* (London, 1693).
[?Con, Alexander,] *An Answer, to a little Book call'd Protestancy to be Embrac'd or, A New and Infallible Method to reduce Romanists from Popery to Protestancy* ([Holyroodhouse,] 1686).
[Cunningham, Alexander,] *Some Questions Resolved concerning Episcopal and Presbyterian Government in Scotland* (London, 1690).
Dalrymple, James, *An Apology for Sir James Dalrymple of Stair, President of the Session* (Edinburgh, 1690).
A Declaration by His Highness the Prince of Orange; for the Keeping of the Peace, &c. in the Kingdom of Scotland (Edinburgh, 1689), Wing W2314.
The Declaration of His Highness William Henry, by the Grace of God, Prince of Orange, &c. of the Reasons Inducing Him to Appear in Arms for Preserving of the Protestant Religion, and for Restoring the Laws and Liberties of the Ancient Kingdom of Scotland (The Hague, 1688).
The Declaration of His Highnes William Henry, by the Grace of God Prince of Orange, &c. of the Reasons Inducing Him to Appear in Armes in the Kingdome of England, for Preserving of the Protestant Religion, and for Restoring the Lawes and Liberties of England, Scotland and Ireland (The Hague, 1688).
[Ferguson, Robert,] *The Late Proceedings and Votes of the Parliament of Scotland* (Glasgow, 1689).
Five Letters from a Gentleman in Scotland to his Friend in London (London, 1689).
[Gordon, James,] *A Request to Roman Catholicks to answer the Queries upon these their following Tenets* (London, 1687).

[Gordon, James,] *Some Charitable Observations on a late Treatise of Church Lands & Tithes* (Edinburgh, 1706).
The Grievances Represented by the Estates of Scotland, to the King's Majesty, to be Redressed in Parliament (Edinburgh, 1689).
His Highness the Prince of Orange his Speech to the Scots Lords and Gentlemen ([Edinburgh,] 1689).
His Majesties Gracious Letter to the Parliament of Scotland (Edinburgh, 1685).
His Majesties Royal Letter to his Privy Council of Scotland concerning His Indulgence (Edinburgh, 1687).
A Late Letter Concerning the Sufferings of the Episcopal Clergy in Scotland (London, 1691).
A Letter directed from the Council of Scotland, to the King ([Edinburgh,] 1680).
A Letter from the Arch-Bishops and Bishops to the King's most excellent Majesty (Edinburgh, 1688).
A Letter from the West to a Member of the Meeting of the Estates of Scotland ([Edinburgh?,] 1689).
A Letter to a Member of the Convention of States in Scotland ([Edinburgh?,] 1689).
A Letter to a Reverend Minister of the Gospel of the Presbyterian Perswasion (Edinburgh, 1689).
Letters of Intercommuning against Mr. James Rennick, a seditious, Vagabond and pretended Preacher (Edinburgh, 1684).
[Mackenzie, George, and George Mackenzie,] *A Memorial for his Highness the Prince of Orange, in Relation to the Affairs of Scotland* (London, 1689).
[Monro, Alexander,] *An Apology for the Clergy of Scotland* (London, 1693).
[Monro, Alexander,] *A Letter to a Friend, giving an Account of all the Treatises that have been Publish'd with relation to the Present Persecution against the Church of Scotland* (London, 1692).
[Monro, Alexander,] *Presbyterian Inquisition; as it was lately Practised against the Professors of the Colledge of Edinburgh* (London, 1691).
[Montgomery, James,] *Great Britain's Just Complaint for her Late Measures, Present Sufferings, and the Future Miseries she is Exposed to* ([London,] 1692).
[Morer, Thomas, John Sage, Alexander Monro,] *An Account of the Present Persecution of the Church of Scotland in several letters* (London, 1690).
A Proclamation, against Field Conventicles, and offering a Revvard for apprehending Iames Renwick, Alexander Shiels, and Houstoun (Edinburgh, 1687).
A Proclamation against Slanderers and Leesing-makers (Edinburgh, 1686).
A Proclamation, against Spreading of False News &c. (Edinburgh, 1688).
A Proclamation, anent Field Conventicles and House Meetings (Edinburgh, 1687).
A Proclamation, appointing a Rendezvous of the Militia-Regiments in several Shires, & calling out the Heretors, &c. (Edinburgh, 1688).

A Proclamation commanding the Return of all His Majesties Subjects, who have taken Arms under, and now are in the Service or Pay of the States-General of the United Provinces of the Netherlands, by Sea or Land (Edinburgh, 1688).

A Proclamation, for calling out Heretors &c. for his Majesties Service (Edinburgh, 1688).

A Proclamation, for Payment of His Majesties Cess and Excise (Edinburgh, 1688).

A Proclamation, for Restoring the Goods of such Persons as were Robbed, and Taken away from them in the late Tumults (Edinburgh, 1688).

A Proclamation, for Suppressing of Tumults in Edinburgh, and Elsewhere (Edinburgh, 1688).

A Proclamation of Privy Council, for Securing the Peace of the City of Edinburgh, and Suppressing and Repressing of Tumults and Insurrections therein, &c. (Edinburgh, 1688).

A Proclamation, offering a Reward of One Hundred Pound Sterling to any who shall bring in the Person of Mr James Renwick (Edinburgh, 1686).

A Proclamation Reviving and Renuing a former Proclamation against Slanderers and Leesing-makers (Edinburgh, 1686).

A Proclamation, taking off the Stop of Execution against Heretors, called out to attend His Majesties Host (Edinburgh, 1688).

[Reid, Robert,] *The Account of the Popes Procession at Aberdene* ([Aberdeen,] 1689).

Renwick, James, *January 22. 1688. Some Notes or Heads of a Sermon* ([Edinburgh?,] [1688?]).

Renwick, James, *January 24. 1688. Some Notes or Heads of a Sermon preached in Fyfe* ([Edinburgh?,] [1688?]).

[Renwick, James, et al.,] *The Testimony of some Persecuted Presbyterian Ministers of the Gospel* ([Edinburgh?,] 1688).

[Renwick, James, Alexander Shields et al.,] *An Informatory Vindication of a Poor, Wasted, Misrepresented Remnant* ([Edinburgh?,] 1707).

[Ridpath, George,] *An Answer to the Scotch Presbyterian Eloquence* (London, 1693).

[Rule, Gilbert,] *A Second Vindication of the Church of Scotland: Being an Answer to Five Pamphlets* (Edinburgh, 1691).

[Rule, Gilbert,] *A Vindication of the Church of Scotland. Being an Answer to a Paper, intituled, Some Questions concerning Episcopal and Presbyterial government in Scotland*, 2nd edn (Edinburgh, 1691).

The Rules of the Schools at the Jesuits in Fanchurch-Street (London, n.d.).

The Rules of the Schools at the Savoy (London, 1687).

The Rules of the Schools of the Royal Colledge at Holy-Rood-House (Holyroodhouse, 1688).

[Sage, John,] *An Account of the Late Establishment of Presbyterian-Government by the Parliament of Scotland* (London, 1693).

[Sage, John,] *The Case of the Present Afflicted Clergy in Scotland truly Represented* (London, 1690).
Sales, Francis de, *An Introduction to a Devout Life, of S. Francis de Sales Bishop and Prince of Geneva* ([Holyroodhouse,] 1687).
Salus Populi Suprema Lex. Or, the Free Thoughts of a Well-Wisher, for a Good Settlement. In a Letter to a Friend ([Edinburgh?,] 1689).
The Scotch Presbyterian Eloquence; or, the Foolishness of their Teaching Discovered from their Books, Sermons and Prayers (London, 1692).
[Shields, Alexander,] *A Hind Let Loose, or an Historical Representation of the Testimonies, of the Church of Scotland* (n.p., 1687).
[Shields, Alexander,] *A Short Memorial of the Sufferings and Grievances, Past and Present, of the Presbyterians in Scotland: particularly of those of them called by Nick-name Cameronians* ([Edinburgh,] 1690).
[Skene, Alexander,] *Memorialls for the Government of the Royall-Burghs in Scotland* (Aberdeen, 1685).
Some Weighty Considerations, Humbly Proposed to the Honourable Members of the Ensuing Assembly of the States of Scotland ([Edinburgh,] 1689).
Speke, Hugh, *The Secret History of the Happy Revolution in 1688* (London, 1715).
To his Grace His Majesties High Commissioner, and the Right Honourable Estates of Parliament. The Petition of the Magistrats and Town Council of Elgin ([Edinburgh, 1700]).
To His Grace, His Majesties High Commissioner, and the Right Honourable the Estates of Parliament. The Petition of the Hospital of the Merchants, and Trades of Glasgow ([Edinburgh, 1695]).
To His Grace, His Majesties High Commissioner, and to the Right Honourable, the Estates of Parliament, the Humble Address of the Presbyterian Ministers, and Professors of the Church of Scotland ([Edinburgh, 1689]), Wing T1363.
To the King's most excellent Majesty, the Humble Address of the Presbyterian Ministers in His Majesties Kingdom of Scotland (Edinburgh, 1687).
Ussher, James, *The Reduction of Episcopacy unto the Form of Synodical Government* ([Edinburgh?,] 1689).
Watson, James, 'The publisher's preface to the printers in Scotland', in [Jean de la Caille,] *The History of the Art of Printing* (Edinburgh, 1713).

Sources published since 1720

Acts of the General Assembly of the Church of Scotland, MDCXXXVIII–MDCCCXLII (Edinburgh, 1843).
Ancient Laws and Customs of the Burghs of Scotland: Volume II: A.D. 1424–1707 (SBRS, 1910).
Anderson, Peter John (ed.), *Charters and Other Writs illustrating the History of the Royal Burgh of Aberdeen, MCLXXI–MDCCCIV* (Aberdeen, 1890).

Armet, C. M. (ed.), *Kirkcudbright Sheriff Court Deeds, 1676–1700*, 2 vols (Edinburgh, 1953).
Armet, Helen (ed.), *Extracts from the Records of the Burgh of Edinburgh, 1689 to 1701* (Edinburgh, 1962).
Bain, Joseph, et al. (eds), *Calendar of the State Papers relating to Scotland and Mary, Queen of Scots, 1547–1603*, 13 vols (Edinburgh, 1898–1969).
Balfour-Melville, E. W. M. (ed.), *An Account of the Proceedings of the Estates in Scotland, 1689–1690*, 2 vols (SHS, 1954–5).
Bell, Robert (ed.), *Siege of the Castle of Edinburgh* (Bannatyne Club, 1828).
Brown, Keith M., et al. (eds), *Records of the Parliaments of Scotland to 1707*, <http://www.rps.ac.uk/> (last accessed 6 July 2017).
Brown, P. Hume, Henry Paton and E. Balfour-Melville (eds), *The Register of the Privy Council of Scotland*, 3rd ser., 16 vols (Edinburgh, 1908–70).
Burnet, Gilbert, *Bishop Burnet's History of his own Time*, ed. Martin J. Routh, 2nd edn, 6 vols (Oxford, 1833).
Calendar of State Papers Preserved in the Public Record Office: Domestic Series: James II, Volume III: June, 1687–February, 1689 (London, 1972).
Carruthers, S. W. (ed.), *The Confession of Faith of the Assembly of Divines at Westminster* (Glasgow, 1978).
Charters of the Royal Burgh of Ayr (Edinburgh, 1883).
Charters, Writs, and Public Documents of the Royal Burgh of Dundee (Dundee, 1880).
Clarke, W. N. (ed.), *A Collection of Letters addressed by Prelates and Individuals of High Rank in Scotland and by Two Bishops of Sodor and Man to Sancroft Archbishop of Canterbury* (Edinburgh, 1848).
Cramond, W., *The Annals of Cullen, 961–1904* (Buckie, 1904).
Cramond, William (ed.), *The Annals of Banff*, 2 vols (New Spalding Club, 1891–3).
Cramond, William (ed.), *The Records of Elgin*, 2 vols (New Spalding Club, 1903–8).
Dickinson, William Croft, and Gordon Donaldson (eds), *A Source Book of Scottish History: Volume Three: 1567–1707*, 2nd edn (London, 1961).
Dilworth, Mark, 'The Scottish mission in 1688–1689', *Innes Review*, 20 (1969), pp. 68–79.
'The Erroll papers', in *Miscellany of the Spalding Club: Volume Second* (Spalding Club, 1842).
'Establishment for the pay of his majesty's standing forces in the kingdom of Scotland. 16 June 1684', in *Miscellany of the Maitland Club: Consisting of Original Papers and Other Documents illustrative of the History and Literature of Scotland: Volume III – Part 1* (Maitland Club, 1842), pp. 73–83.
Extracts from the Council Register of the Burgh of Aberdeen, 1643–1747 (SBRS, 1872).

Extracts from the Records of the Burgh of Glasgow, A.D. 1663–1690 (SBRS, 1905).
Extracts from the Records of the Burgh of Peebles, 1652–1714 (SBRS, 1910).
Extracts from the Records of the Royal Burgh of Lanark: with Charters and Documents relating to the Burgh, A.D. 1150–1722 (SBRS, 1893).
Extracts from the Records of the Royal Burgh of Stirling, A.D. 1667–1752 (Glasgow, 1889).
Forbes, Atholl (ed.), *Curiosities of a Scots Charta Chest, 1600–1800* (Edinburgh, 1897).
Fraser, William, *The Annandale Family Book of the Johnstones, Earls and Marquises of Annandale*, 2 vols (Edinburgh, 1894).
Fraser, William, *The Book of Carlaverock: Memoirs of the Maxwells, Earls of Nithsdale, Lords Maxwell & Herries*, 2 vols (Edinburgh, 1873).
Fraser, William, *The Chiefs of Colquhoun and their Country*, 2 vols (Edinburgh, 1869).
Fraser, William, *The Chiefs of Grant*, 3 vols (Edinburgh, 1883).
Fraser, William, *The Melvilles, Earls of Melville, and the Leslies, Earls of Leven*, 3 vols (Edinburgh, 1890).
Fraser, William, *The Red Book of Grandtully*, 2 vols (Edinburgh, 1868).
Fraser, William, *The Scotts of Buccleuch*, 2 vols (Edinburgh, 1878).
Fraser, William, *The Sutherland Book*, 3 vols (Edinburgh, 1892).
Fraser-Mackintosh, Charles (ed.), *Letters of Two Centuries, chiefly connected with Inverness and the Highlands, from 1616 to 1815* (Inverness, 1890).
Goldie, Mark, et al. (eds), *The Entring Book of Roger Morrice, 1677–1691*, 7 vols (Woodbridge, 2007–9).
Gordon, Alexander (ed.), *Freedom after Ejection: A Review (1690–1692) of Presbyterian and Congregational Nonconformity in England and Wales* (Manchester, 1917).
Grant, James (ed.), *Seafield Correspondence, from 1685 to 1708* (SHS, 1912).
Gunn, George, and Clement B. Gunn (eds), *Records of the Baron Court of Stitchill, 1655–1807* (SHS, 1905).
Hay, Richard Augustine, *Genealogie of the Hayes of Tweeddale* (Edinburgh, 1835).
Hett, Francis Paget (ed.), *The Memoirs of Sir Robert Sibbald (1641–1722)* (London, 1932).
HMC, *Calendar of the Stuart Papers belonging to His Majesty the King, preserved at Windsor Castle*, 7 vols (London, 1902–23).
HMC, *The Manuscripts of the Duke of Athole, K.T., and of the Earl of Home* (London, 1891).
HMC, *The Manuscripts of the Duke of Hamilton, K.T.* (London, 1887).
HMC, *The Manuscripts of the Duke of Roxburghe; Sir H.H. Campbell, Bart.; the Earl of Strathmore; and the Countess Dowager of Seafield* (London, 1894).
HMC, *Report on the Laing Manuscripts preserved in the University of Edinburgh*, ed. Henry Paton, 2 vols (London, 1914–25).

HMC, *Report on the Manuscripts of the Duke of Buccleuch & Queensberry, K.G., K.T., Preserved at Drumlanrig Castle*, 2 vols (London, 1897–1903).
HMC, *Report on the Manuscripts of the Earl of Mar and Kellie*, ed. Henry Paton, 2 vols (London, 1904–30).
HMC, *Tenth Report of the Royal Commission on Historical Manuscripts* [Part 1] (London, 1885).
Hume, David, *A Diary of the Proceedings in the Parliament and Privy Council of Scotland. May 21, MDCC.–March 7, MDCCVII* (Bannatyne Club, 1828).
Japikse, N. (ed.), *Correspondentie van Willem III en van Hans Willem Bentinck, Eersten Graaf van Portland*, 1st part, 2 vols (The Hague, 1927–8).
Jerdan, William (ed.), *Letters from James, Earl of Perth* (Camden Society, 1845).
Johnston, Mary Bruce (trans.), *Rothesay Town Council Records, 1653–1766*, 2 vols (Edinburgh, 1935).
Journals of the House of Commons (London, 1802–).
Journals of the House of Lords (London, 1767–).
Lauder, John, *Historical Notices of Scotish Affairs*, ed. David Laing, 2 vols (Bannatyne Club, 1848).
Lindsay, Colin, earl of Balcarres, *Memoirs touching the Revolution in Scotland, MDCLXXXVIII–MDCXC*, ed. A. W. C. Lindsay (Bannatyne Club, 1841).
'Lists of fees and pensions granted to the officers of state and other servants of the crown etc. in Scotland, MDCLXVII–MDCXCIX', in *Miscellany of the Maitland Club ... Volume III – Part 1*, pp. 147–75.
Luttrell, Narcissus, *A Brief Historical Relation of State Affairs from September 1678 to April 1714*, 6 vols (Oxford, 1857).
Macbean, L. (ed.), *The Kirkcaldy Burgh Records: With the Annals of Kirkcaldy, the Town's Charter, Extracts from Original Documents, and a Description of the Ancient Burgh* (Kirkcaldy, 1908).
Mackay, Hugh, *Memoirs of the War carried on in Scotland and Ireland, M.DC.LXXXIX–M.DC.XCI*, ed. James M. Hog, Patrick F. Tytler and Adam Urquhart (Bannatyne Club, 1833).
Mackay, William (ed.), *Records of the Presbyteries of Inverness and Dingwall, 1643–1688* (SHS, 1896).
Mackay, William, et al. (eds), *Records of Inverness*, 2 vols (New Spalding Club, 1911–24).
Mackenzie, George, *Memoirs of the Affairs of Scotland from the Restoration of King Charles II* (Edinburgh, 1821).
Marwick, James D., and Robert Renwick (eds), *Charters and Other Documents Relating to the City of Glasgow*, 2 vols (SBRS, 1894–1906).
Mears, Natalie, Alasdair Raffe, Stephen Taylor and Philip Williamson with Lucy Bates (eds), *National Prayers: Special Worship since the Reformation: Volume 1: Special Prayers, Fasts and Thanksgivings in the British Isles, 1533–1688* (Church of England Record Society, 2013).
Meikle, Henry W. (ed.), 'An Edinburgh diary', *Book of the Old Edinburgh Club*, 27 (1949), pp. 111–54.

[Melville, William Leslie (ed.),] *Leven and Melville Papers: Letters and State Papers chiefly addressed to George Earl of Melville, Secretary of State for Scotland, 1689–1691* (Bannatyne Club, 1843).

Memorabilia of the City of Perth (Perth, 1806).

Miller, William F., 'Gleanings from the records of the yearly meeting of Aberdeen, 1672–1786', *Journal of the Friends' Historical Society*, 8 (1911), pp. 40–6, 53–80, 113–22.

Mooney, John (ed.), *Charters and Other Records of the City and Royal Burgh of Kirkwall* (Third Spalding Club, 1952).

Munimenta Alme Universitatis Glasguensis: Records of the University of Glasgow from its Foundation till 1727, 4 vols (Maitland Club, 1854).

Muniments of the Royal Burgh of Irvine, 2 vols (Edinburgh, 1890–1).

Murray, John, duke of Atholl, *Chronicles of the Atholl and Tullibardine Families*, 5 vols (Edinburgh, 1908).

Normand, Lawrence, and Gareth Roberts (eds), *Witchcraft in Early Modern Scotland: James VI's* Demonology *and the North Berwick Witches* (Exeter, 2000).

Paul, Robert (ed.), 'The diary of the Rev. George Turnbull, minister of Alloa and Tynighame, 1657–1704', in *Miscellany of the Scottish History Society (First Volume)* (SHS, 1893), pp. 293–445.

Records of the Convention of the Royal Burghs of Scotland, 8 vols (Edinburgh, 1866–1918).

'Register containeing the state and condition of every burgh within the kingdome of Scotland, in the year 1692', in *Miscellany of the Scottish Burgh Records Society* (SBRS, 1881), pp. 51–157.

'Register of the provincial synod of Glasgow and Ayr, A.D. MDCLXXXVII–A.D. MDCXC', in Joseph Robertson (ed.), *Miscellany of the Maitland Club, consisting of Original Papers and Other Documents, Illustrative of the History and Literature of Scotland: Volume IV. Part I* (Maitland Club, 1847), pp. 209–92.

Reliquiae Barclaianae: Correspondence of Colonel David Barclay and Robert Barclay of Urie, and his Son Robert (London, 1870).

Robertson, D., *South Leith Records* (Edinburgh, 1911).

Rogers, Charles, *History of the Chapel Royal of Scotland with the Register of the Chapel Royal of Stirling* (Grampian Club, 1882).

Ruffhead, Owen (ed.), *The Statutes at Large, from Magna Charta to the End of the last Parliament, 1761*, 8 vols (London, 1763–4).

Scott, Andrew Murray (ed.), 'Letters of John Graham of Claverhouse', in *Miscellany of the Scottish History Society: Eleventh Volume* (SHS, 1990), pp. 135–268.

'Setts of the royal burghs of Scotland', in *Miscellany of the Scottish Burgh Records Society*, pp. 159–295.

[Shields, Michael,] *Faithful Contendings Displayed: Being an Historical Relation of the State and Actings of the Suffering Remnant of the Church of Scotland*, ed. John Howie (Glasgow, 1780).

Steel, Annie (ed.), *Records of Annan, 1678–1833* (Annan, 1933).
Stevenson, David (ed.), *The Government of Scotland under the Covenanters, 1637–1651* (SHS, 1982).
Thomson, Thomas, and Cosmo Innes (eds), *Acts of the Parliament of Scotland*, 12 vols (Edinburgh, 1814–75).
Walker, Patrick, *Biographia Presbyteriana*, 2 vols (Edinburgh, 1827).
Warrand, Duncan (ed.), *More Culloden Papers*, 5 vols (Inverness, 1923–30).
Wilson, John B. (ed.), *The Lochmaben Court and Council Book, 1612–1721* (Scottish Record Society, 2001).
Wodrow, Robert, *Analecta: or, Materials for a History of Remarkable Providences*, 4 vols (Maitland Club, 1842–3).
Wodrow, Robert, *The History of the Sufferings of the Church of Scotland from the Restoration to the Revolution*, ed. Robert Burns, 4 vols (Glasgow, 1828–30).
Wood, Marguerite (ed.), *Extracts from the Records of the Burgh of Edinburgh, A.D. 1589 to 1603* (Edinburgh, 1927).
Wood, Marguerite (ed.), *Extracts from the Records of the Burgh of Edinburgh, 1642 to 1655* (Edinburgh, 1938).
Wood, Marguerite (ed.), *Extracts from the Records of the Burgh of Edinburgh, 1655 to 1665* (Edinburgh, 1940).
Wood, Marguerite (ed.), *Extracts from the Records of the Burgh of Edinburgh, 1665 to 1680* (Edinburgh, 1950).
Wood, Marguerite (ed.), *Extracts from the Records of the Burgh of Edinburgh, 1681 to 1689* (Edinburgh, 1954).

SECONDARY WORKS

Published secondary works

Adams, Sharon, 'Brown, John (1626/7–1685)', *ODNB*.
Adams, Sharon, 'Wilson, Margaret (1666/7–1685)', *ODNB*.
Agnew, Andrew, *The Agnews of Lochnaw: A History of the Hereditary Sheriffs of Galloway* (Edinburgh: Adam and Charles Black, 1864).
Allen, Aaron M., 'Conquering the suburbs: politics and work in early modern Edinburgh', *Journal of Urban History*, 37 (2011), pp. 423–43.
Anson, Peter F., *Underground Catholicism in Scotland, 1622–1878* (Montrose: Standard Press, 1970).
Ashley, Maurice, *James II* (London: J. M. Dent, 1977).
Aylmer, Gerald, *The Crown's Servants: Government and Civil Service under Charles II, 1660–1685* (Oxford: Oxford University Press, 2002).
Baker, Keith Michael, 'Revolution 1.0', *Journal of Modern European History*, 11 (2013), pp. 187–219.
Baker, Keith Michael, and Dan Edelstein (eds), *Scripting Revolution: A Historical Approach to the Comparative Study of Revolutions* (Stanford, CA: Stanford University Press, 2015).

Barnes, Robert Paul, 'Scotland and the glorious revolution of 1688', *Albion*, 3 (1971), pp. 116–27.

Beddard, Robert, 'The unexpected whig revolution of 1688', in Robert Beddard (ed.), *The Revolutions of 1688* (Oxford: Clarendon Press, 1991), pp. 11–101.

Beik, William, *Absolutism and Society in Seventeenth-Century France: State Power and Provincial Aristocracy in Languedoc* (Cambridge: Cambridge University Press, 1985).

Bellesheim, Alphons, *History of the Catholic Church of Scotland*, 4 vols (Edinburgh: Blackwood, 1887–90).

Bonney, Richard, *Political Change in France under Richelieu and Mazarin, 1624–1661* (Oxford: Oxford University Press, 1978).

Bowie, Karin, 'Publicity, parties and patronage: parliamentary management and the ratification of the Anglo-Scottish union', in Stewart J. Brown and Christopher A. Whatley (eds), *The Union of 1707: New Dimensions* (Edinburgh: Edinburgh University Press, 2008), pp. 78–93.

Brown, Keith M., *Noble Power in Scotland from the Reformation to the Revolution* (Edinburgh: Edinburgh University Press, 2011).

Brown, Keith Mark, 'Toward political participation and capacity: elections, voting, and representation in early modern Scotland', *Journal of Modern History*, 88 (2016), pp. 1–33.

Brown, P. Hume, *History of Scotland*, 3 vols (Cambridge: Cambridge University Press, 1905–9).

Brown, P. Hume, *Surveys of Scottish History* (Glasgow: James Maclehose and Sons, 1919).

Bruce, Steve, *Choice and Religion: A Critique of Rational Choice Theory* (Oxford: Oxford University Press, 1999).

Brunton, George, and David Haig, *An Historical Account of the Senators of the College of Justice* (Edinburgh: Thomas Clark, 1832).

Burnet, George B., *The Story of Quakerism in Scotland, 1650–1850* (London: James Clarke, 1952).

Capp, Bernard, 'The religious marketplace: public disputations in Civil War and Interregnum England', *English Historical Review*, 129 (2014), pp. 48–78.

Carswell, John, *The Descent on England: A Study of the English Revolution of 1688 and its European Background* (London: Barrie and Rockliff, 1969).

Chandaman, C. D., *The English Public Revenue, 1660–1688* (Oxford: Clarendon Press, 1975).

Childs, John, *The Army, James II, and the Glorious Revolution* (Manchester: Manchester University Press, 1980).

Clarke, Tristram, 'Canaries, James (1653/4–1698)', *ODNB*.

Clarke, Tristram, 'The Williamite episcopalians and the glorious revolution in Scotland', *RSCHS*, 24 (1990–2), pp. 33–51.

Coffey, John, *Persecution and Toleration in Protestant England, 1558–1689* (Harlow: Longman, 2000).

Cohen, I. Bernard, 'The eighteenth-century origins of the concept of scientific revolution', *Journal of the History of Ideas*, 37 (1976), pp. 257–88.
Cowan, Ian B., 'Church and state reformed? The revolution of 1688–9 in Scotland', in Jonathan I. Israel (ed.), *The Anglo-Dutch Moment: Essays on the Glorious Revolution and its World Impact* (Cambridge: Cambridge University Press, 1991), pp. 163–83.
Cowan, Ian B., 'The reluctant revolutionaries: Scotland in 1688', in Eveline Cruickshanks (ed.), *By Force or by Default? The Revolution of 1688–1689* (Edinburgh: John Donald, 1989), pp. 65–81.
Cowan, Ian B., *The Scottish Covenanters, 1660–1688* (London: Victor Gollancz, 1976).
Cowan, Ian B., 'Worship and dissent in Restoration Scotland', *Scotia*, 2 (1978), pp. 61–9.
Cowan, William, 'The Holyrood press, 1686–1688', *Publications of the Edinburgh Bibliographical Society*, 6 (1901–4), pp. 83–100.
Cullen, Karen J., *Famine in Scotland: The 'Ill Years' of the 1690s* (Edinburgh: Edinburgh University Press, 2010).
Cust, Richard, 'The collapse of royal power in England, 1637–1642', in Michael J. Braddick (ed.), *The Oxford Handbook of the English Revolution* (Oxford: Oxford University Press, 2015), pp. 60–76.
Dalrymple, John, *Memoirs of Great Britain and Ireland*, 2nd edn, 2 vols (London: W. Strahan and T. Cadell, 1771–3).
Dalton, Charles, *The Scots Army, 1661–1688* (London: Eyre & Spottiswoode, 1909).
Davidson, Neil, *Discovering the Scottish Revolution, 1692–1746* (London: Pluto Press, 2003).
Dennison, E. Patricia, *Holyrood and Canongate: A Thousand Years of History* (Edinburgh: Birlinn, 2005).
DesBrisay, Gordon, 'Catholics, Quakers and religious persecution in Restoration Aberdeen', *Innes Review*, 47 (1996), pp. 136–68.
Dixon, C. Scott, Dagmar Freist and Mark Greengrass (eds), *Living with Religious Diversity in Early-Modern Europe* (Farnham: Ashgate, 2009).
Donaldson, Gordon, 'Covenant to revolution', in Duncan B. Forrester and Douglas M. Murray (eds), *Studies in the History of Worship in Scotland*, 2nd edn (Edinburgh: T. & T. Clark, 1996), pp. 59–72.
Dunlop, A. Ian, *William Carstares and the Kirk by Law Established* (Edinburgh: Saint Andrew Press, 1967).
Easson, D. E., 'A Scottish parish in Covenanting times', *RSCHS*, 9 (1945–7), pp. 111–25.
Edwards, Roger, *Love & Loyalty: Looking for Glasgow's Early Episcopalians* ([Glasgow:] Roger Edwards, 2015).
Emerson, Roger L., *An Enlightened Duke: The Life of Archibald Campbell (1682–1761), Earl of Ilay, 3rd Duke of Argyll* (Kilkerran: Humming Earth, 2013).

Farguson, Julie, 'Dynastic politics, international protestantism and royal rebellion: Prince George of Denmark and the glorious revolution', *English Historical Review*, 131 (2016), pp. 540–69.

Ferguson, William, *Scotland's Relations with England: A Survey to 1707* (Edinburgh: John Donald, 1977).

Findlay, David, and Alexander Murdoch, 'Revolution to reform: eighteenth-century politics, *c.* 1690–1800', in E. Patricia Dennison, David Ditchburn and Michael Lynch (eds), *Aberdeen before 1800: A New History* (East Linton: Tuckwell Press, 2002), pp. 267–86.

Finke, Roger, 'Religious deregulation: origins and consequences', *Journal of Church and State*, 32 (1990), pp. 609–26.

Finke, Roger, and Rodney Stark, 'Religious economies and sacred canopies: religious mobilization in American cities, 1906', *American Sociological Review*, 53 (1988), pp. 41–9.

Ford, J. D., 'Protestations to parliament for remeid of law', *SHR*, 88 (2009), pp. 57–107.

Foster, Walter Roland, *Bishop and Presbytery: The Church of Scotland, 1661–1688* (London: S.P.C.K., 1958).

Fry, Michael, *The Dundas Despotism* (Edinburgh: Edinburgh University Press, 1992).

Furgol, Edward M., 'Livingstone, George, third earl of Linlithgow (1616–1690)', *ODNB*.

Gardner, Ginny, *The Scottish Exile Community in the Netherlands, 1660–1690* (East Linton: Tuckwell Press, 2004).

Gibson, William, *James II and the Trial of the Seven Bishops* (Basingstoke: Palgrave Macmillan, 2009).

Glaser, Eliane (ed.), *Religious Tolerance in the Atlantic World: Early Modern and Contemporary Perspectives* (Basingstoke: Palgrave Macmillan, 2014).

Glassey, Lionel K. J., *Politics and the Appointment of Justices of the Peace, 1675–1720* (Oxford: Oxford University Press, 1979).

Glassey, Lionel K. J., 'The revolution of 1688 in Scotland', *History Teaching Review Year Book*, 12 (1998), pp. 10–16.

Glassey, Lionel K. J., 'William II and the settlement of religion in Scotland, 1688–1690', *RSCHS*, 23 (1987–9), pp. 317–29.

Glozier, Matthew, 'The earl of Melfort, the court Catholic party and the foundation of the Order of the Thistle, 1687', *SHR*, 79 (2000), pp. 233–8.

Goldie, Mark, 'Absolutism', in George Klosko (ed.), *The Oxford Handbook of the History of Political Philosophy* (Oxford: Oxford University Press, 2011), pp. 282–95.

Goldie, Mark, 'The theory of religious intolerance in Restoration England', in Ole Peter Grell, Jonathan I. Israel and Nicholas Tyacke (eds), *From Persecution to Toleration: The Glorious Revolution and Religion in England* (Oxford: Clarendon Press, 1991), pp. 331–68.

Goldstone, Jack A., *Revolution and Rebellion in the Early Modern World* (Berkeley, CA: University of California Press, 1991).
Goodare, Julian, *The Government of Scotland, 1560–1625* (Oxford: Oxford University Press, 2004).
Goodare, Julian, 'The rise of the Covenanters, 1637–1644', in Braddick (ed.), *Oxford Handbook of the English Revolution*, pp. 43–59.
Goodare, Julian, 'The Scottish revolution', in Sharon Adams and Julian Goodare (eds), *Scotland in the Age of Two Revolutions* (Woodbridge: Boydell, 2014), pp. 79–96.
Goodare, Julian, *State and Society in Early Modern Scotland* (Oxford: Oxford University Press, 1999).
Goodwin, Jeff, and René Rojas, 'Revolutions and regime change', in Donatella Della Porta and Mario Diani (eds), *The Oxford Handbook of Social Movements* (Oxford: Oxford University Press, 2015), pp. 793–804.
Graham, Eric J., *A Maritime History of Scotland, 1650–1790* (East Linton: Tuckwell Press, 2002).
Greaves, Richard L., *Secrets of the Kingdom: British Radicals from the Popish Plot to the Revolution of 1688–1689* (Stanford, CA: Stanford University Press, 1992).
Halliday, James, 'The Club and the revolution in Scotland, 1689–90', *SHR*, 45 (1966), pp. 143–59.
Halliday, Paul D., *Dismembering the Body Politic: Partisan Politics in England's Towns, 1650–1730* (Cambridge: Cambridge University Press, 1998).
Hanlon, Gregory, *Confession and Community in Seventeenth-Century France: Catholic and Protestant Coexistence in Aquitaine* (Philadelphia, PA: University of Pennsylvania Press, 1993).
Hannay, R. K., 'The visitation of St Andrews University in 1690', *SHR*, 13 (1916), pp. 1–15.
Hannay, R. K., 'The visitation of the college of Edinburgh in 1690', *Book of the Old Edinburgh Club*, 8 (1916), pp. 79–100.
Harris, Tim, 'Did the English have a script for revolution in the seventeenth century?', in Baker and Edelstein (eds), *Scripting Revolution*, pp. 25–40.
Harris, Tim, *London Crowds in the Reign of Charles II: Propaganda and Politics from the Restoration until the Exclusion Crisis* (Cambridge: Cambridge University Press, 1987).
Harris, Tim, 'The people, the law, and the constitution in Scotland and England: a comparative approach to the glorious revolution', *Journal of British Studies*, 38 (1999), pp. 28–58.
Harris, Tim, *Rebellion: Britain's First Stuart Kings, 1567–1642* (Oxford: Oxford University Press, 2014).
Harris, Tim, 'Reluctant revolutionaries? The Scots and the revolution of 1688–89', in Howard Nenner (ed.), *Politics and the Political Imagination in Later Stuart Britain: Essays Presented to Lois Green Schwoerer* (Rochester, NY: University of Rochester Press, 1997), pp. 97–117.

Harris, Tim, *Restoration: Charles II and his Kingdoms* (London: Allen Lane, 2005).
Harris, Tim, *Revolution: The Great Crisis of the British Monarchy, 1685–1720* (London: Allen Lane, 2006).
Harrison, Richard D., 'Musgrave, Sir Christopher, fourth baronet (c. 1631–1704)', *ODNB*.
Hay, George, *The Architecture of Scottish Post-Reformation Churches, 1560–1843* (Oxford: Clarendon Press, 1957).
Headley, John M., Hans Joachim Hillerbrand and Anthony Papalas (eds), *Confessionalization in Europe, 1555–1700: Essays in Honor and Memory of Bodo Nischan* (Aldershot: Ashgate, 2004).
Henderson, T. F., 'Meldrum, George (1634?–1709)', rev. John Callow, *ODNB*.
Henderson, T. F., 'Stewart, Alexander, fifth earl of Moray (*bap.* 1634, *d.* 1701)', rev. A. J. Mann, *ODNB*.
Hill, Christopher, 'The word "revolution" in seventeenth-century England', in Richard Ollard and Pamela Tudor-Craig (eds), *For Veronica Wedgwood These: Studies in Seventeenth-Century History* (London: Collins, 1986), pp. 134–51.
Hobsbawm, E. J., 'Revolution', in Roy Porter and Mikuláš Teich (eds), *Revolution in History* (Cambridge: Cambridge University Press, 1986), pp. 5–46.
Hopkins, P. A., 'Sir James Montgomerie of Skelmorlie', in Eveline Cruickshanks and Edward Corp (eds), *The Stuart Court in Exile and the Jacobites* (London: Hambledon Press, 1995), pp. 39–59.
Hopkins, Paul, *Glencoe and the End of the Highland War*, rev. edn (Edinburgh: John Donald, 1998).
Hopkins, Paul, 'Mackenzie, Kenneth, fourth earl of Seaforth and Jacobite first marquess of Seaforth (*bap.* 1661, *d.* 1701)', *ODNB*.
Horwitz, Henry, *Parliament, Policy and Politics in the Reign of William III* (Manchester: Manchester University Press, 1977).
Hosford, David H., *Nottingham, Nobles and the North: Aspects of the Revolution of 1688* (Hamden, CT: Conference on British Studies, 1976).
Houston, R. A., *Social Change in the Age of Enlightenment: Edinburgh, 1660–1760* (Oxford: Clarendon Press, 1994).
Huntington, Samuel P., *Political Order in Changing Societies* (New Haven, CT: Yale University Press, 1968).
Hyman, Elizabeth Hannan, 'A Church militant: Scotland, 1661–1690', *Sixteenth Century Journal*, 26 (1995), pp. 49–74.
Jackson, Clare, '"Assize of error" and the independence of the criminal jury in Restoration Scotland', *Scottish Archives*, 10 (2004), pp. 1–25.
Jackson, Clare, 'Judicial torture, the liberties of the subject, and Anglo-Scottish relations, 1660–1690', in T. C. Smout (ed.), *Anglo-Scottish Relations from 1603 to 1900*, Proceedings of the British Academy, 127 (Oxford: Oxford University Press, 2005), pp. 75–101.

Jackson, Clare, *Restoration Scotland, 1660–1690: Royalist Politics, Religion and Ideas* (Woodbridge: Boydell, 2003).
Jackson, Clare, 'Revolution principles, *ius naturae* and *ius gentium* in early-enlightenment Scotland: the contribution of Sir Francis Grant, Lord Cullen (*c.* 1660–1726)', in T. J. Hochstrasser and P. Schröder (eds), *Early Modern Natural Law Theories: Contexts and Strategies in the Early Enlightenment* (Dordrecht: Kluwer Academic Publishers, 2003), pp. 107–40.
Jackson, Gordon, 'Glasgow in transition, *c.* 1660–*c.* 1740', in T. M. Devine and Gordon Jackson (eds), *Glasgow: Volume 1: Beginnings to 1830* (Manchester: Manchester University Press, 1995), pp. 63–105.
Jerolmack, Colin, and Douglas Porpora, 'Religion, rationality, and experience: a response to the new rational choice theory of religion', *Sociological Theory*, 22 (2004), pp. 140–60.
Joly, A., *Un Converti de Bossuet: James Drummond, Duc de Perth, 1648–1716* (Lille: A l'Economat des Facultés Catholiques, 1933).
Jones, J. R., *The Revolution of 1688 in England* (London: Weidenfeld and Nicolson, 1972).
Kaplan, Benjamin J., *Divided by Faith: Religious Conflict and the Practice of Toleration in Early Modern Europe* (Cambridge, MA: Belknap Press, 2007).
Kennedy, A., 'Rebellion, government and the Scottish response to Argyll's rising of 1685', *Journal of Scottish Historical Studies*, 36 (2016), pp. 40–59.
Kennedy, Allan, *Governing Gaeldom: The Scottish Highlands and the Restoration State, 1660–1688* (Leiden: Brill, 2014).
Kennedy, Allan, 'The urban community in Restoration Scotland: government, society and economy in Inverness, 1660–*c.* 1685', *Northern Scotland*, 5 (2014), pp. 26–49.
Kenyon, J. P., *Robert Spencer, Earl of Sunderland, 1641–1702* (London: Longmans, Green, 1958).
Killen, W. D., *History of Congregations of the Presbyterian Church in Ireland* (Belfast: J. Cleeland, 1886).
Koselleck, Reinhart, 'Historical criteria of the modern concept of revolution', in Reinhart Koselleck, *Futures Past: On the Semantics of Historical Time*, trans. Keith Tribe (Cambridge, MA: MIT Press, 1985), pp. 39–54.
Landsman, Ned C., *Scotland and its First American Colony, 1683–1765* (Princeton, NJ: Princeton University Press, 1985).
Langley, Chris R., *Worship, Civil War and Community, 1638–1660* (London: Routledge, 2016).
Leneman, Leah, *Living in Atholl: A Social History of the Estates, 1685–1785* (Edinburgh: Edinburgh University Press, 1986).
Leneman, Leah, and Rosalind Mitchison, *Sin in the City: Sexuality and Social Control in Urban Scotland, 1660–1780* (Edinburgh: Scottish Cultural Press, 1998).
Lenman, Bruce, *The Jacobite Risings in Britain, 1689–1746* (London, 1980).

Lenman, Bruce, 'The poverty of political theory in the Scottish revolution of 1688–1690', in Lois G. Schwoerer (ed.), *The Revolution of 1688–1689: Changing Perspectives* (Cambridge: Cambridge University Press, 1992), pp. 244–59.

Lenman, Bruce, 'The Scottish nobility and the revolution of 1688–1690', in Beddard (ed.), *Revolutions of 1688*, pp. 137–62.

Lenman, Bruce P., 'Militia, fencible men, and home defence, 1660–1797', in Norman Macdougall (ed.), *Scotland and War, AD 79–1918* (Edinburgh: John Donald, 1991), pp. 170–92.

Levack, Brian, 'Judicial torture in Scotland during the age of Mackenzie', in Hector L. MacQueen (ed.), *Miscellany Four* (Edinburgh: Stair Society, 2002), pp. 185–98.

Levillain, Charles-Edouard, 'London besieged? The City's vulnerability during the glorious revolution', in Jason McElligott (ed.), *Fear, Exclusion and Revolution: Roger Morrice and Britain in the 1680s* (Farnham: Ashgate, 2006), pp. 91–107.

Lynch, Michael, 'The crown and the burghs, 1500–1625', in Michael Lynch (ed.), *The Early Modern Town in Scotland* (London: Croom Helm, 1987), pp. 55–80.

Lynch, Michael, *Edinburgh and the Reformation* (Edinburgh: John Donald, 1981).

Macaulay, Thomas Babbington, *The History of England from the Accession of James the Second*, ed. Charles Harding Firth, 6 vols (London: Macmillan, 1914).

McCallum, John, 'Charity and conflict: poor relief in mid-seventeenth-century Dundee', *SHR*, 95 (2016), pp. 30–56.

MacDonald, Alan R., *The Burghs and Parliament in Scotland, c. 1550–1651* (Aldershot: Ashgate, 2007).

MacDonald, Alan, 'Dundee and the crown, c. 1550–1650', in Charles McKean, Bob Harris and Christopher A. Whatley (eds), *Dundee: Renaissance to Enlightenment* (Dundee: Dundee University Press, 2009), pp. 33–56.

McDowall, William, *History of the Burgh of Dumfries*, 3rd edn (Dumfries: Thomas Hunter, 1906).

Macinnes, Allan I., 'Catholic recusancy and the penal laws, 1603–1707', *RSCHS*, 23 (1987–9), pp. 27–63.

Macinnes, Allan I., *Charles I and the Making of the Covenanting Movement, 1625–1641* (Edinburgh: John Donald, 1991).

Macinnes, Allan I., 'Jacobitism in Scotland: episodic cause or national movement?', *SHR*, 86 (2002), pp. 225–52.

Macinnes, Allan I., *Union and Empire: The Making of the United Kingdom in 1707* (Cambridge: Cambridge University Press, 2007).

Macinnes, Allan I., 'William of Orange – "Disaster for Scotland"?', in Esther Mijers and David Onnekink (eds), *Redefining William III: The Impact of the King-Stadholder in International Context* (Aldershot: Ashgate, 2007), pp. 201–23.

MacIntosh, Gillian H., *The Scottish Parliament under Charles II, 1660–1685* (Edinburgh: Edinburgh University Press, 2007).

Mackay, John, *Life of Lieut. General Hugh Mackay* (Bannatyne Club, 1836).

Mackenzie, William Mackay, *The Scottish Burghs* (Edinburgh: Oliver and Boyd, 1949).

McLay, Keith A. J., 'The Restoration and the glorious revolution, 1660–1702', in Edward M. Spiers, Jeremy A. Crang and Matthew Strickland (eds), *A Military History of Scotland* (Edinburgh: Edinburgh University Press, 2012), pp. 298–325.

McNeill, Peter G. B., 'The independence of the Scottish judiciary', *Juridical Review*, new ser., 3 (1958), pp. 134–47.

McNeill, Peter G. B., and Hector L. MacQueen (eds), *Atlas of Scottish History to 1707* (Edinburgh: Scottish Medievalists, 1996).

M'Ure, John, *A View of the City of Glasgow: or, An Account of its Origin, Rise and Progress* (Glasgow: James Duncan, 1736).

Maitland, William, *The History of Edinburgh, from its Foundation to the Present Time* (Edinburgh: Hamilton, Balfour and Neill, 1753).

Malcolm, Charles A., 'Introduction', in Charles A. Malcolm (ed.), *The Minutes of the Justices of the Peace for Lanarkshire, 1707–1723* (SHS, 1931), pp. ix–lxxxiii.

Mann, Alastair J., 'Inglorious revolution: administrative muddle and constitutional change in the Scottish parliament of William and Mary', *Parliamentary History*, 22 (2003), pp. 121–44.

Mann, Alastair J., *James VII: Duke and King of Scots, 1633–1701* (Edinburgh: John Donald, 2014).

Mann, Alastair J., '"James VII, King of the Articles": political management and parliamentary failure', in Keith M. Brown and Alastair J. Mann (eds), *Parliament and Politics in Scotland, 1567–1707* (Edinburgh: Edinburgh University Press, 2005), pp. 184–207.

Mann, Alastair J., *The Scottish Book Trade, 1500–1720: Print Commerce and Print Control in Early Modern Scotland* (East Linton: Tuckwell Press, 2000).

Marshall, John, *John Locke, Toleration and Early Enlightenment Culture: Religious Intolerance and Arguments for Religious Toleration in Early Modern and 'Early Enlightenment' Europe* (Cambridge: Cambridge University Press, 2006).

Matthew, H. C. G., and Brian Harrison (eds), *Oxford Dictionary of National Biography*, 61 vols (Oxford: Oxford University Press, 2004).

Maxwell, Thomas, 'The Church union attempt at the general assembly of 1692', in Duncan Shaw (ed.), *Reformation and Revolution: Essays Presented to the Very Reverend Principal Emeritus Hugh Watt* (Edinburgh: Saint Andrew Press, 1967), pp. 237–57.

Maxwell, Thomas, 'Presbyterian and episcopalian in 1688', *RSCHS*, 13 (1959–62), pp. 25–37.
Millar, A. H., *Roll of Eminent Burgesses of Dundee, 1513–1886* (Dundee: J. Leng, 1887).
Miller, James, *Inverness* (Edinburgh: Birlinn, 2004).
Miller, John, 'Britain', in John Miller (ed.), *Absolutism in Seventeenth-Century Europe* (Basingstoke: Macmillan Education, 1990), pp. 195–224.
Miller, John, *Cities Divided: Politics and Religion in English Provincial Towns, 1660–1722* (Oxford: Oxford University Press, 2007).
Miller, John, *James II: A Study in Kingship* (London: Methuen, 1978).
Miller, John, 'James II and toleration', in Cruickshanks (ed.), *By Force or by Default?*, pp. 8–27.
Miller, John, 'The militia and the army in the reign of James II', *Historical Journal*, 16 (1973), pp. 659–79.
Miller, John, 'The potential for "absolutism" in later Stuart England', *History*, 69 (1984), pp. 187–207.
Mitchison, Rosalind, *The Old Poor Law in Scotland: The Experience of Poverty, 1574–1845* (Edinburgh: Edinburgh University Press, 2000).
Moore, Barrington, *Social Origins of Dictatorship and Democracy: Lord and Peasant in the Making of the Modern World* (London: Penguin, 1967).
Muirhead, Andrew T. N., *Reformation, Dissent and Diversity: The Story of Scotland's Churches, 1560–1960* (London: Bloomsbury, 2015).
Munck, Thomas, *Seventeenth-Century Europe: State, Conflict and the Social Order in Europe, 1598–1700* (Basingstoke: Macmillan, 1990).
Murdoch, Alexander, 'The importance of being Edinburgh: management and opposition in Edinburgh politics, 1746–1784', *SHR*, 62 (1983), pp. 1–16.
Murdoch, Alexander, *'The People Above': Politics and Administration in Mid-Eighteenth-Century Scotland* (Edinburgh: John Donald, 1980).
Murdoch, Alexander J., 'Politics and the people in the burgh of Dumfries, 1758–1760', *SHR*, 70 (1991), pp. 151–71.
Murray, Athol L., 'The Scottish treasury, 1667–1708', *SHR*, 45 (1966), pp. 89–104.
Mutch, Alistair, *Religion and National Identity: Governing Scottish Presbyterianism in the Eighteenth Century* (Edinburgh: Edinburgh University Press, 2015).
Niggemann, Ulrich, 'Some remarks on the origins of the term "Glorious Revolution"', *The Seventeenth Century*, 27 (2012), pp. 477–87.
Ouston, Hugh, 'York in Edinburgh: James VII and the patronage of learning in Scotland, 1679–1688', in John Dwyer, Roger A. Mason and Alexander Murdoch (eds), *New Perspectives on the Politics and Culture of Early Modern Scotland* (Edinburgh: John Donald, 1982), pp. 133–55.
Pagan, Theodora, *The Convention of the Royal Burghs of Scotland* (Glasgow: Glasgow University Press, 1926).
Paterson, James, *History and Genealogy of the Family of Wauchope of Niddrie-Merschell* (Edinburgh: For private circulation, 1858).

Paterson, Raymond Campbell, *No Tragic Story: The Fall of the House of Campbell* (Edinburgh: John Donald, 2001).
Patrick, Derek J., 'Unconventional procedure: Scottish electoral politics after the revolution', in Brown and Mann (eds), *Parliament and Politics in Scotland*, pp. 208–44.
Pincus, Steve, *1688: The First Modern Revolution* (New Haven, CT: Yale University Press, 2009).
Rachum, Ilan, 'The meaning of "revolution" in the English Revolution (1648–1660)', *Journal of the History of Ideas*, 56 (1995), pp. 195–215.
Raffe, Alasdair, *The Culture of Controversy: Religious Arguments in Scotland, 1660–1714* (Woodbridge: Boydell, 2012).
Raffe, Alasdair, 'Female authority and lay activism in Scottish presbyterianism, 1660–1740', in Sarah Apetrei and Hannah Smith (eds), *Religion and Women in Britain, c. 1660–1760* (Farnham: Ashgate, 2014), pp. 61–78.
Raffe, Alasdair, 'Preaching, reading and publishing the Word in protestant Scotland', in Kevin Killeen, Helen Smith and Rachel Willie (eds), *The Oxford Handbook of the Bible in Early Modern England, c. 1530–1700* (Oxford: Oxford University Press, 2015), pp. 317–31.
Raffe, Alasdair, 'Presbyterianism, secularization, and Scottish politics after the revolution of 1688–1690', *Historical Journal*, 53 (2010), pp. 317–37.
Raffe, Alasdair, 'Presbyterians and episcopalians: the formation of confessional cultures in Scotland, 1660–1715', *English Historical Review*, 125 (2010), pp. 570–98.
Raffe, Alasdair, 'Propaganda, religious controversy and the Williamite revolution in Scotland', *Dutch Crossing*, 29 (2005), pp. 21–42.
Raffe, Alasdair, 'The Restoration, the revolution and the failure of episcopacy in Scotland', in Tim Harris and Stephen Taylor (eds), *The Final Crisis of the Stuart Monarchy: The Revolutions of 1688–91 in their British, Atlantic and European Contexts* (Woodbridge: Boydell, 2013), pp. 87–108.
Raffe, Alasdair, 'Scotland', in Jeremy Gregory (ed.), *The Oxford History of Anglicanism: Volume 2: Establishment and Empire: The Development of Anglicanism, 1662–1829* (Oxford: Oxford University Press, 2017), pp. 150–9.
Raffe, Alasdair, 'Scottish state oaths and the revolution of 1688–1690', in Adams and Goodare (eds), *Scotland in the Age of Two Revolutions*, pp. 173–91.
Raffe, Alasdair, 'Worship and devotion in multiconfessional Scotland, 1686–1689' (forthcoming).
Rait, Robert S., *The Parliaments of Scotland* (Glasgow: Maclehose, Jackson, 1924).
Reid, James Seaton, *History of the Presbyterian Church in Ireland*, new edn, 3 vols (Belfast: William Mullan, 1867).
Riley, P. W. J., *The English Ministers and Scotland, 1707–1727* (London: Athlone Press, 1964).

Riley, P. W. J., *King William and the Scottish Politicians* (Edinburgh: John Donald, 1979).
Riley, P. W. J., *The Union of England and Scotland: A Study in Anglo-Scottish Politics of the Eighteenth Century* (Manchester: Manchester University Press, 1978).
Robertson, A. D., *Lanark: The Burgh and its Councils, 1469–1880* (Lanark: Lanark Town Council, 1974).
Robertson, Barry, *Lordship and Power in the North of Scotland: The Noble House of Huntly, 1603–1690* (Edinburgh: John Donald, 2011).
Rowlands, Guy, *The Dynastic State and the Army under Louis XIV: Royal Service and Private Interest, 1661–1701* (Cambridge: Cambridge University Press, 2002).
Safley, Thomas Max (ed.), *A Companion to Multiconfessionalism in the Early Modern World* (Leiden: Brill, 2011).
Safley, Thomas Max, 'Multiconfessionalism: a brief introduction', in Safley (ed.), *Companion to Multiconfessionalism*, pp. 1–19.
Scott, Hew, *Fasti Ecclesiae Scoticanae: The Succession of Ministers in the Church of Scotland from the Reformation*, rev. edn, 8 vols (Edinburgh: Oliver and Boyd, 1915–50).
Shagan, Ethan H., *The Rule of Moderation: Violence, Religion and the Politics of Restraint in Early Modern England* (Cambridge: Cambridge University Press, 2011).
Shaw, John S., 'Campbell, Archibald, first duke of Argyll (*d.* 1703)', *ODNB*.
Shaw, John Stuart, *The Management of Scottish Society, 1707–1764* (Edinburgh: John Donald, 1983).
Shukman, Ann, *Bishops and Covenanters: The Church in Scotland, 1688–1691* (Edinburgh: John Donald, 2012).
Skocpol, Theda, *States and Social Revolutions: A Comparative Analysis of France, Russia, and China* (Cambridge: Cambridge University Press, 1979).
Smout, T. C., 'The road to union', in Geoffrey Holmes (ed.), *Britain after the Glorious Revolution, 1689–1714* (London: Macmillan, 1969), pp. 176–96.
Snow, Vernon F., 'The concept of revolution in seventeenth-century England', *Historical Journal*, 5 (1962), pp. 167–74.
Sowerby, Scott, *Making Toleration: The Repealers and the Glorious Revolution* (Cambridge, MA: Harvard University Press, 2013).
Speck, W. A., *The Birth of Britain: A New Nation, 1700–1710* (Oxford: Blackwell, 1994).
Speck, W. A., *James II* (Harlow: Pearson Education, 2002).
Speck, W. A., 'James II and VII (1633–1701)', *ODNB*.
Speck, W. A., *Reluctant Revolutionaries: Englishmen and the Revolution of 1688* (Oxford: Oxford University Press, 1988).
Speck, W. A., 'The revolution of 1688 in the north of England', *Northern History*, 25 (1989), pp. 188–204.

Spurlock, R. Scott, *Cromwell and Scotland: Conquest and Religion, 1650–1660* (Edinburgh: John Donald, 2007).

Stark, Rodney, and William Sims Bainbridge, *A Theory of Religion* (New York: Peter Lang, 1987).

Stark, Rodney, and Laurence R. Iannaccone, 'A supply-side reinterpretation of the "secularization" of Europe', *Journal for the Scientific Study of Religion*, 33 (1994), pp. 230–52.

Stephen, Jeffrey, *Defending the Revolution: The Church of Scotland, 1689–1716* (Farnham: Ashgate, 2013).

Stephen, Jeffrey, *Scottish Presbyterians and the Act of Union 1707* (Edinburgh: Edinburgh University Press, 2007).

Stevenson, David, 'The burghs and the Scottish revolution', in Lynch (ed.), *Early Modern Town*, pp. 167–91.

Stewart, Laura A. M., 'Politics and government in the Scottish burghs, 1603–1638', in Julian Goodare and Alasdair A. MacDonald (eds), *Sixteenth-Century Scotland: Essays in Honour of Michael Lynch* (Leiden: Brill, 2008), pp. 427–50.

Stewart, Laura A. M., 'Poor relief in Edinburgh and the famine of 1621–24', *International Review of Scottish Studies*, 30 (2005), pp. 5–41.

Stewart, Laura A. M., *Rethinking the Scottish Revolution: Covenanted Scotland, 1637–1651* (Oxford: Oxford University Press, 2016).

Stewart, Laura A. M., 'The "rise" of the state?', in T. M. Devine and Jenny Wormald (eds), *The Oxford Handbook of Modern Scottish History* (Oxford: Oxford University Press, 2012), pp. 220–35.

Stewart, Laura A. M., *Urban Politics and the British Civil Wars: Edinburgh, 1617–53* (Leiden: Brill, 2006).

Story, Robert Herbert, *William Carstares: A Character and Career of the Revolutionary Epoch* (London: Macmillan, 1874).

Strawhorn, John, *The History of Ayr: Royal Burgh and County Town* (Edinburgh: John Donald, 1989).

Sunter, Robert M., *Patronage and Politics in Scotland, 1707–1832* (Edinburgh: John Donald, 1986).

Terry, Charles Sanford, *John Graham of Claverhouse, Viscount of Dundee, 1648–1689* (London: A. Constable, 1905).

Tilly, Charles, *European Revolutions, 1492–1992* (Oxford: Blackwell, 1993).

Tilly, Charles, *From Mobilization to Revolution* (Reading, MA: Addison-Wesley Publishing, 1978).

Tompson, Richard S., 'James Greenshields and the House of Lords: a reappraisal', in W. M. Gordon and T. D. Fergus (eds), *Legal History in the Making: Proceedings of the Ninth British Legal History Conference* (London: Hambledon Press, 1991), pp. 109–24.

Turner, Stanley Horsfall, *The History of Local Taxation in Scotland* (Edinburgh: W. Blackwood, 1908).

Walker, Peter, *James II and the Three Questions: Religious Toleration and the Landed Classes, 1687–1688* (Oxford: Peter Lang, 2010).
Walsham, Alexandra, *Charitable Hatred: Tolerance and Intolerance in England, 1500–1700* (Manchester: Manchester University Press, 2006).
Walsham, Alexandra, 'Cultures of coexistence in early modern England: history, literature and religious toleration', *The Seventeenth Century*, 28 (2013), pp. 115–37.
Western, J. R., *Monarchy and Revolution: The English State in the 1680s* (London: Blandford, 1972).
Whatley, Christopher A., *Scottish Society, 1707–1830: Beyond Jacobitism, towards Industrialisation* (Manchester: Manchester University Press, 2000).
Whatley, Christopher A., with Derek J. Patrick, *The Scots and the Union* (Edinburgh: Edinburgh University Press, 2006).
Whetstone, Ann E., *Scottish County Government in the Eighteenth and Nineteenth Centuries* (Edinburgh: John Donald, 1981).
Whitley, Laurence A. B., *A Great Grievance: Ecclesiastical Lay Patronage in Scotland until 1750* (Eugene, OR: Wipf and Stock, 2013).
Whyte, Ian D., *Scotland before the Industrial Revolution: An Economic and Social History, c.1050–c.1750* (London: Longman, 1995).
Willcock, John, *A Scots Earl in Covenanting Times: Being Life and Times of Archibald, 9th Earl of Argyll (1629–1685)* (Edinburgh: Andrew Elliot, 1907).
Wykes, David L., 'James II's religious indulgence of 1687 and the early organization of dissent: the building of the first nonconformist meeting-house in Birmingham', *Midland History*, 16 (1991), pp. 86–102.
Young, Margaret D. (ed.), *The Parliaments of Scotland: Burgh and Shire Commissioners*, 2 vols (Edinburgh: Scottish Academic Press, 1992–3).

Unpublished theses

Clarke, Tristram N., 'The Scottish Episcopalians, 1688–1720' (University of Edinburgh Ph.D. thesis, 1987).
Holfelder, Kyle David, 'Factionalism in the Kirk during the Cromwellian Invasion and Occupation of Scotland, 1650 to 1660: the Protester-Resolutioner Controversy' (University of Edinburgh Ph.D. thesis, 1999).
Jardine, Mark, 'The United Societies: Militancy, Martyrdom and the Presbyterian Movement in Late-Restoration Scotland, 1679 to 1688' (University of Edinburgh Ph.D. thesis, 2009).
Lee, Ronald Arthur, 'Government and Politics in Scotland 1661–1681' (University of Glasgow Ph.D. thesis, 1995).
Lennox, Roy Wallace, 'Lauderdale and Scotland: A Study in Restoration Politics and Administration, 1660–1682' (Columbia University Ph.D. thesis, 1977).
McAlister, Kirsty F., 'James VII and the Conduct of Scottish Politics, *c.*1679 to *c.*1686' (University of Strathclyde Ph.D. thesis, 2003).

Moir, Scott, '"Some Godlie, Wyse and Vertious Gentilmen": Communities, State Formation, and the Justices of the Peace in Scotland, 1587–1660 (University of Guelph Ph.D. thesis, 2002).

Patrick, Derek J., 'People and Parliament in Scotland, 1689–1702' (University of St Andrews Ph.D. thesis, 2002).

Toller, John M., '"Now of little significancy": The Convention of the Royal Burghs of Scotland, 1651–1688' (University of Dundee Ph.D. thesis, 2010).

Index

Aberdeen, 40, 60, 68, 86, 87, 89, 94, 111, 117–18, 121, 124–5, 149, 205n, 206n, 211n
  Marischal College, 62
  synod of, 50, 141
  Trinity Church, 38, 60
Abjuration oath (1684), 14, 15, 49
Absolutism, 7, 10–11, 20, 23–30, 35, 41, 62, 80, 104, 122, 129, 135, 138, 147, 157–8, 163
Addresses *see* Petitions
Advocates Library, 13
Ainslie, Adam, 128
Ainslie, Robert, 128
Allegiance, oath of, 13, 16, 18, 20, 24, 34, 133, 136, 142, 143, 162, 207n
Alva, 142
America, 12–13, 44
Anderson, George, 118
Angus *see* Forfarshire
Annan, 95, 121, 215n
Annandale, stewartry of, 14
Annandale, William Johnstone, second earl of, 95, 121
Anne, Queen, 140, 143, 144, 159, 160, 162
Anstruther-Easter, 205n
Anstruther-Wester, 83
Anti-popery *see* Catholics and Catholicism
Arbroath, 91, 93, 123
Argyll, Archibald Campbell, ninth earl of, 13, 15–16, 19, 27, 29, 45, 108, 136, 154
Argyll, Archibald Campbell, tenth earl and first duke of, 58

Argyll, synod of, 43
Argyllshire, 16
Army
  English, 1, 28, 155
  Scottish, 1, 2, 27–8, 29, 97, 108, 109, 135, 136, 137, 139, 147, 152, 153–5, 159
Arran, James Hamilton, earl of, 2
Arran, James Stewart, earl of, 84
Arthur, John, 115
Articles, lords of the, 17–18, 22, 86, 101, 144, 145
Articles of Grievances, 2, 131, 134, 135–8, 140, 144, 145, 151
Assize of error, 137
Atholl, John Murray, marquis of, 16, 19, 109, 112, 118, 133, 134, 146, 153, 154, 207n
Auchterlonie, David, 89, 149–50, 192n
Avondale, 46
Ayrshire, 15, 41, 50, 52, 54, 65, 93, 136

Balcarres, Colin Lindsay, third earl of, 3, 95, 96, 97, 108, 109, 112, 126, 133, 153, 198n
Banchory-Devenick, 61
Banff, 123
Banffshire, 38
Baptism, 10, 35, 57, 59, 66, 70–1, 73, 76, 162
Baptists, 10
Barclay, Robert, 40
Barnes, John, 100, 101
Bass Rock, 97, 112, 153
Bathgate, 70, 73, 77

Index

Bell, John, 100
Bell, William, 100, 128
Bentinck, Hans Willem, 179n
Berwickshire, 44, 52, 108, 205n
Bible, 67, 117
Biggar, 48
Bishops *see* Episcopacy and episcopalians; *see also names of bishops*
Blair, Adam, of Carberry, 95, 97
Blair, William, of Blair, 153
Blair Castle, 153
Bo'ness, 47
Book of Common Prayer
  English (1662), 143, 161–2
  Scottish (1637), 23
Borthwick, 44
Boswell, John, 120
Bothwell Bridge, battle of, 10, 11, 14, 36, 69
Bovier, Andrew, 60
Boyd, William, 122–3
Brand, John, 61
Breadalbane, John Campbell, earl of, 112
Brechin, 82, 84, 114, 150
  diocese of, 60
Brewers and brewing, 27, 99, 101–4, 151
Broun, William, of Nuntoun, 93, 94, 97, 118
Brown, John, 15
Bruce, James, 61
Bruce, Peter, 18, 61–2, 103, 112, 152
Bruce, Robert, bishop of Dunblane, 19
Bullo, William, 52
Burghs
  act of 1672, 13, 17, 81, 82–3, 147, 151–2
  burgess oaths, 60, 94, 127
  character of, 82, 83
  council elections in, 84–6, 111, 117–21, 148–50
  James's policy in, 8, 29, 86–92, 104–5, 158
Burnet, Alexander, archbishop of St Andrews, 12
Burnet, David, 38
Burnet, Gilbert, 24
Burnet, Thomas, 62
Burntisland, 63, 102, 121, 123, 149, 151

Cairncross, Alexander, archbishop of Glasgow, 18, 19, 84, 100
Caithness, George Sinclair, earl of, 90
Cameronians, 14, 16, 22, 31, 33, 36, 46, 47, 49, 64, 65, 67, 85, 122–3, 124, 133
  arguments against multiconfessionalism, 41–2
  violence of, 40, 109, 112, 113–14, 116–17
  see also Boyd, William; Houston, David; Linning, Thomas; Renwick, James; Shields, Alexander; Walker, Patrick
Cambuslang, 45, 49
Campbell, Duncan, 44
Campbell, George, 51
Campbell, John, 51
Canaries, James, 18
Cannon, Alexander, 154
Canongate, 39, 40, 42, 50, 60–1, 111, 112
Cargen, 115
Carlisle, 115
Carolina, 13, 44
Carrington, 52, 53, 54
Carruchan, 115
Carstares, Sarah, 44
Carstares, William, 45
Catholics and Catholicism, 18, 35, 74–5, 109, 124, 135
  burgh magistrates, 81, 92, 93–4, 99–100, 104, 118–19, 120, 121, 123, 126
  converts to, 1, 19, 32, 57–60, 62, 69, 89
  laws against, 11, 16–18, 20, 23–4, 33–4, 80, 101, 144
  revival of, 31, 33, 38–40, 60–2, 122, 135
  violence against, 1, 2, 5, 40, 59, 60–1, 107, 109, 110–15, 131
Cess, 15, 17, 26, 129, 145, 159
Charles I, 4, 23, 80, 84
Charles II, 6, 9, 11–15, 20, 25–7, 28, 31, 35, 36, 46, 85, 99, 124, 137–8
  and absolutism, 7, 10–11, 23
Christie, Alexander, 179n
Church of Scotland
  lay patronage in, 54, 140, 141, 142
  nature of, 9–10, 11, 43, 136, 140–4, 157, 161–2
  settlement of 1661–2, 10, 11, 84, 138, 157, 158
  settlement of 1690, 8, 74, 140–2, 158

see also Episcopacy and episcopalians; Presbyterianism and presbyterians
Civil war, 5, 132, 152–6
Claim of Right (1689), 6, 81, 91, 92, 93, 101, 104, 105, 131, 134–8, 146, 147, 151
and the settlement of 1689–90, 2, 140, 144, 145, 159
Clarendon, Henry Hyde, second earl of, 19
Club, the, 141, 145–6, 147, 159
Cochrane, John, second earl of Dundonald, 22, 55
Cockburn, Adam, of Ormiston, 55
Cockburn, John, 67
Cockburn, William, 194n
Coliart, James, 76–7, 78
Comprehension, 142–3
Confessionalisation, 7
Convention of estates
elections to (1689), 5, 94, 106, 107–8, 125–9, 131, 147
of 1678, 26, 144
of 1689, 2, 4, 5, 6, 8, 13, 52, 81, 82, 89, 106, 112, 130, 131–41, 144, 146, 147–9, 151, 152–3, 155, 158
Convention of royal burghs, 82–3, 85, 87, 89, 95, 96, 100, 147, 151–2
Coronation oath, 12, 14, 135, 159
Corstorphine, 50
Court of session, 11, 17, 19, 34, 58, 109, 136–7, 144, 161–2
Covenanters, 4, 11, 25, 101, 157
Covenants, 16, 55, 66, 67–8 116, 127
Craghead, Robert, 48
Craigie, 51
Crail, 215n
Cramond, 50, 74
Crawford, James, of Mountquhannie, 96, 97, 120
Crawford, Matthew, 64, 65, 67
Crawford, William Lindsay, eighteenth earl of, 55
Crichton, William, 44
Cromarty, 83
Cromdale, 154
Cromwell, Oliver, and Cromwellian regime, 10, 35, 99, 102
Cullen, 155, 215n
Culross, 94, 120, 126, 129, 176n, 198n
Cumbernauld, 53, 72
Cumbrae, 51

Cumulative jurisdiction, act concerning (1681), 12, 135, 137
Cunningham, Alexander, 61
Cunningham, William, 99–100
Cupar, 90–1, 95, 155
Customs, 26, 83, 102, 135
Cuthbert, John, of Drakies, 120

Dalgleish, John, 68
Dalkeith, 70, 75, 78
presbytery of, 44, 52, 54, 69, 142, 178n
Dalmeny, 50
Dalrymple, Sir James, 134
Dalrymple, Sir John, 134, 146
Dalserf, 116
Darien, 159, 160
Deas, Henry, 121, 122
Deprivation of clergy
affecting episcopalians, 68, 74, 141, 142, 143
affecting presbyterians, 10, 43–4
Derry, 48, 153
Deskford, Walter Ogilvy, Lord, 58
Dick, John, 100
Dingwall, 89
presbytery of, 74, 76
Discipline, 8, 48, 57, 74–8, 162, 184n
Douai, 61
Douglas, Colonel James, 15
Douglas, Thomas, 117
Dreghorn, 50
Dron, 72
Drumlanrig, James Douglas, earl of, 95
Drummond, George, of Blair Drummond, 87, 102–3, 112
Drummond, Lieutenant-General William, 15, 17
Dublin, 45, 103
Duff, William, 97
Dumbarton, 13, 91
presbytery of, 43, 48, 76
Dumbarton, George Douglas, earl of, 16, 152
Dumfries, 49, 50–1, 54, 87, 93, 94, 95, 113, 115, 118, 119, 123, 155, 201n
presbytery of, 43, 45, 47, 48, 51
synod of, 164
Dumfriesshire, 14, 45, 48, 52, 65, 117
Dunbar, 90, 91, 95, 98, 117, 124, 194n
presbytery of, 70
Dunbar, Gavin, 93, 118

Dunbartonshire, 14, 116
Dundas, Henry, 161
Dundee, 37, 68, 97, 101, 103, 127, 148, 151
Dundee, John Graham, viscount of, 5, 15, 97, 101, 127, 133, 148, 153–4, 155
Dundonald, John Cochrane, second earl of, 22, 55
Dunfermline, 44
Dunkeld, battle of, 154
Dunlop, William, 44
Dunnottar Castle, 179n
Duns, presbytery of, 73
Dysart, 54, 83

Eadie, David, 89, 118
East New Jersey, 13, 44
Economy, Scottish, 12–13, 17, 82, 83, 138, 151–2, 158, 159, 160
Edinburgh, 12, 13, 27, 32, 37, 42, 43, 44, 50, 52, 61, 69, 74, 75, 108, 117, 126–7, 133, 152, 153, 155, 161
  bishop of *see* Paterson, John
  burgh council, 71, 84, 85, 90, 110–11, 123, 124, 126, 148, 150, 162
  Castle, 152–3
  Catholics in, 38, 39, 40, 60
  diocesan synod of, 62
  Lady Yester's Church, 39
  local taxation in, 102, 103
  Old Kirk parish, 50
  presbytery of, 178n
  significance in the revolution, 6, 107, 113, 130, 155
  town college, 45, 61, 62, 68, 110
  Trinity College parish, 53, 75
  violence in, 18, 34, 59, 110–13, 115
  West Kirk parish, 44, 53, 73
Edinburghshire, 72, 75, 116, 204n
Elders, 46, 48–9, 53, 72, 73, 75, 77–8, 123, 141, 142
Elgin, 95–6, 97, 103, 104, 105, 119, 154
  episcopal synod of, 68
Ellon, presbytery of, 63
Engagement (1648), 84
England, 1, 7, 8, 12, 13, 15, 19, 20, 22, 37, 50, 64, 93, 99, 132, 152, 158, 159
  English Revolution of the 1640s and 1650s, 3, 55
  nature of government in, 24, 26, 27, 28, 29, 87
  revolution in, 1–2, 4–5, 6, 45, 106, 107, 108, 109, 114, 115, 122, 127, 131, 134
  see also Church of England; Union, Anglo-Scottish
Enniskillen, 153
Enzie, 38
Episcopacy and episcopalians, 10, 34, 49, 65–6, 67, 68, 84, 112, 138, 140–4, 150, 157, 160, 161–2
  clergy, 11, 14, 23, 33, 35–7, 40, 46, 51, 56, 57, 60, 68–9, 107, 110, 111, 125
  response to multiconfessionalism, 50, 52–5, 61, 62–3
  violence against, 109, 115–17, 121, 131, 140
  see also Church of Scotland
Erskine, William, 63
Ewn, Ewen McHucheon vic, 74–5
Excise
  act concerning (1685), 15, 24, 25
  local excises, 97, 101–4, 136, 147, 151
  national excise, 26, 27, 87, 97, 101, 145
Exclusion crisis, 12, 110
Execution, public, 14–15, 16, 19, 41, 42, 137
Exile, 24, 33, 44–5, 60, 122, 133, 138

Fall, James, 3
Fast days, 67–8
Ferguson, Robert, 146, 147
Fife, 14, 37, 54, 96, 97, 114, 124
  synod of, 178n
Findlater, James Ogilvy, third earl of, 58
Fleming, Placid, 3
Fleming, Robert, 45
Fletcher, Andrew, 138
Fletcher, James, 127
Fordyce, presbytery of, 63
Forfar, 117–18, 154, 196n
Forfarshire, 97, 103, 153
Fortrose, 90, 126
Fossoway, 45
France, 1, 4, 12, 13, 17, 24, 28, 29, 44, 64, 112, 114, 132, 145, 153
  French Revolution, 3
Fraser, Finlay, 120
Fraser, Michael, 68, 69

Galloway, 92, 113, 114
  synod of, 52, 164
Garden, George, 60, 125
Gedd, Alexander, 149
General assembly, 43, 46, 47, 67, 68, 142, 178n
Gibson, Matthew, 127, 128
Gibson, Walter, 87
Glasgow, 13, 16, 27, 33, 38, 45, 48, 50, 82, 103, 110–11, 117, 122–3, 124, 128, 178n
  archbishop of, 84, 101, 150; see also Cairncross, Alexander; Paterson, John; Ross, Arthur
  Barony parish, 70, 73
  burgh council, 71, 84, 87, 100, 102, 114, 150
  diocesan synod of, 76, 77, 117, 164
  presbytery of, 43, 53
  synod of Glasgow and Ayr, 43, 47, 49, 51, 67
  University of, 3, 44
Glassford, 40, 116
Glencoe massacre, 147
Godden v. *Hales*, 24
Gordon, Charles, 179n
Gordon, George, first duke of, 19, 62, 112, 152–3
Gordon, James, 61
Graham, John, of Claverhouse
  see Dundee, John Graham, viscount of
Grant, Alexander, 96, 97
Gray, James, 116
Gray, John, 44
Greenshields, James, 161–2

Haddington, 95, 97, 119, 124, 128, 129, 155
Haddingtonshire, 27, 67, 116, 124, 138–9
Hague, The, 122
Hall, Sir John, 127, 148
Hamilton, 33, 116
  presbytery of, 43, 45, 46–7, 49
Hamilton, Anne, duchess of Hamilton, 44, 55
Hamilton, Archibald, 49
Hamilton, Katherine, 55
Hamilton, William Douglas, third duke of Hamilton, 17, 19, 22, 37, 133, 141, 145, 146, 150, 153
Hanoverian succession, 159, 160

Hardy, John, 64
Hart, John, 116
Hawick, 76, 77
Hay, James, 102, 103
Hay, Lord David, 2–3
Hay, Patrick, 89, 94
Heriot, Alexander, 75
Heritable jurisdictions, 28–9, 80, 137, 161, 162
Higgins, William, 128
Highlands and highlanders, 16, 29, 38, 108, 109, 137, 143, 153, 154, 155, 168n
Holyroodhouse, 33, 60–1, 109, 111, 112, 113, 130, 198n
  chapel royal, 1, 20, 33, 38–9, 94, 121
  Jesuit school, 33, 38, 39–40, 58, 135
  printing press, 40, 61–2, 135, 172n, 184n
Houston, David, 41, 48, 65
Huguenots, 39, 60, 63
Hunter, Robert, 99

Ilay, Archibald Campbell, earl of, 161
Inchinnan, 16
Indulgences
  English indulgences of 1687 and 1688, 7, 22, 50
  of 1669 and 1672, 10, 11, 31, 35, 36, 42, 43, 66
  of 1679, 11, 31, 36
  of 1687, 7, 20–1, 22, 24, 25, 31–7, 38, 40–2, 43, 44, 45, 46, 49, 52, 53–5, 56–7, 61, 63, 66, 68, 70, 73, 75–9, 92, 93, 94, 127, 135, 136
Inglis, John, 44
Innes, Lewis, 38
Innes, Sir Alexander, of Coxton, 96
Inverkeithing, 122, 149
Inverness, 14, 50, 68–9, 97, 120, 155
Inverness-shire, 169n
Ipswich, 152
Ireland, 13, 33, 41, 45, 48, 52, 64, 65, 109, 114, 119, 153, 154
Irvine, 45, 54–5, 63, 67, 93, 103, 121, 123, 129, 151
  presbytery of, 43, 47, 49, 51, 68
Irving, John, 94
Irving, Thomas, 115

Jackson, Bessie, 78
Jacobites and Jacobitism, 5, 48, 58, 125, 133, 142, 143–4, 145, 148, 149, 150, 153–6, 158, 159, 162
James VI, 23, 84
James VII
  accession of, 13–14, 15
  addresses to, 16, 25, 40, 41, 42–3, 50, 66, 124
  as duke of Albany and York, 9, 11, 12–13, 40, 110
  during revolution, 1–2, 6, 106, 108, 113
  royal government, nature of, 6–8, 19, 23–6, 27–30, 80–1, 86, 104, 135–8, 146, 157–8
  royal revenues, 26–7
Jedburgh, 45, 128
  presbytery of, 77
Johnston, James, 115
Johnston, John (Glasgow), 100
Johnston, John (Peebles), 77, 78
Justices of the peace, 29, 70, 72, 73, 74, 77, 161
Justiciary commissioners, 6, 14, 36, 137

Kelso, 72
Kempis, Thomas à, 62
Kennedy, Hugh, of Shalloch, 100, 150
Kennedy, Thomas (Donaghmore), 48
Kennedy, Thomas (Edinburgh), 85
Kidd, John, 93, 123
Kilbride, 47
Kilcalmonell and Kilberry, 51
Killiecrankie, 119, 153–4, 155
Kilrenny, 83
Kiltearn, 76
Kilwinning, 68
Kincaid, Thomas, 50, 61, 62
Kincardineshire, 37, 126
Kinglassie, 114
Kinross, 45
Kinross-shire, 14, 37, 44, 97
Kintyre, 16, 154
  presbytery of, 43, 51, 78
Kirk sessions, 48–9, 53, 55, 70, 71–3, 74, 75, 76–7, 78, 104–5
Kirkbride, 51
Kirkcaldy, 96–7, 112, 119–20, 198n
  presbytery of, 164
Kirkcudbright, 90, 93, 114, 118
  stewartry of, 14, 51, 52
Kirkliston, 71
Kirkpatrick-Durham, 45
Kirkton, James, 44, 45
Kirkwall, 88, 90, 92

Lamington, 48
Lanark, 85, 98, 119
  presbytery of, 43, 74
Lanarkshire, 14, 40, 48, 52, 65, 75, 109, 116
Langlands, John, 77
Langlands, Robert, 46
Lauder, Sir John, of Fountainhall, 39, 86, 95
Lauderdale, John Maitland, second earl and duke of, 13, 102, 127
Leighton, Robert, bishop of Dunblane, archbishop of Glasgow, 36
Leith, 45, 50, 53, 73
Lennox, Charles, first duke of, 150
Lenzie Easter, 53, 72
Leslie, 55
Leslie, George, 86
Libberton, 180n
Lindsay, William, 142
Linlithgow, 13, 87, 90, 92, 97, 100, 114, 128, 151
  presbytery of, 43, 47, 70, 71, 73
Linlithgow, George Livingstone, third earl of, 97
Linlithgowshire, 52, 116
Linning, Thomas, 47
Little, John, 78
Livingstone, George, Lord, 97, 100, 128
Livingstone, Robert, 180n
Lochaber, 154
Lochmaben, 121, 165
Lochrutton, 51
Locke, John, 78
Lockhart, Cromwell, of Lee, 85, 98
Lockhart, Sir George, 17
London, 1, 2, 3, 4, 5, 6, 8, 40, 59, 93, 106, 110, 114, 117, 121, 123, 125, 139, 140
  as a place of publication, 39, 61, 62, 110
Lothian and Tweeddale, synod of, 43, 163n
Louis XIV, King, 24, 28
Lundie, James, of Strathairlie, 96, 97, 120

McBean, Angus, 68–9
McCalich, John, 76
McCulloch, Sir Godfrey, of Myrton, 58, 93
MacDonald, Alasdair, of Glengarry, 58
MacDonald, Coll, of Keppoch, 58
MacDonald, Daniel, 94, 120
Mackay, General Hugh, 154, 155
Mackenzie, Sir George, of Rosehaugh, 19, 34
Mackie, James, 94, 120, 136, 140, 194n
Maclauchlan, Margaret, 15
Main, Thomas, 92–3
Maitland, Charles, 97, 153
Manor, 68
Mar, Charles Erskine, twenty-first or fifth earl of, 22
Marriage, 8, 35, 57, 70–1, 73, 75, 162, 164
Mary II, Queen, 2, 3, 5, 58, 59, 131, 133, 134, 141, 142, 143, 144, 146
Mary of Modena, Queen, 37
Massie, Andrew, 61
Maxwell, John, of Barncleuch, 93, 94, 115, 118
Maxwell, John, of Lochfoot, 115
Maxwell, Sir John, of Pollok, 153
Meeting houses
  episcopalian, 143
  presbyterian, 33, 37, 43, 44, 45, 47, 49–50, 52, 53, 54, 55, 69, 70, 71, 73, 77, 78
Meldrum, George, 68
Melfort, John Drummond, viscount and earl of, 17, 18, 19, 20, 24–5, 39, 59, 86, 102, 103, 111
Melville, George, first earl of, 141, 145
Menzies, John or William, 112
Merse and Teviotdale, synod of, 164
Mertoun, 44
Militia, 2, 6, 23, 27, 108–9, 112, 124, 137, 152, 155
Milne, Alexander, 100
Ministers
  calls to, 44, 45, 46, 48, 51, 53, 55, 142
  ordination of, 33, 43, 46–7, 49, 51, 68, 128
  see also under Episcopacy and episcopalians; Presbyterianism and presbyterians
Moncrieff, William, 44

Monmouth, James Scott, duke of, 15–16, 138
Monro, Alexander, 62, 111, 112
Montgomery, Sir James, of Skelmorlie, 136, 149
Montrose, 40, 89, 98, 102–3, 117–18, 149–50, 151
Moray, Alexander Stewart, fifth earl of, 17, 18, 19, 58–9, 86, 87, 103
Morrice, Roger, 20
Muir, John, 50, 114
Muir, Robert, 46–7
Muirkirk, 15
Murray, David, 128
Murray, Lord John, 55, 154
Murray, Sir Archibald, of Blackbarony, 128
Murray, Sir Patrick, 3
Musgrave, Sir Christopher, 115

National Covenant *see* Covenants
Netherlands, 12, 15, 24, 27, 45, 47, 108
Newall, Martin, 87
Newton, 142
Newton-on-Ayr, 94
Nicolson, Thomas, 38, 58
Niddrie, 113
Nithsdale, 109, 113
Nithsdale, Lucie Douglas, countess of, 113
North Berwick, 97, 153, 205n
Northumberland, 45

Oath of abjuration *see* Abjuration oath (1684)
Oath of allegiance *see* Allegiance, oath of
Oliphant, George, 89, 94
Ordination *see under* Ministers
Ormiston, 55, 67
Orrock, Alexander, 64
Orwell, 44

Paisley, 55, 76, 89–90, 150
  presbytery of, 43, 44, 76
Panmure, James Maule, fourth earl of, 22, 84, 150
Parliament, British (and English), 140, 160, 161, 162
Parliament, Scottish, 5, 8, 24, 29, 34, 35, 80, 82–3, 95, 98, 102, 104,

113, 123, 124, 136, 137, 138, 144–7, 151, 157, 158–60
  of 1661–3, 11, 108, 135
  of 1681, 9, 11–12, 26, 34, 83, 144
  of 1685, 15–16, 23, 24, 25, 26, 34, 67
  of 1686, 13, 17–18, 19, 20, 23, 24–5, 58, 62, 80, 82, 83, 86–7, 89, 100, 127
  of 1689–1702, 2, 51, 82, 132, 141–3, 144–7, 150, 151–2, 153
  see also names of acts of parliament; Petitions; Union, Anglo-Scottish
Paterson, John, bishop of Edinburgh, archbishop of Glasgow, 11, 17, 59, 62, 74, 76, 77, 87
Paterson, Sir Hugh, of Bannockburn, 103
Paterson, Sir William, 95, 97, 119
Paton, Robert, 51
Peden, Alexander, 15
Peebles, 47, 68, 77, 92, 97, 113, 149
  presbytery of Peebles, 52, 77
  presbytery of Peebles and Biggar, 47–8, 51
Peeblesshire, 52, 116, 117, 128
Penicuik, 54
Pentland rising, 10
Perth, 50, 89, 93–4, 97, 121–2, 127–8, 153, 154–5
Perth, James Drummond, earl of, 1, 17, 18, 19, 24, 39, 58, 59, 61, 86, 87, 88, 94, 106, 111, 112, 120, 196n
Perthshire, 72, 153, 164
Petitions
  to church courts, 46, 47
  to parliament, 52, 89, 140, 141, 148, 151, 152, 155
  to the convention of royal burghs, 100
  to the crown, 16, 25, 40, 41, 42–3, 50, 66, 124
  to the privy council, 52, 96, 97, 119–20, 150
  to William of Orange, 2, 107, 111, 113, 117, 123–4, 125, 138–9, 140, 152
Petre, Sir Edward, 122
Piedmont, 64
Pierstoun, 50
Pitcairn, Alexander, 72
Pitmedden, Sir Alexander Seton, Lord, 19, 208n
Pittenweem, 90

Pollok, 65
Poor relief, 8, 57, 71–4,
Pope-burning, 110–11, 113, 121
Popery *see* Catholics and Catholicism
Presbyterianism and presbyterians, 85, 92–3, 111, 112, 114, 122, 134, 140–4, 149, 150, 157, 159, 161, 162, 164
  and elections to the convention of estates, 125, 127, 128, 129, 133
  general assembly (1690), 43, 47, 67–8
  general meeting (1687–90), 25, 43, 44, 48, 65, 68, 71, 73, 77, 123, 140
  response to multiconfessionalism, 33, 42–55, 56, 61, 63–78, 79
  Restoration presbyterian nonconformity, 10, 11–12, 14–15, 31, 35–6, 97, 137
  toleration of, 17, 20–3, 31–2, 36–7
  see also Church of Scotland
Presbyteries *see names of presbyteries*
Prince, Sir Magnus, 126, 127
Privy council, 1, 2, 11–13, 15–17, 19–20, 22, 32, 37, 38, 61, 70, 74, 108–15, 122, 123, 138, 141, 143, 144, 146, 147
  abolition of, 160, 161
  and the burghs, 81, 85–7, 89–91, 93, 97–100, 103, 115, 117–21, 149, 150, 151
  and the enforcement of religious uniformity, 36–7, 65, 66–7, 69
  secret committee, 16, 17, 19, 23, 97, 108, 118, 146
  see also under Petitions
Proclamations, 12, 13, 18–19, 20–3, 25, 38, 42, 108, 111, 113, 122, 135, 141, 155
Protesters, 35
Providence, 48, 132

Quakers, 20, 32, 33, 35, 40, 55, 56, 60, 63, 74, 109, 116
Queensberry, William Douglas, first duke of, 16, 19, 23, 126, 133, 134, 146
Queensferry, 45, 50, 54, 68, 97

Rabbling, 109, 115–17, 142
Rait, Alexander, 101
Ratho, 72

Rathven, 63
Regensburg, 3
Reid, James, 124–5
Renfrew, 44, 48–9, 71, 91
Renfrewshire, 16, 52, 65, 109
Renwick, James, 14, 41, 42
Resolutioners, 35
Restoration settlement, 10, 11, 138, 157
Revolution of 1688–90
  nature of, 2–3, 4–5, 106–8, 113, 119, 129–30, 155–6
  settlement of 1689–90, 8, 81, 132, 138, 140–52, 156, 157, 158, 161, 162
Riddell, Archibald, 44
Riddell, John, of Hayning, 95
Riots, 1, 18, 34, 59, 60–1, 109, 110, 111–13, 115, 127, 130
Risk, David, 76, 78
Rochester, Laurence Hyde, first earl of, 19
Rogers, Ralph, 44
Ronaldson, George, 75
Roslin, 113
Ross, Arthur, archbishop of St Andrews, 17, 62, 69, 100
Ross, William, twelfth Lord, 55, 145
Ross-shire, 69, 169n
Rothes, Anne, countess of, 55
Rothesay, 92, 148, 165
Roxburgh, 68
Roxburghshire, 52, 70
Royal College of Physicians, 13
Royal ecclesiastical supremacy, 24, 42, 43, 67, 140
  Act of supremacy (1669), 11, 135, 136, 141
Rule, Gilbert, 45, 63
Russell, Robert, 100
Rutherglen, 50, 75, 92
Rye House Plot, 36, 45

Sage, John, 52
St Andrews, 82, 84, 97, 111, 123, 150
  archbishop of *see* Burnet, Alexander; Ross, Arthur; Sharp, James
  University of, 25, 111
Savoy, 64
Scot, George, of Pitlochie, 44
Scott, Robert, 117
Seaforth, Kenneth Mackenzie, fourth earl of, 19, 58, 154
Security, act of (1704), 159

Selkirk, 18, 91, 95
Semple, Gabriel, 45, 48
Sermons, 18, 38, 41, 53, 59, 61, 62, 63–5, 66, 67–9, 114
Sharp, James, archbishop of St Andrews, 69, 97
Sharp, Sir William, of Scotscraig, 97–8
Sharp, Sir William, of Stoneyhill, 97
Sherlock, William, 207n
Shields, Alexander, 41, 114
Shiels, Thomas, 51
Sibbald, Sir Robert, 59
Simpson, John, 77
Simson, Patrick, 44, 48–9
Sinclair, John, 67
Skene, Sir George, of Fintry, 192n
Skirling, 117
Smith, Alexander, 90
Smith, James, 90
Smith, Robert, 128
Solemn League and Covenant *see* Covenants
South Carolina, 13, 44
Spalding, John, 50
Spence, William, 45
Spott, 70, 72, 73, 74, 116–17
Squadrone Volante, 160
Stanfield, Philip, 58
State oaths *see names of oaths*
Steuart, Patrick, of Ballechin, 153, 154
Steuart, Sir James, of Goodtrees, 207n
Stewart, James, 93–4, 121–2, 127
Stirling, 13, 91, 100, 108, 150
  Castle, 112
  presbytery of, 142
Stirling, George, 112, 127, 148
Stirlingshire, 76, 164
Stitchill, 70
Stobhall, 94, 121
Stobo, 52, 53, 77
Strachan, John, 62
Strachan, Robert, 38, 60
Stranraer, 114, 149
Strathblane, 76
Succession, act concerning the (1681), 12, 13–14, 135

Tarbat, Sir George Mackenzie, Viscount, 89, 146, 154
Taxation, 2, 27, 81, 82, 83, 129, 145, 152, 159; *see also* Cess; Excise
Temple, 75
Terregles, 51, 113

Test oath (1681), 11–12, 13, 16–17, 18, 20, 23, 24, 29, 34–5, 49, 67, 68, 85, 92, 93, 125–6, 132, 172n, 194n
Thanksgiving days, 36, 37, 53
Thistle, Order of the, 39
Thomson, David, 68
Thomson, James, 51
Threipland, Sir Patrick, of Fingask, 97, 121, 127–8, 195n
Tinwald and Trailflat, 117
Toleration, 1, 35, 41, 142
   episcopalian toleration act (1712), 8, 160, 162
   see also under Presbyterianism and presbyterians
Torture, 136
Trail, William, 44
Traquair, Charles Stewart, fourth earl of, 19, 112
   House, 113
Treasury, 2, 19, 26, 27, 38–9, 61, 97
Troqueer, 51
Tullideff, William, 63
Tweeddale, John Hay, second earl and first marquis of, 2, 95, 126–7, 138, 140
Tweedsmuir, 51

Uniformity, enforcement of religious, 7, 10, 35, 137, 140
Union, Anglo-Scottish, 13, 138–40, 159–60, 161
   union settlement of 1707–12, 8, 158, 160–3
United Provinces see Netherlands
United Societies see Cameronians
Universities see names of universities

Vadie, Simon, 76
Veitch, Jean, 77

Wales, Charles Francis Edward, prince of, 122

Walker, Patrick, 113
Wallace, John, 111, 112
Wallace, Sir William, of Craigie, 93, 94, 97, 99–100, 118–19
Warner, Patrick, 45, 63–4, 64–5
Watson, James, 61–2, 172n
Watson, Thomas, 78
Wauchope, John, 27
Weir, George, 116
Wemyss, Margaret, countess of, 55
Westminster confession of faith, 42–3, 66, 141
Whigs, 12
Wick, 90
Wigtown, 15, 91, 92, 93
Wigtownshire, 14, 52, 129
William, prince of Orange, 45, 107, 114, 117, 121–2, 131, 132, 139–40
   addresses to, 2, 107, 111, 113, 117, 123–4, 125, 138–9, 140, 152
   as King William II, 140–7, 150, 152, 155–6, 159, 160, 162
   Declaration of Reasons (1688), 81, 107, 122–3, 151, 147
   invasion of England, 1, 3, 4, 6, 45, 58, 106, 107, 110, 113, 127
   Scottish support for, 5, 107, 109, 121, 122–5, 125–6, 131, 132–4, 148, 149, 154
Williamson, David, 44, 73
Williamson, William, 97
Wilson, John, 75
Wilson, Margaret, 15
Wishart, William, 45
Wodrow, Robert, 22, 31, 32–3, 55, 64, 123
Wood, George, 196n
Wood, Hugh, 116
Worship, nature of, 66–7

Yester, John Hay, Lord, 124
York, James, duke of see James VII
Young, Robert, 46

EU representative:
Easy Access System Europe
Mustamäe tee 50, 10621 Tallinn, Estonia
Gpsr.requests@easproject.com

www.ingramcontent.com/pod-product-compliance
Lightning Source LLC
Chambersburg PA
CBHW061709300426
44115CB00014B/2619